High-Performance Browser Networking

Ilya Grigorik

O'REILLY®

Beijing · Cambridge · Farnham · Köln · Sebastopol · Tokyo

High-Performance Browser Networking

by Ilya Grigorik

Printed in the United States of America.

Published by O'Reilly Media, Inc., 1005 Gravenstein Highway North, Sebastopol, CA 95472.

O'Reilly books may be purchased for educational, business, or sales promotional use. Online editions are also available for most titles (*http://my.safaribooksonline.com*). For more information, contact our corporate/institutional sales department: 800-998-9938 or *corporate@oreilly.com*.

Editor: Courtney Nash	**Cover Designer:** Randy Comer
Production Editor: Melanie Yarbrough	**Interior Designer:** David Futato
Proofreader: Julie Van Keuren	**Illustrator:** Kara Ebrahim
Indexer: WordCo Indexing Services	

September 2013:   First Edition

Revision History for the First Edition:

2013-09-09:   First release

See *http://oreilly.com/catalog/errata.csp?isbn=9781449344764* for release details.

ISBN: 978-1-449-34476-4

[LSI]

Table of Contents

Part III.   HTTP

Foreword

"Good developers know how things work. Great developers know why things work."

We all resonate with this adage. We want to be that person who understands and can explain the underpinning of the systems we depend on. And yet, if you're a web developer, you might be moving in the opposite direction.

Web development is becoming more and more specialized. What kind of web developer are you? Frontend? Backend? Ops? Big data analytics? UI/UX? Storage? Video? Messaging? I would add "Performance Engineer" making that list of possible specializations even longer.

It's hard to balance studying the foundations of the technology stack with the need to keep up with the latest innovations. And yet, if we don't understand the foundation our knowledge is hollow, shallow. Knowing how to use the topmost layers of the technology stack isn't enough. When the complex problems need to be solved, when the inexplicable happens, the person who understands the foundation leads the way.

That's why *High Performance Browser Networking* is an important book. If you're a web developer, the foundation of your technology stack is the Web and the myriad of networking protocols it rides on: TCP, TLS, UDP, HTTP, and many others. Each of these protocols has its own performance characteristics and optimizations, and to build high performance applications you need to understand why the network behaves the way it does.

Thank goodness you've found your way to this book. I wish I had this book when I started web programming. I was able to move forward by listening to people who understood the why of networking and read specifications to fill in the gaps. High Performance Browser Networking combines the expertise of a networking guru, Ilya Grigorik, with the necessary information from the many relevant specifications, all woven together in one place.

In *High Performance Browser Networking*, Ilya explains many whys of networking: Why latency is the performance bottleneck. Why TCP isn't always the best transport mechanism and UDP might be your better choice. Why reusing connections is a critical optimization. He then goes even further by providing specific actions for improving networking performance. Want to reduce latency? Terminate sessions at a server closer to the client. Want to increase connection reuse? Enable connection keep-alive. The combination of understanding what to do and why it matters turns this knowledge into action.

Ilya explains the foundation of networking and builds on that to introduce the latest advances in protocols and browsers. The benefits of HTTP 2.0 are explained. XHR is reviewed and its limitations motivate the introduction of Cross-Origin Resource Sharing. Server-Sent Events, WebSockets, and WebRTC are also covered, bringing us up to date on the latest in browser networking.

Viewing the foundation and latest advances in networking from the perspective of performance is what ties the book together. Performance is the context that helps us see the why of networking and translate that into how it affects our website and our users. It transforms abstract specifications into tools that we can wield to optimize our websites and create the best user experience possible. That's important. That's why you should read this book.

—Steve Souders, Head Performance Engineer, Google, 2013

Preface

The web browser is the most widespread deployment platform available to developers today: it is installed on every smartphone, tablet, laptop, desktop, and every other form factor in between. In fact, current cumulative industry growth projections put us on track for 20 billion connected devices by 2020—each with a browser, and at the very least, WiFi or a cellular connection. The type of platform, manufacturer of the device, or the version of the operating system do not matter—each and every device will have a web browser, which by itself is getting more feature rich each day.

The browser of yesterday looks nothing like what we now have access to, thanks to all the recent innovations: HTML and CSS form the presentation layer, JavaScript is the new assembly language of the Web, and new HTML5 APIs are continuing to improve and expose new platform capabilities for delivering engaging, high-performance applications. There is simply no other technology, or platform, that has ever had the reach or the distribution that is made available to us today when we develop for the browser. And where there is big opportunity, innovation always follows.

In fact, there is no better example of the rapid progress and innovation than the networking infrastructure within the browser. Historically, we have been restricted to simple HTTP request-response interactions, and today we have mechanisms for efficient streaming, bidirectional and real-time communication, ability to deliver custom application protocols, and even peer-to-peer videoconferencing and data delivery directly between the peers—all with a few dozen lines of JavaScript.

The net result? Billions of connected devices, a swelling userbase for existing and new online services, and high demand for high-performance web applications. Speed is a feature, and in fact, for some applications it is *the feature*, and delivering a high-performance web application requires a solid foundation in how the browser and the network interact. That is the subject of this book.

About This Book

Our goal is to cover what every developer should know about the network: what protocols are being used and their inherent limitations, how to best optimize your applications for the underlying network, and what networking capabilities the browser offers and when to use them.

In the process, we will look at the internals of TCP, UDP, and TLS protocols, and how to optimize our applications and infrastructure for each one. Then we'll take a deep dive into how the wireless and mobile networks work under the hood—this radio thing, it's very different—and discuss its implications for how we design and architect our applications. Finally, we will dissect how the HTTP protocol works under the hood and investigate the many new and exciting networking capabilities in the browser:

- Upcoming HTTP 2.0 improvements
- New XHR features and capabilities
- Data streaming with Server-Sent Events
- Bidirectional communication with WebSocket
- Peer-to-peer video and audio communication with WebRTC
- Peer-to-peer data exchange with DataChannel

Understanding how the individual bits are delivered, and the properties of each transport and protocol in use are essential knowledge for delivering high-performance applications. After all, if our applications are blocked waiting on the network, then no amount of rendering, JavaScript, or any other form of optimization will help! Our goal is to eliminate this wait time by getting the best possible performance from the network.

High-Performance Browser Networking will be of interest to anyone interested in optimizing the delivery and performance of her applications, and more generally, curious minds that are not satisfied with a simple checklist but want to know how the browser and the underlying protocols actually work under the hood. The "how" and the "why" go hand in hand: we'll cover practical advice about configuration and architecture, and we'll also explore the trade-offs and the underlying reasons for each optimization.

 Our primary focus is on the protocols and their properties with respect to applications running in the browser. However, all the discussions on TCP, UDP, TLS, HTTP, and just about every other protocol we will cover are also directly applicable to native applications, regardless of the platform.

Conventions Used in This Book

The following typographical conventions are used in this book:

Italic

> Indicates new terms, URLs, email addresses, filenames, and file extensions.

`Constant width`

> Used for program listings, as well as within paragraphs to refer to program elements such as variable or function names, databases, data types, environment variables, statements, and keywords.

`Constant width bold`

> Shows commands or other text that should be typed literally by the user.

`Constant width italic`

> Shows text that should be replaced with user-supplied values or by values determined by context.

 This icon signifies a tip, suggestion, or general note.

 This icon indicates a warning or caution.

Safari® Books Online

 *Safari Books Online* is an on-demand digital library that delivers expert content in both book and video form from the world's leading authors in technology and business.

Technology professionals, software developers, web designers, and business and creative professionals use Safari Books Online as their primary resource for research, problem solving, learning, and certification training.

Safari Books Online offers a range of product mixes and pricing programs for organizations, government agencies, and individuals. Subscribers have access to thousands of books, training videos, and prepublication manuscripts in one fully searchable database from publishers like O'Reilly Media, Prentice Hall Professional, Addison-Wesley Professional, Microsoft Press, Sams, Que, Peachpit Press, Focal Press, Cisco Press, John Wiley & Sons, Syngress, Morgan Kaufmann, IBM Redbooks, Packt, Adobe Press, FT Press, Apress, Manning, New Riders, McGraw-Hill, Jones & Bartlett, Course

Technology, and dozens more. For more information about Safari Books Online, please visit us online.

How to Contact Us

Please address comments and questions concerning this book to the publisher:

O'Reilly Media, Inc.
1005 Gravenstein Highway North
Sebastopol, CA 95472
800-998-9938 (in the United States or Canada)
707-829-0515 (international or local)
707-829-0104 (fax)

We have a web page for this book, where we list errata, examples, and any additional information. You can access this page at *http://oreil.ly/high-performance-browser*.

To comment or ask technical questions about this book, send email to *bookques tions@oreilly.com*.

For more information about our books, courses, conferences, and news, see our website at *http://www.oreilly.com*.

Find us on Facebook: *http://facebook.com/oreilly*

Follow us on Twitter: *http://twitter.com/oreillymedia*

Watch us on YouTube: *http://www.youtube.com/oreillymedia*

Networking 101

CHAPTER 1

Primer on Latency and Bandwidth

Speed Is a Feature

The emergence and the fast growth of the web performance optimization (WPO) industry within the past few years is a telltale sign of the growing importance and demand for speed and faster user experiences by the users. And this is not simply a psychological *need for speed* in our ever accelerating and connected world, but a requirement driven by empirical results, as measured with respect to the bottom-line performance of the many online businesses:

- Faster sites lead to better user engagement.
- Faster sites lead to better user retention.
- Faster sites lead to higher conversions.

Simply put, speed is a feature. And to deliver it, we need to understand the many factors and fundamental limitations that are at play. In this chapter, we will focus on the two critical components that dictate the performance of all network traffic: latency and bandwidth (Figure 1-1).

Latency
> The time from the source sending a packet to the destination receiving it

Bandwidth
> Maximum throughput of a logical or physical communication path

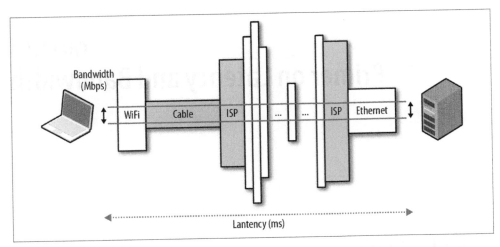

Figure 1-1. Latency and bandwidth

Armed with a better understanding of how bandwidth and latency work together, we will then have the tools to dive deeper into the internals and performance characteristics of TCP, UDP, and all application protocols above them.

Decreasing Transatlantic Latency with Hibernia Express

Latency is an important criteria for many high-frequency trading algorithms in the financial markets, where a small edge of a few milliseconds can translate to millions in loss or profit.

In early 2011, Huawei and Hibernia Atlantic began laying a new 3,000-mile fiber-optic link ("Hibernia Express") across the Atlantic Ocean to connect London to New York, with the sole goal of saving traders 5 milliseconds of latency by taking a shorter route between the cities, as compared with all other existing transatlantic links.

Once operational, the cable will be used by financial institutions only, and will cost over $400M to complete, which translates to $80M per millisecond saved! Latency is expensive—literally and figuratively.

The Many Components of Latency

Latency is the time it takes for a message, or a packet, to travel from its point of origin to the point of destination. That is a simple and useful definition, but it often hides a lot of useful information—every system contains multiple sources, or components, contributing to the overall time it takes for a message to be delivered, and it is important to understand what these components are and what dictates their performance.

Let's take a closer look at some common contributing components for a typical router on the Internet, which is responsible for relaying a message between the client and the server:

Propagation delay
> Amount of time required for a message to travel from the sender to receiver, which is a function of distance over speed with which the signal propagates.

Transmission delay
> Amount of time required to push all the packet's bits into the link, which is a function of the packet's length and data rate of the link.

Processing delay
> Amount of time required to process the packet header, check for bit-level errors, and determine the packet's destination.

Queuing delay
> Amount of time the incoming packet is waiting in the queue until it can be processed.

The total latency between the client and the server is the sum of all the delays just listed. Propagation time is dictated by the distance and the medium through which the signal travels—as we will see, the propagation speed is usually within a small constant factor of the speed of light. On the other hand, transmission delay is dictated by the available data rate of the transmitting link and has nothing to do with the distance between the client and the server. As an example, let's assume we want to transmit a 10 Mb file over two links: 1 Mbps and 100 Mbps. It will take 10 seconds to put the entire file on the "wire" over the 1 Mbps link and only 0.1 seconds over the 100 Mbps link.

Next, once the packet arrives at the router, the router must examine the packet header to determine the outgoing route and may run other checks on the data—this takes time as well. Much of this logic is now often done in hardware, so the delays are very small, but they do exist. And, finally, if the packets are arriving at a faster rate than the router is capable of processing, then the packets are queued inside an incoming buffer. The time data spends queued inside the buffer is, not surprisingly, known as queuing delay.

Each packet traveling over the network will incur many instances of each of these delays. The farther the distance between the source and destination, the more time it will take to propagate. The more intermediate routers we encounter along the way, the higher the processing and transmission delays for each packet. Finally, the higher the load of traffic along the path, the higher the likelihood of our packet being delayed inside an incoming buffer.

Bufferbloat in Your Local Router

Bufferbloat is a term that was coined and popularized by Jim Gettys in 2010, and is a great example of queuing delay affecting the overall performance of the network.

The underlying problem is that many routers are now shipping with large incoming buffers under the assumption that dropping packets should be avoided at all costs. However, this breaks TCP's congestion avoidance mechanisms (which we will cover in the next chapter), and introduces high and variable latency delays into the network.

The good news is that the new CoDel active queue management algorithm has been proposed to address this problem, and is now implemented within the Linux 3.5+ kernels. To learn more, refer to "Controlling Queue Delay" (*http://hpbn.co/aqmacm*) in ACM Queue.

Speed of Light and Propagation Latency

As Einstein outlined in his theory of special relativity, the speed of light is the maximum speed at which all energy, matter, and information can travel. This observation places a hard limit, and a governor, on the propagation time of any network packet.

The good news is the speed of light is high: 299,792,458 meters per second, or 186,282 miles per second. However, and there is always a however, that is the speed of light in a vacuum. Instead, our packets travel through a medium such as a copper wire or a fiber-optic cable, which will slow down the signal (Table 1-1). This ratio of the speed of light and the speed with which the packet travels in a material is known as the refractive index of the material. The larger the value, the slower light travels in that medium.

The typical refractive index value of an optical fiber, through which most of our packets travel for long-distance hops, can vary between 1.4 to 1.6—slowly but surely we are making improvements in the quality of the materials and are able to lower the refractive index. But to keep it simple, the rule of thumb is to assume that the speed of light in fiber is around 200,000,000 meters per second, which corresponds to a refractive index of ~1.5. The remarkable part about this is that we are already within a small constant factor of the maximum speed! An amazing engineering achievement in its own right.

Table 1-1. Signal latencies in vacuum and fiber

Route	Distance	Time, light in vacuum	Time, light in fiber	Round-trip time (RTT) in fiber
New York to San Francisco	4,148 km	14 ms	**21 ms**	42 ms
New York to London	5,585 km	19 ms	**28 ms**	56 ms
New York to Sydney	15,993 km	53 ms	**80 ms**	160 ms
Equatorial circumference	40,075 km	133.7 ms	**200 ms**	200 ms

The speed of light is fast, but it nonetheless takes 160 milliseconds to make the round-trip (RTT) from New York to Sydney. In fact, the numbers in Table 1-1 are also optimistic in that they assume that the packet travels over a fiber-optic cable along the great-circle path (the shortest distance between two points on the globe) between the cities. In practice, no such cable is available, and the packet would take a much longer route between New York and Sydney. Each hop along this route will introduce additional routing, processing, queuing, and transmission delays. As a result, the actual RTT between New York and Sydney, over our existing networks, works out to be in the 200–300 millisecond range. All things considered, that still seems pretty fast, right?

We are not accustomed to measuring our everyday encounters in milliseconds, but studies have shown that most of us will reliably report perceptible "lag" once a delay of over 100–200 milliseconds is introduced into the system. Once the 300 millisecond delay threshold is exceeded, the interaction is often reported as "sluggish," and at the 1,000 milliseconds (1 second) barrier, many users have already performed a mental context switch while waiting for the response—anything from a daydream to thinking about the next urgent task.

The conclusion is simple: to deliver the best experience and to keep our users engaged in the task at hand, we need our applications to respond within hundreds of milliseconds. That doesn't leave us, and especially the network, with much room for error. To succeed, network latency has to be carefully managed and be an explicit design criteria at all stages of development.

Content delivery network (CDN) services provide many benefits, but chief among them is the simple observation that distributing the content around the globe, and serving that content from a nearby location to the client, will allow us to significantly reduce the propagation time of all the data packets.

We may not be able to make the packets travel faster, but we can reduce the distance by strategically positioning our servers closer to the users! Leveraging a CDN to serve your data can offer significant performance benefits.

Last-Mile Latency

Ironically, it is often the last few miles, not the crossing of oceans or continents, where significant latency is introduced: the infamous last-mile problem. To connect your home or office to the Internet, your local ISP needs to route the cables throughout the neighborhood, aggregate the signal, and forward it to a local routing node. In practice, depending on the type of connectivity, routing methodology, and deployed technology, these first few hops can take tens of milliseconds just to get to your ISP's main routers! According to the "Measuring Broadband America" report conducted by the Federal Communications Commission in early 2013, during peak hours:

> Fiber-to-the-home, on average, has the best performance in terms of latency, with 18 ms average during the peak period, with cable having 26 ms latency and DSL 44 ms latency.
>
> — FCC
> *February 2013*

This translates into 18–44 ms of latency just to the closest measuring node within the ISP's core network, before the packet is even routed to its destination! The FCC report is focused on the United States, but last-mile latency is a challenge for all Internet providers, regardless of geography. For the curious, a simple traceroute can often tell you volumes about the topology and performance of your Internet provider.

```
$> traceroute google.com
traceroute to google.com (74.125.224.102), 64 hops max, 52 byte packets
 1  10.1.10.1 (10.1.10.1)  7.120 ms  8.925 ms  1.199 ms ❶
 2  96.157.100.1 (96.157.100.1)  20.894 ms  32.138 ms  28.928 ms
 3  x.santaclara.xxxx.com (68.85.191.29)  9.953 ms  11.359 ms  9.686 ms
 4  x.oakland.xxx.com (68.86.143.98)  24.013 ms 21.423 ms 19.594 ms
 5  68.86.91.205 (68.86.91.205)  16.578 ms  71.938 ms  36.496 ms
 6  x.sanjose.ca.xxx.com (68.86.85.78)  17.135 ms  17.978 ms  22.870 ms
 7  x.529bryant.xxx.com (68.86.87.142)  25.568 ms  22.865 ms  23.392 ms
 8  66.208.228.226 (66.208.228.226)  40.582 ms  16.058 ms  15.629 ms
 9  72.14.232.136 (72.14.232.136)  20.149 ms  20.210 ms  18.020 ms
10  64.233.174.109 (64.233.174.109)  63.946 ms  18.995 ms  18.150 ms
11  x.1e100.net (74.125.224.102)  18.467 ms  17.839 ms  17.958 ms ❷
```

❶ 1st hop: local wireless router

❷ 11th hop: Google server

In the previous example, the packet started in the city of Sunnyvale, bounced to Santa Clara, then Oakland, returned to San Jose, got routed to the "529 Bryant" datacenter, at which point it was routed toward Google and arrived at its destination on the 11th hop. This entire process took, on average, 18 milliseconds. Not bad, all things considered, but in the same time the packet could have traveled across most of the continental USA!

The last-mile latency can vary wildly based on your provider, the deployed technology, topology of the network, and even the time of day. As an end user, if you are looking to improve your web browsing speeds, low latency is worth optimizing for when picking a local ISP.

 Latency, not bandwidth, is the performance bottleneck for most websites! To understand why, we need to understand the mechanics of TCP and HTTP protocols—subjects we'll be covering in subsequent chapters. However, if you are curious, feel free to skip ahead to "More Bandwidth Doesn't Matter (Much)" on page 176.

Measuring Latency with Traceroute

Traceroute is a simple network diagnostics tool for identifying the routing path of the packet and the latency of each network hop in an IP network. To identify the individual hops, it sends a sequence of packets toward the destination with an increasing "hop limit" (1, 2, 3, and so on). When the hop limit is reached, the intermediary returns an ICMP Time Exceeded message, allowing the tool to measure the latency for each network hop.

On Unix platforms the tool can be run from the command line via `traceroute`, and on Windows it is known as `tracert`.

Bandwidth in Core Networks

An optical fiber acts as a simple "light pipe," slightly thicker than a human hair, designed to transmit light between the two ends of the cable. Metal wires are also used but are subject to higher signal loss, electromagnetic interference, and higher lifetime maintenance costs. Chances are, your packets will travel over both types of cable, but for any long-distance hops, they will be transmitted over a fiber-optic link.

Optical fibers have a distinct advantage when it comes to bandwidth because each fiber can carry many different wavelengths (channels) of light through a process known as wavelength-division multiplexing (WDM). Hence, the total bandwidth of a fiber link is the multiple of per-channel data rate and the number of multiplexed channels.

As of early 2010, researchers have been able to multiplex over 400 wavelengths with the peak capacity of 171 Gbit/s per channel, which translates to over 70 Tbit/s of total bandwidth for a single fiber link! We would need thousands of copper wire (electrical) links to match this throughput. Not surprisingly, most long-distance hops, such as subsea data transmission between continents, is now done over fiber-optic links. Each cable carries several strands of fiber (four strands is a common number), which translates into bandwidth capacity in hundreds of terabits per second for each cable.

Bandwidth at the Network Edge

The backbones, or the fiber links, that form the core data paths of the Internet are capable of moving hundreds of terabits per second. However, the available capacity at the edges of the network is much, much less, and varies wildly based on deployed technology: dial-up, DSL, cable, a host of wireless technologies, fiber-to-the-home, and even the performance of the local router. The available bandwidth to the user is a function of the lowest capacity link between the client and the destination server (Figure 1-1).

Akamai Technologies operates a global CDN, with servers positioned around the globe, and provides free quarterly reports at Akamai's website (*http://www.akamai.io*) on average broadband speeds, as seen by their servers. Table 1-2 captures the macro bandwidth trends as of Q1 2013.

Table 1-2. Average bandwidth speeds as seen by Akamai servers in Q1 2013

Rank	Country	Average Mbps	Year-over-year change
-	Global	3.1	17%
1	South Korea	14.2	-10%
2	Japan	11.7	6.8%
3	Hong Kong	10.9	16%
4	Switzerland	10.1	24%
5	Netherlands	9.9	12%
...			
9	United States	8.6	27%

The preceding data excludes traffic from mobile carriers, a topic we will come back to later to examine in closer detail. For now, it should suffice to say that mobile speeds are highly variable and generally slower. However, even with that in mind, the average global broadband bandwidth in early 2013 was just 3.1 Mbps! South Korea led the world with a 14.2 Mbps average throughput, and United States came in 9th place with 8.6 Mbps.

As a reference point, streaming an HD video can require anywhere from 2 to 10 Mbps depending on resolution and the codec. So an average user can stream a lower-resolution video stream at the network edge, but doing so would consume much of their link capacity—not a very promising story for a household with multiple users.

Figuring out where the bandwidth bottleneck is for any given user is often a nontrivial but important exercise. Once again, for the curious, there are a number of online services, such as speedtest.net operated by Ookla (Figure 1-2), which provide upstream and downstream tests to some local server—we will see why picking a local server is important in our discussion on TCP. Running a test on one of these services is a good way to check that your connection meets the advertised speeds of your local ISP.

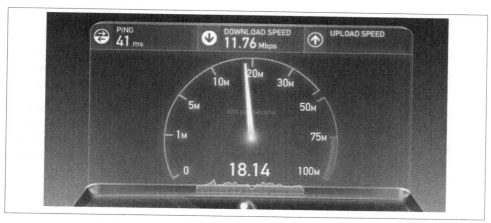

Figure 1-2. Upstream and downstream test (speedtest.net)

However, while a high-bandwidth link to your ISP is desirable, it is also not a guarantee of stable end-to-end performance. The network could be congested at any intermediate node at some point in time due to high demand, hardware failures, a concentrated network attack, or a host of other reasons. High variability of throughput and latency performance is an inherent property of our data networks—predicting, managing, and adapting to the continuously changing "network weather" is a complex task.

Delivering Higher Bandwidth and Lower Latencies

Our demand for higher bandwidth is growing fast, in large part due to the rising popularity of streaming video, which is now responsible for well over half of all Internet traffic. The good news is, while it may not be cheap, there are multiple strategies available for us to grow the available capacity: we can add more fibers into our fiber-optic links, we can deploy more links across the congested routes, or we can improve the WDM techniques to transfer more data through existing links.

TeleGeography, a telecommunications market research and consulting firm, estimates that as of 2011, we are using, on average, just 20% of the available capacity of the deployed subsea fiber links. Even more importantly, between 2007 and 2011, more than half of all the added capacity of the trans-Pacific cables was due to WDM upgrades: same fiber links, better technology on both ends to multiplex the data. Of course, we cannot expect these advances to go on indefinitely, as every medium reaches a point of diminishing returns. Nonetheless, as long as economics of the enterprise permit, there is no fundamental reason why bandwidth throughput cannot be increased over time—if all else fails, we can add more fiber links.

Improving latency, on the other hand, is a very different story. The quality of the fiber links could be improved to get us a little closer to the speed of light: better materials with lower refractive index and faster routers along the way. However, given that our current speeds are within ~1.5 of the speed of light, the most we can expect from this strategy is just a modest 30% improvement. Unfortunately, there is simply no way around the laws of physics: the speed of light places a hard limit on the minimum latency.

Alternatively, since we can't make light travel faster, we can make the distance shorter —the shortest distance between any two points on the globe is defined by the great-circle path between them. However, laying new cables is also not always possible due to the constraints imposed by the physical terrain, social and political reasons, and of course, the associated costs.

As a result, to improve performance of our applications, we need to architect and optimize our protocols and networking code with explicit awareness of the limitations of available bandwidth and the speed of light: we need to reduce round trips, move the data closer to the client, and build applications that can hide the latency through caching, pre-fetching, and a variety of similar techniques, as explained in subsequent chapters.

CHAPTER 2

Building Blocks of TCP

At the heart of the Internet are two protocols, IP and TCP. The IP, or Internet Protocol, is what provides the host-to-host routing and addressing, and TCP, or Transmission Control Protocol, is what provides the abstraction of a reliable network running over an unreliable channel. TCP/IP is also commonly referred to as the Internet Protocol Suite and was first proposed by Vint Cerf and Bob Kahn in their 1974 paper titled "A Protocol for Packet Network Intercommunication."

The original proposal (RFC 675) was revised several times, and in 1981 the v4 specification of TCP/IP was published not as one, but as two separate RFCs:

- RFC 791—Internet Protocol
- RFC 793—Transmission Control Protocol

Since then, there have been a number of enhancements proposed and made to TCP, but the core operation has not changed significantly. TCP quickly replaced previous protocols and is now the protocol of choice for many of the most popular applications: World Wide Web, email, file transfers, and many others.

TCP provides an effective abstraction of a reliable network running over an unreliable channel, hiding most of the complexity of network communication from our applications: retransmission of lost data, in-order delivery, congestion control and avoidance, data integrity, and more. When you work with a TCP stream, you are guaranteed that all bytes sent will be identical with bytes received and that they will arrive in the same order to the client. As such, TCP is optimized for accurate delivery, rather than a timely one. This, as it turns out, also creates some challenges when it comes to optimizing for web performance in the browser.

The HTTP standard does not specify TCP as the only transport protocol. If we wanted, we could deliver HTTP via a datagram socket (User Datagram Protocol or UDP), or any other transport protocol of our choice, but in practice all HTTP traffic on the

Internet today is delivered via TCP due to the many great features it provides out of the box.

Because of this, understanding some of the core mechanisms of TCP is essential knowledge for building an optimized web experience. Chances are you won't be working with TCP sockets directly in your application, but the design choices you make at the application layer will dictate the performance of TCP and the underlying network over which your application is delivered.

Intertwined History of TCP and IP Protocols

We are all familiar with IPv4 and IPv6, but what happened to IPv{1,2,3,5}? The 4 in IPv4 stands for the version 4 of the TCP/IP protocol, which was published in September 1981. The original TCP/IP proposal coupled the two protocols, and it was the v4 draft that officially split the two into separate RFCs. Hence, the v4 in IPv4 is a heritage of its relationship to TCP: there were no prior, standalone IPv1, IPv2, or IPv3 protocols.

When the working group began work on "Internet Protocol next generation" (IPng) in 1994, a new version number was needed, but v5 was already assigned to another experimental protocol: Internet Stream Protocol (ST). As it turns out, ST never took off, which is why few ever heard of it. Hence the 6 in IPv6.

Three-Way Handshake

All TCP connections begin with a three-way handshake (Figure 2-1). Before the client or the server can exchange any application data, they must agree on starting packet sequence numbers, as well as a number of other connection specific variables, from both sides. The sequence numbers are picked randomly from both sides for security reasons.

SYN
> Client picks a random sequence number x and sends a SYN packet, which may also include additional TCP flags and options.

SYN ACK
> Server increments x by one, picks own random sequence number y, appends its own set of flags and options, and dispatches the response.

ACK
> Client increments both x and y by one and completes the handshake by dispatching the last ACK packet in the handshake.

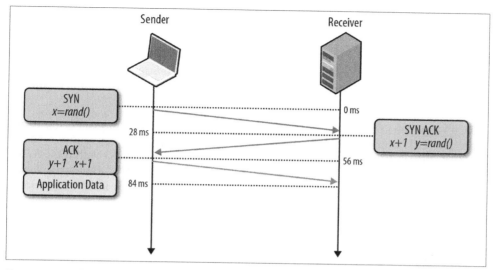

Figure 2-1. Three-way handshake

Once the three-way handshake is complete, the application data can begin to flow between the client and the server. The client can send a data packet immediately after the ACK packet, and the server must wait for the ACK before it can dispatch any data. This startup process applies to every TCP connection and carries an important implication for performance of all network applications using TCP: each new connection will have a full roundtrip of latency before any application data can be transferred.

For example, if our client is in New York, the server is in London, and we are starting a new TCP connection over a fiber link, then the three-way handshake will take a minimum of 56 milliseconds (Table 1-1): 28 milliseconds to propagate the packet in one direction, after which it must return back to New York. Note that bandwidth of the connection plays no role here. Instead, the delay is governed by the latency between the client and the server, which in turn is dominated by the propagation time between New York and London.

The delay imposed by the three-way handshake makes new TCP connections expensive to create, and is one of the big reasons why connection reuse is a critical optimization for any application running over TCP.

TCP Fast Open

The TCP handshake phase has been identified as a significant source of total web browsing latency, in large part due to the prevalence of very short TCP flows required to retrieve dozens to hundreds of assets from various hosts.

TCP Fast Open (TFO) is a mechanism that aims to reduce the latency penalty imposed on new TCP connections. Based on traffic analysis and network emulation done at Google, researchers have shown that TFO, which allows data transfer within the SYN packet, could decrease HTTP transaction network latency by 15%, whole-page load times by over 10% on average, and in some cases by up to 40% in high-latency scenarios.

Both client and server TFO support is now available in Linux 3.7+ kernels, which makes it a viable option for new clients and servers. Having said that, TFO is also not a solution to every problem. While it may help eliminate the roundtrip penalty of the three-way handshake, it also works only in certain cases: there are limits on the maximum size of the data payload within the SYN packet, only certain types of HTTP requests can be sent, and it works only for repeat connections due to a requirement for a cryptographic cookie. For a detailed discussion on the capabilities and limitations of TFO, check the latest IETF draft of "TCP Fast Open."

Congestion Avoidance and Control

In early 1984, John Nagle documented a condition known as "congestion collapse," which could affect any network with asymmetric bandwidth capacity between the nodes:

> Congestion control is a recognized problem in complex networks. We have discovered that the Department of Defense's Internet Protocol (IP), a pure datagram protocol, and Transmission Control Protocol (TCP), a transport layer protocol, when used together, are subject to unusual congestion problems caused by interactions between the transport and datagram layers. In particular, IP gateways are vulnerable to a phenomenon we call "congestion collapse", especially when such gateways connect networks of widely different bandwidth...

> Should the roundtrip time exceed the maximum retransmission interval for any host, that host will begin to introduce more and more copies of the same datagrams into the net. The network is now in serious trouble. Eventually all available buffers in the switching nodes will be full and packets must be dropped. The roundtrip time for packets that are delivered is now at its maximum. Hosts are sending each packet several times, and eventually some copy of each packet arrives at its destination. This is congestion collapse.

This condition is stable. Once the saturation point has been reached, if the algorithm for selecting packets to be dropped is fair, the network will continue to operate in a degraded condition.

— John Nagle
RFC 896

The report concluded that congestion collapse had not yet become a problem for AR-PANET because most nodes had uniform bandwidth, and the backbone had substantial excess capacity. However, neither of these assertions held true for long. In 1986, as the number (5,000+) and the variety of nodes on the network grew, a series of congestion collapse incidents swept throughout the network—in some cases the capacity dropped by a factor of 1,000 and the network became unusable.

To address these issues, multiple mechanisms were implemented in TCP to govern the rate with which the data can be sent in both directions: flow control, congestion control, and congestion avoidance.

 Advanced Research Projects Agency Network (ARPANET) was the precursor to the modern Internet and the world's first operational packet-switched network. The project was officially launched in 1969, and in 1983 the TCP/IP protocols replaced the earlier NCP (Network Control Program) as the principal communication protocols. The rest, as they say, is history.

Flow Control

Flow control is a mechanism to prevent the sender from overwhelming the receiver with data it may not be able to process—the receiver may be busy, under heavy load, or may only be willing to allocate a fixed amount of buffer space. To address this, each side of the TCP connection advertises (Figure 2-2) its own receive window (rwnd), which communicates the size of the available buffer space to hold the incoming data.

When the connection is first established, both sides initiate their rwnd values by using their system default settings. A typical web page will stream the majority of the data from the server to the client, making the client's window the likely bottleneck. However, if a client is streaming large amounts of data to the server, such as in the case of an image or a video upload, then the server receive window may become the limiting factor.

If, for any reason, one of the sides is not able to keep up, then it can advertise a smaller window to the sender. If the window reaches zero, then it is treated as a signal that no more data should be sent until the existing data in the buffer has been cleared by the application layer. This workflow continues throughout the lifetime of every TCP connection: each ACK packet carries the latest rwnd value for each side, allowing both sides to dynamically adjust the data flow rate to the capacity and processing speed of the sender and receiver.

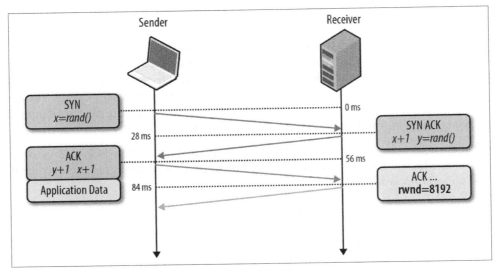

Figure 2-2. Receive window (rwnd) size advertisement

Window Scaling (RFC 1323)

The original TCP specification allocated 16 bits for advertising the receive window size, which places a hard upper bound on the maximum value (2^{16}, or 65,535 bytes) that can be advertised by the sender and receiver. Turns out, this upper bound is often not enough to get optimal performance, especially in networks that exhibit high bandwith delay product; more on this can be found on page 28.

To address this, RFC 1323 was drafted to provide a "TCP window scaling" option, which allows us to raise the maximum receive window size from 65,535 bytes to 1 gigabyte! The window scaling option is communicated during the three-way handshake and carries a value that represents the number of bits to left-shift the 16-bit window size field in future ACKs.

Today, TCP window scaling is enabled by default on all major platforms. However, intermediate nodes, routers, and firewalls can rewrite or even strip this option entirely. If your connection to the server, or the client, is unable to make full use of the available bandwidth, then checking the interaction of your window sizes is always a good place to start. On Linux platforms, the window scaling setting can be checked and enabled via the following commands:

- `$> sysctl net.ipv4.tcp_window_scaling`

- `$> sysctl -w net.ipv4.tcp_window_scaling=1`

Slow-Start

Despite the presence of flow control in TCP, network congestion collapse became a real issue in the mid to late 1980s. The problem was that flow control prevented the sender from overwhelming the receiver, but there was no mechanism to prevent either side from overwhelming the underlying network: neither the sender nor the receiver knows the available bandwidth at the beginning of a new connection, and hence need a mechanism to estimate it and also to adapt their speeds to the continuously changing conditions within the network.

To illustrate one example where such an adaptation is beneficial, imagine you are at home and streaming a large video from a remote server that managed to saturate your downlink to deliver the maximum quality experience. Then another user on your home network opens a new connection to download some software updates. All of the sudden, the amount of available downlink bandwidth to the video stream is much less, and the video server must adjust its data rate—otherwise, if it continues at the same rate, the data will simply pile up at some intermediate gateway and packets will be dropped, leading to inefficient use of the network.

In 1988, Van Jacobson and Michael J. Karels documented several algorithms to address these problems: slow-start, congestion avoidance, fast retransmit, and fast recovery. All four quickly became a mandatory part of the TCP specification. In fact, it is widely held that it was these updates to TCP that prevented an Internet meltdown in the '80s and the early '90s as the traffic continued to grow at an exponential rate.

To understand slow-start, it is best to see it in action. So, once again, let us come back to our client, who is located in New York, attempting to retrieve a file from a server in London. First, the three-way handshake is performed, during which both sides advertise their respective receive window (rwnd) sizes within the ACK packets (Figure 2-2). Once the final ACK packet is put on the wire, we can start exchanging application data.

The only way to estimate the available capacity between the client and the server is to measure it by exchanging data, and this is precisely what slow-start is designed to do. To start, the server initializes a new congestion window (cwnd) variable per TCP connection and sets its initial value to a conservative, system-specified value (initcwnd on Linux).

Congestion window size (cwnd)
> Sender-side limit on the amount of data the sender can have in flight before receiving an acknowledgment (ACK) from the client.

The cwnd variable is not advertised or exchanged between the sender and receiver—in this case, it will be a private variable maintained by the server in London. Further, a new rule is introduced: the maximum amount of data in flight (not ACKed) between the client and the server is the minimum of the rwnd and cwnd variables. So far so good, but how do the server and the client determine optimal values for their congestion window sizes? After all, network conditions vary all the time, even between the same two network nodes, as we saw in the earlier example, and it would be great if we could use the algorithm without having to hand-tune the window sizes for each connection.

The solution is to start slow and to grow the window size as the packets are acknowledged: slow-start! Originally, the cwnd start value was set to 1 network segment; RFC 2581 updated this value to a maximum of 4 segments in April 1999, and most recently the value was increased once more to 10 segments by RFC 6928 in April 2013.

The maximum amount of data in flight for a new TCP connection is the minimum of the rwnd and cwnd values; hence the server can send up to four network segments to the client, at which point it must stop and wait for an acknowledgment. Then, for every received ACK, the slow-start algorithm indicates that the server can increment its cwnd window size by one segment—for every ACKed packet, two new packets can be sent. This phase of the TCP connection is commonly known as the "exponential growth" algorithm (Figure 2-3), as the client and the server are trying to quickly converge on the available bandwidth on the network path between them.

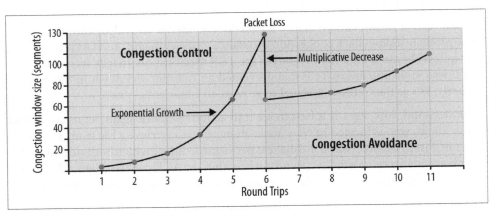

Figure 2-3. Congestion control and congestion avoidance

So why is slow-start an important factor to keep in mind when we are building applications for the browser? Well, HTTP and many other application protocols run over TCP, and no matter the available bandwidth, every TCP connection must go through the slow-start phase—we cannot use the full capacity of the link immediately!

Instead, we start with a small congestion window and double it for every roundtrip—i.e., exponential growth. As a result, the time required to reach a specific throughput target is a function (Equation 2-1) of both the roundtrip time between the client and server and the initial congestion window size.

Equation 2-1. Time to reach the cwnd size of size N

$$Time = RTT \times \left\lceil log_2\left(\frac{N}{initial\ cwnd}\right)\right\rceil$$

For a hands-on example of slow-start impact, let's assume the following scenario:

- Client and server receive windows: 65,535 bytes (64 KB)
- Initial congestion window: 4 segments (RFC 2581)
- Roundtrip time: 56 ms (London to New York)

 We will be using the old (RFC 2581) value of four network segments for the initial congestion window in this and the following examples, as it is still the most common value for most servers. Except, you won't make this mistake—right? The following examples should serve as good motivation for why you should update your servers!

Despite the 64 KB receive window size, the throughput of a new TCP connection is initially limited by the size of the congestion window. In fact, to reach the 64 KB limit, we will need to grow the congestion window size to 45 segments, which will take 224 milliseconds:

$$\frac{65,535\ bytes}{1,460\ bytes} \approx 45\ segments$$

$$56\ ms \times \left\lceil log_2\left(\frac{45}{4}\right)\right\rceil = 224\ ms$$

That's four roundtrips (Figure 2-4), and hundreds of milliseconds of latency, to reach 64 KB of throughput between the client and server! The fact that the client and server may be capable of transferring at Mbps+ data rates has no effect—that's slow-start.

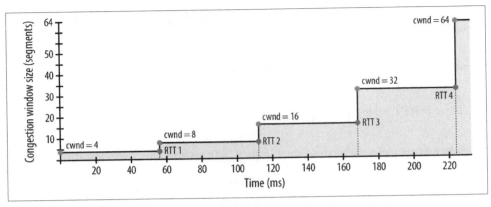

Figure 2-4. Congestion window size growth

To decrease the amount of time it takes to grow the congestion window, we can decrease the roundtrip time between the client and server—e.g., move the server geographically closer to the client. Or we can increase the initial congestion window size to the new RFC 6928 value of 10 segments.

Slow-start is not as big of an issue for large, streaming downloads, as the client and the server will arrive at their maximum window sizes after a few hundred milliseconds and continue to transmit at near maximum speeds—the cost of the slow-start phase is amortized over the lifetime of the larger transfer.

However, for many HTTP connections, which are often short and bursty, it is not unusual for the request to terminate before the maximum window size is reached. As a result, the performance of many web applications is often limited by the roundtrip time between server and client: slow-start limits the available bandwidth throughput, which has an adverse effect on the performance of small transfers.

Slow-Start Restart

In addition to regulating the transmission rate of new connections, TCP also implements a slow-start restart (SSR) mechanism, which resets the congestion window of a connection after it has been idle for a defined period of time. The rationale is simple: the network conditions may have changed while the connection has been idle, and to avoid congestion, the window is reset to a "safe" default.

Not surprisingly, SSR can have a significant impact on performance of long-lived TCP connections that may idle for bursts of time—e.g., HTTP keepalive connections. As a result, it is recommended to disable SSR on the server. On Linux platforms, the SSR setting can be checked and disabled via the following commands:

- `$> sysctl net.ipv4.tcp_slow_start_after_idle`
- `$> sysctl -w net.ipv4.tcp_slow_start_after_idle=0`

To illustrate the impact of the three-way handshake and the slow-start phase on a simple HTTP transfer, let's assume that our client in New York requests a 20 KB file from the server in London over a new TCP connection (Figure 2-5), and the following connection parameters are in place:

- Roundtrip time: 56 ms
- Client and server bandwidth: 5 Mbps
- Client and server receive window: 65,535 bytes
- Initial congestion window: 4 segments (4×1460 bytes ≈ 5.7 KB)
- Server processing time to generate response: 40 ms
- No packet loss, ACK per packet, GET request fits into single segment

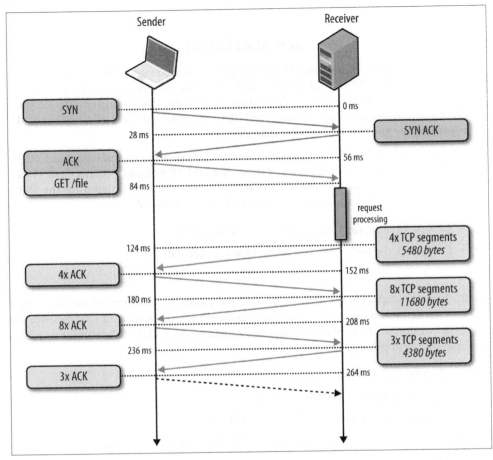

Figure 2-5. Fetching a file over a new TCP connection

0 ms   Client begins the TCP handshake with the SYN packet.

28 ms   Server replies with SYN-ACK and specifies its rwnd size.

56 ms   Client ACKs the SYN-ACK, specifies its rwnd size, and immediately sends the HTTP GET request.

84 ms   Server receives the HTTP request.

124 ms Server completes generating the 20 KB response and sends 4 TCP segments before pausing for an ACK (initial cwnd size is 4).

152 ms Client receives four segments and ACKs each one.

180 ms   Server increments its cwnd for each ACK and sends eight segments.

208 ms   Client receives eight segments and ACKs each one.

236 ms   Server increments its cwnd for each ACK and sends remaining segments.

264 ms   Client receives remaining segments, ACKs each one.

 As an exercise, run through Figure 2-5 with cwnd value set to 10 network segments instead of 4. You should see a full roundtrip of network latency disappear—a 22% improvement in performance!

264 ms to transfer the 20 KB file on a new TCP connection with 56 ms roundtrip time between the client and server! By comparison, let's now assume that the client is able to reuse the same TCP connection (Figure 2-6) and issues the same request once more.

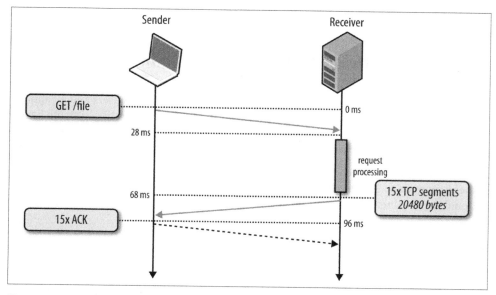

Figure 2-6. Fetching a file over an existing TCP connection

0 ms   Client sends the HTTP request.

28 ms   Server receives the HTTP request.

68 ms   Server completes generating the 20 KB response, but the cwnd value is already greater than the 15 segments required to send the file; hence it dispatches all the segments in one burst.

96 ms   Client receives all 15 segments, ACKs each one.

The same request made on the same connection, but without the cost of the three-way handshake and the penalty of the slow-start phase, now took 96 milliseconds, which translates into a 275% improvement in performance!

In both cases, the fact that both the server and the client have access to 5 Mbps of upstream bandwidth had no impact during the startup phase of the TCP connection. Instead, the latency and the congestion window sizes were the limiting factors.

In fact, the performance gap between the first and the second request dispatched over an existing connection will only widen if we increase the roundtrip time; as an exercise, try it with a few different values. Once you develop an intuition for the mechanics of TCP congestion control, dozens of optimizations such as keepalive, pipelining, and multiplexing will require little further motivation.

Increasing TCP's Initial Congestion Window

Increasing the initial cwnd size on the server to the new RFC 6928 value of 10 segments (IW10) is one of the simplest ways to improve performance for all users and all applications running over TCP. And the good news is that many operating systems have already updated their latest kernels to use the increased value—check the appropriate documentation and release notes.

For Linux, IW10 is the new default for all kernels above 2.6.39. However, don't stop there: upgrade to 3.2+ to also get the benefit of other important updates; see "Proportional Rate Reduction for TCP" on page 27.

Congestion Avoidance

It is important to recognize that TCP is specifically designed to use packet loss as a feedback mechanism to help regulate its performance. In other words, it is not a question of *if*, but rather of *when* the packet loss will occur. Slow-start initializes the connection with a conservative window and, for every roundtrip, doubles the amount of data in flight until it exceeds the receiver's flow-control window, a system-configured congestion threshold (ssthresh) window, or until a packet is lost, at which point the congestion avoidance algorithm (Figure 2-3) takes over.

The implicit assumption in congestion avoidance is that packet loss is indicative of network congestion: somewhere along the path we have encountered a congested link or a router, which was forced to drop the packet, and hence we need to adjust our window to avoid inducing more packet loss to avoid overwhelming the network.

Once the congestion window is reset, congestion avoidance specifies its own algorithms for how to grow the window to minimize further loss. At a certain point, another packet loss event will occur, and the process will repeat once over. If you have ever looked at a throughput trace of a TCP connection and observed a sawtooth pattern within it, now you know why it looks as such: it is the congestion control and avoidance algorithms adjusting the congestion window size to account for packet loss in the network.

Finally, it is worth noting that improving congestion control and avoidance is an active area both for academic research and commercial products: there are adaptations for different network types, different types of data transfers, and so on. Today, depending on your platform, you will likely run one of the many variants: TCP Tahoe and Reno (original implementations), TCP Vegas, TCP New Reno, TCP BIC, TCP CUBIC (default on Linux), or Compound TCP (default on Windows), among many others. However, regardless of the flavor, the core performance implications of congestion control and avoidance hold for all.

Proportional Rate Reduction for TCP

Determining the optimal way to recover from packet loss is a nontrivial exercise: if you are too aggressive, then an intermittent lost packet will have significant impact on throughput of the entire connection, and if you don't adjust quickly enough, then you will induce more packet loss!

Originally, TCP used the Multiplicative Decrease and Additive Increase (AIMD) algorithm: when packet loss occurs, halve the congestion window size, and then slowly increase the window by a fixed amount per roundtrip. However, in many cases AIMD is too conservative, and hence new algorithms were developed.

Proportional Rate Reduction (PRR) is a new algorithm specified by RFC 6937, whose goal is to improve the speed of recovery when a packet is lost. How much better is it? According to measurements done at Google, where the new algorithm was developed, it provides a 3–10% reduction in average latency for connections with packet loss.

PRR is now the default congestion-avoidance algorithm in Linux 3.2+ kernels—another good reason to upgrade your servers!

Bandwidth-Delay Product

The built-in congestion control and congestion avoidance mechanisms in TCP carry another important performance implication: the optimal sender and receiver window sizes must vary based on the roundtrip time and the target data rate between them.

To understand why this is the case, first recall that the maximum amount of unacknowledged, in-flight data between the sender and receiver is defined as the minimum of the receive (rwnd) and congestion (cwnd) window sizes: the current receive windows are communicated in every ACK, and the congestion window is dynamically adjusted by the sender based on the congestion control and avoidance algorithms.

If either the sender or receiver exceeds the maximum amount of unacknowledged data, then it must stop and wait for the other end to ACK some of the packets before proceeding. How long would it have to wait? That's dictated by the roundtrip time between the two!

Bandwidth-delay product (BDP)
> Product of data link's capacity and its end-to-end delay. The result is the maximum amount of unacknowledged data that can be in flight at any point in time.

If either the sender or receiver are frequently forced to stop and wait for ACKs for previous packets, then this would create gaps in the data flow (Figure 2-7), which would consequently limit the maximum throughput of the connection. To address this problem, the window sizes should be made just big enough, such that either side can continue sending data until an ACK arrives back from the client for an earlier packet—no gaps, maximum throughput. Consequently, the optimal window size depends on the roundtrip time! Pick a low window size, and you will limit your connection throughput, regardless of the available or advertised bandwidth between the peers.

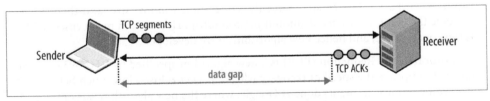

Figure 2-7. Transmission gaps due to low congestion window size

So how big do the flow control (rwnd) and congestion control (cwnd) window values need to be? The actual calculation is a simple one. First, let us assume that the minimum of the cwnd and rwnd window sizes is 16 KB, and the roundtrip time is 100 ms:

$$16 \ \text{KB} = (16 \times 1024 \times 8) \quad = 131,072 \ \text{bits}$$

$$\frac{131,072 \ \text{bits}}{0.1 \ \text{s}} \quad = 1,310,720 \ \text{bits/s}$$

$$1,310,720 \ \text{bits/s} = \frac{1,310,720}{1,000,000} \quad = 1.31 \ \text{Mbps}$$

Regardless of the available bandwidth between the sender and receiver, this TCP connection will not exceed a 1.31 Mbps data rate! To achieve higher throughput we need to raise the minimum window size or lower the roundtrip time.

Similarly, we can compute the optimal window size if we know the roundtrip time and the available bandwidth on both ends. In this scenario, let's assume that the roundtrip time stays the same (100 ms), but the sender has 10 Mbps of available bandwidth, and the receiver is on a high-throughput 100 Mbps+ link. Assuming there is no network congestion between them, our goal is to saturate the 10 Mbps link available to the client:

$$10 \ \text{Mbps} = 10 \times 1,000,000 \quad = 10,000,000 \ \text{bits/s}$$

$$10,000,000 \ \text{bits/s} = \frac{10,000,000}{8 \times 1024} \quad = 1,221 \ \text{KB/s}$$

$$1,221 \ \text{KB/s} \times 0.1 \ \text{s} \quad = 122.1 \ \text{KB}$$

The window size needs to be at least 122.1 KB to saturate the 10 Mbps link. Recall that the maximum receive window size in TCP is 64 KB unless window scaling—see "Window Scaling (RFC 1323)" on page 18—is present: double-check your client and server settings!

The good news is that the window size negotiation and tuning is managed automatically by the network stack and should adjust accordingly. The bad news is sometimes it will still be the limiting factor on TCP performance. If you have ever wondered why your connection is transmitting at a fraction of the available bandwidth, even when you know that both the client and the server are capable of higher rates, then it is likely due to a small window size: a saturated peer advertising low receive window, bad network weather and high packet loss resetting the congestion window, or explicit traffic shaping that could have been applied to limit throughput of your connection.

Head-of-Line Blocking

TCP provides the abstraction of a reliable network running over an unreliable channel, which includes basic packet error checking and correction, in-order delivery, retransmission of lost packets, as well as flow control, congestion control, and congestion avoidance designed to operate the network at the point of greatest efficiency. Combined, these features make TCP the preferred transport for most applications.

However, while TCP is a popular choice, it is not the only, nor necessarily the best choice for every occasion. Specifically, some of the features, such as in-order and reliable packet delivery, are not always necessary and can introduce unnecessary delays and negative performance implications.

To understand why that is the case, recall that every TCP packet carries a unique sequence number when put on the wire, and the data must be passed to the receiver in-order (Figure 2-8). If one of the packets is lost en route to the receiver, then all subsequent packets must be held in the receiver's TCP buffer until the lost packet is retransmitted and arrives at the receiver. Because this work is done within the TCP layer, our application has no visibility into the TCP retransmissions or the queued packet buffers, and must wait for the full sequence before it is able to access the data. Instead, it simply sees a delivery delay when it tries to read the data from the socket. This effect is known as TCP head-of-line (HOL) blocking.

The delay imposed by head-of-line blocking allows our applications to avoid having to deal with packet reordering and reassembly, which makes our application code much simpler. However, this is done at the cost of introducing unpredictable latency variation in the packet arrival times, commonly referred to as *jitter*, which can negatively impact the performance of the application.

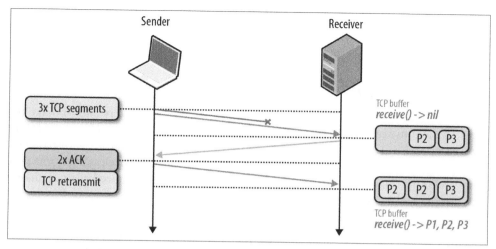

Figure 2-8. TCP Head-of-line blocking

Further, some applications may not even need either reliable delivery or in-order delivery: if every packet is a standalone message, then in-order delivery is strictly unnecessary, and if every message overrides all previous messages, then the requirement for reliable delivery can be removed entirely. Unfortunately, TCP does not provide such configuration—all packets are sequenced and delivered in order.

Applications that can deal with out-of-order delivery or packet loss and that are latency or jitter sensitive are likely better served with an alternate transport, such as UDP.

Packet Loss Is OK

In fact, packet loss is necessary to get the best performance from TCP! A dropped packet acts as a feedback mechanism, which allows the receiver and sender to adjust their sending rates to avoid overwhelming the network, and to minimize latency; see "Bufferbloat in Your Local Router" on page 6. Further, some applications can tolerate packet loss without adverse effects: audio, video, and game state updates are common examples of application data that do not require either reliable or in-order delivery—incidentally, this is also why WebRTC uses UDP as its base transport.

If a packet is lost, then the audio codec can simply insert a minor break in the audio and continue processing the incoming packets. If the gap is small, the user may not even notice, and waiting for the lost packet runs the risk of introducing variable pauses in audio output, which would result in a much worse experience for the user.

Similarly, if we are delivering game state updates for a character in a 3D world, then waiting for a packet describing its state at time T-1, when we already have the packet for time T is often simply unnecessary—ideally, we would receive each and every update, but to avoid gameplay delays, we can accept intermittent loss in favor of lower latency.

Optimizing for TCP

TCP is an adaptive protocol designed to be fair to all network peers and to make the most efficient use of the underlying network. Thus, the best way to optimize TCP is to tune how TCP senses the current network conditions and adapts its behavior based on the type and the requirements of the layers below and above it: wireless networks may need different congestion algorithms, and some applications may need custom quality of service (QoS) semantics to deliver the best experience.

The close interplay of the varying application requirements, and the many knobs in every TCP algorithm, make TCP tuning and optimization an inexhaustible area of academic and commercial research. In this chapter, we have only scratched the surface of the many factors that govern TCP performance. Additional mechanisms, such as selective acknowledgments (SACK), delayed acknowledgments, and fast retransmit, among many others, make each TCP session much more complicated (or interesting, depending on your perspective) to understand, analyze, and tune.

Having said that, while the specific details of each algorithm and feedback mechanism will continue to evolve, the core principles and their implications remain unchanged:

- TCP three-way handshake introduces a full roundtrip of latency.
- TCP slow-start is applied to every new connection.
- TCP flow and congestion control regulate throughput of all connections.
- TCP throughput is regulated by current congestion window size.

As a result, the rate with which a TCP connection can transfer data in modern high-speed networks is often limited by the roundtrip time between the receiver and sender. Further, while bandwidth continues to increase, latency is bounded by the speed of light and is already within a small constant factor of its maximum value. In most cases, latency, not bandwidth, is the bottleneck for TCP—e.g., see Figure 2-5.

Tuning Server Configuration

As a starting point, prior to tuning any specific values for each buffer and timeout variable in TCP, of which there are dozens, you are much better off simply upgrading your hosts to their latest system versions. TCP best practices and underlying algorithms that govern its performance continue to evolve, and most of these changes are only available only in the latest kernels. In short, keep your servers up to date to ensure the optimal interaction between the sender's and receiver's TCP stacks.

On the surface, upgrading server kernel versions seems like trivial advice. However, in practice, it is often met with significant resistance: many existing servers are tuned for specific kernel versions, and system administrators are reluctant to perform the upgrade.

To be fair, every upgrade brings its risks, but to get the best TCP performance, it is also likely the single best investment you can make.

With the latest kernel in place, it is good practice to ensure that your server is configured to use the following best practices:

"Increasing TCP's Initial Congestion Window" on page 26
A larger starting congestion window allows TCP transfers more data in the first roundtrip and significantly accelerates the window growth—an especially critical optimization for bursty and short-lived connections.

"Slow-Start Restart" on page 23
Disabling slow-start after idle will improve performance of long-lived TCP connections, which transfer data in bursts.

"Window Scaling (RFC 1323)" on page 18
Enabling window scaling increases the maximum receive window size and allows high-latency connections to achieve better throughput.

"TCP Fast Open" on page 16
Allows application data to be sent in the initial SYN packet in certain situations. TFO is a new optimization, which requires support both on client and server; investigate if your application can make use of it.

The combination of the preceding settings and the latest kernel will enable the best performance—lower latency and higher throughput—for individual TCP connections.

Depending on your application, you may also need to tune other TCP settings on the server to optimize for high connection rates, memory consumption, or similar criteria. However, these configuration settings are dependent on the platform, application, and hardware—consult your platform documentation as required.

For Linux users, ss is a useful power tool to inspect various statistics for open sockets. From the command line, run ss --options --extended --memory --processes --info to see the current peers and their respective connection settings.

Tuning Application Behavior

Tuning performance of TCP allows the server and client to deliver the best throughput and latency for an individual connection. However, how an application uses each new, or established, TCP connection can have an even greater impact:

- No bit is faster than one that is not sent; send fewer bits.
- We can't make the bits travel faster, but we can move the bits closer.
- TCP connection reuse is critical to improve performance.

Eliminating unnecessary data transfers is, of course, the single best optimization—e.g., eliminating unnecessary resources or ensuring that the minimum number of bits is transferred by applying the appropriate compression algorithm. Following that, locating the bits closer to the client, by geo-distributing servers around the world—e.g., using a CDN—will help reduce latency of network roundtrips and significantly improve TCP performance. Finally, where possible, existing TCP connections should be reused to minimize overhead imposed by slow-start and other congestion mechanisms.

Performance Checklist

Optimizing TCP performance pays high dividends, regardless of the type of application, for every new connection to your servers. A short list to put on the agenda:

- Upgrade server kernel to latest version (Linux: 3.2+).
- Ensure that cwnd size is set to 10.
- Disable slow-start after idle.
- Ensure that window scaling is enabled.
- Eliminate redundant data transfers.
- Compress transferred data.
- Position servers closer to the user to reduce roundtrip times.
- Reuse established TCP connections whenever possible.

CHAPTER 3

Building Blocks of UDP

User Datagram Protocol, or UDP, was added to the core network protocol suite in August of 1980 by Jon Postel, well after the original introduction of TCP/IP, but right at the time when the TCP and IP specifications were being split to become two separate RFCs. This timing is important because, as we will see, the primary feature and appeal of UDP is not in what it introduces, but rather in all the features it chooses to omit. UDP is colloquially referred to as a *null protocol*, and RFC 768, which describes its operation, could indeed fit on a napkin.

Datagram

> A self-contained, independent entity of data carrying sufficient information to be routed from the source to the destination nodes without reliance on earlier exchanges between the nodes and the transporting network.

The words datagram and packet are often used interchangeably, but there are some nuances. While the term "packet" applies to any formatted block of data, the term "datagram" is often reserved for packets delivered via an unreliable service—no delivery guarantees, no failure notifications. Because of this, you will frequently find the more descriptive term "Unreliable" substituted for the official term "User" in the UDP acronym, to form "Unreliable Datagram Protocol." That is also why UDP packets are generally, and more correctly, referred to as datagrams.

Perhaps the most well-known use of UDP, and one that every browser and Internet application depends on, is the Domain Name System (DNS): given a human-friendly computer hostname, we need to discover its IP address before any data exchange can occur. However, even though the browser itself is dependent on UDP, historically the protocol has never been exposed as a first-class transport for pages and applications running within it. That is, until WebRTC entered into the picture.

The new Web Real-Time Communication (WebRTC) standards, jointly developed by the IETF and W3C working groups, are enabling real-time communication, such as voice and video calling and other forms of peer-to-peer (P2P) communication, natively within the browser via UDP. With WebRTC, UDP is now a first-class browser transport with a client-side API! We will investigate WebRTC in-depth in Chapter 18, but before we get there, let's first explore the inner workings of the UDP protocol to understand why and where we may want to use it.

Null Protocol Services

To understand UDP and why it is commonly referred to as a "null protocol," we first need to look at the Internet Protocol (IP), which is located one layer below both TCP and UDP protocols.

The IP layer has the primary task of delivering datagrams from the source to the destination host based on their addresses. To do so, the messages are encapsulated within an IP packet (Figure 3-1) which identifies the source and the destination addresses, as well as a number of other routing parameters .

Once again, the word "datagram" is an important distinction: the IP layer provides no guarantees about message delivery or notifications of failure and hence directly exposes the unreliability of the underlying network to the layers above it. If a routing node along the way drops the IP packet due to congestion, high load, or for other reasons, then it is the responsibility of a protocol above IP to detect it, recover, and retransmit the data —that is, if that is the desired behavior!

Bit	+0..7		+8..15		+16..23	+24..31
0	Version	Header Length	DSCP	ECN	Total Length	
32	Identification			Flags	Fragment Offset	
64	Time To Live		Protocol		Header Checksum	
96	Source IP Address					
128	Destination IP Address					
160	Options (if present)					
...	Payload					

Figure 3-1. IPv4 header (20 bytes)

The UDP protocol encapsulates user messages into its own packet structure (Figure 3-2), which adds only four additional fields: source port, destination port, length of packet, and checksum. Thus, when IP delivers the packet to the destination host, the host is able to unwrap the UDP packet, identify the target application by the destination port, and deliver the message. Nothing more, nothing less.

Bit	+0..7	+8..15	+16..23	+24..31
0	Source Port		Destination Port	
32	Length		Checksum	
...	Payload			

Figure 3-2. UDP header (8 bytes)

In fact, both the source port and the checksum fields are optional fields in UDP datagrams. The IP packet contains its own header checksum, and the application can choose to omit the UDP checksum, which means that all the error detection and error correction can be delegated to the applications above them. At its core, UDP simply provides "application multiplexing" on top of IP by embedding the source and the target application ports of the communicating hosts. With that in mind, we can now summarize all the UDP non-services:

No guarantee of message delivery
　　No acknowledgments, retransmissions, or timeouts

No guarantee of order of delivery
　　No packet sequence numbers, no reordering, no head-of-line blocking

No connection state tracking
　　No connection establishment or teardown state machines

No congestion control
　　No built-in client or network feedback mechanisms

TCP is a byte-stream oriented protocol capable of transmitting application messages spread across multiple packets without any explicit message boundaries within the packets themselves. To achieve this, connection state is allocated on both ends of the connection, and each packet is sequenced, retransmitted when lost, and delivered in order. UDP datagrams, on the other hand, have definitive boundaries: each datagram is carried in a single IP packet, and each application read yields the full message; datagrams cannot be fragmented.

UDP is a simple, stateless protocol, suitable for bootstrapping other application protocols on top: virtually all of the protocol design decisions are left to the application above it. However, before you run away to implement your own protocol to replace TCP, you should think carefully about complications such as UDP interaction with the many layers of deployed middleboxes (NAT traversal), as well as general network protocol design best practices. Without careful engineering and planning, it is not uncommon to start with a bright idea for a new protocol but end up with a poorly implemented version of TCP. The algorithms and the state machines in TCP have been honed and improved over decades and have taken into account dozens of mechanisms that are anything but easy to replicate well.

UDP and Network Address Translators

Unfortunately, IPv4 addresses are only 32 bits long, which provides a maximum of 4.29 billion unique IP addresses. The IP Network Address Translator (NAT) specification was introduced in mid-1994 (RFC 1631) as an interim solution to resolve the looming IPv4 address depletion problem—as the number of hosts on the Internet began to grow exponentially in the early '90s, we could not expect to allocate a unique IP to every host.

The proposed IP reuse solution was to introduce NAT devices at the edge of the network, each of which would be responsible for maintaining a table mapping of local IP and port tuples to one or more globally unique (public) IP and port tuples (Figure 3-3). The local IP address space behind the translator could then be reused among many different networks, thus solving the address depletion problem.

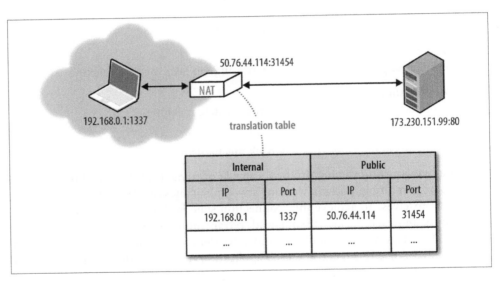

Figure 3-3. IP Network Address Translator

Unfortunately, as it often happens, there is nothing more permanent than a temporary solution. Not only did the NAT devices resolve the immediate problem, but they also quickly became a ubiquitous component of many corporate and home proxies and routers, security appliances, firewalls, and dozens of other hardware and software devices. NAT middleboxes are no longer a temporary solution; rather, they have become an integral part of the Internet infrastructure.

Reserved Private Network Ranges

Internet Assigned Numbers Authority (IANA), which is an entity that oversees global IP address allocation, reserved three well-known ranges for private networks, most often residing behind a NAT device:

Table 3-1. Reserved IP ranges

IP address range	Number of addresses
10.0.0.0–10.255.255.255	16,777,216
172.16.0.0–172.31.255.255	1,048,576
192.168.0.0–192.168.255.255	65,536

One or all of the preceding ranges should look familiar. Chances are, your local router has assigned your computer an IP address from one of those ranges. That's your private IP address on the internal network, which is then translated by the NAT device when communicating with an outside network.

To avoid routing errors and confusion, no public computer is allowed to be assigned an IP address from any of these reserved private network ranges.

Connection-State Timeouts

The issue with NAT translation, at least as far as UDP is concerned, is precisely the routing table that it must maintain to deliver the data. NAT middleboxes rely on connection state, whereas UDP has none. This is a fundamental mismatch and a source of many problems for delivering UDP datagrams. Further, it is now not uncommon for a client to be behind many layers of NATs, which only complicates matters further.

Each TCP connection has a well-defined protocol state machine, which begins with a handshake, followed by application data transfer, and a well-defined exchange to close the connection. Given this flow, each middlebox can observe the state of the connection and create and remove the routing entries as needed. With UDP, there is no handshake or connection termination, and hence there is no connection state machine to monitor.

Delivering outbound UDP traffic does not require any extra work, but routing a reply requires that we have an entry in the translation table, which will tell us the IP and port of the local destination host. Thus, translators have to keep state about each UDP flow, which itself is stateless.

Even worse, the translator is also tasked with figuring out when to drop the translation record, but since UDP has no connection termination sequence, either peer could just stop transmitting datagrams at any point without notice. To address this, UDP routing records are expired on a timer. How often? There is no definitive answer; instead the timeout depends on the vendor, make, version, and configuration of the translator. Consequently, one of the de facto best practices for long-running sessions over UDP is to introduce bidirectional keepalive packets to periodically reset the timers for the translation records in all the NAT devices along the path.

TCP Timeouts and NATs

Technically, there is no need for additional TCP timeouts on NAT devices. The TCP protocol follows a well-defined handshake and termination sequence, which signals when the appropriate translation records can be added and removed.

Unfortunately, in practice, many NAT devices apply similar timeout logic both to TCP and UDP sessions. As a result, in some cases bidirectional keepalive packets are also required for TCP. If your TCP connections are getting dropped, then there is a good chance that an intermediate NAT timeout is to blame.

NAT Traversal

Unpredictable connection state handling is a serious issue created by NATs, but an even larger problem for many applications is the inability to establish a UDP connection at all. This is especially true for P2P applications, such as VoIP, games, and file sharing, which often need to act as both client and server to enable two-way direct communication between the peers.

The first issue is that in the presence of a NAT, the internal client is unaware of its public IP: it knows its internal IP address, and the NAT devices perform the rewriting of the source port and address in every UDP packet, as well as the originating IP address within the IP packet. However, if the client communicates its private IP address as part of its application data with a peer outside of its private network, then the connection will inevitably fail. Hence, the promise of "transparent" translation is no longer true, and the application must first discover its public IP address if it needs to share it with a peer outside its private network.

However, knowing the public IP is also not sufficient to successfully transmit with UDP. Any packet that arrives at the public IP of a NAT device must also have a destination port and an entry in the NAT table that can translate it to an internal destination host IP and port tuple. If this entry does not exist, which is the most likely case if someone simply tries to transmit data from the public network, then the packet is simply dropped (Figure 3-4). The NAT device acts as a simple packet filter since it has no way to automatically determine the internal route, unless explicitly configured by the user through a port-forwarding or similar mechanism.

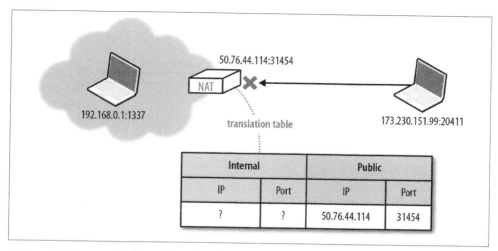

Figure 3-4. *Dropped inbound packet due to missing mapping*

It is important to note that the preceding behavior is not an issue for client applications, which begin their interaction from the internal network and in the process establish the necessary translation records along the path. However, handling inbound connections (acting as a server) from P2P applications such as VoIP, game consoles, file sharing, and so on, in the presence of a NAT, is where we will immediately run into this problem.

To work around this mismatch in UDP and NATs, various traversal techniques (TURN, STUN, ICE) have to be used to establish end-to-end connectivity between the UDP peers on both sides.

STUN, TURN, and ICE

Session Traversal Utilities for NAT (STUN) is a protocol (RFC 5389) that allows the host application to discover the presence of a network address translator on the network, and when present to obtain the allocated public IP and port tuple for the current connection (Figure 3-5). To do so, the protocol requires assistance from a well-known, third-party STUN server that must reside on the public network.

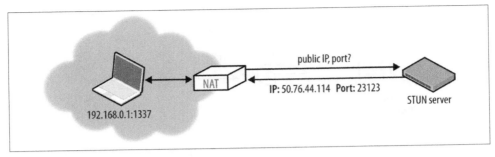

Figure 3-5. STUN query for public IP and port

Assuming the IP address of the STUN server is known (through DNS discovery, or through a manually specified address), the application first sends a binding request to the STUN server. In turn, the STUN server replies with a response that contains the public IP address and port of the client as seen from the public network. This simple workflow addresses several problems we encountered in our earlier discussion:

- The application discovers its public IP and port tuple and is then able to use this information as part of its application data when communicating with its peers.
- The outbound binding request to the STUN server establishes NAT routing entries along the path, such that the inbound packets arriving at the public IP and port tuple can now find their way back to the host application on the internal network.
- The STUN protocol defines a simple mechanism for keepalive pings to keep the NAT routing entries from timing out.

With this mechanism in place, whenever two peers want to talk to each other over UDP, they will first send binding requests to their respective STUN servers, and following a successful response on both sides, they can then use the established public IP and port tuples to exchange data.

However, in practice, STUN is not sufficient to deal with all NAT topologies and network configurations. Further, unfortunately, in some cases UDP may be blocked altogether by a firewall or some other network appliance—not an uncommon scenario for many enterprise networks. To address this issue, whenever STUN fails, we can use the Traversal Using Relays around NAT (TURN) protocol (RFC 5766) as a fallback, which can run over UDP and switch to TCP if all else fails.

They key word in TURN is, of course, "relays." The protocol relies on the presence and availability of a public relay (Figure 3-6) to shuttle the data between the peers.

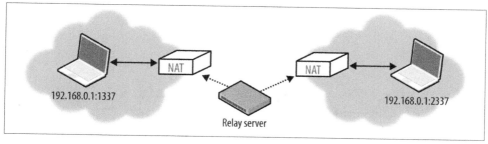

Figure 3-6. TURN relay server

- Both clients begin their connections by sending an allocate request to the same TURN server, followed by permissions negotiation.
- Once the negotiation is complete, both peers communicate by sending their data to the TURN server, which then relays it to the other peer.

Of course, the obvious downside in this exchange is that it is no longer peer-to-peer! TURN is the most reliable way to provide connectivity between any two peers on any networks, but it carries a very high cost of operating the TURN server—at the very least, the relay must have enough capacity to service all the data flows. As a result, TURN is best used as a last resort fallback for cases where direct connectivity fails.

STUN and TURN in Practice

Google's libjingle is an open-source C++ library for building peer-to-peer applications, which takes care of STUN, TURN, and ICE negotiations under the hood. The library is used to power the Google Talk chat application, and the documentation provides a valuable reference point for performance of STUN vs. TURN in the real world:

- 92% of the time the connection can take place directly (STUN).
- 8% of the time the connection requires a relay (TURN).

Unfortunately, even with STUN, a significant fraction of users are unable to establish a direct P2P tunnel. To provide a reliable service, we also need TURN relays, which can acts as a fallback for cases where direct P2P communication is not an option.

Building an effective NAT traversal solution is not for the faint of heart. Thankfully, we can lean on Interactive Connectivity Establishment (ICE) protocol (RFC 5245) to help with this task. ICE is a protocol, and a set of methods, that seek to establish the most efficient tunnel between the participants (Figure 3-7): direct connection where possible, leveraging STUN negotiation where needed, and finally fallback to TURN if all else fails.

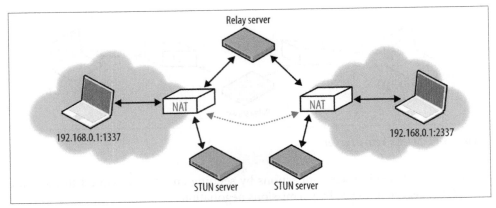

Figure 3-7. ICE attempts direct, STUN, and TURN connectivity options

In practice, if you are building a P2P application over UDP, then you most definitely want to leverage an existing platform API, or a third-party library that implements ICE, STUN, and TURN for you. And now that you are familiar with what each of these protocols does, you can navigate your way through the required setup and configuration!

Optimizing for UDP

UDP is a simple and a commonly used protocol for bootstrapping new transport protocols. In fact, the primary feature of UDP is all the features it omits: no connection state, handshakes, retransmissions, reassembly, reordering, congestion control, congestion avoidance, flow control, or even optional error checking. However, the flexibility that this minimal message-oriented transport layer affords is also a liability for the implementer. Your application will likely have to reimplement some, or many, of these features from scratch, and each must be designed to play well with other peers and protocols on the network.

Unlike TCP, which ships with built-in flow and congestion control and congestion avoidance, UDP applications must implement these mechanisms on their own. Congestion insensitive UDP applications can easily overwhelm the network, which can lead to degraded network performance and, in severe cases, to network congestion collapse.

If you want to leverage UDP for your own application, make sure to research and read the current best practices and recommendations. One such document is the RFC 5405, which specifically focuses on design guidelines for applications delivered via unicast UDP. Here is a short sample of the recommendations:

- Application *must* tolerate a wide range of Internet path conditions.
- Application *should* control rate of transmission.
- Application *should* perform congestion control over all traffic.
- Application *should* use bandwidth similar to TCP.
- Application *should* back off retransmission counters following loss.
- Application *should not* send datagrams that exceed path MTU.
- Application *should* handle datagram loss, duplication, and reordering.
- Application *should* be robust to delivery delays up to 2 minutes.
- Application *should* enable IPv4 UDP checksum, and *must* enable IPv6 checksum.
- Application *may* use keepalives when needed (minimum interval 15 seconds).

Designing a new transport protocol requires a lot of careful thought, planning, and research—do your due diligence. Where possible, leverage an existing library or a framework that has already taken into account NAT traversal, and is able to establish some degree of fairness with other sources of concurrent network traffic.

On that note, good news: WebRTC is just such a framework!

CHAPTER 4

Transport Layer Security (TLS)

The SSL protocol was originally developed at Netscape to enable ecommerce transaction security on the Web, which required encryption to protect customers' personal data, as well as authentication and integrity guarantees to ensure a safe transaction. To achieve this, the SSL protocol was implemented at the application layer, directly on top of TCP (Figure 4-1), enabling protocols above it (HTTP, email, instant messaging, and many others) to operate unchanged while providing communication security when communicating across the network.

When SSL is used correctly, a third-party observer can only infer the connection endpoints, type of encryption, as well as the frequency and an approximate amount of data sent, but cannot read or modify any of the actual data.

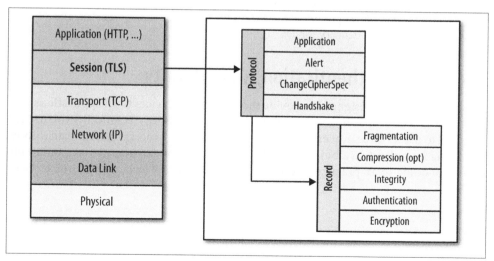

Figure 4-1. Transport Layer Security (TLS)

When the SSL protocol was standardized by the IETF, it was re-named to Transport Layer Security (TLS). Many use the TLS and SSL names interchangeably, but technically, they are different, since each describes a different version of the protocol.

SSL 2.0 was the first publicly released version of the protocol, but it was quickly replaced by SSL 3.0 due to a number of discovered security flaws. Because the SSL protocol was proprietary to Netscape, the IETF formed an effort to standardize the protocol, resulting in RFC 2246, which became known as TLS 1.0 and is effectively an upgrade to SSL 3.0:

> The differences between this protocol and SSL 3.0 are not dramatic, but they are significant to preclude interoperability between TLS 1.0 and SSL 3.0.
>
> — The TLS Protocol
> *RFC 2246*

Since the publication of TLS 1.0 in January 1999, two new versions have been produced by the IETF working group to address found security flaws, as well as to extend the capabilities of the protocol: TLS 1.1 in April 2006 and TLS 1.2 in August 2008. Internally the SSL 3.0 implementation, as well as all subsequent TLS versions, are very similar, and many clients continue to support SSL 3.0 and TLS 1.0 to this day, although there are very good reasons to upgrade to newer versions to protect users from known attacks!

 TLS was designed to operate on top of a reliable transport protocol such as TCP. However, it has also been adapted to run over datagram protocols such as UDP. The Datagram Transport Layer Security (DTLS) protocol, defined in RFC 6347, is based on the TLS protocol and is able to provide similar security guarantees while preserving the datagram delivery model.

Encryption, Authentication, and Integrity

The TLS protocol is designed to provide three essential services to all applications running above it: encryption, authentication, and data integrity. Technically, you are not required to use all three in every situation. You may decide to accept a certificate without validating its authenticity, but you should be well aware of the security risks and implications of doing so. In practice, a secure web application will leverage all three services.

Encryption

A mechanism to obfuscate what is sent from one computer to another.

Authentication

A mechanism to verify the validity of provided identification material.

Integrity

A mechanism to detect message tampering and forgery.

In order to establish a cryptographically secure data channel, the connection peers must agree on which ciphersuites will be used and the keys used to encrypt the data. The TLS protocol specifies a well-defined handshake sequence to perform this exchange, which we will examine in detail in "TLS Handshake" on page 50. The ingenious part of this handshake, and the reason TLS works in practice, is its use of public key cryptography (also known as asymmetric key cryptography), which allows the peers to negotiate a shared secret key without having to establish any prior knowledge of each other, and to do so over an unencrypted channel.

As part of the TLS handshake, the protocol also allows both connection peers to authenticate their identity. When used in the browser, this authentication mechanism allows the client to verify that the server is who it claims to be (e.g., your bank) and not someone simply pretending to be the destination by spoofing its name or IP address. This verification is based on the established chain of trust; see "Chain of Trust and Certificate Authorities" on page 57). In addition, the server can also optionally verify the identity of the client—e.g., a company proxy server can authenticate all employees, each of whom could have his own unique certificate signed by the company.

Finally, with encryption and authentication in place, the TLS protocol also provides its own message framing mechanism and signs each message with a message authentication code (MAC). The MAC algorithm is a one-way cryptographic hash function (effectively a checksum), the keys to which are negotiated by both connection peers. Whenever a TLS record is sent, a MAC value is generated and appended for that message, and the receiver is then able to compute and verify the sent MAC value to ensure message integrity and authenticity.

Combined, all three mechanisms serve as a foundation for secure communication on the Web. All modern web browsers provide support for a variety of ciphersuites, are able to authenticate both the client and server, and transparently perform message integrity checks for every record.

Proxies, Intermediaries, TLS, and New Protocols on the Web

The extensibility and the success of HTTP created a vibrant ecosystem of various proxies and intermediaries on the Web: cache servers, security gateways, web accelerators, content filters, and many others. In some cases we are aware of their presence (explicit proxies), and in others they are completely transparent to the end user.

Unfortunately, the very success and the presence of these servers has created a small problem for anyone who tries to deviate from the HTTP protocol in any way: some proxy servers may simply relay HTTP extensions or alternative wire formats they cannot interpret, others may continue to blindly apply their logic even when they shouldn't, and some, such as security appliances, may infer malicious traffic where there is none.

In other words, in practice, deviating from the well-defined semantics of HTTP on port 80 will often lead to unreliable deployments: some clients will have no problems, while others may fail with unpredictable behaviors—e.g., the same client may see different connectivity behaviors as it migrates between different networks.

Due to these behaviors, new protocols and extensions to HTTP, such as WebSocket, SPDY, and others, often rely on establishing an HTTPS tunnel to bypass the intermediate proxies and provide a reliable deployment model: the encrypted tunnel obfuscates the data from all intermediaries. This solves the immediate problem, but it does have a real downside of not being able to leverage the intermediaries, many of which provide useful services: authentication, caching, security scanning, and so on.

If you have ever wondered why most WebSocket guides will tell you to use HTTPS to deliver data to mobile clients, this is why. As times passes and the intermediaries are upgraded to recognize new protocols, the requirement for HTTPS deployment will also become less relevant—that is, unless your session actually needs the encryption, authentication, and integrity provided by TLS!

TLS Handshake

Before the client and the server can begin exchanging application data over TLS, the encrypted tunnel must be negotiated: the client and the server must agree on the version of the TLS protocol, choose the ciphersuite, and verify certificates if necessary. Unfortunately, each of these steps requires new packet roundtrips (Figure 4-2) between the client and the server, which adds startup latency to all TLS connections.

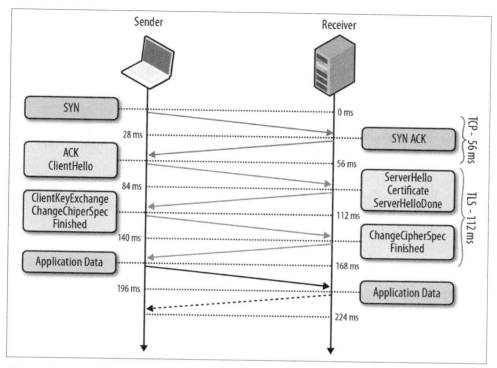

Figure 4-2. TLS handshake protocol

 Figure 4-2 assumes the same 28 millisecond one-way "light in fiber" delay between New York and London as used in previous TCP connection establishment examples; see Table 1-1.

0 ms   TLS runs over a reliable transport (TCP), which means that we must first complete the TCP three-way handshake, which takes one full roundtrip.

56 ms   With the TCP connection in place, the client sends a number of specifications in plain text, such as the version of the TLS protocol it is running, the list of supported ciphersuites, and other TLS options it may want to use.

84 ms   The server picks the TLS protocol version for further communication, decides on a ciphersuite from the list provided by the client, attaches its certificate, and sends the response back to the client. Optionally, the server can also send a request for the client's certificate and parameters for other TLS extensions.

112 ms Assuming both sides are able to negotiate a common version and cipher, and the client is happy with the certificate provided by the server, the client then generates a new symmetric key, encrypts it with the server's public key, and tells the server to switch to encrypted communication going forward. Up until now, all the data has been exchanged in clear text with the exception of the new symmetric key that is encrypted with the server's public key.

140 ms The server decrypts the symmetric key sent by the client, checks message integrity by verifying the MAC, and returns an encrypted "Finished" message back to the client.

168 ms The client decrypts the message with the symmetric key it generated earlier, verifies the MAC, and if all is well, then the tunnel is established and application data can now be sent.

 New TLS connections require two roundtrips for a "full handshake." Alternatively, an "abbreviated handshake" can be used, which requires one roundtrip; see "TLS Session Resumption" on page 55.

Negotiating a secure TLS tunnel is a complicated process, and there are many ways to get it wrong. The good news is all the work just shown will be done for us by the server and the browser, and all we need to do is provide and configure the certificates.

Having said that, while our web applications do not have to drive the preceding exchange, it is nonetheless important to realize that every TLS connection will require up to two extra roundtrips on top of the TCP handshake—that's a long time to wait before any application data can be exchanged! If not managed carefully, delivering application data over TLS can add hundreds, if not thousands of milliseconds of network latency.

Performance of Public vs. Symmetric Key Cryptography

Public-key cryptography is used only during session setup of the TLS tunnel. The server provides its public key to the client, and then the client generates a symmetric key, which it encrypts with the server's public key, and returns the encrypted symmetric key to the server. Finally, the server can decrypt the sent symmetric key with its private key.

Symmetric key cryptography, which uses the shared secret key generated by the client, is then used for all further communication between the client and the server. This is done, in large part, to improve performance—public key cryptography is much more computationally expensive. To illustrate the difference, if you have OpenSSL installed on your computer, you can run the following tests:

- `$> openssl speed rsa`
- `$> openssl speed aes`

Note that the units between the two tests are not directly comparable: the RSA test provides a summary table of operations per second for different key sizes, while AES performance is measured in bytes per second. Nonetheless, it should be easy to see that the number of RSA operations (full TLS handshakes), for a recommended key length of 1,024 or 2,048 bits is the likely bottleneck.

The exact performance numbers vary significantly based on used hardware, number of cores, TLS version, server configuration, and other factors. Don't fall for marketing or an outdated benchmark! Always run the performance tests on your own hardware.

Application Layer Protocol Negotiation (ALPN)

Two network peers may want to use a custom application protocol to communicate with each other. One way to resolve this is to determine the protocol upfront, assign a well-known port to it (e.g., port 80 for HTTP, port 443 for TLS), and configure all clients and servers to use it. However, in practice, this is a slow and impractical process: each port assignment must be approved and, worse, firewalls and other intermediaries often permit traffic only on ports 80 and 443.

As a result, to enable easy deployment of custom protocols, we must reuse ports 80 or 443 and use an additional mechanism to negotiate the application protocol. Port 80 is reserved for HTTP, and the HTTP specification provides a special Upgrade flow for this very purpose. However, the use of Upgrade can add an extra network roundtrip of latency, and in practice is often unreliable in the presence of many intermediaries; see "Proxies, Intermediaries, TLS, and New Protocols on the Web" on page 50.

For a hands-on example of HTTP Upgrade flow, flip ahead to "Efficient HTTP 2.0 Upgrade and Discovery" on page 224.

The solution is, you guessed it, to use port 443, which is reserved for secure HTTPS sessions (running over TLS). The use of an end-to-end encrypted tunnel obfuscates the data from intermediate proxies and enables a quick and reliable way to deploy new and arbitrary application protocols. However, while use of TLS addresses reliability, we still need a way to negotiate the protocol!

An HTTPS session could, of course, reuse the HTTP Upgrade mechanism to perform the require negotiation, but this would result in another full roundtrip of latency. What if we could negotiate the protocol as part of the TLS handshake itself?

As the name implies, Application Layer Protocol Negotiation (ALPN) is a TLS extension that introduces support for application protocol negotiation into the TLS handshake (Figure 4-2), thereby eliminating the need for an extra roundtrip required by the HTTP Upgrade workflow. Specifically, the process is as follows:

- The client appends a new `ProtocolNameList` field, containing the list of supported application protocols, into the `ClientHello` message.
- The server inspects the `ProtocolNameList` field and returns a `ProtocolName` field indicating the selected protocol as part of the `ServerHello` message.

The server may respond with only a single protocol name, and if it does not support any that the client requests, then it may choose to abort the connection. As a result, once the TLS handshake is complete, both the secure tunnel is established, and the client and server are in agreement as to which application protocol will be used, they can begin communicating immediately.

ALPN eliminates the need for the HTTP Upgrade exchange, saving an extra roundtrip of latency. However, note that the TLS handshake itself still must be performed; hence ALPN negotiation is not any faster than HTTP Upgrade over an unencrypted channel. Instead, it ensures that application protocol negotiation over TLS is *not any slower*.

History and Relationship of NPN and ALPN

Next Protocol Negotiation (NPN) is a TLS extension, which was developed as part of the SPDY effort at Google to enable efficient application protocol negotiation during the TLS handshake. Sound familiar? The end result is functionally equivalent to ALPN.

ALPN is a revised and IETF approved version of the NPN extension. In NPN, the server advertised which protocols it supports, and the client then chose and confirmed the protocol. In ALPN, this exchange was reversed: the client now specifies which protocols it supports, and the server then selects and confirms the protocol. The rationale for the change is that this brings ALPN into closer alignment with other protocol negotiation standards.

In other words, ALPN is a successor to NPN, and NPN is deprecated. Clients and servers that rely on NPN negotiation will have to be upgraded to use ALPN instead.

Server Name Indication (SNI)

An encrypted TLS tunnel can be established between any two TCP peers: the client only needs to know the IP address of the other peer to make the connection and perform the

TLS handshake. However, what if the server wants to host multiple independent sites, each with its own TLS certificate, on the same IP address—how does that work? Trick question; it doesn't.

To address the preceding problem, the Server Name Indication (SNI) extension was introduced to the TLS protocol, which allows the client to indicate the hostname the client is attempting to connect to at the start of the handshake. As a result, a web server can inspect the SNI hostname, select the appropriate certificate, and continue the handshake.

TLS, HTTP, and Dedicated IPs

The TLS+SNI workflow is identical to Host header advertisement in HTTP, where the client indicates the hostname of the site it is requesting: the same IP address may host many different domains, and both SNI and Host are required to disambiguate between them.

Unfortunately, many older clients (e.g., most IE versions running on Windows XP, Android 2.2, and others) do not support SNI. As a result, if you need to provide TLS to these older clients, then you may need a dedicated IP address for each and every host.

TLS Session Resumption

The extra latency and computational costs of the full TLS handshake impose a serious performance penalty on all applications that require secure communication. To help mitigate some of the costs, TLS provides an ability to resume or share the same negotiated secret key data between multiple connections.

Session Identifiers

The first Session Identifiers (RFC 5246) resumption mechanism was introduced in SSL 2.0, which allowed the server to create and send a 32-byte session identifier as part of its "ServerHello" message during the full TLS negotiation we saw earlier.

Internally, the server could then maintain a cache of session IDs and the negotiated session parameters for each peer. In turn, the client could then also store the session ID information and include the ID in the "ClientHello" message for a subsequent session, which serves as an indication to the server that the client still remembers the negotiated cipher suite and keys from previous handshake and is able to reuse them. Assuming both the client and the server are able to find the shared session ID parameters in their respective caches, then an abbreviated handshake (Figure 4-3) can take place. Otherwise, a full new session negotiation is required, which will generate a new session ID.

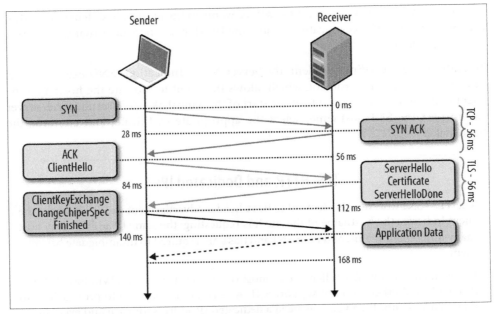

Figure 4-3. Abbreviated TLS handshake protocol

Leveraging session identifiers allows us to remove a full roundtrip, as well as the overhead of public key cryptography, which is used to negotiate the shared secret key. This allows a secure connection to be established quickly and with no loss of security, since we are reusing the previously negotiated session data.

> In practice, most web applications attempt to establish multiple connections to the same host to fetch resources in parallel, which makes session resumption a must-have optimization to reduce latency and computational costs for both sides.
>
> Most modern browsers intentionally wait for the first TLS connection to complete before opening new connections to the same server: subsequent TLS connections can reuse the SSL session parameters to avoid the costly handshake.

However, one of the practical limitations of the Session Identifiers mechanism is the requirement for the server to create and maintain a session cache for every client. This results in several problems on the server, which may see tens of thousands or even millions of unique connections every day: consumed memory for every open TLS connection, a requirement for session ID cache and eviction policies, and nontrivial deployment challenges for popular sites with many servers, which should, ideally, use a shared TLS session cache for best performance.

None of the preceding problems are impossible to solve, and many high-traffic sites are using session identifiers successfully today. But for any multiserver deployment, session identifiers will require some careful thinking and systems architecture to ensure a well operating session cache.

Session Tickets

To address this concern for server-side deployment of TLS session caches, the "Session Ticket" (RFC 5077) replacement mechanism was introduced, which removes the requirement for the server to keep per-client session state. Instead, if the client indicated that it supports Session Tickets, in the last exchange of the full TLS handshake, the server can include a New Session Ticket record, which includes all of the session data encrypted with a secret key known only by the server.

This session ticket is then stored by the client and can be included in the `SessionTick et` extension within the `ClientHello` message of a subsequent session. Thus, all session data is stored only on the client, but the ticket is still safe because it is encrypted with a key known only by the server.

The session identifiers and session ticket mechanisms are respectively commonly referred to as *session caching* and *stateless resumption* mechanisms. The main improvement of stateless resumption is the removal of the server-side session cache, which simplifies deployment by requiring that the client provide the session ticket on every new connection to the server—that is, until the ticket has expired.

 In practice, deploying session tickets across a set of load-balanced servers also requires some careful thinking and systems architecture: all servers must be initialized with the same session key, and an additional mechanism may be needed to periodically rotate the shared key across all servers.

Chain of Trust and Certificate Authorities

Authentication is an integral part of establishing every TLS connection. After all, it is possible to carry out a conversation over an encrypted tunnel with any peer, including an attacker, and unless we can be sure that the computer we are speaking to is the one we trust, then all the encryption work could be for nothing. To understand how we can verify the peer's identity, let's examine a simple authentication workflow between Alice and Bob:

- Both Alice and Bob generate their own public and private keys.
- Both Alice and Bob hide their respective private keys.
- Alice shares her public key with Bob, and Bob shares his with Alice.
- Alice generates a new message for Bob and signs it with her private key.
- Bob uses Alice's public key to verify the provided message signature.

Trust is a key component of the preceding exchange. Specifically, public key encryption allows us to use the public key of the sender to verify that the message was signed with the right private key, but the decision to approve the sender is still one that is based on trust. In the exchange just shown, Alice and Bob could have exchanged their public keys when they met in person, and because they know each other well, they are certain that their exchange was not compromised by an impostor—perhaps they even verified their identities through another, secret (physical) handshake they had established earlier!

Next, Alice receives a message from Charlie, whom she has never met, but who claims to be a friend of Bob's. In fact, to prove that he is friends with Bob, Charlie asked Bob to sign his own public key with Bob's private key and attached this signature with his message (Figure 4-4). In this case, Alice first checks Bob's signature of Charlie's key. She knows Bob's public key and is thus able to verify that Bob did indeed sign Charlie's key. Because she trusts Bob's decision to verify Charlie, she accepts the message and performs a similar integrity check on Charlie's message to ensure that it is, indeed, from Charlie.

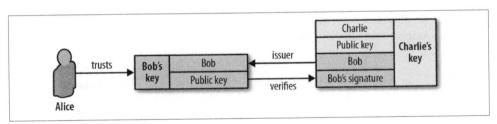

Figure 4-4. Chain of trust for Alice, Bob, and Charlie

What we have just done is established a chain of trust: Alice trusts Bob, Bob trusts Charlie, and by transitive trust, Alice decides to trust Charlie. As long as nobody in the chain gets compromised, this allows us to build and grow the list of trusted parties.

Authentication on the Web and in your browser follows the exact same process as shown. Which means that at this point you should be asking: whom does your browser trust, and whom do you trust when you use the browser? There are at least three answers to this question:

Manually specified certificates
> Every browser and operating system provides a mechanism for you to manually import any certificate you trust. How you obtain the certificate and verify its integrity is completely up to you.

Certificate authorities
> A certificate authority (CA) is a trusted third party that is trusted by both the subject (owner) of the certificate and the party relying upon the certificate.

The browser and the operating system
> Every operating system and most browsers ship with a list of well-known certificate authorities. Thus, you also trust the vendors of this software to provide and maintain a list of trusted parties.

In practice, it would be impractical to store and manually verify each and every key for every website (although you can, if you are so inclined). Hence, the most common solution is to use certificate authorities (CAs) to do this job for us (Figure 4-5): the browser specifies which CAs to trust (root CAs), and the burden is then on the CAs to verify each site they sign, and to audit and verify that these certificates are not misused or compromised. If the security of any site with the CA's certificate is breached, then it is also the responsibility of that CA to revoke the compromised certificate.

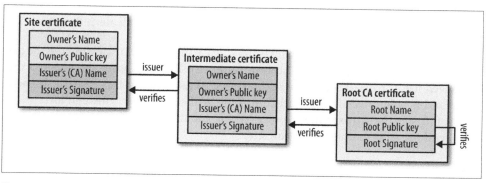

Figure 4-5. CA signing of digital certificates

Every browser allows you to inspect the chain of trust of your secure connection (Figure 4-6), usually accessible by clicking on the lock icon beside the URL.

Figure 4-6. Certificate chain of trust for igvita.com (Google Chrome, v25)

- igvita.com certificate is signed by StartCom Class 1 Primary Intermediate Server.
- StartCom Class 1 Primary Intermediate Server certificate is signed by the StartCom Certification Authority.
- StartCom Certification Authority is a recognized root certificate authority.

The "trust anchor" for the entire chain is the root certificate authority, which in the case just shown, is the StartCom Certification Authority. Every browser ships with a pre-initialized list of trusted certificate authorities ("roots"), and in this case, the browser trusts and is able to verify the StartCom root certificate. Hence, through a transitive chain of trust in the browser, the browser vendor, and the StartCom certificate authority, we extend the trust to our destination site.

Every operating system vendor and every browser provide a public listing of all the certificate authorities they trust by default. If you are curious, use your favorite search engine to find and investigate these lists.

In practice, there are hundreds of well-known and trusted certificate authorities, which is also a common complaint against the system. The large number of CAs creates a potentially large attack surface area against the chain of trust in your browser.

Certificate Revocation

Occasionally the issuer of a certificate will need to revoke or invalidate the certificate due to a number of possible reasons: the private key of the certificate has been compromised, the certificate authority itself has been compromised, or due to a variety of more benign reasons such as a superseding certificate, change in affiliation, and so on. To address this, the certificates themselves contain instructions (Figure 4-7) on how to check if they have been revoked. Hence, to ensure that the chain of trust is not compromised, each peer can check the status of each certificate by following the embedded instructions, along with the signatures, as it walks up the certificate chain.

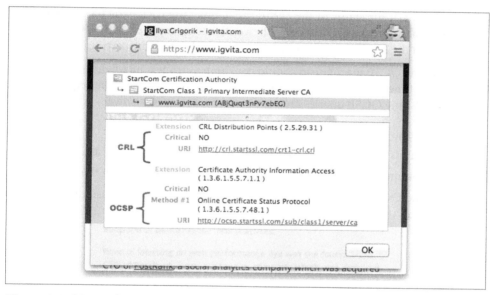

Figure 4-7. CRL and OCSP instructions for igvita.com (Google Chrome, v25)

Certificate Revocation List (CRL)

Certificate Revocation List (CRL) is defined by RFC 5280 and specifies a simple mechanism to check the status of every certificate: each certificate authority maintains and periodically publishes a list of revoked certificate serial numbers. Anyone attempting to verify a certificate is then able to download the revocation list and check the presence of the serial number within it—if it is present, then it has been revoked.

The CRL file itself can be published periodically or on every update and can be delivered via HTTP, or any other file transfer protocol. The list is also signed by the CA, and is usually allowed to be cached for a specified interval. In practice, this workflow works quite well, but there are instances where CRL mechanism may be insufficient:

- The growing number of revocations means that the CRL list will only get longer, and each client must retrieve the entire list of serial numbers.
- There is no mechanism for instant notification of certificate revocation—if the CRL was cached by the client before the certificate was revoked, then the CRL will deem the revoked certificate valid until the cache expires.

Online Certificate Status Protocol (OCSP)

To address some of the limitations of the CRL mechanism, the Online Certificate Status Protocol (OCSP) was introduced by RFC 2560, which provides a mechanism to perform a real-time check for status of the certificate. Unlike the CRL, which contains all the revoked serial numbers, OCSP allows the verifier to query the certificate database directly for just the serial number in question while validating the certificate chain.

As a result, the OCSP mechanism should consume much less bandwidth and is able to provide real-time validation. However, no mechanism is perfect! The requirement to perform real-time OCSP queries creates several problems of its own:

- The CA must be able to handle the load of the real-time queries.
- The CA must ensure that the service is up and globally available at all times.
- The client must block on OCSP requests before proceeding with the navigation.
- Real-time OCSP requests may impair the client's privacy because the CA knows which sites the client is visiting.

In practice, CRL and OCSP mechanisms are complementary, and most certificates will provide instructions and endpoints for both.

The more important part is the client support and behavior: some browsers distribute their own CRL lists, others fetch and cache the CRL files from the CAs. Similarly, some browsers will perform the real-time OCSP check but will differ in their behavior if the OCSP request fails. If you are curious, check your browser and OS certificate revocation settings!

TLS Record Protocol

Not unlike the IP or TCP layers below it, all data exchanged within a TLS session is also framed using a well-defined protocol (Figure 4-8). The TLS Record protocol is responsible for identifying different types of messages (handshake, alert, or data via the "Content Type" field), as well as securing and verifying the integrity of each message.

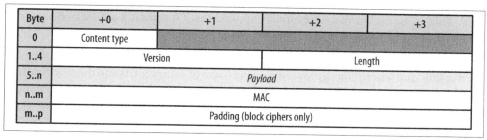

Figure 4-8. TLS record structure

A typical workflow for delivering application data is as follows:

- Record protocol receives application data.
- Received data is divided into blocks: maximum of 2^{14} bytes, or 16 KB per record.
- Application data is optionally compressed.
- Message authentication code (MAC) or HMAC is added.
- Data is encrypted using the negotiated cipher.

Once these steps are complete, the encrypted data is passed down to the TCP layer for transport. On the receiving end, the same workflow, but in reverse, is applied by the peer: decrypt data using negotiated cipher, verify MAC, extract and deliver the data to the application above it.

Once again, the good news is all the work just shown is handled by the TLS layer itself and is completely transparent to most applications. However, the record protocol does introduce a few important implications that you should be aware of:

- Maximum TLS record size is 16 KB
- Each record contains a 5-byte header, a MAC (up to 20 bytes for SSLv3, TLS 1.0, TLS 1.1, and up to 32 bytes for TLS 1.2), and padding if a block cipher is used.
- To decrypt and verify the record, the entire record must be available.

Picking the right record size for your application, if you have the ability to do so, can be an important optimization. Small records incur a larger overhead due to record framing, whereas large records will have to be delivered and reassembled by the TCP layer before they can be processed by the TLS layer and delivered to your application.

Optimizing for TLS

Due to the layered architecture of the network protocols, running an application over TLS is no different from communicating directly over TCP. As such, there are no, or at most minimal, application modifications that you will need to make to deliver it over TLS. That is, assuming you have already applied the "Optimizing for TCP" on page 32 best practices.

However, what you should investigate are the operational pieces of your TLS deployments: how and where you deploy your servers, size of TLS records and memory buffers, certificate sizes, support for abbreviated handshakes, and so on. Getting these parameters right on your servers can make an enormous positive difference in the user experience, as well as in your operational costs.

Computational Costs

Establishing and maintaining an encrypted channel introduces additional computational costs for both peers. Specifically, first there is the asymmetric (public key) encryption used during the TLS handshake (explained on page 50). Then, once a shared secret is established in the handshake, it is used as a symmetric key to encrypt all TLS records.

As we noted earlier, public key cryptography is more computationally expensive when compared with symmetric key cryptography, and in the early days of the Web often required additional hardware to perform "SSL offloading." The good news is this is no longer the case. Modern hardware has made great improvements to help minimize these costs, and what once required additional hardware can now be done directly on the CPU. Large organizations such as Facebook and Google, which offer TLS to hundreds of millions of users, perform all the necessary TLS negotiation and computation in software and on commodity hardware.

> In January this year (2010), Gmail switched to using HTTPS for everything by default. Previously it had been introduced as an option, but now all of our users use HTTPS to secure their email between their browsers and Google, all the time. In order to do this we had to deploy no additional machines and no special hardware. On our production frontend machines, SSL/TLS accounts for less than 1% of the CPU load, less than 10 KB of memory per connection and less than 2% of network overhead. Many people believe that SSL/TLS takes a lot of CPU time and we hope the preceding numbers (public for the first time) will help to dispel that.
>
> If you stop reading now you only need to remember one thing: SSL/TLS is not computationally expensive any more.
>
> — Adam Langley (Google)

> We have deployed TLS at a large scale using both hardware and software load balancers. We have found that modern software-based TLS implementations running on commodity CPUs are fast enough to handle heavy HTTPS traffic load without needing to resort to dedicated cryptographic hardware. We serve all of our HTTPS traffic using software running on commodity hardware.
>
> — Doug Beaver (Facebook)

Previous experiences notwithstanding, techniques such as "TLS Session Resumption" on page 55 are still important optimizations, which will help you decrease the computational costs and latency of public key cryptography performed during the TLS handshake. There is no reason to spend CPU cycles on work that you don't need to do.

 Speaking of optimizing CPU cycles, make sure to upgrade your SSL libraries to the latest release, and build your web server or proxy against them! For example, recent versions of OpenSSL have made significant performance improvements, and chances are your system default OpenSSL libraries are outdated.

Early Termination

The connection setup latency imposed on every TLS connection, new or resumed, is an important area of optimization. First, recall that every TCP connection begins with a three-way handshake (explained on page 14), which takes a full roundtrip for the SYN/SYN-ACK packets. Following that, the TLS handshake (explained on page 50) requires up to two additional roundtrips for the full process, or one roundtrip if TLS session resumption (explained on page 55) can be used.

In the worst case, before any application data can be exchanged, the TCP and TLS connection setup process will take three roundtrips! Following our earlier example of a client in New York and the server in London, with a roundtrip time of 56 milliseconds (Table 1-1), this translates to 168 milliseconds of latency for a full TCP and TLS setup, and 112 milliseconds for a TLS session that is resumed. Even worse, the higher the latency between the peers, the worse the penalty, and 56 milliseconds is definitely an optimistic number!

Because all TLS sessions run over TCP, all the advice for "Optimizing for TCP" on page 32 applies here as well. If TCP connection reuse was an important consideration for unencrypted traffic, then it is a critical optimization for all applications running over TLS—if you can avoid doing the handshake, do so. However, if you have to perform the handshake, then you may want to investigate using the "early termination" technique.

As we discussed in Chapter 1, we cannot expect any dramatic improvements in latency in the future, as our packets are already traveling within a small constant factor of the speed of light. However, while we may not be able to make our packets travel faster, we can make them travel a shorter distance! Early termination is a simple technique of placing your servers closer to the user (Figure 4-9) to minimize the latency cost of each roundtrip between the client and the server.

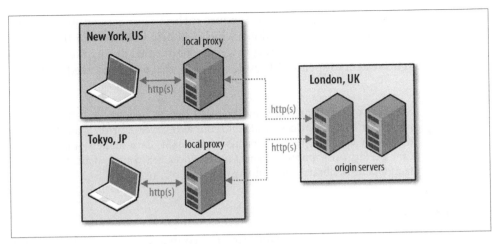

Figure 4-9. Early termination of client connections

The simplest way to accomplish this is to replicate or cache your data and services on servers around the world instead of forcing every user to traverse across oceans and continental links to the origin servers. Of course, this is precisely the service that many content delivery networks (CDNs) are set up to offer. However, the use case for geo-distributed servers does not stop at optimized delivery of static assets.

A nearby server can also terminate the TLS session, which means that the TCP and TLS handshake roundtrips are much quicker and the total connection setup latency is greatly reduced. In turn, the same nearby server can then establish a pool of long-lived, secure connections to the origin servers and proxy all incoming requests and responses to and from the origin servers.

In a nutshell, move the server closer to the client to accelerate TCP and TLS handshakes! Most CDN providers offer this service, and if you are adventurous, you can also deploy your own infrastructure with minimal costs: spin up cloud servers in a few data centers around the globe, configure a proxy server on each to forward requests to your origin, add geographic DNS load balancing, and you are in business.

Uncached Origin Fetch

The technique of using a CDN or a proxy server to fetch a resource, which may need to be customized per user or contains other private data, and hence is not a globally cache-able resource at the edge, is commonly known as an "uncached origin fetch."

While CDNs work best when the data is cached in geo-distributed servers around the world, the uncached origin fetch still provides a very important optimization: the client connection is terminated with the nearby server, which can dramatically reduce the handshake latency costs. In turn, the CDN, or your own proxy server, can maintain a "warm connection pool" to relay the data to the origin servers, allowing you to return a fast response back to the client.

In fact, as an additional layer of optimization, some CDN providers will use nearby servers on both sides of the connection! The client connection is terminated at a nearby CDN node, which then relays the request to the CDN node close to the origin, and the request is then routed to the origin. The extra hop within the CDN network allows the traffic to be routed over the optimized CDN backbone, which can help to further reduce latency between client and origin servers.

Session Caching and Stateless Resumption

Terminating the connection closer to the user is an optimization that will help decrease latency for your users in all cases, but once again, no bit is faster than a bit not sent—send fewer bits. Enabling TLS session caching and stateless resumption will allow you to eliminate an entire roundtrip for repeat visitors.

Session identifiers, on which TLS session caching relies, were introduced in SSL 2.0 and have wide support among most clients and servers. However, if you are configuring SSL/TLS on your server, do not assume that session support will be on by default. In fact, it is more common to have it off on most servers by default—but you know better! You should double-check and verify your configuration:

- Servers with multiple processes or workers should use a shared session cache.
- Size of the shared session cache should be tuned to your levels of traffic.
- A session timeout period should be provided.
- In a multiserver setup, routing the same client IP, or the same TLS session ID, to the same server is one way to provide good session cache utilization.
- Where "sticky" load balancing is not an option, a shared cache should be used between different servers to provide good session cache utilization.
- Check and monitor your SSL/TLS session cache statistics for best performance.

Alternatively, if the client and server both support session tickets, then all session data will be stored on the client, and none of these steps are required—much, much simpler! However, because session tickets are a relatively new extension in TLS, not all clients support it. In practice, and for best results, you should enable both: session tickets will be used for clients that support them, and session identifiers as a fallback for older clients. These mechanisms are not exclusive, and they work together well.

TLS Record Size

All application data delivered via TLS is transported within a record protocol (Figure 4-8). The maximum size of each record is 16 KB, and depending on the chosen cipher, each record will add anywhere from 20 to 40 bytes of overhead for the header, MAC, and optional padding. If the record then fits into a single TCP packet, then we also have to add the IP and TCP overhead: 20-byte header for IP, and 20-byte header for TCP with no options. As a result, there is potential for 60 to 100 bytes of overhead for each record. For a typical maximum transmission unit (MTU) size of 1,500 bytes on the wire, this packet structure translates to a minimum of 6% of framing overhead.

The smaller the record, the higher the framing overhead. However, simply increasing the size of the record to its maximum size (16 KB) is not necessarily a good idea! If the record spans multiple TCP packets, then the TLS layer must wait for all the TCP packets to arrive before it can decrypt the data (Figure 4-10). If any of those TCP packets get lost, reordered, or throttled due to congestion control, then the individual fragments of the TLS record will have to be buffered before they can be decoded, resulting in additional latency. In practice, these delays can create significant bottlenecks for the browser, which prefers to consume data byte by byte and as soon as possible.

```
▽ [8 Reassembled TCP Segments (11221 bytes): #169(1460), #170(1460), #172(1460), #174(1460),
                                              #175(1460), #177(1460), #179(1460), #180(1001)]
    [Frame: 169, payload: 0-1459 (1460 bytes)]
    [Frame: 170, payload: 1460-2919 (1460 bytes)]
    [Frame: 172, payload: 2920-4379 (1460 bytes)]
    [Frame: 174, payload: 4380-5839 (1460 bytes)]
    [Frame: 175, payload: 5840-7299 (1460 bytes)]
    [Frame: 177, payload: 7300-8759 (1460 bytes)]
    [Frame: 179, payload: 8760-10219 (1460 bytes)]
    [Frame: 180, payload: 10220-11220 (1001 bytes)]
    [Segment count: 8]
    [Reassembled TCP length: 11221]
▽ Secure Sockets Layer
  ▽ TLSv1 Record Layer: Application Data Protocol: http
      Content Type: Application Data (23)
      Version: TLS 1.0 (0x0301)
      Length: 11216
      Encrypted Application Data: 07ed92e420530da2e2755a5b5372ef32b53e0d4e7c20c3d8...
```

Figure 4-10. WireShark capture of 11,211-byte TLS record split over 8 TCP segments

Small records incur overhead, large records incur latency, and there is no one answer for the "right" record size. However, for web applications, which are consumed by the browser, the recommended best practice is simple: each TCP packet should carry exactly one TLS record, and the TLS record should occupy the full maximum segment size (MSS) allocated by TCP. In other words, do not use TLS record sizes that span multiple TCP packets, and ship as much data as you can within each record. To determine the optimal TLS record size for your deployment:

- Allocate 20 bytes for IPv4 framing overhead and 40 bytes for IPv6.
- Allocate 20 bytes for TCP framing overhead.
- Allocate 40 bytes for TCP options overhead (timestamps, SACKs).

Assuming a common 1,500-byte starting MTU, this leaves 1,420 bytes for a TLS record delivered over IPv4, and 1,400 bytes for IPv6. To be future-proof, use the IPv6 size: 1,400 bytes, or less if your MTU is lower.

Unfortunately, configuring the TLS record size is not something we can control at the application layer. Instead, this is a setting, and perhaps even a compile-time constant or flag on your TLS server. For details on how to update this value, check the documentation of your server.

 If your servers are handling a large number of TLS connections, then minimizing memory usage per connection can be a vital optimization. By default, popular libraries such as OpenSSL will allocate up to 50 KB of memory per connection, but as with the record size, it may be worth checking the documentation or the source code for how to adjust this value. Google's servers reduce their OpenSSL buffers down to about 5 KB.

TLS Compression

A little-known feature of TLS is built-in support for lossless compression of data transferred within the record protocol: the compression algorithm is negotiated during the TLS handshake, and compression is applied prior to encryption of each record. However, in practice, you should disable TLS compression on your server for several reasons:

- The "CRIME" attack, published in 2012, leverages TLS compression to recover secret authentication cookies and allows the attacker to perform session hijacking.
- Transport-level TLS compression is not content aware and will end up attempting to recompress already compressed data (images, video, etc.).

Double compression will waste CPU time on both the server and the client, and the security breach implications are quite serious: disable TLS compression. In practice, most browsers disable support for TLS compression, but you should nonetheless also explicitly disable it in the configuration of your server to protect your users.

Instead of relying on TLS compression, make sure your server is configured to Gzip all text-based assets and that you are using an optimal compression format for all other media types, such as images, video, and audio.

Certificate-Chain Length

Verifying the chain of trust requires that the browser traverse the chain, starting from the site certificate, and recursively verifying the certificate of the parent until it reaches a trusted root. Hence, the first optimization you should make is to verify that the server does not forget to include all the intermediate certificates when the handshake is performed. If you forget, many browsers will still work, but they will instead be forced to pause the verification and fetch the intermediate certificate on their own, verify it, and then continue. This will most likely require a new DNS lookup, TCP connection, and an HTTP GET request, adding hundreds of milliseconds to your handshake.

How does the browser know from where to fetch it? The child certificate will usually contain the URL for the parent.

Conversely, make sure you do not include unnecessary certificates in your chain! Or, more generally, you should aim to minimize the size of your certificate chain. Recall that server certificates are sent during the TLS handshake, which is likely running over a new TCP connection that is in the early stages of its slow-start algorithm. If the certificate chain exceeds TCP's initial congestion window (Figure 4-11), then we will inadvertently add yet another roundtrip to the handshake: certificate length will overflow the congestion window and cause the server to stop and wait for a client ACK before proceeding.

```
▷ [4 Reassembled TCP Segments (5341 bytes): #98(1402), #99(1460), #101(1176), #102(1303)]
▽ Secure Sockets Layer
  ▽ TLSv1.1 Record Layer: Handshake Protocol: Certificate
      Content Type: Handshake (22)
      Version: TLS 1.1 (0x0302)
      Length: 5327
    ▽ Handshake Protocol: Certificate
        Handshake Type: Certificate (11)
        Length: 5323
        Certificates Length: 5320
      ▷ Certificates (5320 bytes)
```

Figure 4-11. WireShark capture of a 5,323-byte TLS certificate chain

The certificate chain in Figure 4-11 is over 5 KB in size, which will overflow the initial congestion window size of older servers and force another roundtrip of delay into the handshake. One possible solution is to increase the initial congestion window; see "Increasing TCP's Initial Congestion Window" on page 26. In addition, you should investigate if it is possible to reduce the size of the sent certificates:

- Minimize the number of intermediate CAs. Ideally, your sent certificate chain should contain exactly two certificates: your site and the CA's intermediary certificate; use this as a criteria in the selection of your CA. The third certificate, which is the CA root, should already be in the browser's trusted root and hence should not be sent.

- It is not uncommon for many sites to include the root certificate of their CA in the chain, which is entirely unnecessary: if your browser does not already have the certificate in its trust store, then it won't be trusted, and including the root certificate won't change that.

- A carefully managed certificate chain can be as low as 2 or 3 KB in size, while providing all the necessary information to the browser to avoid unnecessary round-trips or out-of-band requests for the certificates themselves. Optimizing your TLS handshake mitigates a critical performance bottleneck, since every new TLS connection is subject to its overhead.

OCSP Stapling

Every new TLS connection requires that the browser must verify the signatures of the sent certificate chain. However, there is one more step we can't forget: the browser also needs to verify that the certificate is not revoked. To do so, it may periodically download and cache the CRL of the certificate authority, but it may also need to dispatch an OCSP request during the verification process for a "real-time" check. Unfortunately, the browser behavior for this process varies wildly:

- Some browsers may use their own update mechanism to push updated CRL lists instead of relying on on-demand requests.

- Some browsers may do only real-time OCSP and CRL checks for Extended Validation (EV) certificates.

- Some browsers may block the TLS handshake on either revocation method, others may not, and this behavior will vary by vendor, platform, and version of the browser.

Unfortunately, it is a complicated space with no single best solution. However, one optimization that can be made for some browsers is OCSP stapling: the server can include (staple) the OCSP response from the CA to its certificate chain, allowing the browser to skip the online check. Moving the OCSP fetch to the server allows the server to cache the signed OCSP response and save the extra request for many clients. However, there are also a few things to watch out for:

- OCSP responses can vary from 400 to 4,000 bytes in size. Stapling this response to your certificate chain may once again overflow your TCP congestion window—pay close attention to the total size.
- Only one OCSP response can be included, which may still mean that the browser will have to issue an OCSP request for other intermediate certificates, if it has not been cached already.

Finally, to enable OCSP stapling, you will need a server that supports it. The good news is popular servers such as Nginx, Apache, and IIS meet this criteria. Check the documentation of your own server for support and configuration instructions.

HTTP Strict Transport Security (HSTS)

HTTP Strict Transport Security is a security policy mechanism that allows the server to declare access rules to a compliant browser via a simple HTTP header—e.g. *Strict-Transport-Security: max-age=31536000*. Specifically, it instructs the user-agent to enforce the following rules:

- All requests to the origin should be sent over HTTPS.
- All insecure links and client requests should be automatically converted to HTTPS on the client before the request is sent.
- In case of a certificate error, an error message is displayed, and the user is not allowed to circumvent the warning.
- *max-age* specifies the lifetime of the specified HSTS ruleset in seconds (e.g., `max-age=31536000` is equal to a 365-day cache lifetime).
- Optionally, the UA can be instructed to remember ("pin") the fingerprint of a host in the specified certificate chain for future access, effectively limiting the scope of authorities who can authenticate the certificate.

HSTS converts the origin to an HTTPS-only destination and helps protect the application from a variety of passive and active network attacks against the user. Performance wise, it also helps eliminate unnecessary HTTP-to-HTTPS redirects by shifting this responsibility to the client, which will automatically rewrite all links to HTTPS.

 As of early 2013, HSTS is supported by Firefox 4+, Chrome 4+, Opera 12+, and Chrome and Firefox for Android. For the latest status, see *caniuse.com/stricttransportsecurity*.

Performance Checklist

As an application developer, you are shielded from virtually all the complexity of TLS. Short of ensuring that you do not mix HTTP and HTTPS content on your pages, your application will run transparently on both. However, the performance of your entire application *will* be affected by the underlying configuration of your server.

The good news is it is never too late to make these optimizations, and once in place, they will pay high dividends for every new connection to your servers! A short list to put on the agenda:

- Get best performance from TCP; see "Optimizing for TCP" on page 32.
- Upgrade TLS libraries to latest release, and (re)build servers against them.
- Enable and configure session caching and stateless resumption
- Monitor your session caching hit rates and adjust configuration accordingly.
- Terminate TLS sessions closer to the user to minimize roundtrip latencies.
- Configure your TLS record size to fit into a single TCP segment.
- Ensure that your certificate chain does not overflow the initial congestion window.
- Remove unnecessary certificates from your chain; minimize the depth.
- Disable TLS compression on your server.
- Configure SNI support on your server.
- Configure OCSP stapling on your server.
- Append HTTP Strict Transport Security header.

Testing and Verification

Finally, to verify and test your configuration, you can use an online service, such as the Qualys SSL Server Test (*http://hpbn.co/qualys*) to scan your public server for common configuration and security flaws. Additionally, you should familiarize yourself with the openssl command-line interface, which will help you inspect the entire handshake and configuration of your server locally.

```
$> openssl s_client -state -CAfile startssl.ca.crt -connect igvita.com:443

CONNECTED(00000003)
SSL_connect:before/connect initialization
SSL_connect:SSLv2/v3 write client hello A
SSL_connect:SSLv3 read server hello A
depth=2 /C=IL/O=StartCom Ltd./OU=Secure Digital Certificate Signing
        /CN=StartCom Certification Authority
verify return:1
```

```
depth=1 /C=IL/O=StartCom Ltd./OU=Secure Digital Certificate Signing
        /CN=StartCom Class 1 Primary Intermediate Server CA
verify return:1
depth=0 /description=ABjQuqt3nPv7ebEG/C=US
        /CN=www.igvita.com/emailAddress=ilya@igvita.com
verify return:1
SSL_connect:SSLv3 read server certificate A
SSL_connect:SSLv3 read server done A ❶
SSL_connect:SSLv3 write client key exchange A
SSL_connect:SSLv3 write change cipher spec A
SSL_connect:SSLv3 write finished A
SSL_connect:SSLv3 flush data
SSL_connect:SSLv3 read finished A
---
Certificate chain ❷
 0 s:/description=ABjQuqt3nPv7ebEG/C=US
     /CN=www.igvita.com/emailAddress=ilya@igvita.com
   i:/C=IL/O=StartCom Ltd./OU=Secure Digital Certificate Signing
     /CN=StartCom Class 1 Primary Intermediate Server CA
 1 s:/C=IL/O=StartCom Ltd./OU=Secure Digital Certificate Signing
     /CN=StartCom Class 1 Primary Intermediate Server CA
   i:/C=IL/O=StartCom Ltd./OU=Secure Digital Certificate Signing
     /CN=StartCom Certification Authority
---
Server certificate
-----BEGIN CERTIFICATE-----
... snip ...
---
No client certificate CA names sent
---
SSL handshake has read 3571 bytes and written 444 bytes ❸
---
New, TLSv1/SSLv3, Cipher is RC4-SHA
Server public key is 2048 bit
Secure Renegotiation IS supported
Compression: NONE
Expansion: NONE
SSL-Session:
    Protocol  : TLSv1
    Cipher    : RC4-SHA
    Session-ID: 269349C84A4702EFA7 ... ❹
    Session-ID-ctx:
    Master-Key: 1F5F5F33D50BE6228A ...
    Key-Arg   : None
    Start Time: 1354037095
    Timeout   : 300 (sec)
    Verify return code: 0 (ok)
---
```

❶   Client completed verification of received certificate chain.

❷   Received certificate chain (two certificates).

❸ Size of received certificate chain.

❹ Issued session identifier for stateful TLS resume.

In the preceding example, we connect to igvita.com on the default TLS port (443), and perform the TLS handshake. Because the s_client makes no assumptions about known root certificates, we manually specify the path to the root certificate of StartSSL Certificate Authority—this is important. Your browser already has StartSSL's root certificate and is thus able to verify the chain, but s_client makes no such assumptions. Try omitting the root certificate, and you will see a verification error in the log.

Inspecting the certificate chain shows that the server sent two certificates, which added up to 3,571 bytes, which is very close to the three- to four-segment initial TCP congestion window size. We should be careful not to overflow it or raise the cwnd size on the server. Finally, we can inspect the negotiated SSL session variables—chosen protocol, cipher, key—and we can also see that the server issued a session identifier for the current session, which may be resumed in the future.

PART II

Performance of Wireless Networks

CHAPTER 5

Introduction to Wireless Networks

Ubiquitous Connectivity

One of the most transformative technology trends of the past decade is the availability and growing expectation of ubiquitous connectivity. Whether it is for checking email, carrying a voice conversation, web browsing, or myriad other use cases, we now expect to be able to access these online services regardless of location, time, or circumstance: on the run, while standing in line, at the office, on a subway, while in flight, and everywhere in between. Today, we are still often forced to be proactive about finding connectivity (e.g., looking for a nearby WiFi hotspot) but without a doubt, the future is about ubiquitous connectivity where access to the Internet is omnipresent.

Wireless networks are at the epicenter of this trend. At its broadest, a wireless network refers to any network not connected by cables, which is what enables the desired convenience and mobility for the user. Not surprisingly, given the myriad different use cases and applications, we should also expect to see dozens of different wireless technologies to meet the needs, each with its own performance characteristics and each optimized for a specific task and context. Today, we already have over a dozen widespread wireless technologies in use: WiFi, Bluetooth, ZigBee, NFC, WiMAX, LTE, HSPA, EV-DO, earlier 3G standards, satellite services, and more.

As such, given the diversity, it is not wise to make sweeping generalizations about performance of wireless networks. However, the good news is that most wireless technologies operate on common principles, have common trade-offs, and are subject to common performance criteria and constraints. Once we uncover and understand these fundamental principles of wireless performance, most of the other pieces will begin to automatically fall into place.

Further, while the mechanics of data delivery via radio communication are fundamentally different from the tethered world, the outcome as experienced by the user is, or should be, all the same—same performance, same results. In the long run all applications are and will be delivered over wireless networks; it just may be the case that some will be accessed more frequently over wireless than others. There is no such thing as a *wired application*, and there is zero demand for such a distinction.

All application should perform well regardless of underlying connectivity. As a user, you should not care about the underlying technology in use, but as developers we must think ahead and architect our applications to anticipate the differences between the different types of networks. And the good news is every optimization that we apply for wireless networks will translate to a better experience in all other contexts. Let's dive in.

Types of Wireless Networks

A network is a group of devices connected to one another. In the case of wireless networks, radio communication is usually the medium of choice. However, even within the radio-powered subset, there are dozens of different technologies designed for use at different scales, topologies, and for dramatically different use cases. One way to illustrate this difference is to partition the use cases based on their "geographic range":

Table 5-1. Types of wireless networks

Type	Range	Applications	Standards
Personal area network (PAN)	Within reach of a person	Cable replacement for peripherals	Bluetooth, ZigBee, NFC
Local area network (LAN)	Within a building or campus	Wireless extension of wired network	IEEE 802.11 (WiFi)
Metropolitan area network (MAN)	Within a city	Wireless inter-network connectivity	IEEE 802.15 (WiMAX)
Wide area network (WAN)	Worldwide	Wireless network access	Cellular (UMTS, LTE, etc.)

The preceding classification is neither complete nor entirely accurate. Many technologies and standards start within a specific use case, such as Bluetooth for PAN applications and cable replacement, and with time acquire more capabilities, reach, and throughput. In fact, the latest drafts of Bluetooth now provide seamless interoperability with 802.11 (WiFi) for high-bandwidth use cases. Similarly, technologies such as WiMAX have their origins as fixed-wireless solutions, but with time acquired additional mobility capabilities, making them a viable alternative to other WAN and cellular technologies.

The point of the classification is not to partition each technology into a separate bin, but to highlight the high-level differences within each use case. Some devices have access to a continuous power source; others must optimize their battery life at all costs. Some require Gbit/s+ data rates; others are built to transfer tens or hundreds of bytes of data (e.g., NFC). Some applications require always-on connectivity, while others are delay and latency tolerant. These and a large number of other criteria are what determine the original characteristics of each type of network. However, once in place, each standard continues to evolve: better battery capacities, faster processors, improved modulation algorithms, and other advancements continue to extend the use cases and performance of each wireless standard.

 Your next application may be delivered over a mobile network, but it may also rely on NFC for payments, Bluetooth for P2P communication via WebRTC, and WiFi for HD streaming. It is not a question of picking, or betting on, just one wireless standard!

Performance Fundamentals of Wireless Networks

Each and every type of wireless technology has its own set of constraints and limitations. However, regardless of the specific wireless technology in use, all communication methods have a maximum channel capacity, which is determined by the same underlying principles. In fact, Claude E. Shannon gave us an exact mathematical model (Equation 5-1) to determine channel capacity, regardless of the technology in use.

Equation 5-1. Channel capacity is the maximum information rate

$$C = BW \times \log_2 \left(1 + \frac{S}{N}\right)$$

- C is the channel capacity and is measured in bits per second.
- BW is the available bandwidth, and is measured in hertz.
- S is signal and N is noise, and they are measured in watts.

Although somewhat simplified, the previous formula captures all the essential insights we need to understand the performance of most wireless networks. Regardless of the name, acronym, or the revision number of the specification, the two fundamental constraints on achievable data rates are the amount of available bandwidth and the signal power between the receiver and the sender.

Bandwidth

Unlike the tethered world, where a dedicated wire can be run between each network peer, radio communication by its very nature uses a shared medium: radio waves, or if you prefer, electromagnetic radiation. Both the sender and receiver must agree up-front on the specific frequency range over which the communication will occur; a well-defined range allows seamless interoperability between devices. For example, the 802.11b and 802.11g standards both use the 2.4–2.5 GHz band across all WiFi devices.

Who determines the frequency range and its allocation? In short, local government (Figure 5-1). In the United States, this process is governed by the Federal Communications Commission (FCC). In fact, due to different government regulations, some wireless technologies may work in one part of the world, but not in others. Different countries may, and often do, assign different spectrum ranges to the same wireless technology.

Politics aside, besides having a common band for interoperability, the most important performance factor is the size of the assigned frequency range. As Shannon's model shows, the overall channel bitrate is directly proportional to the assigned range. Hence, all else being equal, a doubling in available frequency range will double the data rate—e.g., going from 20 to 40 MHz of bandwidth can double the channel data rate, which is exactly how 802.11n is improving its performance over earlier WiFi standards!

Finally, it is also worth noting that not all frequency ranges offer the same performance. Low-frequency signals travel farther and cover large areas (macrocells), but at the cost of requiring larger antennas and having more clients competing for access. On the other hand, high-frequency signals can transfer more data but won't travel as far, resulting in smaller coverage areas (microcells) and a requirement for more infrastructure.

Certain frequency ranges are more valuable than others for some applications. Broadcast-only applications (e.g., broadcast radio) are well suited for low-frequency ranges. On the other hand, two-way communication benefits from use of smaller cells, which provide higher bandwidth and less competition.

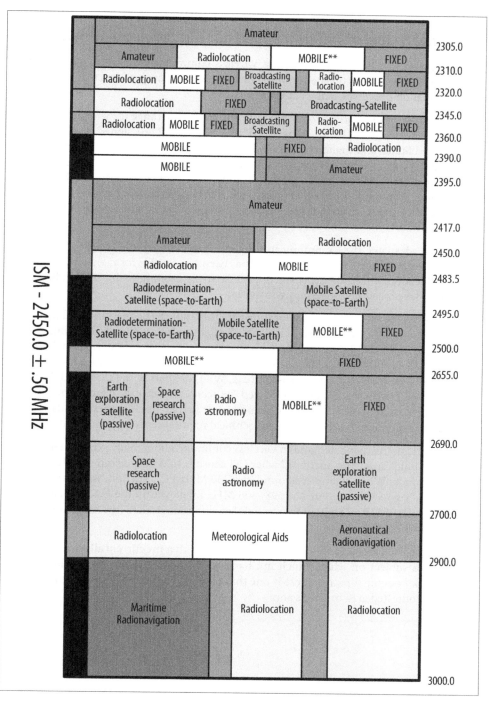

Figure 5-1. *FCC radio spectrum allocation for the 2,300–3,000 MHz band*

A Brief History of Worldwide Spectrum Allocation and Regulation

If you spend any time in the world of wireless communication, you will inevitably stumble into numerous debates on the state and merits of current spectrum allocation and regulation processes. But what is the history?

In the early days of radio, anyone could use any frequency range for whatever purpose she desired. All of that changed when the Radio Act of 1912 was signed into law within the United States and mandated licensed use of the radio spectrum. The original bill was in part motivated by the investigation into the sinking of the Titanic. Some speculate that the disaster could have been averted, or more lives could have been saved, if proper frequencies were monitored by all nearby vessels. Regardless, this new law set a precedent for international and federal legislation of wireless communication. Other countries followed.

A few decades later, the Communications Act of 1934 created the Federal Communications Commission (FCC), and the FCC has been responsible for managing the spectrum allocation within the U.S ever since, effectively "zoning" it by subdividing into ever-smaller parcels designed for exclusive use.

A good example of the different allocations are the "industrial, scientific, and medical" (ISM) radio bands, which were first established at the International Telecommunications Conference in 1947, and as the name implies, were reserved internationally. Both the 2.4–2.5 GHz (100 MHz) and 5.725–5.875 GHz (150 MHz) bands, which power much of our modern wireless communication (e.g., WiFi) are part of the ISM band. Further, both of these ISM bands are also considered "unlicensed spectrum," which allow anyone to operate a wireless network—for commercial or private use—in these bands as long as the hardware used respects specified technical requirements (e.g., transmit power).

Finally, due to the rising demand in wireless communication, many governments have begun to hold "spectrum auctions," where a license is sold to transmit signals over the specific bands. While examples abound, the 700 MHz FCC auction, which took place in 2008, is a good illustration: the 698–806 MHz range within the U.S. was auctioned off for a total of $19.592 billion to over a dozen different bidders (the range was subdivided into blocks). Yes, that is billion with a "b."

Bandwidth is a scarce and expensive commodity. Whether the current allocation process is fair is a subject on which much ink has been spilled and many books have been published. Looking forward, there is one thing we can be sure of: it will continue to be a highly contested area of discussion.

Signal Power

Besides bandwidth, the second fundamental limiting factor in all wireless communication is the signal power between the sender and receiver, also known as the signal-power-to-noise-power, S/N ratio, or SNR. In essence, it is a measure that compares the level of desired signal to the level of background noise and interference. The larger the amount of background noise, the stronger the signal has to be to carry the information.

By its very nature, all radio communication is done over a shared medium, which means that other devices may generate unwanted interference. For example, a microwave oven operating at 2.5 GHz may overlap with the frequency range used by WiFi, creating cross-standard interference. However, other WiFi devices, such as your neighbors' WiFi access point, and even your coworker's laptop accessing the same WiFi network, also create interference for your transmissions.

In the ideal case, you would be the one and only user within a certain frequency range, with no other background noise or interference. Unfortunately, that's unlikely. First, bandwidth is scarce, and second, there are simply too many wireless devices to make that work. Instead, to achieve the desired data rate where interference is present, we can either increase the transmit power, thereby increasing the strength of the signal, or decrease the distance between the transmitter and the receiver—or both, of course.

 Path loss, or path attenuation, is the reduction in signal power with respect to distance traveled—the exact reduction rate depends on the environment. A full discussion on this is outside the scope of this book, but if you are curious, consult your favorite search engine.

To illustrate the relationship between signal, noise, transmit power, and distance, imagine you are in a small room and talking to someone 20 feet away. If nobody else is present, you can hold a conversation at normal volume. However, now add a few dozen people into the same room, such as at a crowded party, each carrying their own conversations. All of the sudden, it would be impossible for you to hear your peer! Of course, you could start speaking louder, but doing so would raise the amount of "noise" for everyone around you. In turn, they would start speaking louder also and further escalate the amount of noise and interference. Before you know it, everyone in the room is only able to communicate from a few feet away from each other (Figure 5-2). If you have ever lost your voice at a rowdy party, or had to lean in to hear a conversation, then you have firsthand experience with SNR.

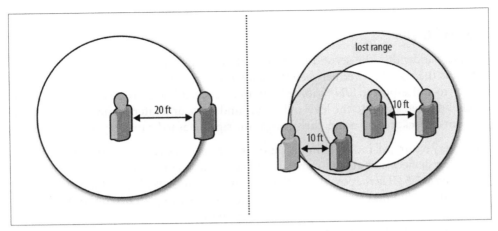

Figure 5-2. Cell-breathing and near-far effects in day-to-day situations

In fact, this scenario illustrates two important effects:

Near-far problem
> A condition in which a receiver captures a strong signal and thereby makes it impossible for the receiver to detect a weaker signal, effectively "crowding out" the weaker signal.

Cell-breathing
> A condition in which the coverage area, or the distance of the signal, expands and shrinks based on the cumulative noise and interference levels.

One, or more loud speakers beside you can block out weaker signals from farther away —the near-far problem. Similarly, the larger the number of other conversations around you, the higher the interference and the smaller the range from which you can discern a useful signal—cell-breathing. Not surprisingly, these same limitations are present in all forms of radio communication as well, regardless of protocol or underlying technology.

Modulation

Available bandwidth and SNR are the two primary, physical factors that dictate the capacity of every wireless channel. However, the algorithm by which the signal is encoded can also have a significant effect.

In a nutshell, our digital alphabet (1's and 0's), needs to be translated into an analog signal (a radio wave). *Modulation* is the process of digital-to-analog conversion, and different "modulation alphabets" can be used to encode the digital signal with different efficiency. The combination of the alphabet and the symbol rate is what then determines the final throughput of the channel. As a hands-on example:

- Receiver and sender can process 1,000 pulses or symbols per second (1,000 baud).
- Each transmitted symbol represents a different bit-sequence, determined by the chosen alphabet (e.g., 2-bit alphabet: 00, 01, 10, 11).
- The bit rate of the channel is 1,000 baud × 2 bits per symbol, or 2,000 bits per second.

The choice of the modulation algorithm depends on the available technology, computing power of both the receiver and sender, as well as the SNR ratio. A higher-order modulation alphabet comes at a cost of reduced robustness to noise and interference—there is no free lunch!

 Don't worry, we are not planning to dive headfirst into the world of signal processing. Rather, it is simply important to understand that the choice of the modulation algorithm does affect the capacity of the wireless channel, but it is also subject to SNR, available processing power, and all other common trade-offs.

Measuring Real-World Wireless Performance

Our brief crash course on signal theory can be summed up as follows: the performance of any wireless network, regardless of the name, acronym, or the revision number, is fundamentally limited by a small number of well-known parameters. Specifically, the amount of allocated bandwidth and the signal-to-noise ratio between receiver and sender. Further, all radio-powered communication is:

- Done over a shared communication medium (radio waves)
- Regulated to use specific bandwidth frequency ranges
- Regulated to use specific transmit power rates
- Subject to continuously changing background noise and interference
- Subject to technical constraints of the chosen wireless technology
- Subject to constraints of the device: form factor, power, etc.

All wireless technologies advertise a peak, or a maximum data rate. For example, the 802.11g standard is capable of 54 Mbit/s, and the 802.11n standard raises the bar up to 600 Mbit/s. Similarly, some mobile carriers are advertising 100+ MBit/s throughput with LTE. However, the most important part that is often overlooked when analyzing all these numbers is the emphasis on *in ideal conditions*.

What are ideal conditions? You guessed it: maximum amount of allotted bandwidth, exclusive use of the frequency spectrum, minimum or no background noise, highest-throughput modulation alphabet, and, increasingly, multiple radio streams (multiple-input and multiple-output, or MIMO) transmitting in parallel. Needless to say, what you see on the label and what you experience in the real world might be (read, will be) very different.

Just a few factors that may affect the performance of your wireless network:

- Amount of distance between receiver and sender
- Amount of background noise in current location
- Amount of interference from users in the same network (intra-cell)
- Amount of interference from users in other, nearby networks (inter-cell)
- Amount of available transmit power, both at receiver and sender
- Amount of processing power and the chosen modulation scheme

In other words, if you want maximum throughput, then try to remove any noise and interference you can control, place your receiver and sender as close as possible, give them all the power they desire, and make sure both select the best modulation method. Or, if you are bent on performance, just run a physical wire between the two! The convenience of wireless communication does have its costs.

Measuring wireless performance is a tricky business. A small change, on the order of a few inches, in the location of the receiver can easily double throughput, and a few instants later the throughput could be halved again because another receiver has just woken up and is now competing for access to the radio channel. By its very nature, wireless performance is highly variable.

Finally, note that all of the previous discussions have been focused exclusively on throughput. Are we omitting latency on purpose? In fact, we have so far, because latency performance in wireless networks is directly tied to the specific technology in use, and that is the subject we turn to next.

CHAPTER 6

WiFi

WiFi operates in the unlicensed ISM spectrum; it is trivial to deploy by anyone, any-where; and the required hardware is simple and cheap. Not surprisingly, it has become one of the most widely deployed and popular wireless standards.

The name itself is a trademark of the WiFi Alliance, which is a trade association estab-lished to promote wireless LAN technologies, as well as to provide interoperability standards and testing. Technically, a device must be submitted to and certified by the WiFi Alliance to carry the WiFi name and logo, but in practice, the name is used to refer to any product based on the IEEE 802.11 standards.

The first 802.11 protocol was drafted in 1997, more or less as a direct adaptation of the Ethernet standard (IEEE 802.3) to the world of wireless communication. However, it wasn't until 1999, when the 802.11b standard was introduced, that the market for WiFi devices took off. The relative simplicity of the technology, easy deployment, conve-nience, and the fact that it operated in the unlicensed 2.4 GHz ISM band allowed anyone to easily provide a "wireless extension" to their existing local area network. Today, most every new desktop, laptop, tablet, smartphone, and just about every other form-factor device is WiFi enabled.

From Ethernet to a Wireless LAN

The 802.11 wireless standards were primarily designed as an adaptation and an exten-sion of the existing Ethernet (802.3) standard. Hence, while Ethernet is commonly re-ferred to as the LAN standard, the 802.11 family (Figure 6-1) is correspondingly com-monly known as the wireless LAN (WLAN). However, for the history geeks, technically much of the Ethernet protocol was inspired by the ALOHAnet protocol, which was the first public demonstration of a wireless network developed in 1971 at the University of Hawaii. In other words, we have come full circle.

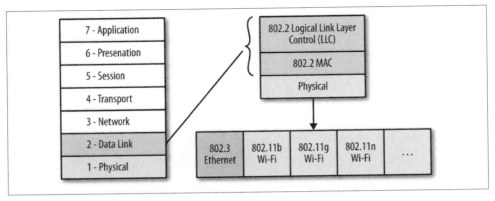

Figure 6-1. 802.3 (Ethernet) and 802.11 (WiFi) data and physical layers

The reason why this distinction is important is due to the mechanics of how the ALOHAnet, and consequently Ethernet and WiFi protocols, schedule all communication. Namely, they all treat the shared medium, regardless of whether it is a wire or the radio waves, as a "random access channel," which means that there is no central process, or scheduler, that controls who or which device is allowed to transmit data at any point in time. Instead, each device decides on its own, and all devices must work together to guarantee good shared channel performance.

The Ethernet standard has historically relied on a probabilistic carrier sense multiple access (CSMA) protocol, which is a complicated name for a simple "listen before you speak" algorithm. In brief, if you have data to send:

- Check whether anyone else is transmitting.
- If the channel is busy, listen until it is free.
- When the channel is free, transmit data immediately.

Of course, it takes time to propagate any signal; hence collisions can still occur. For this reason, the Ethernet standard also added collision detection (CSMA/CD): if a collision is detected, then both parties stop transmitting immediately and sleep for a random interval (with exponential backoff). This way, multiple competing senders won't synchronize and restart their transmissions simultaneously.

WiFi follows a very similar but slightly different model: due to hardware limitations of the radio, it cannot detect collisions while sending data. Hence, WiFi relies on collision avoidance (CSMA/CA), where each sender attempts to avoid collisions by transmitting only when the channel is sensed to be idle, and then sends its full message frame in its entirety. Once the WiFi frame is sent, the sender waits for an explicit acknowledgment from the receiver before proceeding with the next transmission.

There are a few more details, but in a nutshell that's all there is to it: the combination of these techniques is how both Ethernet and WiFi regulate access to the shared medium. In the case of Ethernet, the medium is a physical wire, and in the case of WiFi, it is the shared radio channel.

In practice, the probabilistic access model works very well for lightly loaded networks. In fact, we won't show the math here, but we can prove that to get good channel utilization (minimize number of collisions), the channel load must be kept below 10%. If the load is kept low, we can get good throughput without any explicit coordination or scheduling. However, if the load increases, then the number of collisions will quickly rise, leading to unstable performance of the entire network.

 If you have ever tried to use a highly loaded WiFi network, with many peers competing for access—say, at a large public event, like a conference hall—then chances are, you have firsthand experience with "unstable WiFi performance." Of course, the probabilistic scheduling is not the only factor, but it certainly plays a role.

WiFi Standards and Features

The 802.11b standard launched WiFi into everyday use, but as with any popular technology, the IEEE 802 Standards Committee has not been idle and has actively continued to release new protocols (Table 6-1) with higher throughput, better modulation techniques, multistreaming, and many other new features.

Table 6-1. WiFi release history and roadmap

802.11 protocol	Release	Freq (GHz)	Bandwidth (MHz)	Data rate per stream (Mbit/s)
b	Sep 1999	2.4	20	1, 2, 5.5, 11
g	Jun 2003	2.4	20	6, 9, 12, 18, 24, 36, 48, 54
n	Oct 2009	2.4	20	7.2, 14.4, 21.7, 28.9, 43.3, 57.8, 65, 72.2
n	Oct 2009	5	40	15, 30, 45, 60, 90, 120, 135, 150
ac	~2014	5	20, 40, 80, 160	up to 866.7

Today, the "b" and "g" standards are the most widely deployed and supported. Both utilize the unlicensed 2.4 GHz ISM band, use 20 MHz of bandwidth, and support at most one radio data stream. Depending on your local regulations, the transmit power is also likely fixed at a maximum of 200 mW. Some routers will allow you to adjust this value but will likely override it with a regional maximum.

So how do we increase performance of our future WiFi networks? The "n" and upcoming "ac" standards are doubling the bandwidth from 20 to 40 MHz per channel, using higher-order modulation, and adding multiple radios to transmit multiple streams in parallel—multiple-input and multiple-output (MIMO). All combined, and in ideal conditions, this should enable gigabit-plus throughput with the upcoming "ac" wireless standard.

Measuring and Optimizing WiFi Performance

By this point you should be skeptical of the notion of "ideal conditions," and for good reason. The wide adoption and popularity of WiFi networks also created one of its biggest performance challenges: inter- and intra-cell interference. The WiFi standard does not have any central scheduler, which also means that there are no guarantees on throughput or latency for any client.

The new WiFi Multimedia (WMM) extension enables basic Quality of Service (QoS) within the radio interface for latency-sensitive applications (e.g., voice, video, best effort), but few routers, and even fewer deployed clients, are aware of it. In the meantime, all traffic both within your own network, and in nearby WiFi networks must compete for access for the same shared radio resource.

Your router may allow you to set some Quality of Service (QoS) policy for clients within your own network (e.g., maximum total data rate per client, or by type of traffic), but you nonetheless have no control over traffic generated by other, nearby WiFi networks. The fact that WiFi networks are so easy to deploy is what made them ubiquitous, but the widespread adoption has also created a lot of performance problems: in practice it is now not unusual to find several dozen different and overlapping WiFi networks (Figure 6-2) in any high-density urban or office environment.

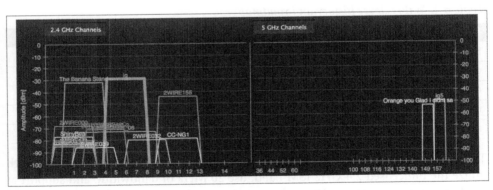

Figure 6-2. inSSIDer visualization of overlapping WiFi networks (2.4 and 5 GHz bands)

The most widely used 2.4 GHz band provides three non-overlapping 20 MHz radio channels: 1, 6, and 11 (Figure 6-3). Although even this assignment is not consistent among all countries. In some, you may be allowed to use higher channels (13, 14), and in others you may be effectively limited to an even smaller subset. However, regardless of local regulations, what this effectively means is that the moment you have more than two or three nearby WiFi networks, some must overlap and hence compete for the same shared bandwidth in the same frequency ranges.

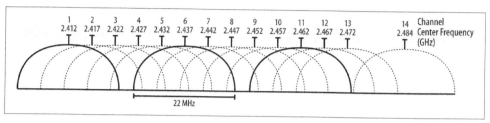

Figure 6-3. Wikipedia illustration of WiFi channels in the 2.4 GHz band

Your 802.11g client and router may be capable of reaching 54 Mbps, but the moment your neighbor, who is occupying the same WiFi channel, starts streaming an HD video over WiFi, your bandwidth is cut in half, or worse. Your access point has no say in this arrangement, and that is a feature, not a bug!

Unfortunately, latency performance fares no better. There are no guarantees for the latency of the first hop between your client and the WiFi access point. In environments with many overlapping networks, you should not be surprised to see high variability, measured in tens and even hundreds of milliseconds for the first wireless hop. You are competing for access to a shared channel with every other wireless peer.

The good news is, if you are an early adopter, then there is a good chance that you can significantly improve performance of your own WiFi network. The 5 GHz band, used by the new 802.11n and 802.11ac standards, offers both a much wider frequency range and is still largely interference free in most environments. That is, at least for the moment, and assuming you don't have too many tech-savvy friends nearby, like yourself! A dual-band router, which is capable of transmitting both on the 2.4 GHz and the 5 GHz bands will likely offer the best of both worlds: compatibility with old clients limited to 2.4 GHz, and much better performance for any client on the 5 GHz band.

Measuring Your WiFi First-Hop Latency

Running a ping to your wireless gateway is a simple way to estimate the latency of your first wireless hop. Your results *will* be different, but just as an example, performing this test in my own home environment with a dual-band 802.11n router yields the following results.

Table 6-2. Latency difference between 2.4GHz and 5GHz WiFi bands

Freq (GHz)	Median (ms)	95% (ms)	99% (ms)
2.4	6.22	34.87	58.91
5	0.90	1.58	7.89

A dramatic performance difference between the overloaded 2.4 GHz band and the mostly open 5 GHz band (Figure 6-2): over a dozen overlapping networks in the 2.4 GHz band is resulting in a 35 ms latency delay (for 95th percentile) for the first hop from my laptop to my wireless router, which is less than 20 feet away!

Putting it all together, what does this tell us about the performance of WiFi?

- WiFi provides no bandwidth or latency guarantees or assignment to its users.
- WiFi provides variable bandwidth based on signal-to-noise in its environment.
- WiFi transmit power is limited to 200 mW, and likely less in your region.
- WiFi has a limited amount of spectrum in 2.4 GHz and the newer 5 GHz bands.
- WiFi access points overlap in their channel assignment by design.
- WiFi access points and peers compete for access to the same radio channel.

There is no such thing as "typical" WiFi performance. The operating range will vary based on the standard, location of the user, used devices, and the local radio environment. If you are lucky, and you are the only WiFi user, then you can expect high throughput, low latency, and low variability in both. But once you are competing for access with other peers, or nearby WiFi networks, then all bets are off—expect high variability for latency and bandwidth.

Packet Loss in WiFi Networks

The probabilistic scheduling of WiFi transmissions can result in a high number of collisions between multiple wireless peers in the area. However, even if that is the case, this does not necessarily translate to higher amounts of observed TCP packet loss. The data and physical layer implementations of all WiFi protocols have their own retransmission and error correction mechanisms, which hide these wireless collisions from higher layers of the networking stack.

In other words, while TCP packet loss is definitely a concern for data delivered over WiFi, the absolute rate observed by TCP is often no higher than that of most wired networks. Instead of direct TCP packet loss, you are much more likely to see higher variability in packet arrival times due to the underlying collisions and retransmissions performed by the lower link and physical layers.

 Prior to 802.11n, the WiFi protocol allowed at most one in-flight frame at any point in time, which had to be ACKed by the link layer before the next frame is sent. With 802.11n, a new "frame aggregation" feature was introduced, which allows multiple WiFi frames to be sent and ACKed at once.

Optimizing for WiFi Networks

The preceding performance characteristics of WiFi may paint an overly stark picture against it. In practice, it seems to work "well enough" in most cases, and the simple convenience that WiFi enables is hard to beat. In fact, you are now more likely to have a device that requires an extra peripheral to get an Ethernet jack for a wired connection than to find a computer, smartphone, or tablet that is not WiFi enabled.

With that in mind, it is worth considering whether your application can benefit from knowing about and optimizing for WiFi networks.

Leverage Unmetered Bandwidth

In practice, a WiFi network is usually an extension to a wired LAN, which is in turn connected via DSL, cable, or fiber to the wide area network. For an average user in the U.S., this translates to 8.6 Mbps of edge bandwidth and a 3.1 Mbps global average (Table 1-2). In other words, most WiFi clients are still likely to be limited by the available WAN bandwidth, not by WiFi itself. That is, when the "radio network weather" is nice!

However, bandwidth bottlenecks aside, this also frequently means that a typical WiFi deployment is backed by an unmetered WAN connection—or, at the very least, a connection with much higher data caps and maximum throughput. While many users may be sensitive to large downloads over their 3G or 4G connections due to associated costs and bandwidth caps, frequently this is not as much of a concern when on WiFi.

Of course, the unmetered assumption is not true in all cases (e.g., a WiFi tethered device backed by a 3G or 4G connection), but in practice it holds true more often than not. Consequently, large downloads, updates, and streaming use cases are best done over

WiFi when possible. Don't be afraid to prompt the user to switch to WiFi on such occasions!

 Many mobile carriers recommend "Wi-Fi offloading" as an explicit strategy for data-intensive applications: prompt the user to switch to WiFi, or leverage WiFi connectivity whenever possible to perform your background syncs and large data transfers.

Adapt to Variable Bandwidth

As we saw, WiFi provides no bandwidth or latency guarantees. The user's router may have some application-level QoS policies, which may provide a degree of fairness to multiple peers on the same wireless network. However, the WiFi radio interface itself has very limited support for QoS. Worse, there are no QoS policies between multiple, overlapping WiFi networks.

As a result, the available bandwidth allocation may change dramatically, on a second-to-second basis, based on small changes in location, activity of nearby wireless peers, and the general radio environment.

As an example, an HD video stream may require several megabits per second of bandwidth (Table 6-3), and while most WiFi standards are sufficient in ideal conditions, in practice you should not be surprised to see, and should anticipate, intermittent drops in throughput. In fact, due to the dynamic nature of available bandwidth, you cannot and should not extrapolate past download bitrate too far into the future. Testing for bandwidth rate just at the beginning of the video will likely result in intermittent buffering pauses as the radio conditions change during playback.

Table 6-3. Sample YouTube video bitrates for H.264 video codec

Container	Video resolution	Encoding	Video bitrate (Mbit/s)
mp4	360p	H.264	0.5
mp4	480p	H.264	1–1.5
mp4	720p	H.264	2–2.9
mp4	1080p	H.264	3–4.3

Instead, while we can't predict the available bandwidth, we can and should adapt based on continuous measurement through techniques such as adaptive bitrate streaming.

Adaptive Bitrate Streaming

While adaptive bitrate streaming is not applicable to all resource types, it is a perfect match for long-lived streams such as video and audio content.

In the case of video, the resource may be encoded and stored at multiple bitrates and then segmented into many parts (e.g., 5–10 second chunks for YouTube videos). Then, while the client is streaming the data, either the client or the server can monitor the download rate of each segment and dynamically switch the bitrate of the next segment to adjust for the varying bandwidth. In fact, in practice many video streaming services begin the stream with a low bitrate segment to get fast playback start and then continuously adjust the bitrate of the following segments based on the available bandwidth.

How many different bitrate levels do you need? The answer depends on your application! But as an example, Netflix encodes each and every stream in over 120 different versions to adjust for the varying screen sizes and available bandwidth bitrates. Delivering a smooth, on-demand video experience is not a trivial exercise.

Adapt to Variable Latency

Just as there are no bandwidth guarantees when on WiFi, similarly, there are no guarantees on the latency of the first wireless hop. Further, things get only more unpredictable if multiple wireless hops are needed, such as in the case when a wireless bridge (relay) access point is used.

In the ideal case, when there is minimum interference and the network is not loaded, the wireless hop can take less than one millisecond with very low variability. However, in practice, in high-density urban and office environments the presence of dozens of competing WiFi access points and peers creates a lot of contention for the same radio frequencies. As a result, you should not be surprised to see a 1–10 millisecond median for the first wireless hop, with a long latency tail: expect an occasional 10–50 millisecond delay and, in the worst case, even as high as hundreds of milliseconds.

If your application is latency sensitive, then you may need to think carefully about adapting its behavior when running over a WiFi network. In fact, this may be a good reason to consider WebRTC, which offers the option of an unreliable UDP transport. Of course, switching transports won't fix the radio network, but it can help lower the protocol and application induced latency overhead.

CHAPTER 7

Mobile Networks

As of early 2013, there are now an estimated 6.4 billion worldwide cellular connections. For 2012 alone, IDC market intelligence reports show an estimated 1.1 billion shipments for smart connected devices—smartphones, tablets, laptops, PCs, and so on. However, even more remarkable are the hockey stick growth projections for the years to come: the same IDC reports forecast the new device shipment numbers to climb to over 1.8 billion by 2016, and other cumulative forecasts estimate a total of over 20 billion connected devices by 2020.

With an estimated human population of 7 billion in 2012, rising to 7.5 billion by 2020, these trends illustrate our insatiable appetite for smart connected devices: apparently, most of us are not satisfied with just one.

However, the absolute number of connected devices is only one small part of the overall story. Implicit in this growth is also the insatiable demand for high-speed connectivity, ubiquitous wireless broadband access, and the connected services that must power all of these new devices! This is where, and why, we must turn our conversation to the performance of the various cellular technologies, such as GSM, CDMA, HSPA, and LTE. Chances are, most of your users will be using one of these technologies, some exclusively, to access your site or service. The stakes are high, we have to get this right, and mobile networks definitely pose their own set of performance challenges.

Brief History of the G's

Navigating the forest of the various cellular standards, release versions, and the pros and cons of each could occupy not chapters, but entire books. Our goal here is much more humble: we need to develop an intuition for the operating parameters, and their implications, of the major past and future milestones (Table 7-1) of the dominant wireless technologies in the market.

Table 7-1. Generations of mobile networks

Generation	Peak data rate	Description
1G	no data	Analog systems
2G	Kbit/s	First digital systems as overlays or parallel to analog systems
3G	Mbit/s	Dedicated digital networks deployed in parallel to analog systems
4G	Gbit/s	Digital and packet-only networks

The first important realization is that the underlying standards for each wireless generation are expressed in terms of *peak spectral efficiency* (bps/Hz), which is then translated to impressive numbers such as Gbit/s+ peak data rates for 4G networks. However, you should now recognize the key word in the previous sentence: *peak!* Think back to our earlier discussion on "Measuring Real-World Wireless Performance" on page 87—peak data rates are achieved in ideal conditions.

Regardless of the standard, the real performance of every network will vary by provider, their configuration of the network, the number of active users in a given cell, the radio environment in a specific location, the device in use, plus all the other factors that affect wireless performance. With that in mind, while there are no guarantees for data rates in real-world environments, a simple but effective strategy to calibrate your performance expectations (Table 7-2) is to assume much closer to the lower bound for data throughput, and toward the higher bound for packet latency for every generation.

Table 7-2. Data rates and latency for an active mobile connection

Generation	Data rate	Latency
2G	100–400 Kbit/s	300–1000 ms
3G	0.5–5 Mbit/s	100–500 ms
4G	1–50 Mbit/s	< 100 ms

To complicate matters further, the classification of any given network as 3G or 4G is definitely too coarse, and correspondingly so is the expected throughput and latency. To understand why this is the case, and where the industry is heading, we first need to take a quick survey of the history of the different technologies and the key players behind their evolution.

First Data Services with 2G

The first commercial 1G network was launched in Japan in 1979. It was an analog system and offered no data capabilities. In 1991, the first 2G network was launched in Finland based on the emerging GSM (Global System for Mobile Communications, originally Groupe Spécial Mobile) standard, which introduced digital signaling within the radio network. This enabled first circuit-switched mobile data services, such as text messaging (SMS), and packet delivery at a whopping peak data rate of 9.6 Kbit/s!

It wasn't until the mid 1990s, when general packet radio service (GPRS) was first introduced to the GSM standard that wireless Internet access became a practical, albeit still very slow, possibility: with GPRS, you could now reach 172 Kbit/s, with typical roundtrip latency hovering in high hundreds of milliseconds. The combination of GPRS and earlier 2G voice technologies is often described as 2.5G. A few years later, these networks were enhanced by EDGE (Enhanced Data rates for GSM Evolution), which increased the peak data rates to 384 Kbit/s. The first EDGE networks (2.75G) were launched in the U.S. in 2003.

At this point, a pause and some reflection is warranted. Wireless communication is many decades old, but practical, consumer-oriented data services over mobile networks are a recent phenomenon! 2.75G networks are barely a decade old, which is recent history, and are also still widely used around the world. Yet, most of us now simply can't imagine living without high-speed wireless access. The rate of adoption, and the evolution of the wireless technologies, has been nothing short of breathtaking.

3GPP and 3GPP2 Partnerships

Once the consumer demand for wireless data services began to grow, the question of radio network interoperability became a hot issue for everyone involved. For one, the telecom providers must buy and deploy the hardware for the radio access network (RAN), which requires significant capital investments and ongoing maintenance—standard hardware means lower costs. Similarly, without industry-wide standards, the users would be restricted to their home networks, limiting the use cases and convenience of mobile data access.

In response, the European Telecommunication Standards Institute (ETSI) developed the GSM standard in the early 1990's, which was quickly adopted by many European countries and around the globe. In fact, GSM would go on to become the most widely deployed wireless standard, by some estimates, covering 80%–85% of the market (Figure 7-1). But it wasn't the only one. In parallel, the IS-95 standard developed by Qualcomm also captured 10%–15% of the market, most notably with many network deployments across North America. As a result, a device designed for the IS-95 radio network cannot operate on the GSM network, and vice versa—an unfortunate property that is familiar to many international travelers.

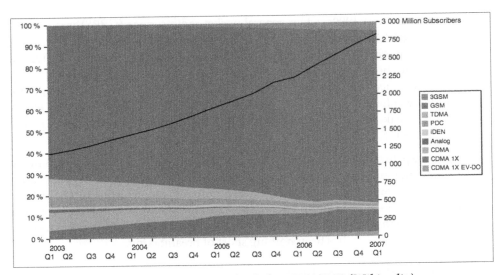

Figure 7-1. Market share of mobile standards for 2003–2007 (Wikipedia)

In 1998, recognizing the need for global evolution of the deployed standards, as well as defining the requirements for the next generation (3G) networks, the participants in GSM and IS-95 standards organizations formed two global partnership projects:

3rd Generation Partnership Project (3GPP)
> Responsible for developing the Universal Mobile Telecommunication System (UMTS), which is the 3G upgrade to GSM networks. Later, it also assumed maintenance of the GSM standard and development of the new LTE standards.

3rd Generation Partnership Project 2 (3GPP2)
> Responsible for developing the 3G specifications based on the CDMA2000 technology, which is a successor to the IS-95 standard developed by Qualcomm.

Consequently, the development of both types of standards (Table 7-3) and associated network infrastructure has proceeded in parallel. Perhaps not directly in lockstep, but nonetheless following mostly similar evolution of the underlying technologies.

Table 7-3. Cellular network standards developed by 3GPP and 3GPP2

Generation	Organization	Release
2G	3GPP	GSM
	3GPP2	IS-95 (cdmaOne)
2.5G, 2.75G	3GPP	GPRS, EDGE (EGPRS)
	3GPP2	CDMA2000
3G	3GPP	UMTS
	3GPP2	CDMA 2000 1x EV-DO Release 0

Generation	Organization	Release
3.5G, 3.75G, 3.9G	3GPP	HSPA, HSPA+, LTE
	3GPP2	EV-DO Revision A, EV-DO Revision B, EV-DO Advanced
4G	3GPP	LTE-Advanced, HSPA+ Revision 11+

Chances are, you should see some familiar labels on the list: EV-DO, HSPA, LTE. Many network operators have invested significant marketing resources, and continue to do so, to promote these technologies as their "latest and fastest mobile data networks." However, our interest and the reason for this historical detour is not for the marketing, but for the macro observations of the evolution of the mobile wireless industry:

- There are two dominant, deployed mobile network types around the world.
- 3GPP and 3GPP2 manage the evolution of each technology.
- 3GPP and 3GPP2 standards are not device interoperable.

There is no one 4G or 3G technology. The International Telecommunication Union (ITU) sets the international standards and performance characteristics, such as data rates and latency, for each wireless generation, and the 3GPP and 3GPP2 organizations then define the standards to meet and exceed these expectations within the context of their respective technologies.

 How do you know which network type your carrier is using? Simple. Does your phone have a SIM card? If so, then it is a 3GPP technology that evolved from GSM. To find out more detailed information about the network, check your carrier's FAQ, or if your phone allows it, check the network information directly on your phone.

For Android users, open your phone dial screen and type in: *#*#4636#*#*. If your phone allows it, it should open a diagnostics screen where you can inspect the status and type of your mobile connection, battery diagnostics, and more.

Evolution of 3G Technologies

In the context of 3G networks, we have two dominant and competing standards: UMTS and CDMA-based networks, which are developed by 3GPP and 3GPP2, respectively. However as the earlier table of cellular standards (Table 7-3) shows, each is also split into several transitional milestones: 3.5G, 3.75G, and 3.9G technologies.

Why couldn't we simply jump to 4G instead? Well, standards take a long time to develop, but even more importantly, there are big financial costs for deploying new network infrastructure. As we will see, 4G requires an entirely different radio interface and parallel infrastructure to 3G. Because of this, and also for the benefit of the many users who have purchased 3G handsets, both 3GPP and 3GPP2 have continued to evolve the existing 3G standards, which also enables the operators to incrementally upgrade their existing networks to deliver better performance to their existing users.

Not surprisingly, the throughput, latency, and other performance characteristics of the various 3G networks have improved, sometimes dramatically, with every new release. In fact, technically, LTE is considered a 3.9G transitional standard! However, before we get to LTE, let's take a closer look at the various 3GPP and 3GPP2 milestones.

Evolution of 3GPP technologies

Table 7-4. 3GPP release history

Release	Date	Summary
99	1999	First release of the UMTS standard
4	2001	Introduced an all-IP core network
5	2002	Introduced High-Speed Packet Downlink Access (HSDPA)
6	2004	Introduced High-Speed Packet Uplink Access (HSUPA)
7	2007	Introduced High-Speed Packet Access Evolution (HSPA+)
8	2008	Introduced new LTE System Architecture Evolution (SAE)
9	2009	Improvements to SAE and WiMAX interoperability
10	2010	Introduced 4G LTE-Advanced architecture

In the case of networks following the 3GPP standards, the combination of HSDPA and HSUPA releases is often known and marketed as a High-Speed Packet Access (HSPA) network. This combination of the two releases enabled low single-digit Mbit/s throughput in real-world deployments, which was a significant step up from the early 3G speeds. HSPA networks are often labeled as 3.5G.

From there, the next upgrade was HSPA+ (3.75G), which offered significantly lower latencies thanks to a simplified core network architecture and data rates in mid to high single-digit Mbit/s throughput in real-world deployments. However, as we will see, release 7, which introduced HSPA+, was not the end of the line for this technology. In fact, the HSPA+ standards have been continuously refined since then and are now competing head to head with LTE and LTE-Advanced!

Evolution of 3GPP2 technologies

Table 7-5. 3GPP2 release history of the CDMA2000 1x EV-DO standard

Release	Date	Summary
Rel. 0	1999	First release of the 1x EV-DO standard
Rev. A	2001	Upgrade to peak data-rate, lower latency, and QoS
Rev. B	2004	Introduced multicarrier capabilities to Rev. A
Rev. C	2007	Improved core network efficiency and performance

The CDMA2000 EV-DO standard developed by 3GPP2 followed a similar network upgrade path. The first release (Rel. 0) enabled low single digit Mbit/s downlink throughput but very low uplink speeds. The uplink performance was addressed with Rev. A, and both uplink and downlink speeds were further improved in Rev. B. Hence, a Rev. B network was able to deliver mid to high single-digit Mbit/s performance to its users, which makes it comparable to HSPA and early HSPA+ networks—aka, 3.5–3.75G.

The Rev. C release is also frequently referred to as EV-DO Advanced and offers significant operational improvements in capacity and performance. However, the adoption of EV-DO Advanced has not been nearly as strong as that of HSPA+. Why? If you paid close attention to the standards generation table (Table 7-3), you may have noticed that 3GPP2 does not have an official and competing 4G standard!

While 3GPP2 could have continued to evolve its CDMA technologies, at some point both the network operators and the network vendors agreed on 3GPP LTE as a *common 4G successor* to all types of networks. For this reason, many of the CDMA network operators are also some of the first to invest into early LTE infrastructure, in part to be able to compete with ongoing HSPA+ improvements.

In other words, most mobile operators around the world are converging on HSPA+ and LTE as the future mobile wireless standards—that's the good news. Having said that, don't hold your breath. Existing 2G and 3–3.75G technologies are still powering the vast majority of deployed mobile radio networks, and even more importantly, will remain operational for at least another decade.

3G is often described as "mobile broadband." However, broadband is a relative term. Some pin it as a communication bandwidth of at least 256 Kbit/s, others as that exceeding 640 Kbit/s, but the truth is that the value keeps changing based on the experience we are trying to achieve. As the services evolve and demand higher throughput, so does the definition of broadband.

In that light, it might be more useful to think of 3G standards as those targeting and exceeding the Mbit/s bandwidth threshold. How far over the Mbit/s barrier? Well, that depends on the release version of the standard (as we saw earlier), the carrier configuration of the network, and the capabilities of the device in use.

IMT-Advanced 4G Requirements

Before we dissect the various 4G technologies, it is important to understand what stands behind the "4G" label. Just as with 3G, there is no one 4G technology. Rather, 4G is a set of requirements (IMT-Advanced) that was developed and published by the ITU back in 2008. Any technology that meets these requirements can be labeled as 4G.

Some example requirements of IMT-Advanced include the following:

- Based on an IP packet switched network
- Interoperable with previous wireless standards (3G and 2G)
- 100 Mbit/s data rate for mobile clients and Gbit/s+ when stationary
- Sub 100 ms control-plane latency and sub 10 ms user-plane latency
- Dynamic allocation and sharing of network resources between users
- Use of variable bandwidth allocation, from 5 to 20 MHz

The actual list is much, much longer but the preceding captures the highlights important for our discussion: much higher throughput and significantly lower latencies when compared to earlier generations. Armed with these criteria, we now know how to classify a 4G network—right? Not so fast, that would be too easy! The marketing departments also had to have their say.

LTE-Advanced is a standard that was specifically developed to satisfy all the IMT-Advanced criteria. In fact, it was also the first 3GPP standard to do so. However, if you were paying close attention, you would have noticed that LTE (release 8) and LTE-Advanced (release 10) are, in fact, different standards. Technically, LTE should really be considered a 3.9G transitional standard, even though it lays much of the necessary groundwork to meet the 4G requirements—it is almost there, but not quite!

However, this is where the marketing steps in. The 3G and 4G trademarks are held by the ITU, and hence their use should correspond to defined requirements for each generation. Except the carriers won a marketing coup and were able to redefine the "4G" trademark to include a set of technologies that are *significantly close* to the 4G requirements. For this reason, LTE (release 8) and most HSPA+ networks, which do not meet the actual technical 4G requirements, are nonetheless marketed as "4G."

What about the real (LTE-Advanced) 4G deployments? Those are coming, but it remains to be seen how these networks will be marketed in light of their earlier predecessors. Regardless, the point is, the "4G" label as it is used today by many carriers is ambiguous, and you should read the fine print to understand the technology behind it.

Long Term Evolution (LTE)

Despite the continuous evolution of the 3G standards, the increased demand for high data transmission speeds and lower latencies exposed a number of inherent design limitations in the earlier UMTS technologies. To address this, 3GPP set out to redesign both the core and the radio networks, which led to the creation of the aptly named Long Term Evolution (LTE) standard:

- All IP core network
- Simplified network architecture to lower costs
- Low latencies in user (<10 ms) and control planes (<100 ms)
- New radio interface and modulation for high throughput (100 Mbps)
- Ability to use larger bandwidth allocations and carrier aggregation
- MIMO as a requirement for all devices

Not surprisingly, the preceding list should read similar to the IMT-Advanced requirements we saw earlier. LTE (release 8) laid the groundwork for the new network architecture, and LTE-Advanced (release 10) delivered the necessary improvements to meet the true 4G requirements set by IMT-Advanced.

At this point it is important to note that due to radio and core network implementation differences, LTE networks are not simple upgrades to existing 3G infrastructure. Instead, LTE networks must be deployed in parallel and on separate spectrum from existing 3G infrastructure. However, since LTE is a common successor to both UMTS and CDMA standards, it does provide a way to interoperate with both: an LTE subscriber can be seamlessly handed off to a 3G network and be migrated back where LTE infrastructure is available.

Finally, as the name implies, LTE is definitely the long-term evolution plan for virtually all future mobile networks. The only question is, how distant is this future? A few carriers have already begun investing into LTE infrastructure, and many others are beginning to look for the spectrum, funds, or both, to do so. However, current industry estimates show that this migration will indeed be a *long-term one*—perhaps over the course of the next decade or so. In the meantime, HSPA+ is set to take the center stage.

 Every LTE-capable device must have multiple radios for mandatory MIMO support. However, each device will also need separate radio interfaces for earlier 3G and 2G networks. If you are counting, that translates to three or four radios in every handset! For higher data rates with LTE, you will need 4x MIMO, which brings the total to five or six radios. You were wondering why your battery is drained so quickly?

HSPA+ is Leading Worldwide 4G Adoption

HSPA+ was first introduced in 3GPP release 7, back in 2007. However, while the popular attention quickly shifted toward LTE, which was first introduced in 3GPP release 8 in 2008, what is often overlooked is that the development of HSPA+ did not cease and continued to coevolve in parallel. In fact, HSPA+ release 10 meets many of the IMT-Advanced criteria. But, you may ask, if we have LTE and everyone is in agreement that it is *the standard* for future mobile networks, why continue to develop and invest into HSPA+? As usual, the answer is a simple one: cost.

3GPP 3G technologies command the lion's share of the established wireless market around the world, which translates into huge existing infrastructure investments by the carriers around the globe. Migrating to LTE requires development of new radio networks, which once again translates into significant capital expenditures. By contrast, HSPA+ offers a much more capital efficient route: the carriers can deploy incremental upgrades to their existing networks and get comparable performance.

Cost-effectiveness is the name of the game and the reason why current industry projections (Figure 7-2) show HSPA+ as responsible for the majority of 4G upgrades around the world for years to come. In the meantime, CDMA technologies developed by 3GPP2 will continue to coexist, although their number of subscriptions is projected to start declining slowly, while new LTE deployments will proceed in parallel with different rates in different regions—in part due to cost constraints, and in part due to different regulation and the availability of required radio spectrum.

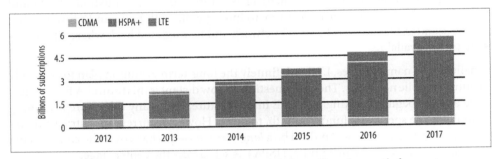

Figure 7-2. 4G Americas: HSPA+ and LTE mobile broadband growth forecast

For a variety of reasons, North America appears to be the leader in LTE adoption: current industry projections show the number of LTE subscribers in U.S. and Canada surpassing that of HSPA by 2016 (Figure 7-3). However, the rate of LTE adoption in North America appears to be significantly more aggressive than in most other countries. Within the global context, HSPA+ is set to be the dominant mobile wireless technology of the current decade.

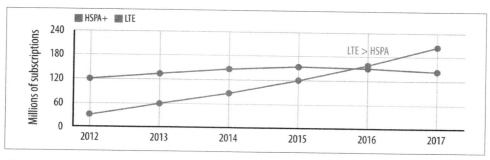

Figure 7-3. 4G Americas: U.S./Canada HSPA+ and LTE growth forecast

While many are first surprised by the trends in the HSPA+ vs. LTE adoption, this is not an unexpected outcome. If nothing else, it serves to illustrate an important point: it takes roughly a decade from the first specification of a new wireless standard to its mainstream availability in real-world wireless networks.

By extension, it is a fairly safe bet that we will be talking about LTE-Advanced in earnest by the early 2020s! Unfortunately, deploying new radio infrastructure is a costly and time-consuming proposition.

Building for the Multigeneration Future

Crystal ball gazing is a dangerous practice in our industry. However, by this point we have covered enough to make some reasonable predictions about what we can and should expect out of the currently deployed mobile networks, as well as where we might be in a few years' time.

First, the wireless standards are evolving quickly, but the physical rollout of these networks is both a costly and a time-consuming exercise. Further, once deployed, the network must be maintained for significant amounts of time to recoup the costs and to keep existing customers online. In other words, while there is a lot of hype and marketing around 4G, older-generation networks will continue to operate for at least another decade. When building for the mobile web, plan accordingly.

Ironically, while 4G networks provide significant improvements for IP data delivery, 3G networks are still much more efficient in handling the old-fashioned voice traffic! Voice over LTE (VoLTE) is currently in active development and aims to enable efficient and reliable voice over 4G, but most current 4G deployments still rely on the older, circuit-switched infrastructure for voice delivery.

Consequently, when building applications for mobile networks, we cannot target a single type or generation of network, or worse, hope for specific throughput or latency performance. As we saw, the actual performance of any network is highly variable, based on deployed release, infrastructure, radio conditions, and a dozen other variables. Our applications should adapt to the continuously changing conditions within the network: throughput, latency, and even the availability of the radio connection. When the user is on the go, it is highly likely that he may transition between multiple generations of networks (LTE, HSPA+, HSPA, EV-DO, and even GPRS Edge) based on the available coverage and signal strength. If the application fails to account for this, then the user experience will suffer.

The good news is HSPA+ and LTE adoption is growing very fast, which enables an entirely new class of high-throughput and latency-sensitive applications previously not possible. Both are effectively on par in throughput and latency (Table 7-6): mid to high digit Mbps throughput in real-world environments, and sub-100-millisecond latency, which makes them comparable to many home and office WiFi networks.

Table 7-6. HSPA+, LTE, and LTE-Advanced comparison

	HSPA+	LTE	LTE-Advanced
Peak downlink speed (Mbit/s)	168	300	3,000
Peak uplink speed (Mbit/s)	22	75	1,500
Maximum MIMO streams	2	4	8
Idle to connected latency (ms)	< 100	< 100	< 50
Dormant to active latency (ms)	< 50	< 50	< 10
User-plane one-way latency (ms)	< 10	< 5	< 5

However, while 4G wireless performance is often compared to that of WiFi, or wired broadband, it would be incorrect to assume that we can get away with treating them as the same environments: that they are definitely not.

For example, most users and developers expect an "always on" experience where the device is permanently connected to the Internet and is ready to instantaneously react to user input or an incoming data packet. This assumption holds true in the tethered world but is definitely incorrect for mobile networks. Practical constraints such as battery life and device capabilities mean that we must design our applications with explicit awareness of the constraints of mobile networks. To understand these differences, let's dig a little deeper.

User-Plane One-way Latency

User-plane one-way latency is the target time specified by the LTE standard for the one-way transit between a packet being available in the wireless device and the same packet being available at the radio tower. In other words, it is the one-way latency of the first wireless hop when the device is in the high-power continuous reception state. Every application packet will incur this cost—no shortcuts.

Device Features and Capabilities

What is often forgotten is that the deployed radio network is only half of the equation. It goes without saying that devices from different manufacturers and release dates will have very different characteristics: CPU speeds and core counts, amount of available memory, storage capacity, GPU, and more. Each of these factors will affect the overall performance of the device and the applications running on it.

However, even with all of these variables accounted for, when it comes to network performance, there is one more section that is often overlooked: radio capabilities. Specifically, the device that the user is holding in her hands must also be able to take advantage of the deployed radio infrastructure! The carrier may deploy the latest LTE infrastructure, but a device designed for an earlier release may simply not be able to take advantage of it, and vice versa.

User Equipment Category

Both the 3GPP and 3GPP2 standards continue to evolve and enhance the radio interface requirements: modulation schemes, number of radios, and so on. To get the best performance out of any network, the device must also meet the specified user equipment (UE) category requirements for each type of network. In fact, for each release, there are often multiple UE categories, each of which will offer very different radio performance.

An obvious and important question is, why? Once again, the answer is a simple one: cost. Availability of multiple categories of devices enables device differentiation, various price points for price-sensitive users, and ability to adapt to deployed network infrastructure on the ground.

The HSPA standard alone specifies over 36 possible UE categories! Hence, just saying that you have an "HSPA capable device" (Table 7-7) is not enough—you need to read the fine print. For example, assuming the radio network is capable, to get the 42.2 Mbps/s throughput, you would also need a category 20 (2x MIMO), or category 24 (dual-cell) device. Finally, to confuse matters further, a category 21 device does not automatically guarantee higher throughput over a category 20 handset.

Table 7-7. Sample 3GPP HSPA user equipment (UE) categories

3GPP Release	Category	MIMO, Multicell	Peak data rate (Mbit/s)
5	8	—	7.2
5	10	—	14.0
7	14	—	21.1
8	20	2x MIMO	42.2
8	21	Dual-cell	23.4
8	24	Dual-cell	42.2
10	32	Quad-cell + MIMO	168.8

Similarly, the LTE standard defines its own set of user equipment categories (Table 7-8): a high-end smartphone is likely to be a category 3–5 device, but it will also likely share the network with a lot of cheaper category 1–2 neighbors. Higher UE categories, which require 4x and even 8x MIMO, are more likely to be found in specialized devices—powering that many radios simultaneously consumes a lot of power, which may not be very practical for something in your pocket!

Table 7-8. LTE user equipment (UE) categories

3GPP release	Category	MIMO	Peak downlink (Mbit/s)	Peak uplink (Mbit/s)
8	1	1x	10.3	5.2
8	2	2x	51.0	25.5
8	3	2x	102.0	51.0
8	4	2x	150.8	51.0
8	5	4x	299.6	75.4
10	6	2x or 4x	301.5	51.0
10	7	2x or 4x	301.5	102.0
10	8	8x	2998.6	1497.8

In practice, most of the early LTE deployments are targeting category 1–3 devices, with early LTE-Advanced networks focusing on category 3 as their primary UE type.

If you own an LTE or an HSPA+ device, do you know its category classification? And once you figure that out, do you know which 3GPP release your network operator is running? To get the best performance, the two must match. Otherwise, you will be limited either by the capabilities of the radio network or the device in use.

Deciphering the Radio Specification on a Mobile Device

If you have ever read the technical specification of your mobile device, you would have no doubt noticed a long and confusing list of frequencies and technology types under the connectivity section. Well, now we should know enough to decipher this list! As an example, let's take a look at the specification for Google's Nexus 4:

- GSM/EDGE/GPRS (850, 900, 1800, 1900 MHz)
- 3G (850, 900, 1700, 1900, 2100 MHz)
- HSPA+ 42

The first line tells us that the device can operate on 2G networks and is GPRS (2.5G) and EDGE (2.75G) capable—hundreds of Kbit/s peak data rates. The list of frequencies indicates the bands on which the radio is able to operate, to account for the different regulations and network deployments around the world.

The second line is similar, except that it doesn't indicate much in terms of maximum 3G throughput. But that is exactly what the third line reveals: HSPA+ indicates that the phone can operate on 3.75G networks, and the "42" tells us that it is either a category 20 device with MIMO, or a category 24 dual-cell device with maximum data rate of 42.2 Mbps in the downlink—that is, if the network allows it. In fact, Nexus 4 is a category 24 dual-cell device.

Finally, this phone is not LTE capable; for that it would need another radio interface, in addition to the 2G and 3G radios. Many mobile phones are already miracles of miniaturization, but this fact is only more impressive when you realize that most modern phones don't just have one radio: most have somewhere between two and four!

Radio Resource Controller (RRC)

Both 3G and 4G networks have a unique feature that is not present in tethered and even WiFi networks. The Radio Resource Controller (RRC) mediates all connection management between the device in use and the radio base station (Figure 7-4). Understanding why it exists, and how it affects the performance of every device on a mobile network, is critical to building high-performance mobile applications. The RRC has direct impact on latency, throughput, and battery life of the device in use.

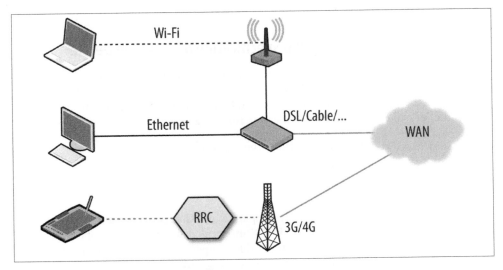

Figure 7-4. Radio Resource Controller

When using a physical connection, such as an Ethernet cable, your computer has a direct and an always-on network link, which allows either side of this connection to send data packets at any time; this is the best possible case for minimizing latency. As we saw in "From Ethernet to a Wireless LAN" on page 89, the WiFi standard follows a similar model, where each device is able to transmit at any point in time. This too provides minimum latency in the best case, but due to the use of the shared radio medium can also lead to high collision rates and unpredictable performance if there are many active users. Further, because any WiFi peer could start transmitting at any time, all others must also be ready to receive. The radio is always on, which consumes a lot of power.

In practice, keeping the WiFi radio active at all times is simply too expensive, as battery capacity is a limited resource on most devices. Hence, WiFi offers a small power optimization where the access point broadcasts a delivery traffic indication message (DTIM) within a periodic beacon frame to indicate that it will be transmitting data for certain clients immediately after. In turn, the clients can listen for these DTIM frames as hints for when the radio should be ready to receive, and otherwise the radio can sleep until the next DTIM transmission. This lowers battery use but adds extra latency.

 The upcoming WiFi Multimedia (WMM) standard will further improve the power efficiency of WiFi devices with the help of the new PowerSave mechanisms such as NoAck and APSD (Automatic Power Save Delivery).

Therein lies the problem for 3G and 4G networks: network efficiency and power. Or rather, lack of power, due to the fact that mobile devices are constrained by their battery capacity and a requirement for high network efficiency among a significantly larger number of active users in the cell. This is why the RRC exists.

As the name implies, the Radio Resource Controller assumes full responsibility over scheduling of who talks when, allocated bandwidth, the signal power used, the power state of each device, and a dozen other variables. Simply put, the RRC is the brains of the radio access network. Want to send data over the wireless channel? You must first ask the RRC to allocate some radio resources for you. Have incoming data from the Internet? The RRC will notify you for when to listen to receive the inbound packets.

The good news is all the RRC management is performed by the network. The bad news is, while you can't necessarily control the RRC via an API, if you do want to optimize your application for 3G and 4G networks, then you need to be aware of and work within the constraints imposed by the RRC.

 The RRC lives within the radio network. In 2G and 3G networks, the RRC lived in the core carrier network, and in 4G the RRC logic has been moved directly to the serving radio tower (eNodeB) to improve performance and reduce coordination latency.

3G, 4G, and WiFi Power Requirements

The radio is one of the most power-hungry components of any handset. In fact, the screen is the only component that consumes higher amounts of power when active—emphasis on active. In practice, the screen is off for significant periods of time, whereas the radio must maintain the illusion of an "always-on" experience such that the user is reachable at any point in time.

One way to achieve this goal is to keep the radio active at all times, but even with the latest advances in battery capacity, doing so would drain the battery in a matter of hours. Worse, latest iterations of the 3G and 4G standards require parallel transmissions (MIMO, Multicell, etc.), which is equivalent to powering multiple radios at once. In practice, a balance must be struck between keeping the radio active to service low-latency interactive traffic and cycling into low-power states to enable reasonable battery performance.

How do the different technologies compare, and which is better for battery life? There is no one single answer. With WiFi, each device sets its own transmit power, which is usually in the 30–200 mW range. By comparison, the transmit power of the 3G/4G radio is managed by the network and can consume as low as 15 mW when in an idle state. However, to account for larger range and interference, the same radio can require 1,000–3,500 mW when transmitting in a high-power state!

In practice, when transferring large amounts of data, WiFi is often far more efficient if the signal strength is good. But if the device is mostly idle, then the 3G/4G radio is more effective. For best performance, ideally we would want dynamic switching between the different connection types. However, at least for the moment, no such mechanism exists. This is an active area of research, both in the industry and academia.

So how does the battery and power management affect networking performance? Signal power (explained on page 85) is one of the primary levers to achieve higher throughput. However, high transmit power consumes significant amounts of energy and hence may be throttled to achieve better battery life. Similarly, powering down the radio may also tear down the radio link to the radio tower altogether, which means that in the event of a new transmission, a series of control messages must be first exchanged to reestablish the radio context, which can add tens and even hundreds of milliseconds of latency.

Both throughput and latency performance are directly impacted by the power management profile of the device in use. In fact, and this is key, in 3G and 4G networks the radio power management is controlled by the RRC: not only does it tell you when to communicate, but it will also tell you the transmit power and when to cycle into different power states.

LTE RRC State Machine

The radio state of every LTE device is controlled by the radio tower currently servicing the user. In fact, the 3GPP standard defines a well-specified state machine, which describes the possible power states of each device connected to the network (Figure 7-5). The network operator can make modifications to the parameters that trigger the state transitions, but the state machine itself is the same across all LTE deployments.

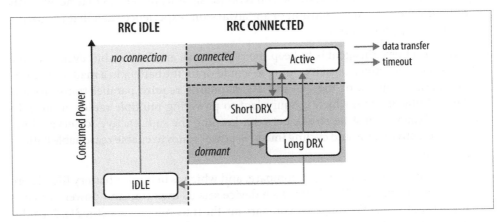

Figure 7-5. LTE RRC state machine

RRC Idle

Device radio is in a low-power state (<15 mW) and only listening to control traffic. No radio resources are assigned to the client within the carrier network.

RRC Connected

Device radio is in a high-power state (1000–3500 mW) while it either transmits data or waits for data, and dedicated radio resources are allocated by the radio network.

The device is either idle, in which case it is only listening to control channel broadcasts, such as paging notifications of inbound traffic, or connected, in which case the network has an established context and resource assignment for the client.

When in an idle state, the device cannot send or receive any data. To do so, it must first synchronize itself to the network by listening to the network broadcasts and then issue a request to the RRC to be moved to the "connected" state. This negotiation can take several roundtrips to establish, and the 3GPP LTE specification allocates a target of 100 milliseconds or less for this state transition. In LTE-Advanced, the target time was further reduced to 50 milliseconds.

Once in a connected state, a network context is established between the radio tower and the LTE device, and data can be transferred. However, once either side completes the intended data transfer, how does the RRC know when to transition the device to a lower power state? Trick question—it doesn't!

IP traffic is bursty, optimized TCP connections are long-lived, and UDP traffic provides no "end of transmission" indicator by design. As a result, and not unlike the NAT connection-state timeouts solution covered on page 39, the RRC state machine depends on a collection of timers to trigger the RRC state transitions.

Finally, because the connected state requires such high amounts of power, multiple substates are available (Figure 7-5) to allow for more efficient operation:

Continuous reception

Highest power state, established network context, allocated network resources.

Short Discontinuous Reception (Short DRX)

Established network context, no allocated network resources.

Long Discontinuous Reception (Long DRX)

Established network context, no allocated network resources.

In the high-power state, the RRC creates a reservation for the device to receive and transmit data over the wireless interface and notifies the device for what these time-slots are, the transmit power that must be used, the modulation scheme, and a dozen other variables. Then, if the device has been idle for a configured period of time, it is transitioned to a Short DRX power state, where the network context is still maintained, but no specific radio resources are assigned. When in Short DRX state, the device only listens to periodic broadcasts from the network, which allows it to preserve the battery —not unlike the DTIM interval in WiFi.

What Are "Assigned Radio Resources"?

In LTE, just as in most other modern wireless standards, there are shared uplink and downlink radio channels, the access to which is controlled by the RRC. When in a connected state, the RRC tells each and every device which timeslots are assigned to whom, which transmit power must be used, modulation, plus a dozen other variables.

If the mobile device does not have an assignment for these resources by the RRC, then it cannot transmit or receive any user data. Consequently, when in a DRX state, the device is synchronized to the RRC, but no uplink or downlink resources are allocated to it: the device is "half awake."

If the radio remains idle long enough, it is then transitioned to the Long DRX state, which is identical to the Short DRX state, except that the device sleeps for longer periods of time between waking up to listen to the broadcasts (Figure 7-6).

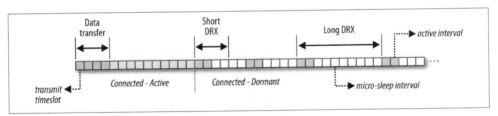

Figure 7-6. Discontinuous reception: Short DRX and Long DRX

What happens if the network or the mobile device must transmit data when the radio is in one of Short or Long DRX (dormant) states? The device and the RRC must first exchange control messages to negotiate when to transmit and when to listen to radio broadcasts. For LTE, this negotiation time ("dormant to connected") is specified as less than 50 milliseconds, and further tightened to less than 10 milliseconds for LTE-Advanced.

So what does this all mean in practice? Depending on which power state the radio is in, an LTE device may first require anywhere from 10 to 100 milliseconds (Table 7-9) of latency to negotiate the required resources with the RRC. Following that, application data can be transferred over the wireless link, through the carrier's network, and then out to the public Internet. Planning for these delays, especially when designing latency-sensitive applications, can be all the difference between "unpredictable performance" and an optimized mobile application.

Table 7-9. LTE and LTE-Advanced RRC latency

	LTE	LTE-Advanced
Idle to connected latency	< 100 ms	< 50 ms
DRX to connected latency	< 50 ms	< 10 ms
User-plane one-way latency	< 5 ms	< 5 ms

HSPA and HSPA+ (UMTS) RRC State Machine

Earlier generation 3GPP networks prior to LTE and LTE-Advanced have a very similar RRC state machine that is also maintained by the radio network. That's the good news. The bad news is the state machine for earlier generations is a bit more complicated (Figure 7-7), and the latencies are much, much higher. In fact, one reason why LTE offers better performance is precisely due to the simplified architecture and improved performance of the RRC state transitions.

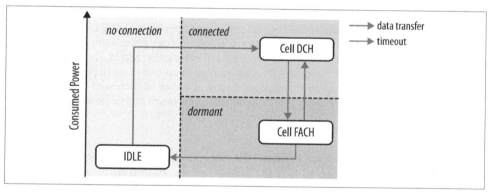

Figure 7-7. UMTS RRC state machine: HSPA, HSPA+

Idle

> Similar to idle in LTE. The device radio is in a low-power state and only listening to control traffic from the network. No radio resources are assigned to the client within the carrier network.

Cell DCH

> Similar to connected LTE mode when in continuous reception. The device is in a high-power state, and network resources are assigned both for upstream and downstream data transfer.

Cell FACH

> An intermediate power state, which consumes significantly less power than DCH. The device does not have dedicated network resources but is nonetheless able to

transmit small amounts of user data through a shared low-speed channel (with speeds of typically less than 20 Kbps).

Idle and DCH states are nearly identical to that of idle and connected in LTE. However, the intermediate FACH state is unique to UMTS networks (HSPA, HSPA+) and allows the use of a common channel for small data transfers: slow, steady, and consuming roughly half the power of the DCH state. In practice, this state was designed to handle non-interactive traffic, such as periodic polling and status checks done by many background applications.

Not surprisingly, the transition from DCH to FACH is triggered by a timer. However, once in FACH, what triggers a promotion back to DCH? Each device maintains a buffer of data to be sent, and as long as the buffer does not exceed a network-configured threshold, typically anywhere from 100 to 1,000 bytes, then the device can remain in the intermediate state. Finally, if no data is transferred while in FACH for some period of time, another timer transitions the device down to the idle state.

 Unlike LTE, which offers two intermediate states (Short DRX and Long DRX), UMTS devices have just a single intermediate state: FACH. However, even though LTE offers a theoretically higher degree of power control, the radios themselves tend to consume more power in LTE devices; higher throughput comes at a cost of increased battery consumption. Hence, LTE devices still have a much higher power profile than their 3G predecessors.

Individual power states aside, perhaps the biggest difference between the earlier-generation 3G networks and LTE is the latency of the state transitions. Where LTE targets sub-hundred milliseconds for idle to connected states, the same transition from idle to DCH can take up to two seconds and require tens of control messages between the 3G device and the RRC! FACH to DCH is not much better either, requiring up to one and a half seconds for the state transition.

The good news is the latest HSPA+ networks have made significant improvements in this department and are now competitive with LTE (Table 7-6). However, we can't count on ubiquitous access to 4G or HSPA+ networks; older generation 3G networks will continue to exist for at least another decade. Hence, all mobile applications should plan for multisecond RRC latency delays when accessing the network over a 3G interface.

EV-DO (CDMA) RRC State Machine

While 3GPP standards such as HSPA, HSPA+, and LTE are the dominant network standards around the globe, it is important that we don't forget the 3GPP2 CDMA based networks. The growth curve for EV-DO networks may look comparatively flat, but even so, current industry projections show nearly half a billion CDMA powered wireless subscriptions by 2017.

Not surprisingly, regardless of the differences in the standards, the fundamental limitations are the same in UMTS- and CDMA-based networks: battery power is a constraining resource, radios are expensive to operate, and network efficiency is an important goal. Consequently, CDMA networks also have an RRC state machine (Figure 7-8), which controls the radio state of each device.

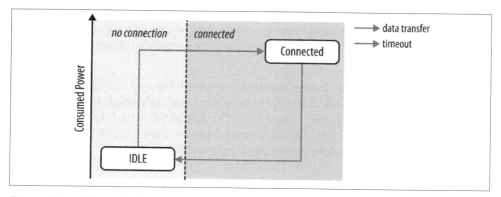

Figure 7-8. CDMA RRC state machine: EV-DO (Rev. 0—DO Advanced)

Idle
> Similar to idle in 3GPP standards. The device radio is in a low-power state and only listening to control traffic from the network. No radio resources are assigned to the client within the carrier network.

Connected
> Similar to connected LTE mode and DCH in HSPA. The device is in a high-power state and network resources are assigned for both upstream and downstream data transfers.

This is definitely the simplest RRC state machine out of all the ones we have examined: the device is either in a high-power state, with allocated network resources, or it is idle. Further, all network transfers require a transition to a connected state, the latency for which is similar to that of HSPA networks: hundreds to thousands of milliseconds depending on the revision of the deployed infrastructure. There are no other intermediate states, and transitions back to idle are also controlled via carrier configured timeouts.

Inefficiency of Periodic Transfers

An important consequence of the timeout-driven radio state transitions, regardless of the generation or the underlying standard, is that it is very easy to construct network access patterns that can yield both poor user experience for interactive traffic and poor battery performance. In fact, all you have to do is wait long enough for the radio to transition to a lower-power state, and then trigger a network access to force an RRC transition!

To illustrate the problem, let's assume that the device is on an HSPA+ network, which is configured to move from DCH to FACH state after 10 seconds of radio inactivity. Next, we load an application that schedules an intermittent transfer, such as a real-time analytics beacon, on an 11-second interval. What's the net result? The device may end up spending hundreds of milliseconds in data transfer and otherwise idle while in a high-power state. Worse, it would transition into the low-power state only to be woken up again a few hundred milliseconds later—worst-case scenario for latency and battery performance.

Every radio transmission, no matter how small, forces a transition to a high-power state. Then, once the transmission is done, the radio will remain in this high-power state until the inactivity timer has expired (Figure 7-9). The size of the actual data transfer does not influence the timer. Further, the device may then also have to cycle through several more intermediate states before it can return back to idle.

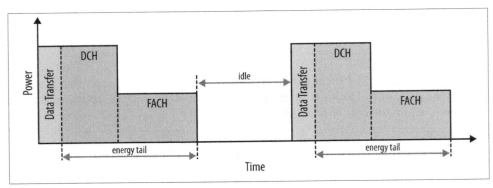

Figure 7-9. HSPA+ energy tail due to DCH > FACH > IDLE transitions

The "energy tails" generated by the timer-driven state transitions make periodic transfers a very inefficient network access pattern on mobile networks. First, you have to pay the latency cost of the state transition, then the transfer happens, and finally the radio idles, wasting power, until all the timers fire and the device can return to the low-power state.

End-to-End Carrier Architecture

Now that we have familiarized ourselves with the RRC and device capabilities, it is useful to zoom out and consider the overall end-to-end architecture of a carrier network. Our goal here is not to become experts in the nomenclature and function of every component, of which there are dozens, but rather to highlight the components that have a direct impact on how the data flows through the carrier network and reasons why it may affect the performance of our applications.

The specific infrastructure and names of various logical and physical components within a carrier network depend on the generation and type of deployed network: EV-DO vs. HSPA vs. LTE, and so on. However, there are also many similarities among all of them, and in this chapter we'll examine the high-level architecture of an LTE network.

Why LTE? First, it is the most likely architecture for new carrier deployments. Second, and even more importantly, one of the key features of LTE is its simplified architecture: fewer components and fewer dependencies also enable improved performance.

Radio Access Network (RAN)

The radio access network (RAN) is the first big logical component of every carrier network (Figure 7-10), whose primary responsibility is to mediate access to the provisioned radio channel and shuttle the data packets to and from the user's device. In fact, this is the component controlled and mediated by the Radio Resource Controller. In LTE, each radio base station (eNodeB) hosts the RRC, which maintains the RRC state machine and performs all resource assignment for each active user in its cell.

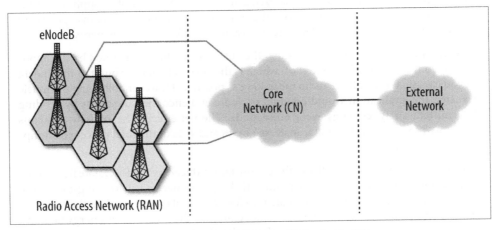

Figure 7-10. LTE radio access network: tracking cells and eNodeBs

Whenever a user has a stronger signal from a nearby cell, or if his current cell is overloaded, he may be handed off to a neighboring tower. However, while this sounds simple on paper, the hand-off procedure is also the reason for much of the additional complexity within every carrier network. If all users always remained in the same fixed position, and stayed within reach of a single tower, then a static routing topology would suffice. However, as we all know, that is simply not the case: users are mobile and must be migrated from tower to tower, and the migration process should not interrupt any voice or data traffic. Needless to say, this is a nontrivial problem.

First of all, if the user's device can be associated with any radio tower, how do we know where to route the incoming packets? Of course, there is no magic: the radio access network must communicate with the core network to keep track of the location of every user. Further, to handle the transparent handoff, it must also be able to dynamically update its existing tunnels and routes without interrupting any existing, user-initiated voice and data sessions.

 In LTE, a tower-to-tower handoff can be performed within hundreds of milliseconds, which will yield a slight pause in data delivery at the physical layer, but otherwise this procedure is completely transparent to the user and to all applications running on her device. In earlier-generation networks, this same process can take up to several seconds.

However, we're not done yet. Radio handoffs can be a frequent occurrence, especially in high-density urban and office environments, and requiring the user's device to continuously perform the cell handoff negotiations, even when the device is idle, would consume a lot of energy on the device. Hence, an additional layer of indirection was added: one or more radio towers are said to form a "tracking area," which is a logical grouping of towers defined by the carrier network.

The core network must know the location of the user, but frequently it knows only the tracking area and not the specific tower currently servicing the user—as we will see, this has important implications on the latency of inbound data packets. In turn, the device is allowed to migrate between towers within the same tracking area with no overhead: if the device is in idle RRC state, no notifications are emitted by the device or the radio network, which saves energy on the mobile handset.

Core Network (CN)

The core network (Figure 7-11), which is also known as the Evolved Packet Core (EPC) in LTE is responsible for the data routing, accounting, and policy management. Put simply, it is the piece that connects the radio network to the public Internet.

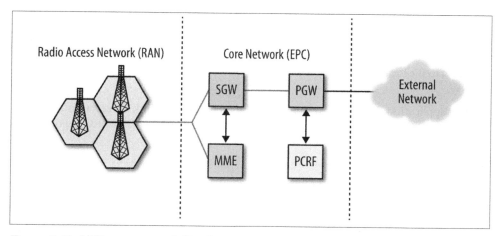

Figure 7-11. LTE core network (EPC): PGW, PCRF, SGW, and MME

First, we have the packet gateway (PGW), which is the public gateway that connects the mobile carrier to the public Internet. The PGW is the termination point for all external connections, regardless of the protocol. When a mobile device is connected to the carrier network, the IP address of the device is allocated and maintained by the PGW.

Each device within the carrier network has an internal identifier, which is independent of the assigned IP address. In turn, once a packet is received by the PGW, it is encapsulated and tunneled through the EPC to the radio access network. LTE uses Stream

Control Transmission Protocol (SCTP) for control-plane traffic and a combination of GPRS Tunneling Protocol (GTP) and UDP for all other data.

Physical Layer vs. Application Layer Connectivity

The fact that the device IP address is allocated and maintained by the PGW has a number of important implications. First, it means that a wireless device can be easily associated with multiple IP addresses. Conversely, if the IP addresses are at a premium, then multiple devices can share the same IP address but be allocated different ports for outgoing and incoming traffic: the PGW acts as a NAT. In fact, the latter case is quite common. The same carrier IP address can be assigned to dozens, if not hundreds, of devices within its network.

Consequently, traffic from the same device may originate from multiple public carrier IP addresses. Don't be surprised to see the same client request resources from different IPs! With IPv6, this behavior may change, and each device may finally get a unique IP address. Having said that, few carriers support IPv6 today, and the rollout and adoption of IPv6 remains very slow.

However, IP assignment aside, it is arguably even more important to recognize that because it is the PGW that terminates all connections, the device radio state is not tied to application layer connectivity: tearing down the radio context within the radio network terminates the physical radio link between the device and the radio tower, but this does not affect the state of any TCP or UDP sessions. The device radio can be idle, with no link to the local radio tower, while the established connections are maintained by the PGW.

Once application data must be delivered, the physical radio link is reestablished, and communication resumes with no side effects other than the incurred RRC negotiation delays required to reestablish the radio context.

The PGW also performs all the common policy enforcement, such as packet filtering and inspection, QoS assignment, DoS protection, and more. The Policy and Charging Rules Function (PCRF) component is responsible for maintaining and evaluating these rules for the packet gateway. PCRF is a logical component, meaning it can be part of the PGW, or it can stand on its own.

Now, let's say the PGW has received a packet from the public Internet for one of the mobile devices on its network; where does it route the data? The PGW has no knowledge of the actual location of the user, nor the different tracking areas within the radio access network. This next step is the responsibility of the Serving Gateway (SGW) and the Mobility Management Entity (MME).

The PGW routes all of its packets to the SGW. However, to make matters even more complicated, the SGW may not know the exact location of the user either. This function is, in fact, one of the core responsibilities of the MME. The Mobility Management Entity component is effectively a user database, which manages all the state for every user on the network: their location on the network, type of account, billing status, enabled services, plus all other user metadata. Whenever a user's location within the network changes, the location update is sent to the MME; when the user turns on their phone, the authentication is performed by the MME, and so on.

Hence, when a packet arrives at the SGW, a query to the MME is sent for the location of the user. Then, once the MME returns the answer, which contains the tracking area and the ID of the specific tower serving the target device, the SGW can establish a connection to the tower if none exists and route the user data to the radio access network.

In a nutshell, that is all there is to it. This high-level architecture is effectively the same in all the different generations of mobile data networks. The names of the logical components may differ, but fundamentally all mobile networks are subject to the following workflow:

- Data arrives at the external packet gateway, which connects the core network to the public Internet.
- A set of routing and packet policies is applied at the packet gateway.
- Data is routed from the public gateway to one or more serving gateways, which act as mobility anchors for the devices within the radio network.
- A user database service performs the authentication, billing, provisioning of services, and location tracking of each user on the network.
- Once the location of the user within the radio network is determined, the data is routed from the serving gateway to the appropriate radio tower.
- The radio tower performs the necessary resource assignment and negotiation with the target device and then delivers the data over the radio interface.

Simplified and Unified Architecture of the LTE Core Network

One of the main features of LTE is its new Evolved Packet Core (EPC) network, which is based on an IP-only architecture designed to carry both voice and data over the same, unified network. This design allows more cost-effective operation for the carrier but also places much stronger performance requirements on the network: voice requires low latency, and 4G speeds require much higher throughput.

How does the EPC achieve these goals? There are a large number of architectural improvements, but one of the primary differences to previous-generation networks is the simplified architecture of the LTE core network: some components were removed, others were collapsed into fewer logical components, and a lot of the decision making has been moved to the edges of the network.

For example, in LTE the RRC is maintained by the radio tower (eNodeB), whereas in earlier generations the RRC was managed higher up in the network (at the serving gateway), which imposed additional latency and performance bottlenecks on all control traffic within the network.

Backhaul Capacity and Latency

An important factor in the performance of any carrier network is the provisioned connectivity and capacity between all the logical and physical components. The LTE radio interface may be capable of reaching up to 100 Mbps between the user and the radio tower, but once the signal is received by the radio tower, sufficient capacity must be available to transport all this data through the carrier network and toward its actual destination. Plus, let's not forget that a single tower should be able to service many active users simultaneously!

Delivering a true 4G experience is not a simple matter of deploying the new radio network. The core network must also be upgraded, sufficient capacity links must be present between the EPC and the radio network, and all the EPC components must be able to process much higher data rates with much lower latencies than in any previous generation network.

 In practice, a single radio tower may serve up to three nearby radio cells, which can easily add up to hundreds of active users. With 10+ Mbps data rate requirements per user, each tower needs a dedicated fiber link!

Needless to say, all of these requirements make 4G networks a costly proposition to the carrier: running fiber to all the radio stations, high-performance routers, and so on. In practice, it is now not unusual to find the overall performance of the network being limited not by the radio interface, but by the available backhaul capacity of the carrier network.

These performance bottlenecks are not something we can control as developers of mobile applications, but they do, once again, illustrate an important fact: the architecture of our IP networks is based on a best effort delivery model, which makes no guarantees about end-to-end performance. Once we remove the bottleneck from the first hop, which is the wireless interface, we move the bottleneck to the next slowest link in the network, either within the carrier network or somewhere else on the path toward our destination. In fact, this is nothing new; recall our earlier discussion on "Last-Mile Latency" on page 8 in wired networks.

Just because you are connected over a 4G interface doesn't mean you are guaranteed the maximum throughput offered by the radio interface. Instead, our applications must adapt to the continuously changing network weather over the wireless channel, within the carrier network, and on the public Internet.

Packet Flow in a Mobile Network

One of the primary complaints about designing applications for the mobile web is the high variability in latency. Well, now that we have covered the RRC and the high-level architecture of a mobile network, we can finally connect the dots and see the end-to-end flow of the data packets, which should also explain why this variability exists. Even better, as we will see, much of the variability is actually very much predictable!

Initiating a Request

To start, let's assume that the user has already authenticated with a 4G network and the mobile device is idle. Next, the user types in a URL and hits "Go." What happens next?

First, because the phone is in idle RRC state, the radio must synchronize with the nearby radio tower and send a request for a new radio context to be established (Figure 7-12, step 1)—this negotiation requires several roundtrips between the handset and the radio tower, which may take up to 100 milliseconds. For earlier-generation networks, where the RRC is managed by the serving gateway, this negotiation latency is much higher—up to several seconds.

Once the radio context is established, the device has a resource assignment from the radio tower and is able to transmit data (step 2) at a specified rate and signal power. The time to transmit a packet of data from the user's radio to the tower is known as the "user-plane one-way latency" and takes up to five milliseconds for 4G networks. Hence, the first packet incurs a much higher delay due to the need to perform the RRC transition, but packets immediately after incur only the constant first-hop latency cost, as long as the radio stays in the high-power state.

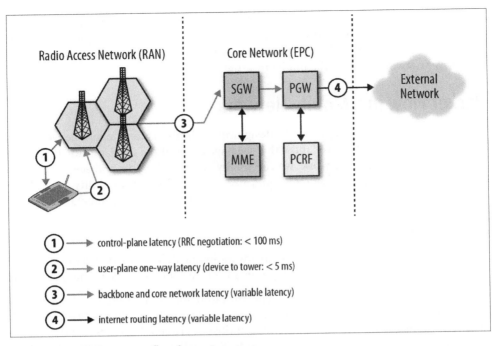

Radio Access Network (RAN)

Core Network (EPC)

SGW   PGW   ④   External Network

MME   PCRF

③

①

②

① ——→ control-plane latency (RRC negotiation: < 100 ms)

② ——→ user-plane one-way latency (device to tower: < 5 ms)

③ ——→ backbone and core network latency (variable latency)

④ ——→ internet routing latency (variable latency)

Figure 7-12. LTE request flow latencies

However, we are not done yet, as we have only transferred our packets from the device to the radio tower! From here, the packets have to travel through the core network—through the SGW to the PGW (step 3)—and out to the public Internet (step 4). Unfortunately, the 4G standards make no guarantees on latency of this path, and hence this latency will vary from carrier to carrier.

> In practice, the end-to-end latency of many deployed 4G networks tends to be in the 30–100 ms range once the device is in a connected state—that is to say, without the control plane latency incurred by the initial packet. Hence, if up to 5 ms of the total time is accounted for on the first wireless hop, then the rest (25–95 ms) is the routing and transit overhead within the core network of the carrier.

Next, let's say the browser has fetched the requested page and the user is engaging with the content. The radio has been idle for a few dozen seconds, which means that the RRC has likely moved the user into a DRX state ("LTE RRC State Machine" on page 116) to conserve battery power and to free up network resources for other users. At this point, the user decides to navigate to a different destination in the browser and hence triggers a new request. What happens now?

Nearly the same workflow is repeated as we just saw, except that because the device was in a dormant (DRX) state, a slightly quicker negotiation (Figure 7-12, step 1) can take place between the device and the radio tower—up to 50 milliseconds (Table 7-9) for dormant to connected.

In summary, a user initiating a new request incurs several different latencies:

Control-plane latency
> Fixed, one-time latency cost incurred for RRC negotiation and state transitions: <100 ms for idle to active, and <50 ms for dormant to active.

User-plane latency
> Fixed cost for every application packet transferred between the device and the radio tower: <5 ms.

Core network latency
> Carrier dependent cost for transporting the packet from the radio tower to the packet gateway: in practice, 30–100 ms.

Internet routing latency
> Variable latency cost between the carrier's packet gateway and the destination address on the public Internet.

The first two latencies are bounded by the 4G requirements, the core network latency is carrier specific, and the final piece is something you can influence by strategically positioning your servers closer to the user; see the earlier discussion on "Speed of Light and Propagation Latency" on page 6.

Latency and Jitter in Mobile Networks

One frequently shared complaint about mobile networks is the variability, or jitter, in packet latency. And it is certainly true that there are many contributing components that can impact latency. However, once you factor in the control plane cost for RRC state transitions incurred by the first packet, you will likely find that the performance is, in fact, much more predictable than you would otherwise expect.

In LTE, the control plane overhead is up to 100 milliseconds. With LTE-Advanced, this number is further lowered to 50 milliseconds. However, in earlier-generation networks, this same negotiation can take seconds!

Core network routing latency is the second, and often very large, contributing factor to the overall packet latency in mobile networks. The specific delays incurred within the core network vary by generation of the network, as well as the specific infrastructure deployed by the carrier. However, while few carriers openly advertise their latency performance—perhaps because it is nothing to be proud of—it usually can be found in their technical FAQs.

For example, AT&T, which is the largest mobile provider in the U.S., sets the following expectations, which are typical for the industry at large, for core network latency for the various generations within its network:

Table 7-10. AT&T latencies for deployed 2G–4G networks

	LTE	HSPA+	HSPA	EDGE	GPRS
Latency	40–50 ms	100–200 ms	150–400 ms	600–750 ms	600–750 ms

By comparison, the circumference of Earth at the equator is 24,901 miles, which takes 133.7 ms for light to travel. In other words, it may not be entirely unreasonable to think of most mobile requests as requiring, on average, at least one trip around the globe!

Inbound Data Flow

Now let's examine the opposite scenario: the user's device is idle, but a data packet must be routed from the PGW to the user (Figure 7-13). Once again, recall that all connections are terminated at the PGW, which means that the device can be idle, with its radio off, but the connection the device may have established earlier, such as a long-lived TCP session, can still be active at the PGW.

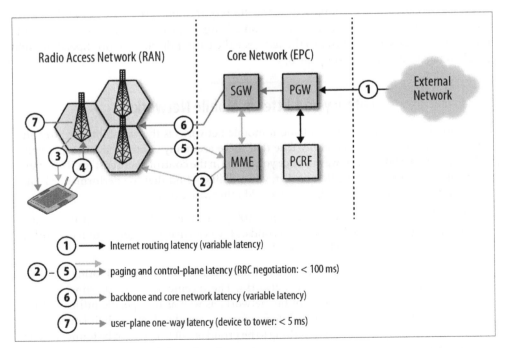

Figure 7-13. LTE inbound data flow latencies

As we saw earlier, the PGW routes the inbound packet to the SGW (step 1), which in turn queries the MME. However, the MME may not know the exact tower currently servicing the user; recall that a collection of radio towers form a "tracking area." Whenever a user enters a different tracking area, its location is updated in the MME, but tower handoffs within the same tracking area do not trigger an update to the MME.

Instead, if the device is idle, the MME sends a paging message (step 2) to all the towers in the tracking area, which in turn all broadcast a notification (step 3) on a shared radio channel, indicating that the device should reestablish its radio context to receive the inbound data. The device periodically wakes to listen to the paging messages, and if it finds itself on the paging list, then it initiates the negotiation (step 4) with the radio tower to reestablish the radio context.

Once the radio context is established, the tower that performed the negotiation sends a message back (step 5) to the MME indicating where the user is, the MME returns the answer to the serving gateway, and the gateway finally routes the message (step 6) to the tower, which then delivers (step 7) the message to the device! Phew.

Once the device is in a connected state, a direct tunnel is established between the radio tower and the serving gateway, which means that further incoming packets are routed directly to the tower without the paging overhead, skipping steps 2–5. Once again, the first packet incurs a much higher latency cost on mobile networks! Plan for it.

The preceding packet workflow is transparent to IP and all layers above it, including our applications: the packets are buffered by the PGW, SGW, and the eNodeB at each stage until they can be routed to the device. In practice, this translates to observable latency jitter in packet arrival times, with the first packet incurring the highest delays due to control-plane negotiation.

Heterogeneous Networks (HetNets)

Existing 4G radio and modulation technologies are already within reach of the theoretical limits of the wireless channel. Hence, the next order of magnitude in wireless performance will not come from improvements in the radio interfaces, but rather from smarter topologies of the wireless networks—specifically, through wide deployment of multilayer heterogeneous networks (HetNets), which will also require many improvements in the intra-cell coordination, handoff, and interference management.

The core idea behind HetNets is a simple one: instead of relying on just the macro coverage of a large geographic area, which creates a lot of competition for all users, we can also cover the area with many small cells (Figure 7-14), each of which can minimize path loss, require lower transmit power, and enable better performance for all users.

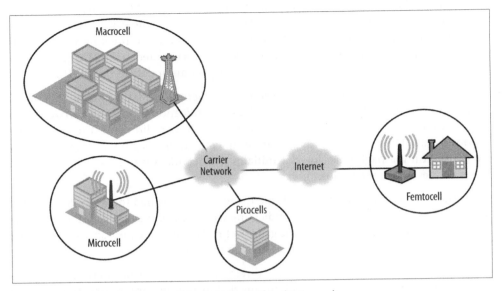

Figure 7-14. Heterogeneous network infographic (Ericsson)

A single macrocell can cover up to tens of square miles in low-density wireless environments, but in practice, in high-density urban and office settings, can be limited to anywhere from just 50 to 300 meters! In other words, it can cover a small block, or a few buildings. By comparison, microcells are designed to cover a specific building; picocells can service one or more separate floors, and femtocells can cover a small apartment and leverage your existing broadband service as the wireless backhaul.

However, note that HetNets are not simply replacing the macrocells with many small cells. Instead, HetNets are layering multiple cells on top of one another! By deploying overlapping layers of wireless networks, HetNets can provide much better network capacity and improved coverage for all users. However, the outstanding challenges are in minimizing interference, providing sufficient uplink capacity, and creating and improving protocols for seamless handoff between the various layers of networks.

What does this mean for the developers building mobile applications? Expect the number of handoffs between different cells to increase significantly and adapt accordingly: the latency and throughput performance may vary significantly.

Modeling and Managing Wireless Network Capacity

Picocells are often used by mobile carriers to extend coverage to indoor and outdoor areas where signal quality may be poor, or to add network capacity in areas with very dense phone usage—e.g., a large public area, a conference hall, stadium, train station, and so on. Some picocells may be deployed permanently, while others may be put up for a specific occasion: wireless capacity planning and modeling (Figure 7-15) is both an art and a science!

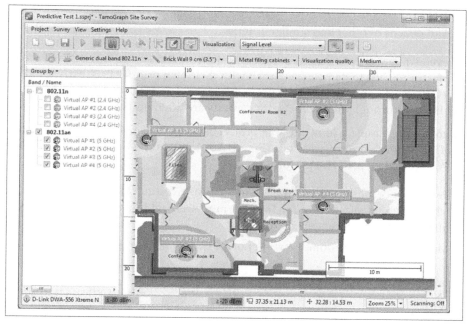

Figure 7-15. Wireless capacity planning with TamoGraph

Dedicated modeling software, such as TamoGraph Site Survey shown earlier, is often used to model the physical environment, number of active users, and the wireless technology in use (WiFi in the previous example) to help determine the required number, placement, and configuration of networks.

Real-World 3G, 4G, and WiFi Performance

By this point, one has to wonder whether all the extra protocols, gateways, and negotiation mechanisms within a 3G or 4G network are worth the additional complexity. By comparison, WiFi implementation is much simpler and seems to work well enough, doesn't it? Answering this question requires a lot of caveats, since as we saw, measuring wireless performance is subject to dozens of environmental and technology considerations. Further, the answer also depends on chosen evaluation criteria:

- Importance of battery performance vs. network performance.
- Per user and network-wide throughput performance.
- Latency and packet jitter performance.
- Cost and feasibility of deployment.
- Ability to meet government and policy requirements.
- And dozens of other and similar criteria…

However, while there are dozens of different stakeholders (users, carriers, and handset manufacturers, just to name a few), each with their own priority lists, early tests of the new 4G networks are showing very promising results. In fact, key metrics such as network latency, throughput, and network capacity are often outperforming WiFi!

As a concrete example, a joint research project between the University of Michigan and AT&T Labs ran a country-wide test (Figure 7-16) within the U.S., comparing 4G, 3G, and WiFi (802.11g, 2.4GHz) performance:

- Performance measurements were done against 46 distinct Measurement Lab nodes, which is an open platform for Internet measurement tools, and via the MobiPerf open-source measurement client.
- Measurements were done over a period of two months in late 2011 by 3,300 users.

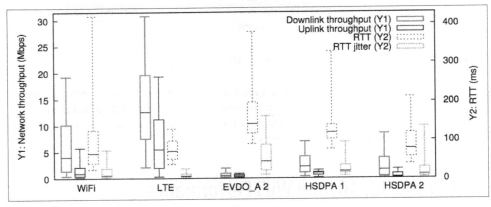

Figure 7-16. Test result analysis of WiFi, LTE, and 3G performance

The box-and-whisker plot for each connection type packs a lot of useful information into a small graphic: the whiskers show the range of the entire distribution, the box shows the 25%–75% quantiles of the distribution, and the black horizontal line within the box is the median.

Of course, a single test does not prove a universal rule, especially when it comes to performance, but the results are nonetheless very promising: early LTE networks are showing great network throughput performance, and even more impressively, much more stable RTT and packet jitter latencies when compared with other wireless standards.

In other words, at least with respect to this test, LTE offers comparable and better performance than WiFi, which also shows that improved performance is possible, and all the extra complexity is paying off! The mobile web doesn't have to be slow. In fact, we have all the reasons to believe that we can and will make it faster.

 For full details of the 4G performance study, analysis, and conclusions, refer to "A Close Examination of Performance and Power Characteristics of 4G LTE Networks" presented at MobiSys 2012.

CHAPTER 8

Optimizing for Mobile Networks

First off, minimizing latency through keepalive connections, geo-positioning your servers and data closer to the client, optimizing your TLS deployments, and all the other protocol optimizations we have covered are only more important on mobile applications, where both latency and throughput are always at a premium. Similarly, all the web application performance best practices are equally applicable. Feel free to flip ahead to Chapter 10; we'll wait.

However, mobile networks also pose some new and unique requirements for our performance strategy. Designing applications for the mobile web requires careful planning and consideration of the presentation of the content within the constraints of the form factor of the device, the unique performance properties of the radio interface, and the impact on the battery life. The three are inextricably linked.

Perhaps because it is the easiest to control, the presentation layer, with topics such as responsive design, tends to receive the most attention. However, where most applications fall short, it is often due to the incorrect design assumptions about networking performance: the application protocols are the same, but the differences in the physical delivery layers impose a number of constraints that, if unaccounted for, will lead to slow response times, high latency variability, and ultimately a compromised experience for the user. To add insult to injury, poor networking decisions will also have an outsized negative impact on the battery life of the device.

There is no universal solution for these three constraints. There are best practices for the presentation layer, the networking, and the battery life performance, but frequently they are at odds; it is up to you and your application to find the balance in your requirements. One thing is for sure: simply disregarding any one of them won't get you far.

With that in mind, we won't elaborate too much on the presentation layer, as that varies with every platform and type of application—plus, there are plenty of existing books dedicated to this subject. But, regardless of the make or the operating system, the radio and battery constraints imposed by mobile networks are universal, and that is what we will focus on in this chapter.

 Throughout this chapter and especially in the following pages, the term "mobile application" is used in its broadest definition: all of our discussions on the performance of mobile networks are equally applicable to native applications, regardless of the platform, and applications running in your browser, regardless of the browser vendor.

Preserve Battery Power

When it comes to mobile, conserving power is a critical concern for everyone involved: device manufacturers, carriers, application developers, and the end users of our applications. When in doubt, or wondering why or how certain mobile behaviors were put in place, ask a simple question: how does it impact or improve the battery life? In fact, this is a great question to ask for any and every feature in your application also.

Networking performance on mobile networks is inherently linked to battery performance. In fact, the physical layers of the radio interface are specifically built to optimize the battery life against the following constraints:

- Radio use at full power can drain a full battery in a matter of hours.
- Radio power requirements are going up with every wireless generation.
- Radio is often second in power consumption only to the screen.
- Radio use has a nonlinear energy profile with respect to data transferred.

With that in mind, mobile applications should aim to minimize their use of the radio interface. To be clear, that is not to say that you should avoid using the radio entirely; after all we are building connected applications that rely on access to the network! However, because keeping the radio active is so expensive in terms of battery life, our applications should maximize the amount of transferred data while the radio is on and then seek to minimize the number of additional data transfers.

 Even though WiFi uses a radio interface to transfer data, it is important to realize that the underlying mechanics of WiFi, and consequently the latency, throughput, and power profiles of WiFi, when compared with 2G, 3G, and 4G mobile networks are fundamentally different; see our earlier discussion on "3G, 4G, and WiFi Power Requirements" on page 115. Consequently, the networking behavior can and often should be different when on WiFi vs. mobile networks.

Measuring Energy Use with AT&T Application Resource Optimizer

Despite the high emphasis on optimizing energy use, most platforms currently lack the necessary tools to help developers measure and optimize their applications. Thankfully, there are third-party tools that can help, such as the free Application Resource Optimizer (ARO) toolkit developed by AT&T.

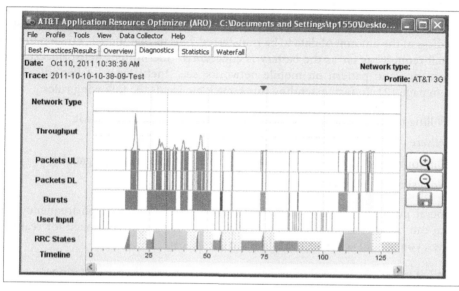

Figure 8-1. AT&T Application Resource Optimizer

ARO consists of two components: a collector and an analyzer. The collector is an Android application that runs in the background (on a real phone, or within an emulator) and captures the transferred data packets, radio activity, and other interactions with the phone. To capture a trace, load the collector, hit Record, interact with your application, and then copy the trace to your system.

Once a trace is available, you can open it with the analyzer to get insights into radio states, energy consumption, and traffic patterns of your application. One of the great features about the analyzer is that it will also provide recommendations for common performance pitfalls, such as missing compression, redundant data transfers, and more.

Two important things to note: the battery consumption and radio states are generated via a specified model of the device and the type of radio network. In other words, the generated numbers are not exact measurements from the device in use but estimates based on specified parameters in the model. On the upside, this allows you to import different device and network models and compare their energy use—e.g., 3G vs. 4G.

Finally, the collector is Android only, but the ARO analyzer can also accept any regular packet trace (pcap) file produced by `tcpdump` or a compatible tool; iOS users will have to use the `tcpdump` method.

To get started with ARO, head to *http://hpbn.co/attaro*.

Eliminate Periodic and Inefficient Data Transfers

The fact that the mobile radio incurs a fixed power cost to cycle into the full power state, regardless of the amount of data to be transferred, tells us that there is no such thing as a "small request" as far as the battery is concerned. Intermittent network access is a performance anti-pattern on mobile networks; see "Inefficiency of Periodic Transfers" on page 121. In fact, extending this same logic yields the following rules:

- Polling is exceptionally expensive on mobile networks; minimize it.
- Where possible, push delivery and notifications should be used.
- Outbound and inbound requests should be coalesced and aggregated.
- Noncritical requests should be deferred until the radio is active.

In general, push delivery is more efficient than polling. However, a high-frequency push stream can be just as, if not more, expensive. Whenever there is a need for real-time updates, you should consider the following questions:

- What is the best interval of updates and does it match user expectations?
- Instead of a fixed update interval, can an adaptive strategy be used?
- Can the inbound or outbound requests be aggregated into fewer network calls?
- Can the inbound or outbound requests be deferred until later?

 For push delivery, native applications have access to platform-specific push delivery services, which should be used when possible. For web applications, server-sent events (SSEs) and WebSocket delivery can be used to minimize latency and protocol overhead. Avoid polling and costly XHR techniques when possible.

A simple aggregation strategy of bundling multiple notifications into a single push event, based on an adaptive interval, user preference, or even the battery level on the device, can make a significant improvement to the power profile of any application, especially background applications, which often rely on this type of network access pattern.

Nagle and Efficient Server Push

TCP aficionados will undoubtedly recognize the request aggregation and bundling advice as Nagle's algorithm, except reimplemented at the application layer! Nagle's algorithm attempts to combine multiple small TCP messages into a single packet to reduce protocol overhead and the number of packets on the wire. Not surprisingly, our mobile applications can benefit a great deal from leveraging the same technique.

A simple implementation of such a strategy is to aggregate messages on the server by time, count, or size, instead of triggering an individual push for each one. A more involved, but significantly more efficient, strategy is to push updates only when the radio is already active on the client—e.g., defer the messages until the client initiates a request or leverage a third-party service that is aware of the client's radio state.

For example, services such as Google Cloud Messaging (GCM) for Android and Chrome offer message delivery APIs which can aggregate messages and deliver updates only when the device is active: the server pushes its messages to GCM, and GCM determines the optimal delivery schedule.

Unfortunately, today there is no cross-browser API to deliver a GCM-like experience to all clients. However, the W3C Push API (see *http://www.w3.org/TR/push-api/*) should address this use case in the future.

Intermittent beacon requests such as audience measurement pings and real-time analytics can easily negate all of your careful battery optimizations. These pings are mostly harmless on wired and even WiFi networks but carry an outsized cost on mobile networks. Do these beacons need to happen instantaneously? There is a good chance that you can easily log and defer these requests until next time the radio is active. Piggyback your background pings, and pay close attention to the network access patterns of third-party libraries and snippets in your code.

Finally, while we have so far focused on the battery, intermittent network access required for techniques such as progressive enhancement and incremental loading also carries a large latency cost due to the RRC state transitions! Recall that every state transition incurs a high control-plane latency cost in mobile networks, which may inject hundreds or thousands of extra milliseconds of latency—an especially expensive proposition for user-initiated and interactive traffic.

Calculating the Energy Cost of Background Updates

To illustrate the impact of periodic polling on battery life, let's do some simple math. The numbers are not exact but are within range of a typical 3G/4G mobile handset:

- 5 watt-hours, or 18,000 joules of battery capacity (5 Wh × 3600 J / Wh)
- 10 joules of consumed energy to cycle radio from idle to connected and back
- 1 minute polling interval consumes 600 joules of energy per hour (60 × 10 J)
- 600 joules of energy is ~3% of total battery capacity (600 J / 18, 000 J)

~3% of available battery capacity per hour for a single application! All it would take is a couple of applications with non-overlapping polling intervals to drain your battery by midday. Although, to be fair, a push application with frequent, unbuffered updates can have an even higher energy consumption profile.

Battery life optimization and frequency of updates are inherently at odds. Consider the requirements of your specific application to determine the optimal strategy: bundling of updates, adaptive update intervals, pull vs. push, and so on. Then, measure the impact with ARO or a similar tool and adjust accordingly.

Eliminate Unnecessary Application Keepalives

The connection state and the lifecycle of any TCP or UDP connection is independent of the radio state on the device: the radio can be in a low-power state while the connections are maintained by the carrier network. Then, when a new packet arrives from the external network, the carrier radio network will notify the device, promote its radio to a connected state, and resume the data transfer.

The application does not need to keep the radio "active" to ensure that connections are not dropped. Unnecessary application keepalives can have an enormous negative impact on battery life performance and are often put in place due to simple misunderstanding of how the mobile radio works. Refer to "Physical Layer vs. Application Layer Connectivity" on page 126 and "Packet Flow in a Mobile Network" on page 129.

 Most mobile carriers set a 5–30 minute NAT connection timeout. Hence, you may need a periodic (5 minute) keepalive to keep an idle connection from being dropped. If you find yourself requiring more frequent keepalives, check your own server, proxy, and load balancer configuration first!

Anticipate Network Latency Overhead

A single HTTP request for a required resource may incur anywhere from hundreds to thousands of milliseconds of network latency overhead in a mobile network. In part, this is due to the high roundtrip latencies, but we also can't forget the overhead (Figure 8-2) of DNS, TCP, TLS, and control-plane costs!

Figure 8-2. Components of a "simple" HTTP request

In the best case, the radio is already in a high-power state, the DNS is pre-resolved, and an existing TCP connection is available: the client may be able to reuse an existing connection and avoid the overhead of establishing a new connection. However, if the connection is busy, or nonexistent, then we must incur a number of additional roundtrips before any application data can be sent.

To illustrate the impact of these extra network roundtrips, let's assume an optimistic 100 ms roundtrip time for 4G and a 200 ms roundtrip time for 3.5G+ networks:

Table 8-1. Latency overhead of a single HTTP request

	3G	4G
Control plane	200–2,500 ms	50–100 ms
DNS lookup	200 ms	100 ms
TCP handshake	200 ms	100 ms
TLS handshake	200–400 ms	100–200 ms
HTTP request	200 ms	100 ms
Total latency overhead	**200–3500 ms**	**100–600 ms**

The RRC control-plane latency alone can add anywhere from hundreds to thousands of milliseconds of overhead to reestablish the radio context on a 3G network! Once the radio is active, we may need to resolve the hostname to an IP address and then perform the TCP handshake—two network roundtrips. Then, if a secure tunnel is required, we may need up to two extra network roundtrips (see "TLS Session Resumption" on page 55). Finally, the HTTP request can be sent, which adds a minimum of another roundtrip.

We have not accounted for the server response time or the size of the response, which may require several roundtrips, and yet we have already incurred up to half a dozen roundtrips. Multiply that by the roundtrip time, and we are looking at entire seconds of latency overhead for 3G, and roughly half a second for 4G networks.

Account for RRC State Transitions

If the mobile device has been idle for more than a few seconds, you should assume and anticipate that the first packet will incur hundreds, or even thousands of milliseconds of extra RRC latency. As a rule of thumb, add 100 ms for 4G, 150–500 ms for 3.5G+, and 500–2,500 ms for 3G networks, as a one-time, control-plane latency cost.

The RRC is specifically designed to help mitigate some of the cost of operating the power-hungry radio. However, what we gain in battery life is offset by increases in latency and lower throughput due to the presence of the various timers, counters, and the consequent overhead of required network negotiation to transition between the different radio states. However, the RRC is also a fact of life on mobile networks–there is no way around it–and if you want to build optimized applications for the mobile web, you must design with the RRC in mind.

A quick summary of what we have learned about the RRC:

- RRC state machines are different for every wireless standard.
- RRC state machines are managed by the radio network for each device.
- RRC state promotions to high power occur when data must be transferred.
- RRC state demotions to lower power occur on network-configured timeouts.
- (4G) LTE state transitions can take 10 to 100 milliseconds.
- (4G) HSPA+ state transitions are competitive with LTE.
- (3G) HSPA and CDMA state transitions can take several seconds.
- Every network transfer, no matter the size, incurs an energy tail.

We have already covered why preserving battery is such an important goal for mobile applications, and we have also highlighted the inefficiency of intermittent transfers, which are a direct result of the timeout-driven RRC state transitions. However, there is one more thing you need to take away: if the device radio has been idle, then initiating a new data transfer on mobile networks will incur an additional latency delay, which may take anywhere from 100 milliseconds on latest-generation networks to up to several seconds on older 3G and 2G networks.

While the network presents the illusion of an always-on experience to our applications, the physical or the radio layer controlled by the RRC is continuously connecting and disconnecting. On the surface, this is not an issue, but the delays imposed by the RRC are, in fact, often easily noticeable by many users when unaccounted for.

Decouple User Interactions from Network Communication

A well-designed application can *feel fast* by providing instant feedback even if the underlying connection is slow or the request is taking a long time to complete. Do not couple user interactions, user feedback, and network communication. To deliver the best experience, the application should acknowledge user input within hundreds of milliseconds; see "Speed, Performance, and Human Perception" on page 170.

If a network request is required, then initiate it in the background, and provide immediate UI feedback to acknowledge user input. The control plane latency alone will often push your application over the allotted budget for providing instant user feedback. Plan for high latencies—you cannot "fix" the latency imposed by the core network and the RRC—and work with your design team to ensure that they are aware of these limitations when designing the application.

Design for Variable Network Interface Availability

Users dislike slow applications, but broken applications, due to transient network errors, are the worst experience of all. Your mobile application must be robust in the face of common networking failures: unreachable hosts, sudden drops in throughput or increases in latency, or outright loss of connectivity. Unlike the tethered world, you simply cannot assume that once the connection is established, it will remain established. The user may be on the move and may enter an area with high amounts of interference, many active users, or plain poor coverage.

Further, just as you cannot design your pages just for the latest browsers, you cannot design your application just for the latest-generation mobile networks. As we have covered earlier ("Building for the Multigeneration Future" on page 109), even users with the latest handsets will continuously transition between 4G, 3G, and even 2G networks based on the continuously changing conditions of their radio environments. Your application should subscribe to these interface transitions and adjust accordingly.

The application can subscribe to navigator.onLine notifications to monitor connection status. For a good introduction, also see Paul Kinlan's article on HTML5Rocks: Working Off the Grid with HTML5 Offline (*http://hpbn.co/offline*).

Change is the only constant in mobile networks. Radio channel quality is always changing based on distance from the tower, congestion from nearby users, ambient interference, and dozens of other factors. With that in mind, while it may be tempting to perform various forms of bandwidth and latency estimation to optimize your mobile application, the results should be treated, at best, as transient data points.

The iPhone 4 "antennagate" serves as a great illustration of the unpredictable nature of radio performance: reception quality was affected by the physical location of your hand in regards to the phone's antenna, which gave birth to the infamous "You're holding it wrong."

Latency and bandwidth estimates on mobile networks are stable on the order of tens to hundreds of milliseconds, at most a second, but not more. Hence, while optimizations such as adaptive bitrate streaming are still useful for long-lived streams, such as video, which is adapted in data chunks spanning a few seconds, these bandwidth estimates should definitely not be cached or used later to make decisions about the available throughput: even on 4G, you may measure your throughput as just a few hundred Kbit/s, and then move your radio a few inches and get Mbit/s+ performance!

Streaming Applications on Mobile Networks

Streaming applications on mobile networks are a tricky problem. If you need to perform a large download and have confidence that the entire file will be used, then you should download the entire file in one shot and then leave the radio idle for as long as possible—e.g., the behavior of music file downloads in the Pandora application we covered earlier.

However, if you cannot stream the full file (e.g., an HD video) due to size or user behavior constraints, then you should leverage adaptive bitrate streaming to continuously adjust to changes in network throughput. You *will* incur high battery cost, but at least you will deliver the best user experience while doing so! Alternatively, consider prompting the user to switch to WiFi.

End-to-end bandwidth and latency estimation is a hard problem on any network, but doubly so on mobile networks. Avoid it, because you will get it wrong. Instead, use coarse-grained information about the generation of the network, and adjust your code accordingly. To be clear, knowing the generation or type of mobile network does not make any end-to-end performance guarantees, but it does tell you important data about the latency of the first wireless hop and the end-to-end performance of the carrier network; see "Latency and Jitter in Mobile Networks" on page 131 and Table 7-6.

Finally, throughput and latency aside, you should plan for loss of connectivity: assume this case is not an exception but the rule. Your application should remain operational, to the extent possible, when the network is unavailable or a transient failure happens and should adapt based on request type and specific error:

- Do not cache or attempt to guess the state of the network.
- Dispatch the request, listen for failures, and diagnose what happened.

- Transient errors will happen; plan for them, and use a retry strategy.
- Listen to connection state to anticipate the best request strategy.
- Use a backoff algorithm for request retries; do not spin forever.
- If offline, log and dispatch the request later if possible.
- Leverage HTML5 AppCache and localStorage for offline mode.

With the growing adoption of HetNet infrastructure, the frequency of cell handoffs is set to rise dramatically, which makes monitoring your connection state and type only more important.

Burst Your Data and Return to Idle

Mobile radio interface is optimized for bursty transfers, which is a property you should leverage whenever possible: group your requests together and download as much as possible, as quickly as possible, and then let the radio return to an idle state. This strategy will deliver the best network throughput and maximize battery life of the device.

The only accurate way to estimate the network's speed is, well, to use it! Latest-generation networks, such as LTE and HSPA+, perform dynamic allocation of resources in one-millisecond intervals and prioritize bursty data flows. To go fast, keep it simple: batch and pre-fetch as much data as you can, and let the network do the rest.

An important corollary is that progressive loading of resources may do more harm than good on mobile networks. By downloading content in small chunks, we expose our applications to higher variability both in throughput and latency, not to mention the much higher energy costs to operate the radio. Instead, anticipate what your users will need next, download the content ahead of time, and let the radio idle:

- If you need to fetch a large music or a video file, consider downloading the entire file upfront, instead of streaming in chunks.
- Prefetch application content and invest in metrics and statistical models to help identify which content is appropriate to download ahead of time.
- Prefetch third-party content, such as ads, ahead of time and add application logic to show and update their state when necessary.
- Eliminate unnecessary intermittent transfers. See "46% of Battery Consumption to Transfer 0.2% of Total Bytes" on page 123.

Building and Evaluating a Prefetch Model

Content pre-fetching will *always* create a natural tension: on one hand, you want to download as few bytes as possible, and on the other you want to minimize your latency and throughput variability and reduce your impact on the battery. Which is more important? Wrong question. The answer is always contextual to your application and the metric you choose to use to determine the effectiveness of your pre-fetch strategy.

The important takeaway is that there are, at a minimum, three variables to balance: number of transferred bytes, impact on the battery, and variability in network throughput and latency. Further, as we saw, these variables are not exclusive: transferring a larger batch of bytes in a single transfer may give you better throughput.

An application with a highly predictable usage pattern can make use of aggressive prefetching, minimize battery consumption, improve user experience, and simultaneously avoid incurring a large byte overhead. Conversely, a poorly implemented pre-fetch strategy can download a lot of unnecessary data and hurt the overall experience for the user.

To determine how your application should behave, first determine your primary goals and the primary usage patterns of your application. Then use that data to implement a pre-fetch strategy and gather metrics to validate the assumptions of your model. Rinse, lather, and repeat.

Offload to WiFi Networks

Current industry estimates show that almost 90% of the worldwide wireless traffic is expected to originate indoors, and frequently in areas with WiFi connectivity within reach. Hence, while the latest 4G networks may compete with WiFi over peak throughput and latency, very frequently they still impose a monthly data cap: mobile access is metered and often expensive to the user. Further, WiFi connections are more battery efficient (see "3G, 4G, and WiFi Power Requirements" on page 115) for large transfers and do not require an RRC.

Whenever possible, and especially if you are building a data-intensive application, you should leverage WiFi connectivity when available, and if not, then consider prompting the user to enable WiFi on her device to improve experience and minimize costs.

Apply Protocol and Application Best Practices

One of the great properties of the layered architecture of our network infrastructure is that it abstracts the physical delivery from the transport layer, and the transport layer abstracts the routing and data delivery from the application protocols. This separation provides great API abstractions, but for best end-to-end performance, we still need to consider the entire stack.

Throughout this chapter, we have focused on the unique properties of the physical layer of mobile networks, such as the presence of the RRC, concerns over the battery life of the device, and incurred routing latencies in mobile networks. However, on top of this physical layer reside the transport and session protocols we have covered in earlier chapters, and all of their optimizations are just as critical, perhaps doubly so:

- "Optimizing for TCP" on page 32
- "Optimizing for UDP" on page 44
- "Optimizing for TLS" on page 63

Minimizing latency by reusing keepalive connections, geo-positioning servers and data closer to the client, optimizing TLS deployments, and all the other optimizations we outlined earlier are even more important on mobile networks, where roundtrip latencies are high and bandwidth is always at a premium.

Of course, our optimization strategy does not stop with transport and session protocols; they are simply the foundation. From there, we must also consider the performance implications of different application protocols (HTTP 1.0, 1.1, and 2.0), as well as general web application best practices—keep reading, we are not done yet!

HTTP

PART III
HTTP

CHAPTER 9

Brief History of HTTP

The Hypertext Transfer Protocol (HTTP) is one of the most ubiquitous and widely adopted application protocols on the Internet: it is the common language between clients and servers, enabling the modern web. From its simple beginnings as a single keyword and document path, it has become the protocol of choice not just for browsers, but for virtually every Internet-connected software and hardware application.

In this chapter, we will take a brief historical tour of the evolution of the HTTP protocol. A full discussion of the varying HTTP semantics is outside the scope of this book, but an understanding of the key design changes of HTTP, and the motivations behind each, will give us the necessary background for our discussions on HTTP performance, especially in the context of the many upcoming improvements in HTTP 2.0.

HTTP 0.9: The One-Line Protocol

The original HTTP proposal by Tim Berners-Lee was designed with *simplicity in mind* as to help with the adoption of his other nascent idea: the World Wide Web. The strategy appears to have worked: aspiring protocol designers, take note.

In 1991, Berners-Lee outlined the motivation for the new protocol and listed several high-level design goals: file transfer functionality, ability to request an index search of a hypertext archive, format negotiation, and an ability to refer the client to another server. To prove the theory in action, a simple prototype was built, which implemented a small subset of the proposed functionality:

- Client request is a single ASCII character string.
- Client request is terminated by a carriage return (CRLF).
- Server response is an ASCII character stream.

- Server response is a hypertext markup language (HTML).
- Connection is terminated after the document transfer is complete.

However, even that sounds a lot more complicated than it really is. What these rules enable is an extremely simple, Telnet-friendly protocol, which some web servers support to this very day:

```
$> telnet google.com 80

Connected to 74.125.xxx.xxx

GET /about/

(hypertext response)
(connection closed)
```

The request consists of a single line: GET method and the path of the requested document. The response is a single hypertext document—no headers or any other metadata, just the HTML. It really couldn't get any simpler. Further, since the previous interaction is a subset of the intended protocol, it unofficially acquired the HTTP 0.9 label. The rest, as they say, is history.

From these humble beginnings in 1991, HTTP took on a life of its own and evolved rapidly over the coming years. Let us quickly recap the features of HTTP 0.9:

- Client-server, request-response protocol.
- ASCII protocol, running over a TCP/IP link.
- Designed to transfer hypertext documents (HTML).
- The connection between server and client is closed after every request.

 Popular web servers, such as Apache and Nginx, still support the HTTP 0.9 protocol—in part, because there is not much to it! If you are curious, open up a Telnet session and try accessing google.com, or your own favorite site, via HTTP 0.9 and inspect the behavior and the limitations of this early protocol.

HTTP 1.0: Rapid Growth and Informational RFC

The period from 1991 to 1995 is one of rapid coevolution of the HTML specification, a new breed of software known as a "web browser," and the emergence and quick growth of the consumer-oriented public Internet infrastructure.

The Perfect Storm: Internet Boom of the Early 1990s

Building on Tim Berner-Lee's initial browser prototype, a team at the National Center of Supercomputing Applications (NCSA) decided to implement their own version. With that, the first popular browser was born: NCSA Mosaic. One of the programmers on the NCSA team, Marc Andreessen, partnered with Jim Clark to found Mosaic Communications in October 1994. The company was later renamed Netscape, and it shipped Netscape Navigator 1.0 in December 1994. By this point, it was already clear that the World Wide Web was bound to be *much more* than just an academic curiosity.

In fact, that same year the first World Wide Web conference was organized in Geneva, Switzerland, which led to the creation of the World Wide Web Consortium (W3C) to help guide the evolution of HTML. Similarly, a parallel HTTP Working Group (HTTP-WG) was established within the IETF to focus on improving the HTTP protocol. Both of these groups continue to be instrumental to the evolution of the Web.

Finally, to create the perfect storm, CompuServe, AOL, and Prodigy began providing dial-up Internet access to the public within the same 1994–1995 time frame. Riding on this wave of rapid adoption, Netscape made history with a wildly successful IPO on August 9, 1995—the Internet boom had arrived, and everyone wanted a piece of it!

The growing list of desired capabilities of the nascent Web and their use cases on the public Web quickly exposed many of the fundamental limitations of HTTP 0.9: we needed a protocol that could serve more than just hypertext documents, provide richer metadata about the request and the response, enable content negotiation, and more. In turn, the nascent community of web developers responded by producing a large number of experimental HTTP server and client implementations through an ad hoc process: implement, deploy, and see if other people adopt it.

From this period of rapid experimentation, a set of best practices and common patterns began to emerge, and in May 1996 the HTTP Working Group (HTTP-WG) published RFC 1945, which documented the "common usage" of the many HTTP 1.0 implementations found in the wild. Note that this was only an informational RFC: HTTP 1.0 as we know it is not a formal specification or an Internet standard!

Having said that, an example HTTP 1.0 request should look very familiar:

```
$> telnet website.org 80

Connected to xxx.xxx.xxx.xxx

GET /rfc/rfc1945.txt HTTP/1.0 ❶
User-Agent: CERN-LineMode/2.15 libwww/2.17b3
Accept: */*

HTTP/1.0 200 OK ❷
Content-Type: text/plain
Content-Length: 137582
Expires: Thu, 01 Dec 1997 16:00:00 GMT
Last-Modified: Wed, 1 May 1996 12:45:26 GMT
Server: Apache 0.84

(plain-text response)
(connection closed)
```

❶ Request line with HTTP version number, followed by request headers

❷ Response status, followed by response headers

The preceding exchange is not an exhaustive list of HTTP 1.0 capabilities, but it does illustrate some of the key protocol changes:

- Request may consist of multiple newline separated header fields.
- Response object is prefixed with a response status line.
- Response object has its own set of newline separated header fields.
- Response object is not limited to hypertext.
- The connection between server and client is closed after every request.

Both the request and response headers were kept as ASCII encoded, but the response object itself could be of any type: an HTML file, a plain text file, an image, or any other content type. Hence, the "hypertext transfer" part of HTTP became a misnomer not long after its introduction. In reality, HTTP has quickly evolved to become a *hypermedia transport*, but the original name stuck.

In addition to media type negotiation, the RFC also documented a number of other commonly implemented capabilities: content encoding, character set support, multipart types, authorization, caching, proxy behaviors, date formats, and more.

Almost every server on the Web today can and will still speak HTTP 1.0. Except that, by now, you should know better! Requiring a new TCP connection per request imposes a significant performance penalty on HTTP 1.0; see "Three-Way Handshake" on page 14, followed by "Slow-Start" on page 19.

HTTP 1.1: Internet Standard

The work on turning HTTP into an official IETF Internet standard proceeded in parallel with the documentation effort around HTTP 1.0 and happened over a period of roughly four years: between 1995 and 1999. In fact, the first official HTTP 1.1 standard is defined in RFC 2068, which was officially released in January 1997, roughly six months after the publication of HTTP 1.0. Then, two and a half years later, in June of 1999, a number of improvements and updates were incorporated into the standard and were released as RFC 2616.

The HTTP 1.1 standard resolved a lot of the protocol ambiguities found in earlier versions and introduced a number of critical performance optimizations: keepalive connections, chunked encoding transfers, byte-range requests, additional caching mechanisms, transfer encodings, and request pipelining.

With these capabilities in place, we can now inspect a typical HTTP 1.1 session as performed by any modern HTTP browser and client:

```
$> telnet website.org 80
Connected to xxx.xxx.xxx.xxx

GET /index.html HTTP/1.1 ❶
Host: website.org
User-Agent: Mozilla/5.0 (Macintosh; Intel Mac OS X 10_7_4)... (snip)
Accept: text/html,application/xhtml+xml,application/xml;q=0.9,*/*;q=0.8
Accept-Encoding: gzip,deflate,sdch
Accept-Language: en-US,en;q=0.8
Accept-Charset: ISO-8859-1,utf-8;q=0.7,*;q=0.3
Cookie: __qca=P0-800083390... (snip)

HTTP/1.1 200 OK ❷
Server: nginx/1.0.11
Connection: keep-alive
Content-Type: text/html; charset=utf-8
Via: HTTP/1.1 GWA
Date: Wed, 25 Jul 2012 20:23:35 GMT
Expires: Wed, 25 Jul 2012 20:23:35 GMT
Cache-Control: max-age=0, no-cache
Transfer-Encoding: chunked

100 ❸
<!doctype html>
```

```
(snip)

100
(snip)

0 ❹

GET /favicon.ico HTTP/1.1 ❺
Host: www.website.org
User-Agent: Mozilla/5.0 (Macintosh; Intel Mac OS X 10_7_4)... (snip)
Accept: */*
Referer: http://website.org/
Connection: close ❻
Accept-Encoding: gzip,deflate,sdch
Accept-Language: en-US,en;q=0.8
Accept-Charset: ISO-8859-1,utf-8;q=0.7,*;q=0.3
Cookie: __qca=P0-800083390... (snip)

HTTP/1.1 200 OK ❼
Server: nginx/1.0.11
Content-Type: image/x-icon
Content-Length: 3638
Connection: close
Last-Modified: Thu, 19 Jul 2012 17:51:44 GMT
Cache-Control: max-age=315360000
Accept-Ranges: bytes
Via: HTTP/1.1 GWA
Date: Sat, 21 Jul 2012 21:35:22 GMT
Expires: Thu, 31 Dec 2037 23:55:55 GMT
Etag: W/PSA-GAu26oXbDi

(icon data)
(connection closed)
```

❶   Request for HTML file, with encoding, charset, and cookie metadata

❷   Chunked response for original HTML request

❸   Number of octets in the chunk expressed as an ASCII hexadecimal number (256
    bytes)

❹   End of chunked stream response

❺   Request for an icon file made on same TCP connection

❻   Inform server that the connection will not be reused

❼   Icon response, followed by connection close

Phew, there is a lot going on in there! The first and most obvious difference is that we
have two object requests, one for an HTML page and one for an image, both delivered
over a single connection. This is connection keepalive in action, which allows us to reuse

the existing TCP connection for multiple requests to the same host and deliver a much faster end-user experience; see "Optimizing for TCP" on page 32.

To terminate the persistent connection, notice that the second client request sends an explicit close token to the server via the Connection header. Similarly, the server can notify the client of the intent to close the current TCP connection once the response is transferred. Technically, either side can terminate the TCP connection without such signal at any point, but clients and servers should provide it whenever possible to enable better connection reuse strategies on both sides.

HTTP 1.1 changed the semantics of the HTTP protocol to use connection keepalive by default. Meaning, unless told otherwise (via Connection: close header), the server should keep the connection open by default.

However, this same functionality was also backported to HTTP 1.0 and enabled via the Connection: Keep-Alive header. Hence, if you are using HTTP 1.1, technically you don't need the Connection: Keep-Alive header, but many clients choose to provide it nonetheless.

Additionally, the HTTP 1.1 protocol added content, encoding, character set, and even language negotiation, transfer encoding, caching directives, client cookies, plus a dozen other capabilities that can be negotiated on each request.

We are not going to dwell on the semantics of every HTTP 1.1 feature. This is a subject for a dedicated book, and many great ones have been written already. Instead, the previous example serves as a good illustration of both the quick progress and evolution of HTTP, as well as the intricate and complicated dance of every client-server exchange. There is a lot going on in there!

For a good reference on all the inner workings of the HTTP protocol, check out O'Reilly's *HTTP: The Definitive Guide* by David Gourley and Brian Totty.

HTTP 2.0: Improving Transport Performance

Since its publication, RFC 2616 has served as a foundation for the unprecedented growth of the Internet: billions of devices of all shapes and sizes, from desktop computers to the tiny web devices in our pockets, speak HTTP every day to deliver news, video, and millions of other web applications we have all come to depend on in our lives.

What began as a simple, one-line protocol for retrieving hypertext quickly evolved into a generic hypermedia transport, and now a decade later can be used to power just about any use case you can imagine. Both the ubiquity of servers that can speak the protocol and the wide availability of clients to consume it means that many applications are now designed and deployed exclusively on top of HTTP.

Need a protocol to control your coffee pot? RFC 2324 has you covered with the Hyper Text Coffee Pot Control Protocol (HTCPCP/1.0)—originally an April Fools' Day joke by IETF, and increasingly anything but a joke in our new hyper-connected world.

> The Hypertext Transfer Protocol (HTTP) is an application-level protocol for distributed, collaborative, hypermedia information systems. It is a generic, stateless, protocol that can be used for many tasks beyond its use for hypertext, such as name servers and distributed object management systems, through extension of its request methods, error codes and headers. A feature of HTTP is the typing and negotiation of data representation, allowing systems to be built independently of the data being transferred.
>
> — RFC 2616: HTTP/1.1
> *June 1999*

The simplicity of the HTTP protocol is what enabled its original adoption and rapid growth. In fact, it is now not unusual to find embedded devices—sensors, actuators, and coffee pots alike—using HTTP as their primary control and data protocols. But under the weight of its own success and as we increasingly continue to migrate our everyday interactions to the Web—social, email, news, and video, and increasingly our entire personal and job workspaces—it has also begun to show signs of stress. Users and web developers alike are now demanding near real-time responsiveness and protocol performance from HTTP 1.1, which it simply cannot meet without some modifications.

To meet these new challenges, HTTP must continue to evolve, and hence the HTTPbis working group announced a new initiative for HTTP 2.0 in early 2012:

> There is emerging implementation experience and interest in a protocol that retains the semantics of HTTP without the legacy of HTTP/1.x message framing and syntax, which have been identified as hampering performance and encouraging misuse of the underlying transport.
>
> The working group will produce a specification of a new expression of HTTP's current semantics in ordered, bi-directional streams. As with HTTP/1.x, the primary target transport is TCP, but it should be possible to use other transports.
>
> — HTTP 2.0 charter
> *January 2012*

The primary focus of HTTP 2.0 is on improving transport performance and enabling both lower latency and higher throughput. The major version increment sounds like a big step, which it is and will be as far as performance is concerned, but it is important to note that none of the high-level protocol semantics are affected: all HTTP headers, values, and use cases are the same.

Any existing website or application can and will be delivered over HTTP 2.0 without modification: you do not need to modify your application markup to take advantage of

HTTP 2.0. The HTTP servers will have to speak HTTP 2.0, but that should be a transparent upgrade for the majority of users. The only difference if the working group meets its goal, should be that our applications are delivered with lower latency and better utilization of the network link!

Having said that, let's not get ahead of ourselves. Before we get to the new HTTP 2.0 protocol features, it is worth taking a step back and examining our existing deployment and performance best practices for HTTP 1.1. The HTTP 2.0 working group is making fast progress on the new specification, but even if the final standard was already done and ready, we would still have to support older HTTP 1.1 clients for the foreseeable future—realistically, a decade or more.

CHAPTER 10

Primer on Web Performance

In any complex system, a large part of the performance optimization process is the untangling of the interactions between the many distinct and separate layers of the system, each with its own set of constraints and limitations. So far, we have examined a number of individual networking components in close detail—different physical delivery methods and transport protocols—and now we can turn our attention to the larger, end-to-end picture of web performance optimization:

- Impact of latency and bandwidth on web performance
- Transport protocol (TCP) constraints imposed on HTTP
- Features and shortcomings of the HTTP protocol itself
- Web application trends and performance requirements
- Browser constraints and optimizations

Optimizing the interaction among all the different layers is not unlike solving a family of equations, each dependent on the others, but nonetheless yielding many possible solutions. There is no one fixed set of recommendations or best practices, and the individual components continue to evolve: browsers are getting faster, user connectivity profiles change, and web applications continue to grow in their scope, ambition, and complexity.

Hence, before we dive into enumerating and analyzing individual performance best practices, it is important to step back and define what the problem really is: what a modern web application is, what tools we have at our disposal, how we measure web-performance, and which parts of the system are helping and hindering our progress.

Hypertext, Web Pages, and Web Applications

The evolution of the Web over the course of the last few decades has given us at least three different classes of experience: the hypertext document, rich media web page, and interactive web application. Admittedly, the line between the latter two may at times be blurry to the user, but from a performance point of view, each requires a very different approach to our conversation, metrics, and the definition of performance.

Hypertext document
> Hypertext documents were the genesis of the World Wide Web, the plain text version with some basic formatting and support for hyperlinks. This may not sound exciting by modern standards, but it proved the premise, vision, and the great utility of the World Wide Web.

Web page
> The HTML working group and the early browser vendors extended the definition of hypertext to support additional hypermedia resources, such as images and audio, and added many other primitives for richer layouts. The era of the *web page* has arrived, allowing us to produce rich visual layouts with various media types: visually beautiful but mostly non-interactive, not unlike a printed page.

Web application
> Addition of JavaScript and later revolutions of Dynamic HTML (DHTML) and AJAX shook things up once more and transformed the simple web page into an interactive *web application*, which allowed it to respond to the user directly within the browser. This paved the way for the first full-fledged browser applications, such as Outlook Web Access (originator of XMLHTTP support in IE5), ushering in a new era of complex dependency graphs of scripts, stylesheets, and markup.

An HTTP 0.9 session consisted of a single document request, which was perfectly sufficient for delivery of hypertext: single document, one TCP connection, followed by connection close. Consequently, tuning for performance was as simple as optimizing for a single HTTP request over a short-lived TCP connection.

The advent of the *web page* changed the formula from delivery of a single document to the document plus its dependent resources. Consequently, HTTP 1.0 introduced the notion of HTTP metadata (headers), and HTTP 1.1 enhanced it with a variety of performance-oriented primitives, such as well-defined caching, keepalive, and more. Hence, multiple TCP connections are now potentially at play, and the key performance metric has shifted from *document load time* to *page load time*, which is commonly abbreviated as PLT.

The simplest definition of PLT is "the time until the loading spinner stops spinning in the browser." A more technical definition is time to onload event in the browser, which is an event fired by the browser once the document and all of its dependent resources (JavaScript, images, etc.) have finished loading.

Finally, the web application transformed the simple web page, which used media as an enhancement to the primary content in the markup, into a complex dependency graph: markup defines the basic structure, stylesheets define the layout, and scripts build up the resulting interactive application and respond to user input, potentially modifying both styles and markup in the process.

Consequently, page load time, which has been the de facto metric of the web performance world, is also an increasingly insufficient performance benchmark: we are no longer building pages, we are building dynamic and interactive web applications. Instead of, or in addition to, measuring the time to load each and every resource (PLT), we are now interested in answering application-specific questions:

- What are the milestones in the loading progress of the application?
- What are the times to first interaction by the user?
- What are the interactions the user should engage in?
- What are the engagement and conversion rates for each user?

The success of your performance and optimization strategy is directly correlated to your ability to define and iterate on application-specific benchmarks and criteria. Nothing beats application-specific knowledge and measurements, especially when linked to bottom-line goals and metrics of your business.

DOM, CSSOM, and JavaScript

What exactly do we mean by "complex dependency graph of scripts, stylesheets, and markup" found in a modern web application? To answer this question, we need to take a quick detour into browser architecture and investigate how the parsing, layout, and scripting pipelines have to come together to paint the pixels to the screen.

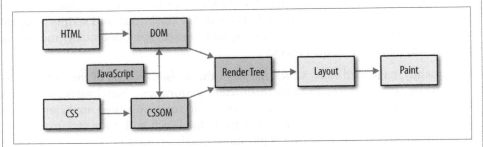

Figure 10-1. Browser processing pipeline: HTML, CSS, and JavaScript

The parsing of the HTML document is what constructs the Document Object Model (DOM). In parallel, there is an oft-forgotten cousin, the CSS Object Model (CSSOM), which is constructed from the specified stylesheet rules and resources. The two are then combined to create the "render tree," at which point the browser has enough information to perform a layout and paint something to the screen. So far, so good.

However, this is where we must, unfortunately, introduce our favorite friend and foe: JavaScript. Script execution can issue a synchronous `doc.write` and block DOM parsing and construction. Similarly, scripts can query for a computed style of any object, which means that JavaScript can also block on CSS. Consequently, the construction of DOM and CSSOM objects is frequently intertwined: DOM construction cannot proceed until JavaScript is executed, and JavaScript execution cannot proceed until CSSOM is available.

The performance of your application, especially the first load and the "time to render" depends directly on how this dependency graph between markup, stylesheets, and JavaScript is resolved. Incidentally, recall the popular "styles at the top, scripts at the bottom" best practice? Now you know why! Rendering and script execution are blocked on stylesheets; get the CSS down to the user as quickly as you can.

Anatomy of a Modern Web Application

What does a modern web application look like after all? HTTP Archive (*http://httparch ive.org/*) can help us answer this question. The project tracks how the Web is built by periodically crawling the most popular sites (300,000+ from Alexa Top 1M) and recording and aggregating analytics on the number of used resources, content types, headers, and other metadata for each individual destination.

An average web application, as of early 2013, is composed of the following:

- 90 requests, fetched from 15 hosts, with 1,311 KB total transfer size
  - HTML: 10 requests, 52 KB
  - Images: 55 requests, 812 KB
  - JavaScript: 15 requests, 216 KB
  - CSS: 5 requests, 36 KB
  - Other: 5 requests, 195 KB

By the time you read this, the preceding numbers have already changed and have grown even larger (Figure 10-2); the upward climb has been a stable and reliable trend with no signs of stopping. However, exact request and kilobyte count aside, it is the order of magnitude of these individual components that warrants some careful contemplation: an average web application is now well over 1 MB in size and is composed of roughly 100 sub-resources delivered from over 15 different hosts!

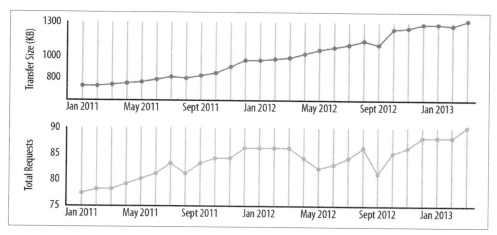

Figure 10-2. Average transfer size and number of requests (HTTP Archive)

Unlike their desktop counterparts, web applications do not require a separate installation process: type in the URL, hit Enter, and we are up and running! However, desktop applications pay the installation cost just once, whereas web applications are running the "installation process" on each and every visit—resource downloads, DOM and CSSOM construction, and JavaScript execution. No wonder web performance is such a fast-growing field and a hot topic of discussion! Hundreds of resources, megabytes of data, dozens of different hosts, all of which must come together in hundreds of milliseconds to facilitate the desired instant web experience.

Speed, Performance, and Human Perception

Speed and performance are relative terms. Each application dictates its own set of requirements based on business criteria, context, user expectations, and the complexity of the task that must be performed. Having said that, if the application must react and respond to a user, then we must plan and design for specific, *user-centric perceptual processing time constants*. Despite the ever-accelerating pace of life, or at least the feeling of it, our reaction times remain constant (Table 10-1), regardless of type of application (online or offline), or medium (laptop, desktop, or mobile device).

Table 10-1. Time and user perception

Delay	User perception
0–100 ms	Instant
100–300 ms	Small perceptible delay
300–1000 ms	Machine is working
1,000+ ms	Likely mental context switch
10,000+ ms	Task is abandoned

 The preceding table helps explain the unofficial rule of thumb in the web performance community: render pages, or at the very least provide visual feedback, in under 250 milliseconds to keep the user engaged!

For an application to feel instant, a perceptible response to user input must be provided within hundreds of milliseconds. After a second or more, the user's flow and engagement with the initiated task is broken, and after 10 seconds have passed, unless progress feedback is provided, the task is frequently abandoned.

Now, add up the network latency of a DNS lookup, followed by a TCP handshake, and another few roundtrips for a typical web page request, and much, if not all, of our 100–1,000 millisecond latency budget can be easily spent on just the networking overhead; see Figure 8-2. No wonder so many users, especially when on a mobile or a wireless network, are demanding faster web browsing performance!

Jakob Nielsen's *Usability Engineering* and Steven Seow's *Designing and Engineering Time* are both excellent resources that every developer and designer should read! Time is measured objectively but perceived subjectively, and *experiences can be engineered* to improve perceived performance.

Translating Web Performance to Dollars and Cents

Speed is a feature, and it is not simply speed for speed's sake. Well-publicized studies from Google, Microsoft, and Amazon all show that web performance translates directly to dollars and cents—e.g., a 2,000 ms delay on Bing search pages decreased per-user revenue by 4.3%!

Similarly, an Aberdeen study of over 160 organizations determined that an extra *one-second* delay in page load times led to 7% loss in conversions, 11% fewer page views, and a 16% decrease in customer satisfaction!

Faster sites yield more page views, higher engagement, and higher conversion rates. However, don't just take our word for it, or put your faith into well-cited industry benchmarks: measure the impact of web performance on your own site, and against your own conversion metrics. If you're wondering how, then keep reading, or skip ahead to "Synthetic and Real-User Performance Measurement" on page 179.

Analyzing the Resource Waterfall

No discussion on web performance is complete without a mention of the resource waterfall. In fact, the resource waterfall is likely the single most insightful network performance and diagnostics tool at our disposal. Every browser provides some instrumentation to see the resource waterfall, and there are great online tools, such as WebPageTest (*http://www.webpagetest.org/*), which can render it online for a wide variety of different browsers.

WebPageTest.org is an open-source project and a free web service that provides a system for testing the performance of web pages from multiple locations around the world: the browser runs within a virtual machine and can be configured and scripted with a variety of connection and browser-oriented settings. Following the test, the results are then available through a web interface, which makes WebPageTest an indispensable power tool in your web performance toolkit.

To start, it is important to recognize that every HTTP request is composed of a number of separate stages (Figure 10-3): DNS resolution, TCP connection handshake, TLS negotiation (if required), dispatch of the HTTP request, followed by content download. The visual display of these individual stages may differ slightly within each browser, but to keep things simple, we will use the WebPageTest version in this chapter. Make sure to familiarize yourself with the meaning of each color in your favorite browser.

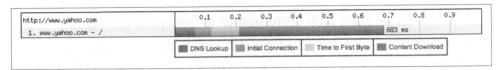

Figure 10-3. Components of an HTTP request (WebPageTest)

Close analysis of Figure 10-3 shows that the Yahoo! homepage took 683 ms to download, and over 200 ms of that time was spent waiting on the network, which amounts to 30% of total latency of the request! However, the document request is only the beginning since, as we know, a modern web application also needs a wide variety of resources (Figure 10-4) to produce the final output. To be exact, to load the Yahoo! homepage, the browser will require 52 resources, fetched from 30 different hosts, all adding up to 486 KB in total.

The resource waterfall reveals a number of important insights about the structure of the page and the browser processing pipeline. First off, notice that while the content of the *www.yahoo.com* document is being fetched, new HTTP requests are being dispatched: HTML parsing is performed incrementally, allowing the browser to discover required resources early and dispatch the necessary requests in parallel. Hence, the scheduling of when the resource is fetched is in large part determined by the structure of the markup. The browser may reprioritize some requests, but the incremental discovery of each resource in the document is what creates the distinct resource "waterfall effect."

Second, notice that the "Start Render" (green vertical line) occurs well before all the resources are fully loaded, allowing the user to begin interacting with the page while the page is being built. In fact, the "Document Complete" event (blue vertical line), also fires early and well before the remaining assets are loaded. In other words, the browser spinner has stopped spinning, the user is able to continue with his task, but the Yahoo! homepage is progressively filling in additional content, such as advertising and social widgets, in the background.

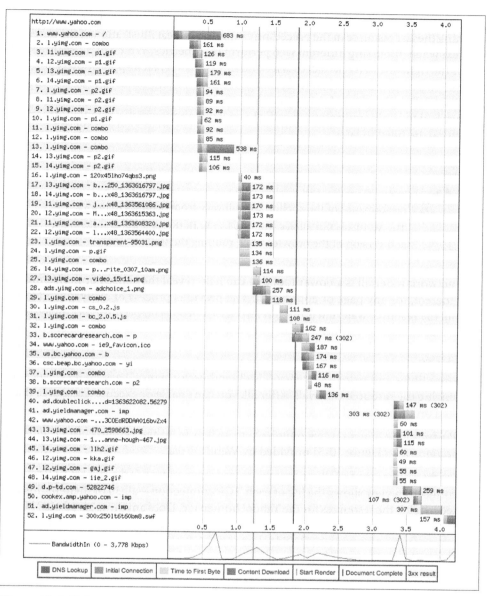

Figure 10-4. Yahoo.com resource waterfall (WebPageTest, March 2013)

The difference between the first render time, document complete, and the time to finish fetching the last resource in the preceding example is a great illustration of the necessary context when discussing different web performance metrics. Which of those three metrics is the right one to track? There is no one single answer; each application is different! Yahoo! engineers have chosen to optimize the page to take advantage of incremental loading to allow the user to begin consuming the important content earlier, and in doing so they had to apply application-specific knowledge about which content is critical and which can be filled in later.

 Different browsers implement different logic for when, and in which order, the individual resource requests are dispatched. As a result, the performance of the application will vary from browser to browser.

Tip: WebPageTest allows you to select both the location and the make and version of the browser when running the test!

The network waterfall is a power tool that can help reveal the chosen optimizations, or lack thereof, for any page or application. The previous process of analyzing and optimizing the resource waterfall is often referred to as *front-end performance* analysis and optimization. However, the name may be an unfortunate choice, as it misleads many to believe that all performance bottlenecks are now on the client. In reality, while Java-Script, CSS, and rendering pipelines are critical and resource-intensive steps, the server response times and network latency ("back-end performance") are no less critical for optimizing the resource waterfall. After all, you can't parse or execute a resource that is blocked on the network!

To illustrate this in action, we only have to switch from the *resource waterfall* to the *connection view* (Figure 10-5) provided by WebPageTest.

Unlike the resource waterfall, where each record represents an individual HTTP request, the connection view shows the life of each TCP connection—all 30 of them in this case —used to fetch the resources for the Yahoo! homepage. Does anything stand out? Notice that the download time, indicated in blue, is but a small fraction of the total latency of each connection: there are 15 DNS lookups, 30 TCP handshakes, and a lot of network latency (indicated in green) while waiting to receive the first byte of each response.

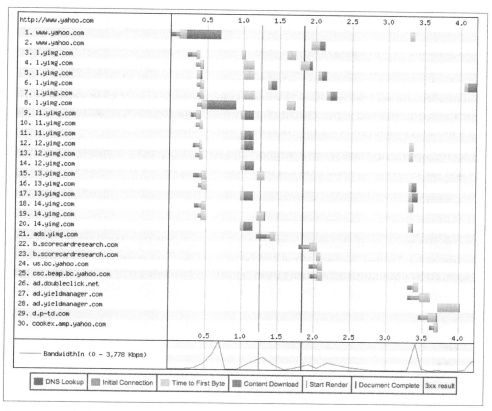

Figure 10-5. Yahoo.com resource waterfall (WebPageTest, March 2013)

 Wondering why some requests are showing the green bar (time to first byte) only? Many responses are very small, and consequently the download time does not register on the diagram. In fact, for many requests, response times are often dominated by the roundtrip latency and server processing times.

Finally, we have saved the best for last. The *real* surprise to many is found at the bottom of the connection view: examine the bandwidth utilization chart in Figure 10-5. With the exception of a few short data bursts, the utilization of the available connection is very low—it appears that we are not limited by bandwidth of our connection! Is this an anomaly, or worse, a browser bug? Unfortunately, it is neither. Turns out, bandwidth is not the limiting performance factor for most web applications. Instead, the bottleneck is the network roundtrip latency between the client and the server.

Performance Pillars: Computing, Rendering, Networking

The execution of a web program primarily involves three tasks: fetching resources, page layout and rendering, and JavaScript execution. The rendering and scripting steps follow a single-threaded, interleaved model of execution; it is not possible to perform concurrent modifications of the resulting Document Object Model (DOM). Hence, optimizing how the rendering and script execution runtimes work together, as we saw in "DOM, CSSOM, and JavaScript" on page 168, is of critical importance.

However, optimizing JavaScript execution and rendering pipelines also won't do much good if the browser is blocked on the network, waiting for the resources to arrive. Fast and efficient delivery of network resources is the performance keystone of each and every application running in the browser.

But, one might ask, Internet speeds are getting faster by the day, so won't this problem solve itself? Yes, our applications are growing larger, but if the global average speed is already at 3.1 Mbps ("Bandwidth at the Network Edge" on page 10) and growing, as evidenced by ubiquitous advertising by every ISP and mobile carrier, why bother, right? Unfortunately, as you might intuit, and as the Yahoo! example shows, if that were the case then you wouldn't be reading this book. Let's take a closer look.

 For a detailed discussion of the trends and interplay of bandwidth and latency, refer back to the "Primer on Latency and Bandwidth" in Chapter 1.

More Bandwidth Doesn't Matter (Much)

Hold your horses; of course bandwidth matters! After all, every commercial by our local ISP and mobile carrier continues to remind us of its many benefits: faster downloads, uploads, and streaming, all at up to speeds of *[insert latest number here]* Mbps!

Access to higher bandwidth data rates is always good, especially for cases that involve bulk data transfers: video and audio streaming or any other type of large data transfer. However, when it comes to everyday web browsing, which requires fetching hundreds of relatively small resources from dozens of different hosts, roundtrip latency is the limiting factor:

- Streaming an HD video from the Yahoo! homepage is bandwidth limited.
- Loading and rendering the Yahoo! homepage is latency limited.

Depending on the quality and the encoding of the video you are trying to stream, you may need anywhere from a few hundred Kbps to several Mbps in bandwidth capacity —e.g., 3+ Mbps for an HD 1080p video stream. This data rate is now within reach for many users, which is evidenced by the growing popularity of streaming video services such as Netflix. Why, then, would downloading a much, much smaller web application be such a challenge for a connection capable of streaming an HD movie?

Latency as a Performance Bottleneck

We have already covered all the necessary topics in preceding chapters to make a good qualitative theory as to why latency may be the limiting factor for everyday web browsing. However, a picture is worth a thousand words, so let's examine the results of a quantitative study performed by Mike Belshe (Figure 10-6), one of the creators of the SPDY protocol, on the impact of varying bandwidth vs. latency on the page load times of some of the most popular destinations on the Web.

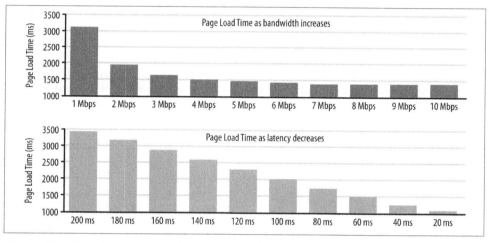

Figure 10-6. Page load time vs. bandwidth and latency

 This study by Mike Belshe served as a launching point for the development of the SPDY protocol at Google, which later became the foundation of the HTTP 2.0 protocol.

In the first test, the connection latency is held fixed, and the connection bandwidth is incrementally increased from 1 Mbps up to 10 Mbps. Notice that at first, upgrading the connection from 1 to 2 Mbps nearly halves the page loading time—exactly the result we want to see. However, following that, each incremental improvement in bandwidth yields diminishing returns. By the time the available bandwidth exceeds 5 Mbps, we are looking at single-digit percent improvements, and upgrading from 5 Mbps to 10 Mbps results in a mere 5% improvement in page loading times!

Akamai's broadband speed report ("Bandwidth at the Network Edge" on page 10) shows that an average consumer in the United States is already accessing the Web with 5 Mbps + of available bandwidth—a number that many other countries are quickly approaching or have surpassed already. Ergo, we are led to conclude that an average consumer in the United States would not benefit *much* from upgrading the available bandwidth of her connection if she is interested in improving her web browsing speeds. She may be able to stream or upload larger media files more quickly, but the pages containing those files will not load noticeably faster: *bandwidth doesn't matter, much.*

However, the latency experiment tells an entirely different story: for every 20 millisecond improvement in latency, we have a linear improvement in page loading times! Perhaps it is latency we should be optimizing for when deciding on an ISP, and not just bandwidth?

> To speed up the Internet at large, we should look for more ways to bring down RTT. What if we could reduce cross-atlantic RTTs from 150 ms to 100 ms? This would have a larger effect on the speed of the internet than increasing a user's bandwidth from 3.9 Mbps to 10 Mbps or even 1 Gbps.
>
> Another approach to reducing page load times would be to reduce the number of round trips required per page load. Today, web pages require a certain amount of back and forth between the client and server. The number of round trips is largely due to the handshakes to start communicating between client and server (e.g. DNS, TCP, HTTP), and also round trips induced by the communication protocols (e.g. TCP slow start). If we can improve protocols to transfer this data with fewer round trips, we should also be able to improve page load times. This is one of the goals of SPDY.
>
> — Mike Belshe
> *More Bandwidth Doesn't Matter (Much)*

The previous results are a surprise to many, but they really should not be, as they are a direct consequence of the performance characteristics of the underlying protocols: TCP handshakes, flow and congestion control, and head-of-line blocking due to packet loss. Most of the HTTP data flows consist of small, bursty data transfers, whereas TCP is optimized for long-lived connections and bulk data transfers. Network roundtrip time is the limiting factor in TCP throughput and performance in most cases; see "Optimizing for TCP" on page 32. Consequently, latency is also the performance bottleneck for HTTP and most web applications delivered over it.

If latency is the limiting performance factor for most wired connections then, as you might intuit, it is an even more important performance bottleneck for wireless clients: wireless latencies are significantly higher, making networking optimization a critical priority for the mobile web.

Synthetic and Real-User Performance Measurement

If we can measure it, we can improve it. The question is, are we measuring the right criteria, and is the process sound? As we noted earlier, measuring the performance of a modern web application is a nontrivial challenge: there is no one single metric that holds true for every application, which means that we must carefully define custom metrics in each case. Then, once the criteria are established, we must gather the performance data, which should be done through a combination of synthetic and real-user performance measurement.

Broadly speaking, synthetic testing refers to any process with a controlled measurement environment: a local build process running through a performance suite, load testing against staging infrastructure, or a set of geo-distributed monitoring servers that periodically perform a set of scripted actions and log the outcomes. Each and every one of these tests may test a different piece of the infrastructure (e.g., application server throughput, database performance, DNS timing, and so on), and serves as a stable baseline to help detect regressions or narrow in on a specific component of the system.

> When configured well, synthetic testing provides a controlled and reproducible performance testing environment, which makes it a great fit for identifying and fixing performance regressions before they reach the user. Tip: identify your key performance metrics and set a "budget" for each one as part of your synthetic testing. If the budget is exceeded, raise an alarm!

However, synthetic testing is not sufficient to identify all performance bottlenecks. Specifically, the problem is that the gathered measurements are not representative of the wide diversity of the real-world factors that will determine the final user experience with the application. Some contributing factors to this gap include the following:

- Scenario and page selection: replicating real user navigation patterns is hard.
- Browser cache: performance may vary widely based on the state of the user's cache.
- Intermediaries: performance may vary based on intermediate proxies and caches.
- Diversity of hardware: wide range of CPU, GPU, and memory performance.
- Diversity of browsers: wide range of browser versions, both old and new.
- Connectivity: continuously changing bandwidth and latency of real connections.

The combination of these and similar factors means that in addition to synthetic testing, we must augment our performance strategy with real-user measurement (RUM) to capture actual performance of our application as experienced by the user. The good news is the W3C Web Performance Working Group has made this part of our

data-gathering process a simple one by introducing the Navigation Timing API
(Figure 10-7), which is now supported across many of the modern desktop and mobile
browsers.

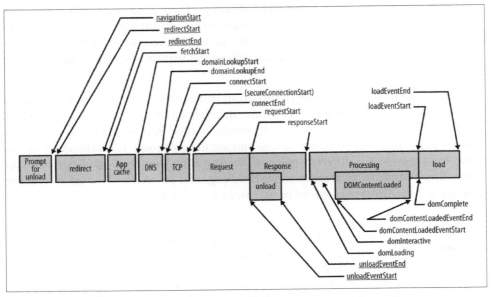

Figure 10-7. User-specific performance timers exposed by Navigation Timing

 As of early 2013, Navigation Timing is supported by IE9+, Chrome 6+,
and Firefox 7+ across desktop and mobile platforms. The notable
omissions are the Safari and Opera browsers. For the latest status, see
caniuse.com/nav-timing.

The real benefit of Navigation Timing is that it exposes a lot of previously inaccessible
data, such as DNS and TCP connect times, with high precision (microsecond timestamps), via a standardized `performance.timing` object in each browser. Hence, the
data gathering process is very simple: load the page, grab the timing object from the
user's browser, and beacon it back to your analytics servers! By capturing this data, we
can observe real-world performance of our applications as seen by real users, on real
hardware, and across a wide variety of different networks.

Analyzing Real User Measurement Data

When analyzing performance data, always look at the underlying distribution of the data: throw away the averages and focus on the histograms, medians, and quantiles. Averages lead to meaningless metrics when analyzing skewed and multimodal distributions. Figure 10-8 shows a hands-on, real-world example of both types of distributions on a single site: skewed distribution for the page load time and a multimodal distribution for the server response time (the two modes are due to cached vs. uncached page generation time by the application server).

Page Load Time Bucket (sec)	Page Load Sample	Percentage of total
0 - 1	22	5.35%
1 - 3	116	28.22%
3 - 7	148	36.01%
7 - 13	66	16.06%
13 - 21	22	5.35%
21 - 35	14	3.41%
35 - 60	10	2.43%

Server Response Time Bucket (sec)	Response Sample	Percentage of total
0 - 0.01	18	4.40%
0.01 - 0.10	33	8.07%
0.10 - 0.50	168	41.08%
0.50 - 1	22	5.38%
1 - 2	124	30.32%
2 - 5	38	9.29%
5+	6	1.47%

Figure 10-8. Page load time (skewed) and response time (multimodal) distributions for igvita.com

Ensure that your analytics tool can provide the right statistical metrics for your performance data. The preceding data was taken from Google Analytics, which provides a histogram view within the standard Site Speed reports. Google Analytics automatically gathers Navigation Timing data when the analytics tracker is installed. Similarly, there are a wide variety of other analytics vendors who offer Navigation Timing data gathering and reporting.

Finally, in addition to Navigation Timing, the W3C Performance Group also standardized two other APIs: User Timing and Resource Timing. Whereas Navigation Timing provides performance timers for root documents only, Resource Timing provides similar performance data for each resource on the page, allowing us to gather the full performance profile of the page. Similarly, User Timing provides a simple JavaScript API to mark and measure application-specific performance metrics with the help of the same high-resolution timers:

```javascript
function init() {
  performance.mark("startTask1"); ❶
  applicationCode1(); ❷
  performance.mark("endTask1");

  logPerformance();
}

function logPerformance() {
  var perfEntries = performance.getEntriesByType("mark");
  for (var i = 0; i < perfEntries.length; i++) { ❸
    console.log("Name: " + perfEntries[i].name +
                " Entry Type: " + perfEntries[i].entryType +
                " Start Time: " + perfEntries[i].startTime +
                " Duration: "   + perfEntries[i].duration  + "\n");
  }
  console.log(performance.timing); ❹
}
```

❶ Store (mark) timestamp with associated name (startTask1).

❷ Execute application code.

❸ Iterate and log user timing data.

❹ Log Navigation Timing object for current page.

The combination of Navigation, Resource, and User timing APIs provides all the necessary tools to instrument and conduct real-user performance measurement for every web application; there is no longer any excuse not to do it right. We optimize what we measure, and RUM and synthetic testing are complementary approaches to help you identify regressions and real-world bottlenecks in the performance and the user experience of your applications.

Custom and application-specific metrics are the key to establishing a sound performance strategy. There is no generic way to measure or define the quality of user experience. Instead, we must define and instrument specific milestones and events in each application, a process that requires collaboration between all the stakeholders in the project: business owners, designers, and developers.

Browser Optimization

We would be remiss if we didn't mention that a modern browser is much more than a simple network socket manager. Performance is one of the primary competitive features for each browser vendor, and given that the networking performance is such a critical criteria, it should not surprise you that the browsers are getting smarter every day: pre-resolving likely DNS lookups, pre-connecting to likely destinations, pre-fetching and prioritizing critical resources on the page, and more.

The exact list of performed optimizations will differ by browser vendor, but at their core the optimizations can be grouped into two broad classes:

Document-aware optimization
> The networking stack is integrated with the document, CSS, and JavaScript parsing pipelines to help identify and prioritize critical network assets, dispatch them early, and get the page to an interactive state as soon as possible. This is often done via resource priority assignments, lookahead parsing, and similar techniques.

Speculative optimization
> The browser may learn user navigation patterns over time and perform speculative optimizations in an attempt to predict the likely user actions by pre-resolving DNS names, pre-connecting to likely hostnames, and so on.

The good news is all of these optimizations are done automatically on our behalf and often lead to hundreds of milliseconds of saved network latency. Having said that, it is important to understand how and why these optimizations work under the hood, because we *can* assist the browser and help it do an even better job at accelerating our applications. There are four techniques employed by most browsers:

Resource pre-fetching and prioritization
> Document, CSS, and JavaScript parsers may communicate extra information to the network stack to indicate the relative priority of each resource: blocking resources required for first rendering are given high priority, while low-priority requests may be temporarily held back in a queue.

DNS pre-resolve
> Likely hostnames are pre-resolved ahead of time to avoid DNS latency on a future HTTP request. A pre-resolve may be triggered through learned navigation history, a user action such as hovering over a link, or other signals on the page.

TCP pre-connect
> Following a DNS resolution, the browser may speculatively open the TCP connection in an anticipation of an HTTP request. If it guesses right, it can eliminate another full roundtrip (TCP handshake) of network latency.

Page pre-rendering

Some browsers allow you to hint the likely next destination and can pre-render the entire page in a hidden tab, such that it can be instantly swapped in when the user initiates the navigation.

 For a deep dive into how these and other networking optimizations are implemented in Google Chrome, see High Performance Networking in Google Chrome (*http://hpbn.co/chrome-networking*).

From the outside, a modern browser network stack presents itself as simple resource-fetching mechanism, but from the inside, it is an elaborate and a fascinating case study for how to optimize for web performance. So how can we assist the browser in this quest? To start, pay close attention to the structure and the delivery of each page:

- Critical resources such as CSS and JavaScript should be discoverable as early as possible in the document.
- CSS should be delivered as early as possible to unblock rendering and JavaScript execution.
- Noncritical JavaScript should be deferred to avoid blocking DOM and CSSOM construction.
- The HTML document is parsed incrementally by the parser; hence the document should be periodically flushed for best performance.

Further, aside from optimizing the structure of the page, we can also embed additional hints into the document itself to tip off the browser about additional optimizations it can perform on our behalf:

```
<link rel="dns-prefetch" href="//hostname_to_resolve.com"> ❶
<link rel="subresource"  href="/javascript/myapp.js"> ❷
<link rel="prefetch"     href="/images/big.jpeg"> ❸
<link rel="prerender"    href="//example.org/next_page.html"> ❹
```

❶ Pre-resolve specified hostname.

❷ Prefetch critical resource found later on this page.

❸ Prefetch resource for this or future navigation.

❹ Prerender specified page in anticipation of next user destination.

Each of these is a hint for a speculative optimization. The browser does not guarantee that it will act on it, but it may use the hint to optimize its loading strategy. Unfortunately, not all browsers support all hints (Table 10-2), but if they don't, then the hint is treated as a no-op and is harmless; make use of each of the techniques just shown where possible.

Table 10-2. Speculative browser optimization hints

Browser	dns-prefetch	subresource	prefetch	prerender
Firefox	3.5+	n/a	3.5+	n/a
Chrome	1.0+	1.0+	1.0+	13+
Safari	5.01+	n/a	n/a	n/a
IE	9+ (prefetch)	n/a	10+	11+

 Internet Explorer 9 supports DNS pre-fetching, but calls it *prefetch*. In Internet Explorer 10+, *dns-prefetch* and *prefetch* are equivalent, resulting in a DNS pre-fetch in both cases.

To most users and even web developers, the DNS, TCP, and SSL delays are entirely transparent and are negotiated at network layers to which few of us descend. And yet each of these steps is critical to the overall user experience, since each extra network roundtrip can add tens or hundreds of milliseconds of network latency. By helping the browser anticipate these roundtrips, we can remove these bottlenecks and deliver much faster and better web applications.

Optimizing Time to First Byte (TTFB) for Google Search

The HTML document is parsed incrementally by the browser, which means that the server can and should flush available document markup as frequently as possible. This enables the client to discover and begin fetching critical resources as soon as possible.

Google Search offers one of the best examples of the benefits of this technique: when a search request arrives, the server immediately flushes the static header of the search page prior to even analyzing the query. After all, why should it wait, the header is the same for every search page! Then, while the client is parsing the header markup, the search query is dispatched to the search index, and the remainder of the document, which includes the search results, is delivered to the user once the results are ready. At this point, the dynamic parts of the header, such as the name of the logged-in user, are filled in via JavaScript.

CHAPTER 11

HTTP 1.X

A discussion on optimization strategies for HTTP 1.0 is a simple one: all HTTP 1.0 deployments should be upgraded to HTTP 1.1; end of story.

Improving performance of HTTP was one the key design goals for the HTTP 1.1 working group, and the standard introduced a large number of critical performance enhancements and features. A few of the best known include the following:

- Persistent connections to allow connection reuse
- Chunked transfer encoding to allow response streaming
- Request pipelining to allow parallel request processing
- Byte serving to allow range-based resource requests
- Improved and much better-specified caching mechanisms

This list is incomplete, and a full discussion of the technical details of each and every HTTP 1.1 enhancement deserves a separate book. Once again, check out *HTTP: The Definitive Guide* by David Gourley and Brian Totty. Similarly, speaking of good reference books, Steve Souders' *High Performance Web Sites* offers great advice in the form of 14 rules, half of which are networking optimizations:

Reduce DNS lookups
Every hostname resolution requires a network roundtrip, imposing latency on the request and blocking the request while the lookup is in progress.

Make fewer HTTP requests
No request is faster than a request not made: eliminate unnecessary resources on your pages.

Use a Content Delivery Network
> Locating the data geographically closer to the client can significantly reduce the network latency of every TCP connection and improve throughput.

Add an Expires header and configure ETags
> Relevant resources should be cached to avoid re-requesting the same bytes on each and every page. An Expires header can be used to specify the cache lifetime of the object, allowing it to be retrieved directly from the user's cache and eliminating the HTTP request entirely. ETags and Last-Modified headers provide an efficient cache revalidation mechanism—effectively a fingerprint or a timestamp of the last update.

Gzip assets
> All text-based assets should be compressed with Gzip when transferred between the client and the server. On average, Gzip will reduce the file size by 60–80%, which makes it one of the simpler (configuration flag on the server) and high-benefit optimizations you can do.

Avoid HTTP redirects
> HTTP redirects can be extremely costly, especially when they redirect the client to a different hostname, which results in additional DNS lookup, TCP connection latency, and so on.

Each of the preceding recommendations has stood the test of time and is as true today as when the book was first published in 2007. That is no coincidence, because all of them highlight two fundamental recommendations: eliminate and reduce unnecessary network latency, and minimize the amount of transferred bytes. Both are *evergreen optimizations*, which will always ring true for any application.

However, the same can't be said for all HTTP 1.1 features and best practices. Unfortunately, some HTTP 1.1 features, like request pipelining, have effectively failed due to lack of support, and other protocol limitations, such as head-of-line response blocking, created further cracks in the foundation. In turn, the web developer community—always an inventive lot—has created and popularized a number of homebrew optimizations: domain sharding, concatenation, spriting, and inlining among dozens of others.

For many web developers, all of these are matter-of-fact optimizations: familiar, necessary, and universally accepted. However, in reality, these techniques should be seen for what they really are: stopgap workarounds for existing limitations in the HTTP 1.1 protocol. We shouldn't have to worry about concatenating files, spriting images, sharding domains, or inlining assets. Unfortunately, "shouldn't" is not a pragmatic stance to take: these optimizations exist for good reasons, and we have to rely on them until the underlying issues are fixed in the next revision of the protocol.

Benefits of Keepalive Connections

One of the primary performance improvements of HTTP 1.1 was the introduction of persistent, or keepalive HTTP connections—both names refer to the same feature. We saw keepalive in action in "HTTP 1.1: Internet Standard" on page 159, but let's illustrate why this feature is such a critical component of our performance strategy.

To keep things simple, let's restrict ourselves to a maximum of one TCP connection and examine the scenario (Figure 11-1) where we need to fetch just two small (<4 KB each) resources: an HTML document and a supporting CSS file, each taking some arbitrary amount of time on the server (40 and 20 ms, respectively).

> Figure 11-1 assumes the same 28 millisecond one-way "light in fiber" delay between New York and London as used in previous TCP connection establishment examples; see Table 1-1.

Each TCP connection begins with a TCP three-way handshake, which takes a full roundtrip of latency between the client and the server. Following that, we will incur a minimum of another roundtrip of latency due to the two-way propagation delay of the HTTP request and response. Finally, we have to add the server processing time to get the total time for every request.

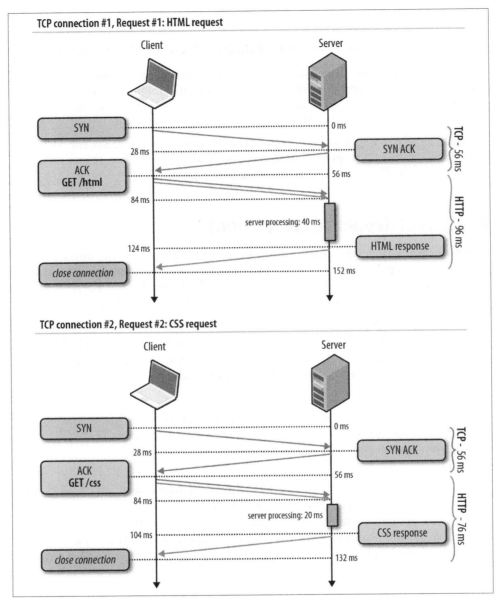

Figure 11-1. Fetching HTML and CSS via separate TCP connections

We cannot predict the server processing time, since that will vary by resource and the back-end behind it, but it is worth highlighting that the minimum total time for an HTTP request delivered via a new TCP connection is two network roundtrips: one for the handshake, one for the request-response cycle. This is a fixed cost imposed on all non-persistent HTTP sessions.

 The faster your server processing time, the higher the impact of the fixed latency overhead of every network request! To prove this, try changing the roundtrip and server times in the previous example.

Hence, a simple optimization is to reuse the underlying connection! Adding support for HTTP keepalive (Figure 11-2) allows us to eliminate the second TCP three-way handshake, avoid another round of TCP slow-start, and save a full roundtrip of network latency.

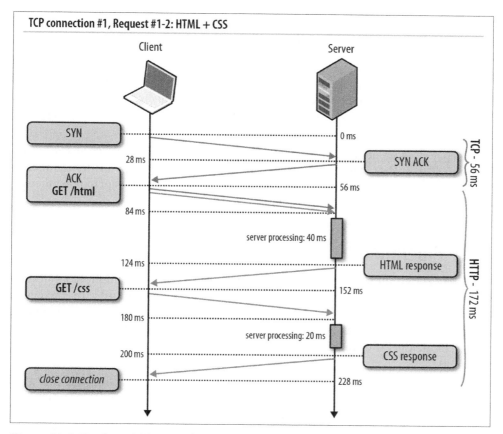

Figure 11-2. Fetching HTML and CSS with connection keepalive

In our example with two requests, the total savings is just a single roundtrip of latency, but let's now consider the general case with a single TCP connection and N HTTP requests:

- Without keepalive, each request will incur two roundtrips of latency.
- With keepalive, the first request incurs two roundtrips, and all following requests incur just one roundtrip of latency.

The total latency savings for N requests is $(N-1) \times RTT$ when connection keepalive is enabled. Finally, recall that the average value of N is 90 resources and growing ("Anatomy of a Modern Web Application" on page 168), and we quickly arrive at potential latency savings measured in seconds! Needless to say, persistent HTTP is a critical optimization for every web application.

Connection Reuse on the Client and Server

The good news is all modern browsers will attempt to use persistent HTTP connections automatically as long as the server is willing to cooperate. Check your application and proxy server configurations to ensure that they support keepalive. For best results, use HTTP 1.1, where keepalive is enabled by default, and if you are stuck with HTTP 1.0, then look into using the `Connection: Keep-Alive` header.

Also, pay close attention to the default behavior of HTTP libraries and frameworks, as many will often default to non-keepalive behavior, mostly because it provides a "simpler API." Whenever you are working with raw HTTP connections, attempt to reuse them: the performance benefits are significant!

HTTP Pipelining

Persistent HTTP allows us to reuse an existing connection between multiple application requests, but it implies a strict first in, first out (FIFO) queuing order on the client: dispatch request, wait for the full response, dispatch next request from the client queue. HTTP pipelining is a small but important optimization to this workflow, which allows us to relocate the FIFO queue from the client (request queuing) to the server (response queuing).

To understand why this is beneficial, let's revisit Figure 11-2. First, observe that once the first request is processed by the server, there is an entire roundtrip of latency—response propagation latency, followed by request propagation latency—during which the server is idle. Instead, what if the server could begin processing the second request immediately after it finished the first one? Or, even better, perhaps it could even process both in parallel, on multiple threads, or with the help of multiple workers.

By dispatching our requests early, without blocking on each individual response, we can eliminate another full roundtrip of network latency, taking us from two roundtrips per request with no connection keepalive, down to two network roundtrips (Figure 11-3) of latency overhead for the entire queue of requests!

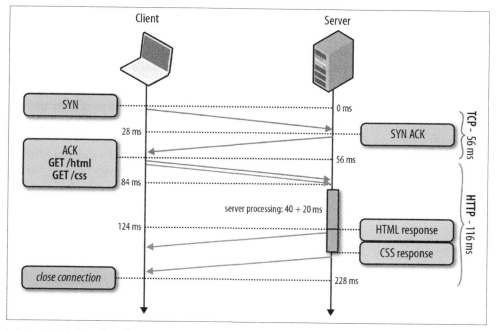

Figure 11-3. Pipelined HTTP requests with server-side FIFO queue

 Eliminating the wait time imposed by response and request propagation latencies is one of the primary benefits of HTTP 1.1 pipelining. However, the ability to process the requests in parallel can have just as big, if not bigger, impact on the performance of your application.

At this point, let's pause and revisit our performance gains so far. We began with two distinct TCP connections for each request (Figure 11-1), which resulted in 284 milliseconds of total latency. With keepalive enabled (Figure 11-2), we were able to eliminate an extra handshake roundtrip, bringing the total down to 228 milliseconds. Finally, with HTTP pipelining in place, we eliminated another network roundtrip in between requests. Hence, we went from 284 milliseconds down to 172 milliseconds, a 40% reduction in total latency, all through simple protocol optimization.

Further, note that the 40% improvement is not a fixed performance gain. This number is specific to our chosen network latencies and the two requests in our example. As an exercise for the reader, try a few additional scenarios with higher latencies and more requests. You may be surprised to discover that the savings can be much, much larger. In fact, the larger the network latency, and the more requests, the higher the savings. It is worth proving to yourself that this is indeed the case! Ergo, the larger the application, the larger the impact of networking optimization.

However, we are not done yet. The eagle-eyed among you have likely spotted another opportunity for optimization: parallel request processing on the server. In theory, there is no reason why the server could not have processed both pipelined requests (Figure 11-3) in parallel, eliminating another 20 milliseconds of latency.

Unfortunately, this optimization introduces a lot of subtle implications and illustrates an important limitation of the HTTP 1.x protocol: strict serialization of returned responses. Specifically, HTTP 1.x does not allow data from multiple responses to be interleaved (multiplexed) on the same connection, forcing each response to be returned in full before the bytes for the next response can be transferred. To illustrate this in action, let's consider the case (Figure 11-4) where the server processes both of our requests in parallel.

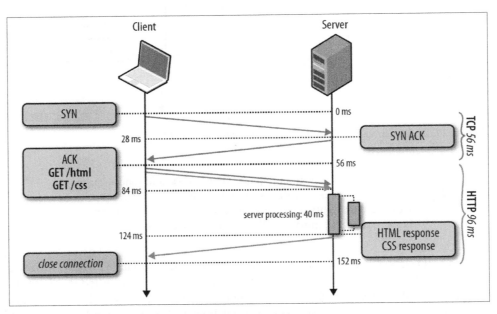

Figure 11-4. Pipelined HTTP requests with parallel processing

Figure 11-4 demonstrates the following:

- Both HTML and CSS requests arrive in parallel, but HTML request is first.
- Server begins processing both in parallel. HTML: 40 ms, CSS: 20 ms.

- CSS request completes first but must be buffered until HTML response is sent.
- Once HTML response is sent, CSS response is flushed from the server buffers.

Even though the client issued both requests in parallel, and the CSS resource is available first, the server must wait to send the full HTML response before it can proceed with delivery of the CSS asset. This scenario is commonly known as *head-of-line blocking* and results in suboptimal delivery: underutilized network links, server buffering costs, and worst of all, unpredictable latency delays for the client. What if the first request hangs indefinitely or simply takes a very long time to generate on the server? With HTTP 1.1, all requests behind it are blocked and have to wait.

 We have already encountered head-of-line blocking when discussing TCP: due to the requirement for strict in-order delivery, a lost TCP packet will block all packets with higher sequence numbers until it is retransmitted, inducing extra application latency; see TCP "Head-of-Line Blocking" on page 30.

In practice, due to lack of multiplexing, HTTP pipelining creates many subtle and undocumented implications for HTTP servers, intermediaries, and clients:

- A single slow response blocks all requests behind it.
- When processing in parallel, servers must buffer pipelined responses, which may exhaust server resources—e.g., what if one of the responses is very large? This exposes an attack vector against the server!
- A failed response may terminate the TCP connection, forcing the client to rerequest all the subsequent resources, which may cause duplicate processing.
- Detecting pipelining compatibility reliably, where intermediaries may be present, is a nontrivial problem.
- Some intermediaries do not support pipelining and may abort the connection, while others may serialize all requests.

Due to these and similar complications, and lack of guidance in the HTTP 1.1 standard for these cases, HTTP pipelining adoption has remained very limited despite its many benefits. Today, some browsers support pipelining, usually as an advanced configuration option, but most have it disabled. In other words, if the web browser is the primary delivery vehicle for your web application, then we can't count on HTTP pipelining to help with performance.

Using HTTP Pipelining Outside the Browser

Before we discount the benefits of HTTP pipelining entirely, it is important to note that it can still be used, and with great results, in situations where you control the capabilities of both the client and the server. In fact, Apple's iTunes case study is a case in point: "Delivering 3× Performance Improvement for iTunes Users" on page 189. This performance feat was accomplished by switching to persistent HTTP and enabling HTTP pipelining both on the server and within the custom iTunes client.

A quick checklist for enabling pipelining in your own application:

- Your HTTP client must support pipelining.
- Your HTTP server must support pipelining.
- Your application must handle aborted connections and retries.
- Your application must handle idempotency concerns of aborted requests.
- Your application must protect itself from broken intermediaries.

In practice, the best way to deploy HTTP pipelining is to create a secure (HTTPS) tunnel between the client and server. That's the most reliable way to avoid interference from intermediaries that may not understand or support pipelined requests.

Using Multiple TCP Connections

In absence of multiplexing in HTTP 1.x, the browser could naively queue all HTTP requests on the client, sending one after another over a single, persistent connection. However, in practice, this is too slow. Hence, the browser vendors are left with no other choice than to open multiple TCP sessions in parallel. How many? In practice, most modern browsers, both desktop and mobile, open up to six connections per host.

Before we go any further, it is worth contemplating the implications, both positive and negative, of opening multiple TCP connections in parallel. Let's consider the maximum case with six independent connections per host:

- The client can dispatch up to six requests in parallel.
- The server can process up to six requests in parallel.
- The cumulative number of packets that can be sent in the first roundtrip (TCP cwnd) is increased by a factor of six.

The maximum request parallelism, in absence of pipelining, is the same as the number of open connections. Further, the TCP congestion window is also effectively multiplied by the number of open connections, allowing the client to circumvent the configured packet limit dictated by TCP slow-start. So far, this seems like a convenient workaround! However, let's now consider some of the costs:

- Additional sockets consuming resources on the client, server, and all intermediaries: extra memory buffers and CPU overhead
- Competition for shared bandwidth between parallel TCP streams
- Much higher implementation complexity for handling collections of sockets
- Limited application parallelism even in light of parallel TCP streams

In practice, the CPU and memory costs are nontrivial, resulting in much higher per-client overhead on both client and server—higher operational costs. Similarly, we raise the implementation complexity on the client—higher development costs. Finally, this approach still delivers only limited benefits as far as application parallelism is concerned. It's not the right long-term solution. Having said that, there are three valid reasons why we have to use it today:

1. As a workaround for limitations of the application protocol (HTTP)
2. As a workaround for low starting congestion window size in TCP
3. As a workaround for clients that cannot use TCP window scaling (see "Bandwidth-Delay Product" on page 28)

Both TCP considerations (window scaling and cwnd) are best addressed by a simple upgrade to the latest OS kernel release; see "Optimizing for TCP" on page 32. The cwnd value has been recently raised to 10 packets, and all the latest platforms provide robust support for TCP window scaling. That's the good news. The bad news is there is no simple workaround for fixing multiplexing in HTTP 1.x.

As long as we need to support HTTP 1.x clients, we are stuck with having to juggle multiple TCP streams. Which brings us to the next obvious question: why and how did the browsers settle on six connections per host? Unfortunately, as you may have guessed, the number is based on a collection of trade-offs: the higher the limit, the higher the client and server overhead, but at the additional benefit of higher request parallelism. Six connections per host is simply a safe middle ground. For some sites, this may provide great results; for many it is insufficient.

Exhausting Client and Server Resources

Limiting the maximum number of connections per host allows the browser to provide a safety check against an unintentional (or intentional) denial of service (DoS) attack. In absence of such limit, the client could saturate all available resources on the server.

Ironically, this same safety check enables the reverse attack on some browsers: if the maximum connection limit is exceeded on the client, then all further client requests are blocked. As an experiment, open six parallel downloads to a single host, and then issue a seventh request: it will hang until one of the previous requests has completed.

Saturating the client connection limit may seem like a benign security flaw, but it is increasingly a real deployment problem for applications that rely on real-time delivery mechanisms, such as WebSocket, Server Sent Events and hanging XHRs: each of these sessions occupies a full TCP stream, even while no data is transferred—remember, no multiplexing! Hence, if you're not careful, you can create a self-imposed DoS attack against your own application.

Domain Sharding

A gap in the HTTP 1.X protocol has forced browser vendors to introduce and maintain a connection pool of up to six TCP streams per host. The good news is all of the connection management is handled by the browser itself. As an application developer, you don't have to modify your application at all. The bad news is six parallel streams may still not be enough for your application.

According to HTTP Archive, an average page is now composed of 90+ individual resources, which if delivered all by the same host would still result in significant queuing delays (Figure 11-5). Hence, why limit ourselves to the same host? Instead of serving all resources from the same origin (e.g., *www.example.com*), we can manually "shard" them across multiple subdomains: *{shard1, shardn}.example.com*. Because the hostnames are different, we are implicitly increasing the browser's connection limit to achieve a higher level of parallelism. The more shards we use, the higher the parallelism!

Name	Method	Status	Type	...	...	Time	Start Time	302 ms	453 ms	604 ms	755 ms
localhost	GET	200	text/html	...	...	17 ms					
01.jpeg	GET	202	image/jpeg	...	...	242 ms					
02.jpeg	GET	202	image/jpeg	...	...	243 ms					
03.jpeg	GET	202	image/jpeg	...	...	242 ms					
04.jpeg	GET	202	image/jpeg	...	...	241 ms					
05.jpeg	GET	202	image/jpeg	...	...	235 ms					
06.jpeg	GET	202	image/jpeg	...	...	235 ms					
07.jpeg	GET	202	image/jpeg	...	...	475 ms					
08.jpeg	GET	202	image/jpeg	...	...	563 ms					
09.jpeg	GET	202	image/jpeg	...	...	561 ms					
10.jpeg	GET	202	image/jpeg	...	...	561 ms					
11.jpeg	GET	202	image/jpeg	...	...	561 ms					
12.jpeg	GET	202	image/jpeg	...	...	561 ms					

Figure 11-5. Staggered resource downloads due to six-connection limit per origin

Of course, there is no free lunch, and domain sharding is not an exception: every new hostname will require an additional DNS lookup, consume additional resources on both sides for each additional socket, and, worst of all, require the site author to manually manage where and how the resources are split.

 In practice, it is not uncommon to have multiple hostnames (e.g., *shard1.example.com, shard2.example.com*) resolve to the same IP address. The shards are CNAME DNS records pointing to the same server, and browser connection limits are enforced with respect to the hostname, not the IP. Alternatively, the shards could point to a CDN or any other reachable server.

What is the formula for the optimal number of shards? Trick question, as there is no such simple equation. The answer depends on the number of resources on the page (which varies per page) and the available bandwidth and latency of the client's connection (which varies per client). Hence, the best we can do is make an informed guess and use some fixed number of shards. With luck, the added complexity will translate to a net win for most clients.

In practice, domain sharding is often overused, resulting in tens of underutilized TCP streams, many of them never escaping TCP slow-start, and in the worst case, actually slowing down the user experience. Further, the costs are even higher when HTTPS must be used, due to the extra network roundtrips incurred by the TLS handshake. A few considerations to keep in mind:

- Get the most out of TCP first; see "Optimizing for TCP" on page 32.
- The browser will automatically open up to six connections on your behalf.
- Number, size, and response time of each resource will affect the optimal number of shards.
- Client latency and bandwidth will affect the optimal number of shards.
- Domain sharding can hurt performance due to additional DNS lookups and TCP slow-start.

Domain sharding is a legitimate but also an imperfect optimization. Always begin with the minimum number of shards (none), and then carefully increase the number and measure the impact on your application metrics. In practice, very few sites actually benefit from more than a dozen connections, and if you do find yourself at the top end of that range, then you may see a much larger benefit by reducing the number of resources or consolidating them into fewer requests.

The extra overhead of DNS lookups and TCP slow-start affects high-latency clients the most, which means that mobile (3G and 4G) clients are often affected the most by overzealous use of domain sharding!

Measuring and Controlling Protocol Overhead

HTTP 0.9 started with a simple, one-line ASCII request to fetch a hypertext document, which incurred minimal overhead. HTTP 1.0 extended the protocol by adding the notion of request and response headers to allow both sides to exchange additional request and response metadata. Finally, HTTP 1.1 made this format a standard: headers are easily extensible by any server or client and are always sent as plain text to remain compatible with previous versions of HTTP.

Today, each browser-initiated HTTP request will carry an additional 500–800 bytes of HTTP metadata: user-agent string, accept and transfer headers that rarely change, caching directives, and so on. Even worse, the 500–800 bytes is optimistic, since it omits the largest offender: HTTP cookies, which are now commonly used for session management, personalization, analytics, and more. Combined, all of this uncompressed HTTP metadata can, and often does, add up to multiple kilobytes of protocol overhead for each and every HTTP request.

RFC 2616 (HTTP 1.1) does not define any limit on the size of the HTTP headers. However, in practice, many servers and proxies will try to enforce either an 8 KB or a 16 KB limit.

The growing list of HTTP headers is not bad in and of itself, as most headers exist for a good reason. However, the fact that all HTTP headers are transferred in plain text (without any compression), can lead to high overhead costs for each and every request, which can be a serious bottleneck for some applications. For example, the rise of API-driven web applications, which frequently communicate with compact serialized messages (e.g., JSON payloads) means that it is now not uncommon to see the HTTP overhead exceed the payload data by an order of magnitude:

```
$> curl --trace-ascii - -d'{"msg":"hello"}' http://www.igvita.com/api

== Info: Connected to www.igvita.com
=> Send header, 218 bytes ❶
POST /api HTTP/1.1
User-Agent: curl/7.24.0 (x86_64-apple-darwin12.0) libcurl/7.24.0 ...
Host: www.igvita.com
Accept: */*
Content-Length: 15 ❷
Content-Type: application/x-www-form-urlencoded
=> Send data, 15 bytes (0xf)
```

```
{"msg":"hello"}

<= Recv header, 134 bytes ❸
HTTP/1.1 204 No Content
Server: nginx/1.0.11
Via: HTTP/1.1 GWA
Date: Thu, 20 Sep 2012 05:41:30 GMT
Cache-Control: max-age=0, no-cache
```

❶ HTTP request headers: 218 bytes

❷ 15-byte application payload ({"msg":"hello"})

❸ 204 response from the server: 134 bytes

In the preceding example, our brief 15-character JSON message is wrapped in 352 bytes of HTTP headers, all transferred as plain text on the wire—96% protocol byte overhead, and that is the best case without any cookies. Reducing the transferred header data, which is highly repetitive and uncompressed, could save entire roundtrips of network latency and significantly improve the performance of many web applications.

> Cookies are a common performance bottleneck for many applications; many developers forget that they add significant overhead to each request. See "Eliminate Unnecessary Request Bytes" on page 238 for a full discussion.

Concatenation and Spriting

The fastest request is a request not made. Reducing the number of total requests is the best performance optimization, regardless of protocol used or application in question. However, if eliminating the request is not an option, then an alternative strategy for HTTP 1.x is to bundle multiple resources into a single network request:

Concatenation
    Multiple JavaScript or CSS files are combined into a single resource.

Spriting
    Multiple images are combined into a larger, composite image.

In the case of JavaScript and CSS, we can safely concatenate multiple files without affecting the behavior and the execution of the code as long as the execution order is maintained. Similarly, multiple images can be combined into an "image sprite," and CSS can then be used to select and position the appropriate parts of the sprite within the browser viewport. The benefits of both of these techniques are twofold:

Reduced protocol overhead

By combining files into a single resource, we eliminate the protocol overhead associated with each file, which, as we saw earlier, can easily add up to kilobytes of uncompressed data transfers.

Application-layer pipelining

The net result of both techniques, as far as byte delivery is concerned, is the same as if HTTP pipelining was available: data from multiple responses is streamed back to back, eliminating extra network latency. Hence, we have simply moved the pipelining logic one layer higher and into our application.

Both concatenation and spriting techniques are examples of content-aware application layer optimizations, which can yield significant performance improvements by reducing the networking overhead costs. However, these same techniques also introduce extra application complexity by requiring additional preprocessing, deployment considerations, and code (e.g., extra CSS markup for managing sprites). Further, bundling multiple independent resources may also have a significant *negative impact* on cache performance and execution speed of the page.

To understand why these techniques may hurt performance, consider the not-unusual case of an application with a few dozen individual JavaScript and CSS files, all combined into two requests in a production environment, one for the CSS and one for the JavaScript assets:

- All resources of the same type will live under the same URL (and cache key).
- Combined bundle may contain resources that are not required for the current page.
- A single update to any one individual file will require invalidating and downloading the full asset bundle, resulting in high byte overhead costs.
- Both JavaScript and CSS are parsed and executed only when the transfer is finished, potentially delaying the execution speed of your application.

In practice, most web applications are not single pages but collections of different views, each with different resource requirements but also with significant overlap: common CSS, JavaScript, and images. Hence, combining all assets into a single bundle often results in loading and processing of unnecessary bytes on the wire—although this can be seen as a form of pre-fetching, but at the cost of slower initial startup.

Updates are an even larger problem for many applications. A single update to an image sprite or a combined JavaScript file may result in hundreds of kilobytes of new data transfers. We sacrifice modularity and cache granularity, which can quickly backfire if there is high churn on the asset, and especially if the bundle is large. If such is the case for your application, consider separating the "stable core," such as frameworks and libraries, into separate bundles.

Memory use can also become a problem. In the case of image sprites, the browser must decode the entire image and keep it in memory, regardless of the actual size of displayed area. The browser does not magically clip the rest of the bitmap from memory!

Calculating Image Memory Requirements

All decoded images are stored as memory-backed RGBA bitmaps within the browser. In turn, each RGBA image pixel requires four bytes of memory: one byte each for red, green, and blue channels, and one byte for the alpha (transparency) channel. Hence, the total memory used is simply pixel width × pixel height × 4 bytes.

As an exercise, how much memory will a 800 × 600 pixel bitmap require?

800 × 600 × 4 bytes = 1,920,000 bytes ≈ 1.83 MB

On resource-constrained devices, such as mobile handsets, the memory overhead can quickly become your new bottleneck. This is especially true for image-heavy applications, such as games, which often depend on large numbers of image assets.

Finally, why would the execution speed be affected? Unfortunately, unlike HTML processing, which is parsed incrementally as soon as the bytes arrive on the client, both JavaScript and CSS parsing and execution is held back until the entire file is downloaded —neither JavaScript nor CSS processing models allow incremental execution.

CSS and JavaScript Bundle Size vs. Execution Performance

The larger the CSS bundle, the longer the browser will be blocked before it can construct the CSSOM, possibly delaying the first paint event of the page. Similarly, large JavaScript bundles may also negatively impact the execution speed of the page; small files allow "incremental" execution.

Unfortunately, there is no "ideal" size for a CSS or a JavaScript bundle. However, tests performed by the Google PageSpeed team indicate that 30–50 KB (compressed) is a good range to target per JavaScript bundle—large enough to mitigate some of the networking overhead associated with small individual files, but still allowing for incremental and tiered execution. Your results may vary based on type and number of scripts in use.

In summary, concatenation and spriting are application-layer optimizations for the limitations of the underlying HTTP 1.x protocol: lack of reliable pipelining support and high request overhead. Both techniques can deliver significant performance improvements when applied correctly, but at the cost of added application complexity and with many additional caveats for caching, update costs, and even speed of execution and rendering of the page. Apply these optimizations carefully, measure the results, and consider the following questions in the context of your own application:

- Is your application blocked on many small, individual resource downloads?
- Can your application benefit from selectively combining some requests?
- Will lost cache granularity negatively affect your users?
- Will combined image assets cause high memory overhead?
- Will the time to first render suffer from delayed execution?

Finding the right balance among all of these criteria is an imperfect science.

Optimizing Gmail Performance

Gmail is a JavaScript-heavy application that has always pushed the performance boundaries of all modern browsers. To speed up first-load performance, the team has tried a variety of techniques, which now include these:

- Separating and delivering first-paint critical CSS from the rest of the CSS
- Separating and delivering smaller JavaScript chunks for incremental execution
- Custom out-of-band update mechanism, in which the client downloads the new JavaScript in the background and the update is applied on page refresh

The size of the Gmail userbase turns a simple JavaScript update into a self-inflicted DoS attack, as all open browsers update their scripts. Instead, Gmail preloads the updated files in the background while the user is interacting with the older version of the page, which allows it to spread the load, and also to deliver a faster experience on next refresh. This process is repeated one or more times each day.

Then, to further accelerate the first-load experience, the team inlines the critical CSS and JavaScript into the HTML document itself and then incrementally loads the remaining JavaScript files in chunks to accelerate script execution—that's the progress bar that is shown as the site first loads!

Resource Inlining

Resource inlining is another popular optimization that helps reduce the number of outbound requests by embedding the resource within the document itself: JavaScript and CSS code can be included directly in the page via the appropriate script and style HTML blocks, and other resources, such as images and even audio or PDF files, can be inlined via the data URI scheme (*data:[mediatype][;base64],data*):

```
<img src="data:image/gif;base64,R0lGODlhAQABAIAAAAA
        AAAAAACH5BAAAAAAALAAAAAABAAEAAAICTAEAOw=="
    alt="1x1 transparent (GIF) pixel" />
```

 The previous example embeds a 1×1 transparent GIF pixel within the document, but any other MIME type, as long as the browser understands it, could be similarly inlined within the page: PDF, audio, video, etc. However, some browsers enforce a limit on the size of data URIs: IE8 has a maximum limit of 32 KB.

Data URIs are useful for small and ideally unique assets. When a resource is inlined within a page, it is by definition part of the page and cannot be cached individually by the browser, a CDN, or any caching proxy as a standalone resource. Hence, if the same resource is inlined across multiple pages, then the same resource will have to be transferred as part of each and every page, increasing the overall size of each page. Further, if the inlined resource is updated, then all pages on which it previously appeared must be invalidated and refetched by the client.

Finally, while text-based resources such as CSS and JavaScript are easily inlined directly into the page with no extra overhead, base64 encoding must be used for non-text assets, which adds a significant overhead: 33% byte expansion as compared with the original resource!

 Base64 encodes any byte stream into an ASCII string via 64 ASCII symbols, plus whitespace. In the process, base64 expands encoded stream by a factor of 4/3, incurring a 33% byte overhead.

In practice, a common rule of thumb is to consider inlining for resources under 1–2 KB, as resources below this threshold often incur higher HTTP overhead than the resource itself. However, if the inlined resource changes frequently, then this may lead to an unnecessarily high cache invalidation rate of host document: inlining is an imperfect science. A few criteria to consider if your application has many small, individual files:

- If the files are small, and limited to specific pages, then consider inlining.
- If the small files are frequently reused across pages, then consider bundling.
- If the small files have high update frequency, then keep them separate.
- Minimize the protocol overhead by reducing the size of HTTP cookies.

CHAPTER 12

HTTP 2.0

HTTP 2.0 will make our applications faster, simpler, and more robust—a rare combination—by allowing us to undo many of the HTTP 1.1 workarounds previously done within our applications and address these concerns within the transport layer itself. Even better, it also opens up a whole host of entirely new opportunities to optimize our applications and improve performance!

The primary goals for HTTP 2.0 are to reduce latency by enabling full request and response multiplexing, minimize protocol overhead via efficient compression of HTTP header fields, and add support for request prioritization and server push. To implement these requirements, there is a large supporting cast of other protocol enhancements, such as new flow control, error handling, and upgrade mechanisms, but these are the most important features that every web developer should understand and leverage in his applications.

HTTP 2.0 does not modify the application semantics of HTTP in any way. All the core concepts, such as HTTP methods, status codes, URIs, and header fields, remain in place. Instead, HTTP 2.0 modifies how the data is formatted (framed) and transported between the client and server, both of whom manage the entire process, and hides all the complexity from our applications within the new framing layer. As a result, all existing applications can be delivered without modification. That's the good news.

However, we are not just interested in delivering a working application; our goal is to deliver the best performance! HTTP 2.0 enables a number of new optimizations our applications can leverage, which were previously not possible, and our job is to make the best of them. Let's take a closer look under the hood.

Standard under construction

HTTP 2.0 is under active construction: core architectural designs, principles, and features are well defined, but the same cannot be said for specific, low-level implementation details. For this reason, our discussion will focus on the architecture and its implications, with a very brief look at the wire format—just enough to understand how the protocol works and its implications.

For the latest draft and status of the HTTP 2.0 standard, visit the IETF tracker (*http://tools.ietf.org/html/draft-ietf-httpbis-http2*).

History and Relationship to SPDY

SPDY is an experimental protocol, developed at Google and announced in mid-2009, whose primary goal was to try to reduce the load latency of web pages by addressing some of the well-known performance limitations of HTTP 1.1. Specifically, the outlined project goals were set as follows:

- Target a 50% reduction in page load time (PLT).
- Avoid the need for any changes to content by website authors.
- Minimize deployment complexity, avoid changes in network infrastructure.
- Develop this new protocol in partnership with the open-source community.
- Gather real performance data to (in)validate the experimental protocol.

To achieve the 50% PLT improvement, SPDY aimed to make more efficient use of the underlying TCP connection by introducing a new binary framing layer to enable request and response multiplexing, prioritization, and to minimize and eliminate unnecessary network latency; see "Latency as a Performance Bottleneck" on page 177.

Not long after the initial announcement, Mike Belshe and Roberto Peon, both software engineers at Google, shared their first results, documentation, and source code for the experimental implementation of the new SPDY protocol:

> So far we have only tested SPDY in lab conditions. The initial results are very encouraging: when we download the top 25 websites over simulated home network connections, we see a significant improvement in performance—pages loaded up to 55% faster.
>
> — A 2x Faster Web
> *Chromium Blog*

Fast-forward a few years to 2012, and the new experimental protocol was supported in Chrome, Firefox, and Opera, and many large web destinations (e.g., Google, Twitter,

Facebook) were offering SPDY to compatible clients. In other words, SPDY proved to offer great performance benefits and was on track to become a de facto standard through growing industry adoption. As a result, the HTTP Working Group (HTTP-WG) kicked off the new HTTP 2.0 effort in early 2012 to take the lessons learned from SPDY and apply them to the official standard.

The Road to HTTP 2.0

SPDY was the catalyst for HTTP 2.0, but SPDY *is not* HTTP 2.0. An open call for HTTP 2.0 proposals was made in early 2012, and following much discussion within the HTTP-WG, the SPDY specification was adopted as a starting point for further work on the standard. Since then, many changes and improvements have been and will continue to be made to the official HTTP 2.0 standard.

However, before we get too far ahead, it is worth reviewing the drafted charter for HTTP 2.0, as it highlights the scope and the key design criteria of the protocol:

It is expected that HTTP/2.0 will:

- Substantially and measurably improve end-user perceived latency in most cases, over HTTP 1.1 using TCP.

- Address the "head of line blocking" problem in HTTP.

- Not require multiple connections to a server to enable parallelism, thus improving its use of TCP, especially regarding congestion control.

- Retain the semantics of HTTP 1.1, leveraging existing documentation, including (but not limited to) HTTP methods, status codes, URIs, and where appropriate, header fields.

- Clearly define how HTTP 2.0 interacts with HTTP 1.x, especially in intermediaries.

- Clearly identify any new extensibility points and policy for their appropriate use.

The resulting specification(s) are expected to meet these goals for common existing deployments of HTTP; in particular, Web browsing (desktop and mobile), non-browsers ("HTTP APIs"), Web serving (at a variety of scales), and intermediation (by proxies, corporate firewalls, "reverse" proxies and Content Delivery Networks). Likewise, current and future semantic extensions to HTTP/1.x (e.g., headers, methods, status codes, cache directives) should be supported in the new protocol.

— HTTPbis WG charter
HTTP 2.0

In short, HTTP 2.0 aims to address the well-known performance limitations of preceding standards, but it is also extending, not replacing, the previous 1.x standards. The application semantics of HTTP are the same, and no changes are being made to the offered functionality or core concepts such as HTTP methods, status codes, URIs, and header fields; these changes are explicitly out of scope. With that in mind, is the "2.0" really warranted?

The reason for the major revision increment to 2.0 is due to the change in how the data is exchanged between the client and server. To achieve the outlined performance goals, HTTP 2.0 adds a new binary framing layer, which is not backward compatible with previous HTTP 1.x servers and clients. Hence, 2.0.

 Unless you are implementing a web server, or a custom client, by working with raw TCP sockets, then chances are you may not even notice any of the actual technical changes in HTTP 2.0: all the new, low-level framing is performed by the browser and server on your behalf. Perhaps the only difference may be the availability of new and optional API capabilities like server push!

Finally, it is important to discuss the timeline for HTTP 2.0. Developing a major revision of a protocol underlying all web communication is a nontrivial task, and one that requires a lot of careful thought, experimentation, and coordination. As such, crystal ball gazing for HTTP 2.0 timelines is dangerous business: it will be ready when it's ready. Having said that, the HTTP-WG is making good progress, and the current official milestones are set as follows:

- March 2012: Call for proposals for HTTP 2.0
- September 2012: First draft of HTTP 2.0
- July 2013: First implementation draft of HTTP 2.0
- April 2014: Working Group last call for HTTP 2.0
- November 2014: Submit HTTP 2.0 to IESG as a Proposed Standard

The big gap between 2012 and 2014 is where the bulk of the editorial and experimental work is planned to happen. Depending on the progress, and the feedback from implementers and the industry at large, the dates will be adjusted as needed. The good news is, as of 2013, the schedule looks well on track!

Coevolution of HTTP 2.0 and SPDY

The HTTP working group adopted the SPDY v2 draft as the starting point for the HTTP 2.0 standard in the summer of 2012. However, the work on SPDY did not stop when this happened. Instead, SPDY continued to coevolve in parallel:

- SPDY v3 was released in 2012 with updated framing format and first implementation of flow control.

- SPDY v4 will be released in 2013–2014 with updated framing format (once more), improved prioritization, flow control, and server push implementations.

The motivation to continue development of SPDY is simple: it is a vehicle for experimenting with new features and proposals for HTTP 2.0. What looks good on paper may not work in practice and vice versa, and SPDY offered a route to test and evaluate each proposal before its inclusion in the HTTP 2.0 standard.

This incremental development process and coevolution of SPDY and HTTP 2.0 results in a lot of work for the implementers, but in practice, it also offers many benefits: more robust and extensively tested specification and client and server implementations that are also coevolving in parallel. In fact, by the time HTTP 2.0 is marked as "ready," we will already have well-tested implementations of popular clients and servers! At which point, SPDY can be retired and HTTP 2.0 will take center stage.

Design and Technical Goals

HTTP 1.x was intentionally designed for simplicity of implementation: HTTP 0.9 was a one-line protocol to bootstrap the World Wide Web; HTTP 1.0 documented the popular extensions to 0.9 in an informational standard; HTTP 1.1 introduced an official IETF standard; see Chapter 9. As such, HTTP 0.9-1.x delivered exactly what it set out to do: HTTP is one of the most ubiquitous and widely adopted application protocols on the Internet.

Unfortunately, implementation simplicity also came at a cost of application performance, which is the exact gap that HTTP 2.0 is designed to fill:

> The HTTP/2.0 encapsulation enables more efficient use of network resources and reduced perception of latency by allowing header field compression and multiple concurrent messages on the same connection. It also introduces unsolicited push of representations from servers to clients.
>
> — HTTP/2.0
> *Draft 4*

HTTP 2.0 is a work in progress, which means that the specific details of how the bits are encoded within each frame, the names of individual fields, and similar low-level details may change. However, while the "how" will continue to evolve, the core design and technical goals are what matters most for our discussion; these are well understood and agreed upon.

Binary Framing Layer

At the core of all performance enhancements of HTTP 2.0 is the new *binary framing layer* (Figure 12-1), which dictates how the HTTP messages are encapsulated and transferred between the client and server.

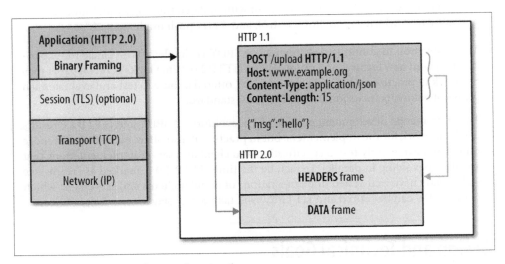

Figure 12-1. HTTP 2.0 binary framing layer

The "layer" refers to a design choice to introduce a new mechanism between the socket interface and the higher HTTP API exposed to our applications: the HTTP semantics, such as verbs, methods, and headers, are unaffected, but the way they are encoded while in transit is what's different. Unlike the newline delimited plaintext HTTP 1.x protocol, all HTTP 2.0 communication is split into smaller messages and frames, each of which is encoded in binary format.

As a result, both client and server must use the new binary encoding mechanism to understand each other: an HTTP 1.x client won't understand an HTTP 2.0 only server, and vice versa. Thankfully, our applications remain blissfully unaware of all these changes, as the client and server perform all the necessary framing work on our behalf.

 HTTPS is another great example of binary framing in action: all HTTP messages are transparently encoded and decoded on our behalf ("TLS Record Protocol" on page 62), enabling secure communication between the client and server, without requiring any modifications of our applications. HTTP 2.0 works in a similar way.

Streams, Messages, and Frames

The introduction of the new binary framing mechanism changes how the data is exchanged (Figure 12-2) between the client and server. To describe this process, we need to introduce some new HTTP 2.0 terminology:

Stream

A bidirectional flow of bytes within an established connection.

Message

A complete sequence of frames that map to a logical message.

Frame

The smallest unit of communication in HTTP 2.0, each containing a frame header, which at minimum identifies the stream to which the frame belongs.

All HTTP 2.0 communication is performed within a connection that can carry any number of bidirectional streams. In turn, each stream communicates in messages, which consist of one or multiple frames, each of which may be interleaved and then reassembled via the embedded stream identifier in the header of each individual frame.

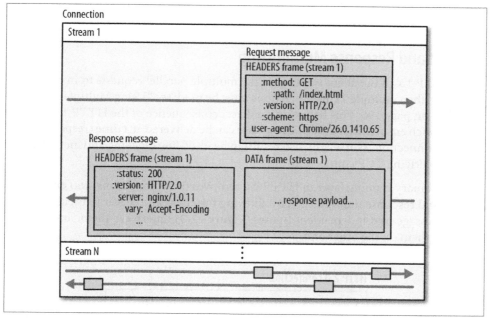

Figure 12-2. HTTP 2.0 streams, messages, and frames

 All HTTP 2.0 frames use binary encoding, and header data is compressed. As such, the preceding diagram illustrates the relationship between streams, messages, and frames, not their exact encoding on the wire—for that, skip to "Brief Introduction to Binary Framing" on page 226.

There is a lot of information packed into those few terse sentences. Let's review it one more time. The terminology of streams, messages, and frames is essential knowledge for understanding HTTP 2.0:

- All *communication* is performed with a single TCP connection.
- The *stream* is a virtual channel within a connection, which carries bidirectional messages. Each stream has a unique integer identifier (1, 2, ..., N).
- The *message* is a logical HTTP message, such as a request, or response, which consists of one or more frames.
- The *frame* is the smallest unit of communication, which carries a specific type of data—e.g., HTTP headers, payload, and so on.

In short, HTTP 2.0 breaks down the HTTP protocol communication into small individual frames, which map to messages within a logical stream. In turn, many streams can be exchanging messages, in parallel, within a single TCP connection.

Request and Response Multiplexing

With HTTP 1.x, if the client wants to make multiple parallel requests to improve performance, then multiple TCP connections must be used; see "Using Multiple TCP Connections" on page 196. This behavior is a direct consequence of the HTTP 1.x delivery model, which ensures that only one response can be delivered at a time (response queuing) per connection. Worse, this also results in head-of-line blocking and inefficient use of the underlying TCP connection.

The new binary framing layer in HTTP 2.0 removes these limitations, and enables full request and response multiplexing, by allowing the client and server to break down an HTTP message into independent frames (Figure 12-3), interleave them, and then reassemble them on the other end.

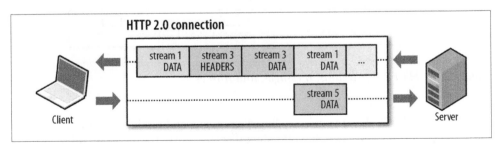

Figure 12-3. HTTP 2.0 request and response multiplexing within a shared connection

The snapshot in Figure 12-3 captures multiple streams in flight within the same connection: the client is transmitting a DATA frame (stream 5) to the server, while the server is transmitting an interleaved sequence of frames to the client for streams 1 and 3. As a result, there are three parallel request-response exchanges in flight!

The ability to break down an HTTP message into independent frames, interleave them, and then reassemble them on the other end is the single most important enhancement of HTTP 2.0. In fact, it introduces a ripple effect of numerous performance benefits across the entire stack of all web technologies, enabling us to do the following:

- Interleave multiple *requests* in parallel without blocking on any one
- Interleave multiple *responses* in parallel without blocking on any one
- Use a single *single connection* to deliver multiple requests and responses in parallel
- Deliver lower page load times by eliminating unnecessary latency
- Remove unnecessary HTTP 1.x workarounds from our application code
- *And much more...*

The new binary framing layer in HTTP 2.0 resolves the head-of-line blocking problem found in HTTP 1.1 and eliminates the need for multiple connections to enable parallel processing and delivery of requests and responses. As a result, this makes our applications faster, simpler, and cheaper to deploy.

Support for request and response multiplexing allows us to eliminate many of the HTTP 1.x workarounds, such as concatenated files, image sprites, and domain sharding; see "Optimizing for HTTP 1.x" on page 241. Similarly, by lowering the number of required TCP connections, HTTP 2.0 also lowers the CPU and memory costs for both the client and server.

Request Prioritization

Once an HTTP message can be split into many individual frames, the exact order in which the frames are interleaved and delivered can be optimized to further improve the performance of our applications. To facilitate this, each stream can be assigned a 31-bit priority value:

- 0 represents the highest priority stream.
- 2^{31} - 1 represents the lowest priority stream.

With priorities in place, the client and server can apply different strategies to process individual streams, messages, and frames in an optimal order: the server can prioritize stream processing by controlling the allocation of resources (CPU, memory, bandwidth), and once the response data is available, prioritize delivery of high-priority frames to the client.

Browser Request Prioritization and HTTP 2.0

Not all resources have equal priority when rendering a page in the browser: the HTML document itself is critical to construct the DOM; the CSS is required to construct the CSSOM; both DOM and CSSOM construction can be blocked on JavaScript resources (see "DOM, CSSOM, and JavaScript" on page 168); and remaining resources, such as images, are often fetched with lower priority.

To accelerate the load time of the page, all modern browsers prioritize requests based on type of asset, its location on the page, and even learned priority from previous visits —e.g., if the rendering was blocked on a certain asset in a previous visit, then the same asset may be prioritized higher in the future.

With HTTP 1.x, the browser has limited ability to leverage above priority data: the protocol does not support multiplexing, and there is no way to communicate request priority to the server. Instead, it must rely on use of parallel connections, which enables limited parallelism of up to six requests per origin. As a result, requests are queued on the client until a connection is available, which adds unnecessary network latency. In theory, "HTTP Pipelining" on page 192 tried to partially address this problem, but in practice it has failed to gain adoption.

HTTP 2.0 resolves all these inefficiencies: the browser can immediately dispatch each request the moment the resource is discovered, specify the priority of each stream, and let the server determine the optimal response delivery. This eliminates unnecessary request queuing latency and allows us to make the most efficient use of each connection.

HTTP 2.0 does not specify any specific algorithm for dealing with priorities, it just provides the mechanism by which the priority data can be exchanged between client and server. As such, priorities are hints, and the prioritization strategy can vary based on the implementation of client and server: the client should provide good priority data, and the server should adapt its processing and delivery based on indicated stream priorities.

As a result, while you may not control the quality of sent priority data from the client, chances are you can control the server; choose your HTTP 2.0 server carefully! To illustrate the point, let's consider the following questions:

- What if the server disregards all priority information?
- Should higher-priority streams always take precedence?
- Are there cases where different priority streams should be interleaved?

If the server disregards all priority information, then it may unintentionally slow the application—e.g., block browser rendering—which may be waiting for critical CSS and JavaScript, by sending images instead. However, dictating a strict priority ordering may also generate suboptimal scenarios, as it may reintroduce the head-of-line blocking problem—e.g., a single slow request unnecessarily blocking delivery of other resources.

Frames from multiple priority levels can and should be interleaved by the server. Where possible, high-priority streams should be given precedence, both during the processing stage and with respect to the bandwidth allocation between client and server. However, to make the best use of the underlying connection, a mix of priority levels is required.

One Connection Per Origin

With the new binary framing mechanism in place, HTTP 2.0 no longer needs multiple TCP connections to multiplex streams in parallel; each stream is split into many frames, which can be interleaved and prioritized. As a result, all HTTP 2.0 connections are persistent, and only one connection should be used between the client and server.

> Through lab measurements, we have seen consistent latency benefits by using fewer connections from the client. The overall number of packets sent by HTTP 2.0 can be as much as 40% less than HTTP. Handling large numbers of concurrent connections on the server also does become a scalability problem, and HTTP 2.0 reduces this load.
>
> — HTTP/2.0
> *Draft 2*

One connection per origin significantly reduces the associated overhead: fewer sockets to manage along the connection path, smaller memory footprint, and better connection throughput. Plus, many other benefits at all layers of the stack:

- Consistent prioritization between all streams
- Better compression through use of a single compression context
- Improved impact on network congestion due to fewer TCP connections
- Less time in slow-start and faster congestion and loss recovery

 Most HTTP transfers are short and bursty, whereas TCP is optimized for long-lived, bulk data transfers. By reusing the same connection between all streams, HTTP 2.0 is able to make more efficient use of the TCP connection.

The move to HTTP 2.0 should not only reduce the network latency, but also help improve throughput and reduce the operational costs!

Packet Loss, high-RTT Links, and HTTP 2.0 Performance

Wait, I hear you say, we listed the benefits of using one TCP connection per origin, but aren't there some potential downsides? Yes, there are.

- We have eliminated head-of-line blocking from HTTP, but there is still head-of-line blocking at the TCP level (see "Head-of-Line Blocking" on page 30).
- Effects of bandwidth-delay product may limit connection throughput if TCP window scaling is disabled.
- When packet loss occurs, the TCP congestion window size is reduced (see "Congestion Avoidance" on page 26), which reduces the maximum throughput of the entire connection.

Each of the items in this list may adversely affect both the throughput and latency performance of an HTTP 2.0 connection. However, despite these limitations, experimental evidence shows that the use of a single TCP connection is still the best deployment strategy for HTTP 2.0:

> In tests so far, the negative effects of head-of-line blocking (especially in the presence of packet loss) is outweighed by the benefits of compression and prioritization.

> — HTTP/2.0
> *Draft 2*

As with all performance optimization processes, the moment you remove one performance bottleneck, you unlock the next one. In the case of HTTP 2.0, TCP may be it. Which is why, once again, a well-tuned TCP stack on the server is such a critical optimization criteria for HTTP 2.0.

There is ongoing research to address these concerns and to improve TCP performance in general: TCP Fast Open, Proportional Rate Reduction, increased initial congestion window, and more. Having said that, it is important to acknowledge that HTTP 2.0, like its predecessors, does not mandate the use of TCP. Other transports, such as UDP, are not outside the realm of possibility.

Flow Control

Multiplexing multiple streams over the same TCP connection introduces contention for shared bandwidth resources. Stream priorities can help determine the relative order of delivery, but priorities alone are insufficient to control how the resource allocation is performed between the streams or multiple connections. To address this, HTTP 2.0 provides a simple mechanism for stream and connection flow control:

- Flow control is hop-by-hop, not end-to-end.
- Flow control is based on window update frames: receiver advertises how many bytes it is prepared to receive on a stream and for the entire connection.
- Flow control window size is updated by a `WINDOW_UPDATE` frame, which specifies the stream ID and the window size increment value.
- Flow control is directional: receiver may choose to set any window size that it desires for each stream and for the entire connection.
- Flow control can be disabled by a receiver, both for an individual stream or for the entire connection.

 When the HTTP 2.0 connection is established, the client and server exchange `SETTINGS` frames, which set the flow control window sizes in both directions. Optionally, either side can also disable flow control on an individual stream or the entire connection.

Does the preceding list remind you of TCP flow control? It should; the mechanism is effectively identical—see "Flow Control" on page 17. However, because TCP flow control cannot differentiate among the many streams within a single HTTP 2.0 connection, it is insufficient on its own. Hence the reason for HTTP 2.0 flow control.

The HTTP 2.0 standard does not specify any specific algorithm, values, or when the `WINDOW_UPDATE` frames should be sent: the implementers are able to select their own algorithm to match their use case and deliver the best performance.

 In addition to priority, which determines the relative order of delivery, flow control can regulate the amount of resources consumed by each stream within an HTTP 2.0 connection: the receiver can advertise a lower window size on a specific stream to limit the rate at which the data is delivered!

Server Push

A powerful new feature of HTTP 2.0 is the ability of the server to send multiple replies for a single client request. That is, in addition to the response for the original request, the server can *push* additional resources to the client (Figure 12-4), without the client having to explicitly request each one!

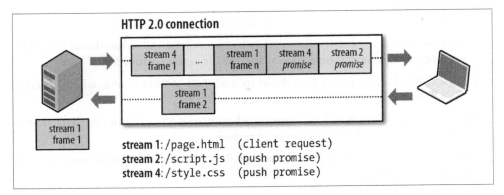

Figure 12-4. Server initiates new streams (promises) for push resources

 When the HTTP 2.0 connection is established, the client and server exchange SETTINGS frames, which can limit the maximum number of concurrent streams in both directions. As a result, the client can limit the number of pushed streams or disable server push entirely by setting this value to zero.

Why would we need such a mechanism? A typical web application consists of dozens of resources, all of which are discovered by the client by examining the document provided by the server. As a result, why not eliminate the extra latency and let the server push the associated resources to the client ahead of time? The server already knows which resources the client will require; that's server push. In fact, if you have ever inlined a CSS, JavaScript, or any other asset via a data URI (see "Resource Inlining" on page 204), then you already have hands-on experience with server push!

By manually inlining the resource into the document, we are, in effect, pushing that resource to the client, without waiting for the client to request it. The only difference with HTTP 2.0 is that we can now move this workflow out of the application and into the HTTP protocol itself, which offers important benefits:

- Pushed resources can be cached by the client.
- Pushed resources can be declined by the client.
- Pushed resources can be reused across different pages.
- Pushed resources can be prioritized by the server.

All pushed resources are subject to the same-origin policy. As a result, the server cannot push arbitrary third-party content to the client; the server must be authoritative for the provided content.

In effect, server push obsoletes most of the cases where inlining is used with HTTP 1.x. The only case where direct resource inlining still makes sense is if the inlined resource is needed on only a single page, and the resource does not incur high encoding overhead; see "Resource Inlining" on page 204. In all other cases, your application should be using HTTP 2.0 server push!

PUSH_PROMISE

All server push streams are initiated via a PUSH_PROMISE frame, which signals the server's intent to push the described resource to the client, in addition to the response for the original request. The PUSH_PROMISE frames contain just the HTTP headers of the promised resource.

Once the client receives a PUSH_PROMISE frame, it has the option to decline the stream if it wants to (e.g., the resource is already in cache), which is an important improvement over HTTP 1.x. Resource inlining, which is a popular "optimization" for HTTP 1.x, is equivalent to a "forced push": the client cannot cancel it, and it also cannot individually cache the inlined resource.

Finally, a few restrictions on server push. First, the server must respect the request-response cycle and push resources only in response to a request; the server cannot initiate server push streams arbitrarily. Second, PUSH_PROMISE frames must be sent before returning the response to eliminate race conditions with the client—e.g., the client requesting the same resource the server is about to push.

Implementing HTTP 2.0 server push

Server push opens many new possibilities for optimized delivery of our applications. However, how does the server determine which resources can or should be pushed? As with prioritization, the HTTP 2.0 standard does not specify any specific algorithm and the decision is left to the implementers. As a result, there are many possible strategies, each of which can be tailored to the context of the application or the server in use:

- The application can explicitly initiate server push within its application code. This requires tight coupling with the HTTP 2.0 server in use but provides full control to the developer.

- The application can signal to the server the associated resources it wants pushed via an additional HTTP header. This decouples the application from the HTTP 2.0

server API—e.g., Apache's mod_spdy looks for X-Associated-Content header, which lists the resources to be pushed.

- The server can automatically learn the associated resources without relying on the application. The server can parse the document and infer the resources to be pushed, or it can analyze the incoming traffic and make the appropriate decisions—e.g., the server can collect the dependency data based on the Referrer header, and then automatically push the critical resources to the client.

This is not a complete list of strategies, but it illustrates the wide range of possibilities: from hands on with the low-level API and all the way through to fully automated implementation. Similarly, should the server push the same resources every time, or could it implement a smarter strategy? The server can be smart and try to infer which resources are in cache based on its own model, client cookie, or another mechanism, and act accordingly. Long story short, server push opens up a lot of new opportunities for innovation.

Finally, it is important to note that pushed resources go directly into the client's cache, just as if the client initiated the request. There is no client-side API, or JavaScript callbacks, that serve as notifications that a push resource has arrived. The entire mechanism is transparent to web applications running within the browser.

Header Compression

Each HTTP transfer carries a set of headers that describe the transferred resource and its properties. In HTTP 1.x, this metadata is always sent as plain text and adds anywhere from 500–800 bytes of overhead per request, and kilobytes more if HTTP cookies are required; see "Measuring and Controlling Protocol Overhead" on page 200. To reduce this overhead and improve performance, HTTP 2.0 compresses header metadata:

- Instead of retransmitting the same data on each request and response, HTTP 2.0 uses "header tables" on both the client and server to track and store previously sent key-value pairs.

- Header tables persist for the entire HTTP 2.0 connection and are incrementally updated both by the client and server.

- Each new header key-value pair is either appended to the existing table or replaces a previous value in the table.

As a result, both sides of the HTTP 2.0 connection know which headers have been sent, and their previous values, which allows a new set of headers to be coded as a simple difference (Figure 12-5) from the previous set.

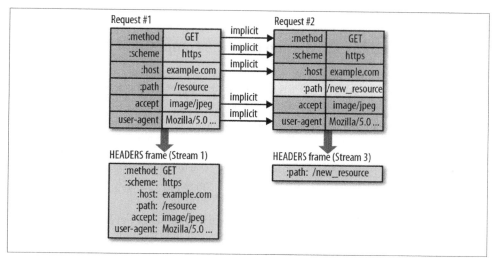

Figure 12-5. Differential coding of HTTP 2.0 headers

 The definitions of the request and response header fields in HTTP 2.0 remain unchanged, with a few minor exceptions: all header keys are lowercase, and the request line is now split into individual :meth od, :scheme, :host, and :path key-value pairs.

In the previous example, the second request needs to communicate only the single path header that has changed between requests; all other headers are inherited from the previous working set. As a result, HTTP 2.0 avoids transmitting redundant header data, which significantly reduces the overhead of each request.

Common key-value pairs that rarely change throughout the lifetime of a connection (e.g., user-agent, accept header, and so on), need to be transmitted only once. In fact, if no headers change between requests (e.g., a polling request requesting the same re-source), then the header overhead is zero bytes. All headers are automatically inherited from the previous request!

SPDY, CRIME, and HTTP 2.0 Compression

Early versions of SPDY used zlib, with a custom dictionary, to compress all HTTP headers, which delivered 85%–88% reduction in the size of the transferred header data, and a significant improvement in page load time latency:

> On the lower-bandwidth DSL link, in which the upload link is only 375 Kbps, request header compression in particular, led to significant page load time improvements for certain sites (i.e., those that issued large number of resource requests). We found a reduction of 45–1142 ms in page load time simply due to header compression.
>
> — SPDY whitepaper
> *chromium.org*

However, in the summer of 2012, a "CRIME" security attack was published against TLS and SPDY compression algorithms, which could result in session hijacking. As a result, the zlib compression algorithm was disabled and was eventually replaced with the new indexing table algorithm described earlier, which addresses the security concerns and, in practice, delivers comparable performance.

For full details of the HTTP 2.0 compression algorithm, see *http://tools.ietf.org/html/ draft-ietf-httpbis-header-compression*.

Efficient HTTP 2.0 Upgrade and Discovery

The switch to HTTP 2.0 cannot happen overnight: millions of servers must be updated to use the new binary framing, and billions of clients must similarly update their browsers and networking libraries.

The good news is, most modern browsers use efficient background update mechanisms, which will enable HTTP 2.0 support quickly and with minimal intervention for a large portion of existing users. However, despite this, some users will be stuck on older browsers, and servers and intermediaries will also have to be updated to support HTTP 2.0, which is a much longer, and labor- and capital-intensive, process.

HTTP 1.x will be around for at least another decade, and most servers and clients will have to support both 1.x and 2.0 standards. As a result, an HTTP 2.0 capable client must be able to discover whether the server, and any and all intermediaries, support the HTTP 2.0 protocol when initiating a new connection. There are three cases to consider:

- Initiating a new HTTPS connection via TLS and ALPN
- Initiating a new HTTP connection *with* prior knowledge
- Initiating a new HTTP connection *without* prior knowledge

Application Layer Protocol Negotiation (ALPN) is used to discover and negotiate HTTP 2.0 support as part of the regular HTTPS negotiation; see "TLS Handshake" on page 50 and "Application Layer Protocol Negotiation (ALPN)" on page 53. Reducing network latency is a critical criteria for HTTP 2.0, and for this reason ALPN negotiation is always used when establishing an HTTPS connection.

Establishing an HTTP 2.0 connection over a regular, non-encrypted channel will require a bit more work. Because both HTTP 1.0 and HTTP 2.0 run on the same port (80), in absence of any other information about server support for HTTP 2.0, the client will have to use the *HTTP Upgrade* mechanism to negotiate the appropriate protocol:

```
GET /page HTTP/1.1
Host: server.example.com
Connection: Upgrade, HTTP2-Settings
Upgrade: HTTP/2.0 ❶
HTTP2-Settings: (SETTINGS payload) ❷

HTTP/1.1 200 OK ❸
Content-length: 243
Content-type: text/html

(... HTTP 1.1 response ...)

        (or)

HTTP/1.1 101 Switching Protocols ❹
Connection: Upgrade
Upgrade: HTTP/2.0

(... HTTP 2.0 response ...)
```

❶ Initial HTTP 1.1 request with HTTP 2.0 upgrade header

❷ Base64 URL encoding of HTTP/2.0 SETTINGS payload

❸ Server declines upgrade, returns response via HTTP 1.1

❹ Server accepts HTTP 2.0 upgrade, switches to new framing

Using the preceding Upgrade flow, if the server does not support HTTP 2.0, then it can immediately respond to the request with HTTP 1.1 response. Alternatively, it can confirm the HTTP 2.0 upgrade by returning the 101 Switching Protocols response in HTTP 1.1 format and then immediately switch to HTTP 2.0 and return the response using the new binary framing protocol. In either case, no extra roundtrips are incurred.

To confirm that both the server and client are knowingly electing to speak HTTP 2.0, both also have to send a "connection header," which is a well-known sequence of bytes defined in the standard. This exchange acts as a "fail-fast" mechanism to avoid clients, servers, and intermediaries that sometimes accept the requested upgrade without understanding the new protocol. This exchange does not incur any extra roundtrips, just a few extra bytes at the beginning of the connection.

Finally, if the client chooses to, it may also remember or obtain the information about HTTP 2.0 support through some other means—e.g., DNS record, manual configuration, and so on—instead of having to rely on the Upgrade workflow. Armed with this knowledge, it may choose to send HTTP 2.0 frames right from the start, over an unencrypted channel, and hope for the best. In the worst case, the connection will fail and the client will fall back to Upgrade workflow or switch to a TLS tunnel with ALPN negotiation.

Deploying HTTP 2.0 with TLS and ALPN

Prior knowledge of HTTP 2.0 support on the server does not guarantee that the connection will be established reliably next time around. When communicating in the clear, the support for HTTP 2.0 must be present end to end, and if any of the intermediaries fail this criteria, then the connection may not succeed.

As a result, while HTTP 2.0 does not require the use of TLS, in practice, it is the most reliable way to deploy it in the presence of large number of existing intermediaries; see "Proxies, Intermediaries, TLS, and New Protocols on the Web" on page 50. For best results, any HTTP 2.0 deployment should start with and support TLS with ALPN negotiation, in addition to the regular HTTP Upgrade workflow.

Brief Introduction to Binary Framing

At the core of all HTTP 2.0 improvements is the new binary, length-prefixed framing layer. Compared with the newline delimited plaintext HTTP 1.x, binary framing offers more compact representation and is both easier and more efficient to process in code.

Once an HTTP 2.0 connection is established, the client and server communicate by exchanging *frames*, which serve as the smallest unit of communication within the protocol. All frames share a common 8-byte header (Figure 12-6), which contains the length of the frame, its type, a bit field for flags, and a 31-bit stream identifier.

Bit	+0..7	+8..15	+16..23	+24..31
0	Length		Type	Flags
32	R	Stream Identifier		
...	Frame Payload			

Figure 12-6. Common 8-byte frame header

- The 16-bit length prefix tells us that a single frame can carry $2^{16} - 1$ bytes of data: ~64 KB, which excludes the 8-byte header size.
- The 8-bit type field determines how the rest of the frame is interpreted.
- The 8-bit flags field allows different frame types to define frame-specific messaging flags.
- The 1-bit reserved field is always set to 0.
- The 31-bit stream identifier uniquely identifies the HTTP 2.0 stream.

 When debugging HTTP 2.0 traffic, some may prefer to work with their favorite hex viewer. Alternatively, there are plug-ins for Wireshark and similar tools that present a much easier and human-friendly representation—e.g., Google Chrome allows you to inspect the decoded exchange in chrome://internals#spdy.

Given this knowledge of the shared HTTP 2.0 frame header, we can now write a simple parser that can examine any HTTP 2.0 bytestream and identify different frame types, report their flags, and report the length of each by examining the first eight bytes of every frame. Further, because each frame is length-prefixed, the parser can skip ahead to the beginning of the next frame both quickly and efficiently, a big performance improvement over HTTP 1.x.

Once the frame type is known, the remainder of the frame can be interpreted by the parser. The HTTP 2.0 standard defines the following types:

DATA   Used to transport HTTP message bodies

HEADERS   Used to communicate additional header fields for a stream

PRIORITY   Used to assign or reassign priority of referenced resource

RST_STREAM   Used to signal abnormal termination of a stream

SETTINGS	Used to signal configuration data about how two endpoints may communicate
PUSH_PROMISE	Used to signal a promise to create a stream and serve referenced resource
PING	Used to measure the roundtrip time and perform "liveness" checks
GOAWAY	Used to inform the peer to stop creating streams for current connection
WINDOW_UPDATE	Used to implement flow control on a per-stream or per-connection basis
CONTINUATION	Used to continue a sequence of header block fragments

The GOAWAY frame allows the server to indicate to the client the last processed stream ID, which eliminates a number of request races and allows the browser to intelligently retry or cancel "in-flight" requests. An important and necessary feature for enabling safe multiplexing!

The exact implementation of the preceding taxonomy of frames is mostly only relevant to server and client implementers, who need to worry about the semantics of flow control, error handling, connection termination, and many other details. And the good news is that all of these are covered extensively in the official standard. If you are curious, check out the latest draft.

Having said that, even though the framing layer is hidden from our applications, it is useful for us to go just one step further and look at the two most common workflows: initiating a new stream and exchanging application data. Having an intuition for how a request, or a response, is translated into individual frames can help answer a lot of questions about HTTP 2.0 performance.

Fixed vs. Variable Length Fields and HTTP 2.0

HTTP 2.0 uses fixed-length fields exclusively. The overhead of an HTTP 2.0 frame is low (8-byte header for a data frame), and variable-length encoding savings do not offset the required complexity for the parsers, nor do they have a significant impact on the used bandwidth or latency of the exchange.

If variable length encoding could reduce the overhead by 50%, for a 1,400-byte network packet on a 1 Mbps connection, this would amount to just 4 saved bytes (0.3%) and less than 100 nanoseconds of latency for a single frame.

Initiating a New Stream

Before any application data can be sent, a new stream must be created and the appropriate metadata, such as stream priority and HTTP headers, must be sent. With HTTP 2.0, both the client and the server can initiate new streams; hence there are two cases to consider:

- The client initiates a new request by sending a HEADERS frame (Figure 12-7), which includes the common header with a new stream ID, an optional 31-bit priority value, and a set of HTTP header key-value pairs within its payload.

- The server initiates a push stream by sending a PUSH_PROMISE frame, which is effectively identical to a HEADERS frame, except that it carries an extra "promised stream ID," instead of a priority value.

Bit		+0..7	+8..15	+16..23	+24..31
0		Length		Type (1)	Flags
32	R	Stream Identifier			
64	R	Priority			
...		Header Block			

Figure 12-7. HEADERS frame with optional priority

Both types of frames are used to communicate only the metadata about each new stream; the payload is delivered independently, within the DATA frames. Also, because both sides can initiate new streams, the stream counters are offset: client-initiated streams have even-numbered stream IDs and server-initiated streams have odd-numbered stream IDs. This offset eliminates collisions in stream IDs between the server and the client: each keeps a simple counter, and increments it when initiating a new stream.

Because stream metadata delivery is separate from application data, the client and server can manage each with different priorities—e.g., "control traffic" can be delivered with higher priority, and flow control is applied only to DATA frames.

Sending Application Data

Once a new stream is created and the HTTP headers are sent, DATA frames (Figure 12-8) are used to send the application payload if one is present. The payload can be split between multiple DATA frames, with the last frame indicating the end of message by toggling the END_STREAM flag in the header of the frame.

Bit	+0..7		+8..15	+16..23	+24..31
0		Length		Type (0)	Flags
32	R		Stream Identifier		
...			HTTP payload		

Figure 12-8. DATA frame

No extra encoding or compression is performed on the payload. The choice of the encoding mechanism is deferred to the application or server—e.g., plain text, gzip compression, or the choice of image or video compression format. And with that, there is literally nothing more to say about the DATA frame! The entire frame consists of the common 8-byte header, followed by the HTTP payload.

 Technically, the length field of the DATA frame allows payloads of up to $2^{16} - 1$ (65535) bytes per frame. However, to reduce head-of-line blocking, the HTTP 2.0 standard requires that DATA frames not exceed $2^{14} - 1$ (16383) bytes per frame—messages that exceed this threshold must be broken up into multiple DATA frames.

Analyzing HTTP 2.0 Frame Data Flow

With basic knowledge of the different frame types, we can now revisit the diagram (Figure 12-9) we encountered earlier in "Request and Response Multiplexing" on page 214 and analyze the data flow.

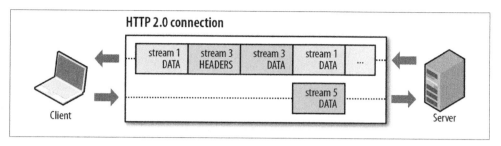

Figure 12-9. HTTP 2.0 request and response multiplexing within a shared connection

- There are three active streams: 1, 3, and 5.
- All three stream IDs are odd; all three are client-initiated streams.
- There are no server-initiated streams in this exchange.
- The server is sending multiple DATA frames for stream 1, which carry the application response to the client's earlier request. This also indicates that the response HEAD ERS frame was transferred earlier.
- The server has interleaved a HEADERS and DATA frame for stream 3 between the DATA frames for stream 1—response multiplexing in action!
- The client is transferring a DATA frame for stream 5, which indicates that a HEAD ERS frame was transferred earlier.

In short, the preceding connection is currently multiplexing three streams in parallel, each at various stages of the processing cycle. The server determines the order of the frames, and we do not have to worry about the type or content of each stream. Stream 1 could be a large data transfer or a video stream, but it does not block the other streams within the shared connection!

CHAPTER 13

Optimizing Application Delivery

High-performance browser networking relies on a host of networking technologies (Figure 13-1), and the overall performance of our applications is the sum total of each of their parts.

We cannot control the network weather between the client and server, nor the client hardware or the configuration of their device, but the rest is in our hands: TCP and TLS optimizations on the server, and dozens of application optimizations to account for the peculiarities of the different physical layers, versions of HTTP protocol in use, as well as general application best practices. Granted, getting it all right is not an easy task, but it is a rewarding one! Let's pull it all together.

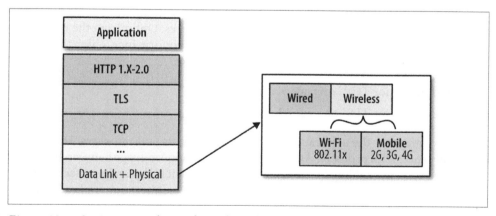

Figure 13-1. Optimization layers for web application delivery

The physical properties of the communication channel set hard performance limits on every application: speed of light and distance between client and server dictate the propagation latency, and the choice of medium (wired vs. wireless) determines the processing, transmission, queuing, and other delays incurred by each data packet. In fact, the performance of most web applications is limited by latency, not bandwidth, and while bandwidth speeds will continue to increase, unfortunately the same can't be said for latency:

- "The Many Components of Latency" on page 4
- "Delivering Higher Bandwidth and Lower Latencies" on page 11
- "Latency as a Performance Bottleneck" on page 177

As a result, while we cannot make the bits travel any faster, it is crucial that we apply all the possible optimizations at the transport and application layers to eliminate unnecessary roundtrips, requests, and minimize the distance traveled by each packet—i.e., position the servers closer to the client.

Every application can benefit from optimizing for the unique properties of the physical layer in wireless networks, where latencies are high and bandwidth is always at a premium. At the API layer, the differences between the wired and wireless networks are entirely transparent, but ignoring them is a recipe for poor performance. Simple optimizations in how and when we schedule resource downloads, beacons, and the rest can translate to significant impact on the experienced latency, battery life, and overall user experience of our applications:

- "Optimizing for WiFi Networks" on page 95
- Optimizing for mobile networks: Chapter 8

Moving up the stack from the physical layer, we must ensure that each and every server is configured to use the latest TCP and TLS best practices. Optimizing the underlying protocols ensures that each client is able to get the best performance—high throughput and low latency—when communicating with the server:

- "Optimizing for TCP" on page 32
- "Optimizing for TLS" on page 63

Finally, we arrive at the application layer. By all accounts and measures, HTTP is an incredibly successful protocol. After all, it is the common language between billions of clients and servers, enabling the modern Web. However, it is also an imperfect protocol, which means that we must take special care in how we architect our applications:

- We must work around the limitations of HTTP 1.x.
- We must learn how to leverage new performance enhancements in HTTP 2.0.
- We must be vigilant about applying the evergreen performance best practices.

The secret to a successful and sustainable web performance strategy is simple: measure first, link business goals to performance metrics, apply optimizations, lather, rinse, and repeat. Developing and investing into appropriate measurement tools and application metrics is top priority; see "Synthetic and Real-User Performance Measurement" on page 179.

Evergreen Performance Best Practices

Regardless of the type of network or the type or version of the networking protocols in use, all applications should always seek to eliminate or reduce unnecessary network latency and minimize the amount of transferred bytes. These two criteria are the evergreen performance best practices that serve as the foundation for dozens of familiar performance rules:

Reduce DNS lookups
> Every hostname resolution requires a network roundtrip, imposing latency on the request and blocking the request while the lookup is in progress.

Reuse TCP connections
> Leverage connection keepalive whenever possible to eliminate the TCP handshake and slow-start latency overhead; see "Slow-Start" on page 19.

Minimize number of HTTP redirects
> HTTP redirects can be extremely costly, especially when they redirect the client to a different hostname, which results in additional DNS lookup, TCP handshake latency, and so on. The optimal number of redirects is zero.

Use a Content Delivery Network (CDN)
> Locating the data geographically closer to the client can significantly reduce the network latency of every TCP connection and improve throughput. This advice applies both to static and dynamic content; see "Uncached Origin Fetch" on page 66.

Eliminate unnecessary resources
> No request is faster than a request not made.

By this point, all of these recommendations should require no explanation: latency is the bottleneck, and the fastest byte is a byte not sent. However, HTTP also provides a number of additional mechanisms, such as caching and compression, as well as its own set of version-specific performance quirks:

Cache resources on the client
> Application resources should be cached to avoid re-requesting the same bytes each time the resources are required.

Compress assets during transfer
> Application resources should be transferred with the minimum number of bytes: always apply the best compression method for each transferred asset.

Eliminate unnecessary request bytes
> Reducing the transferred HTTP header data (i.e., HTTP cookies) can save entire roundtrips of network latency.

Parallelize request and response processing
> Request and response queuing latency, both on the client and server, often goes unnoticed, but contributes significant and unnecessary latency delays.

Apply protocol-specific optimizations
> HTTP 1.x offers limited parallelism, which requires that we bundle resources, split delivery across domains, and more. By contrast, HTTP 2.0 performs best when a single connection is used and HTTP 1.x specific optimizations are removed.

Each of these warrants closer examination. Let's dive in.

Cache Resources on the Client

The fastest network request is a request not made. Maintaining a cache of previously downloaded data allows the client to use a local copy of the resource, thereby eliminating the request. For resources delivered over HTTP, make sure the appropriate cache headers are in place:

- `Cache-Control` header can specify the cache lifetime (max-age) of the resource.
- `Last-Modified` and `ETag` headers provide validation mechanisms.

Whenever possible, you should specify an explicit cache lifetime for each resource, which allows the client to use a local copy, instead of re-requesting the same object all the time. Similarly, specify a validation mechanism to allow the client to check if the expired resource has been updated: if the resource has not changed, we can eliminate the data transfer.

Finally, note that you need to specify both the cache lifetime and the validation method! A common mistake is to provide only one of the two, which results in either redundant transfers of resources that have not changed (i.e., missing validation), or redundant validation checks each time the resource is used (i.e., missing cache lifetime).

Web Caching on Smartphones: Ideal vs. Reality

Caching of HTTP resources has been one of the top performance optimizations ever since the very early versions of the HTTP protocol. However, while seemingly everyone is aware of its benefits, real-world studies continue to discover that it is nonetheless an often-omitted optimization! A recent joint study by AT&T Labs Research and University of Michigan reports:

> Our findings suggest that redundant transfers contribute 18% and 20% of the total HTTP traffic volume in the two datasets. Also they are responsible for 17% of the bytes, 7% of the radio energy consumption, 6% of the signaling load, and 9% of the radio resource utilization of all cellular data traffic in the second dataset. Most of such redundant transfers are caused by the smartphone web caching implementation that does not fully support or strictly follow the protocol specification, or by developers not fully utilizing the caching support provided by the libraries.
>
> — Web Caching on Smartphones
> *MobiSys 2012*

Is your application fetching unnecessary resources over and over again? As evidence shows, that's not a rhetorical question. Double-check your application and, even better, add some tests to catch any regressions in the future.

Compress Transferred Data

Leveraging a local cache allows the client to avoid fetching duplicate content on each request. However, if and when the resource must be fetched, either because it has expired, it is new, or it cannot be cached, then it should be transferred with the minimum number of bytes. Always apply the best compression method for each asset.

The size of text-based assets, such as HTML, CSS, and JavaScript, can be reduced by 60%–80% on average when compressed with Gzip. Images, on the other hand, require a more nuanced consideration:

- Images account for over half the transferred bytes of an average page.
- Image files can be made smaller by eliminating unnecessary metadata.
- Images should be resized on the server to avoid shipping unnecessary bytes.
- An optimal image format should be chosen based on type of image.
- Lossy compression should be used whenever possible.

Different image formats can yield dramatically different compression ratios on the same image file, because different formats are optimized for different use cases. In fact, picking the wrong image format (e.g., using PNG for a photo instead of JPEG or WebP) can easily translate into hundreds and even thousands of unnecessary kilobytes of transferred data. Invest into tools and automation to help determine the optimal format!

Once the right image format is selected, ensure that the dimensions of the files are no larger than they need to be. Resizing an oversized image on the client negatively impacts the CPU, GPU, and memory requirements (see "Calculating Image Memory Requirements" on page 203), in addition to unnecessarily increasing the transfer size.

Finally, with the right format and image dimensions in place, investigate using a lossy image format, such as JPEG or WebP, with various compression levels: higher compression can yield significant byte savings with minimal or no perceptible change in image quality, especially on smaller (mobile) screens.

WebP: New Image Format for the Web

WebP is a new image format developed at Google and supported by Chrome and Opera browsers, which offers improved lossless and lossy compression on the Web:

- WebP lossless images are 26% smaller in size compared with PNGs.
- WebP lossy images are 25%–34% smaller in size compared with JPEGs.
- WebP supports lossless transparency with just 22% additional bytes.

With an average page now over 1 megabyte in size, and images responsible for over half of the transferred bytes, a 20%–30% savings offered by WebP quickly translates to hundreds of kilobytes saved per page. The format does require a higher amount of CPU time for image decoding on the client (~1.4x compared with JPEG), but the byte savings offset the extra processing time. Plus, due to data caps and high data rates, for many users saving bytes is a top priority.

In fact, one of the primary ways services such as Chrome Data Compression Proxy and Opera Turbo achieve bandwidth reduction for their users is through re-encoding each and every image to WebP. On average, Chrome Data Compression Proxy has been shown to reduce data usage by 50%, which indicates that we have a lot of room for better compression within our applications!

Eliminate Unnecessary Request Bytes

HTTP is a stateless protocol, which means that the server is not required to retain any information about the client between different requests. However, many applications require state for session management, personalization, analytics, and more. To enable this functionality, the HTTP State Management Mechanism (RFC 2965) extension allows any website to associate and update "cookie" metadata for its origin: the provided data is saved by the browser and is then automatically appended onto every request to the origin within the `Cookie` header.

The standard does not specify a maximum limit on the size of a cookie, but in practice most browsers enforce a 4 KB limit. However, the standard also allows the site to associate many cookies per origin. As a result, it is possible to associate tens of kilobytes of arbitrary metadata, split across multiple cookies, for each origin! Needless to say, this can have significant performance implications for your application:

- Associated cookie data is automatically sent by the browser on each request.
- In HTTP 1.x, all HTTP headers, including cookies, are transferred uncompressed.
- In HTTP 2.0, compression is applied, but the potential overhead is still high.
- In the worst case, large HTTP cookies can add entire roundtrips of network latency by exceeding the initial TCP congestion window.

Cookie size should be monitored judiciously: transfer the minimum amount of required data, such as a secure session token, and leverage a shared session cache on the server to look up other metadata. And even better, eliminate cookies entirely wherever possible —chances are, you do not need client-specific metadata when requesting static assets, such as images, scripts, and stylesheets.

> When using HTTP 1.x, a common best practice is to designate a dedicated "cookie-free" origin, which can be used to deliver responses that do not need client-specific optimization.

Parallelize Request and Response Processing

In order to achieve the fastest response times within your application, all resource requests should be dispatched as soon as possible. However, another important point to consider is how these requests, and their respective responses, will be processed on the server. After all, if all of our requests are then serially queued by the server, then we are once again incurring unnecessary latency. Here's how to get the best performance:

- Use connection keepalive and upgrade from HTTP 1.0 to HTTP 1.1.
- Leverage multiple HTTP 1.1 connections where necessary for parallel downloads.
- Leverage HTTP 1.1 pipelining whenever possible.
- Investigate upgrading to HTTP 2.0 to improve performance.
- Ensure that the server has sufficient resources to process requests in parallel.

Without connection keepalive, a new TCP connection is required for each HTTP request, which incurs significant overhead due to the TCP handshake and slow-start. For best results, use HTTP 1.1, and reuse existing TCP connections whenever possible. Then, on rare occasions where HTTP pipelining can be used, do so, or even better, consider upgrading to HTTP 2.0 to get the best performance.

Identifying the sources of unnecessary client and server latency is both an art and a science: examine the client resource waterfall (see "Analyzing the Resource Waterfall" on page 171), as well as your server logs. Common pitfalls often include the following:

- Underprovisioned servers, forcing unnecessary processing latency.
- Underprovisioned proxy and load-balancer capacity, forcing delayed delivery of the request (queuing latency) to the application server.
- Blocking resources on the client forcing delayed construction of the page; see "DOM, CSSOM, and JavaScript" on page 168.

Optimizing Resource Loading in the Browser

The browser will automatically determine the optimal loading order for each resource in the document, and we can both assist and hinder the browser in this process:

- We can provide hints to assist the browser; see "Browser Optimization" on page 183.
- We can hinder by hiding resources from the browser.

Modern browsers are all designed to scan the contents of HTML and CSS files as efficiently and as soon as possible. However, the document parser is also frequently blocked while waiting for a script or other blocking resources to download before it can proceed. During this time, the browser uses a "preload scanner," which speculatively looks ahead in the source for resource downloads that could be dispatched early to reduce overall latency.

Note that the use of the preload scanner is a speculative optimization, and it is used only when the document parser is blocked. However, in practice, it yields significant benefits: based on experimental data with Google Chrome, it offers a ~20% improvement in page loading times and rendering speeds!

Unfortunately, these optimizations do not apply for resources that are scheduled via JavaScript; the preload scanner cannot speculatively execute scripts. As a result, moving resource scheduling logic into scripts may offer the benefit of more granular control to the application, but in doing so, it will hide the resource from the preload scanner, a trade-off that warrants close examination.

Optimizing for HTTP 1.x

The order in which we optimize HTTP 1.x deployments is important: configure servers to deliver the best possible TCP and TLS performance, then carefully review and apply mobile and evergreen application best practices: measure, iterate.

With the evergreen optimizations in place, and with good performance instrumentation within the application, evaluate whether the application can benefit from applying HTTP 1.x specific optimizations (read, *workarounds*):

Leverage HTTP pipelining
> If your application controls both the client and the server, then pipelining can help eliminate significant amounts of network latency.

Apply domain sharding
> If your application performance is limited by the default six connections per origin limit, consider splitting resources across multiple origins.

Bundle resources to reduce HTTP requests
> Techniques such as concatenation and spriting can both help minimize the protocol overhead and deliver pipelining-like performance benefits.

Inline small resource
> Consider embedding small resources directly into the parent document to minimize the number of requests.

Pipelining has limited support, and each of the remaining optimizations comes with its own set of benefits and trade-offs. In fact, it is often overlooked that each of these optimizations can hurt performance when applied too aggressively, or incorrectly; review Chapter 11 for an in-depth discussion. Be pragmatic, instrument your application, measure impact carefully and iterate. Distrust any one-size-fits-all advice.

 And one last thing…consider upgrading to HTTP 2.0, as it eliminates the need for most of the HTTP 1.x-specific optimizations previously outlined! Not only will your application load faster with HTTP 2.0, but it will also be simpler and easier to work with.

Optimizing for HTTP 2.0

The primary focus of HTTP 2.0 is on improving transport performance and enabling lower latency and higher throughput between the client and server. Not surprisingly, getting the best possible performance out of TCP and TLS, as well as eliminating other unnecessary network latency, has never been as important. At a minimum:

- Server should start with a TCP cwnd of 10 segments.
- Server should support TLS with ALPN negotiation (NPN for SPDY).
- Server should support TLS resumption to minimize handshake latency.

In short, review "Optimizing for TCP" on page 32 and "Optimizing for TLS" on page 63. Getting the best performance out of HTTP 2.0, especially in light of the one-connection-per-origin recommendation, requires a well-tuned network stack.

Next up—surprise—apply the mobile and other evergreen application best practices: send fewer bytes, eliminate requests, and adapt resource scheduling for wireless networks. Reducing the amount of data transferred and eliminating unnecessary network latency are the best optimizations you can do for any application, web or native, regardless of the version of the transport protocol.

Finally, undo and unlearn the bad habits of domain sharding, concatenation, and image spriting; these workarounds are no longer required with HTTP 2.0. In fact, they will hurt performance rather than help! Instead, we can now rely on built-in multiplexing and new features such as server push.

Early Adopter Guide to HTTP 2.0 and SPDY

The official HTTP 2.0 standard is a work in progress. In the meantime, SPDY is the "production" version of the protocol (see "Coevolution of HTTP 2.0 and SPDY" on page 210), which offers wide and fast-growing client and server support and years of real-world production testing. You may be an early adopter, but you are in good company.

Finally, while SPDY and HTTP 2.0 specifications are not exactly in sync, they do share all the same core features and optimizations. All of our discussion in this and previous sections are equally applicable to both.

Removing 1.x Optimizations

The optimization strategy for HTTP 2.0 diverges significantly from HTTP 1.x. Instead of having to worry about the various limitations of the HTTP 1.x protocol, we can now undo many of the previously necessary workarounds:

Use a single connection per origin
> HTTP 2.0 improves performance by maximizing throughput of a single TCP connection. In fact, use of multiple connections (e.g., domain sharding) is a performance anti-pattern for HTTP 2.0, as it reduces the effectiveness of header compression and request prioritization provided by the protocol.

Remove unnecessary concatenation and image spriting

Resource bundling has many downsides, such as expensive cache invalidations, larger memory requirements, deferred execution, and increased application complexity. With HTTP 2.0, many small resources can be multiplexed in parallel, which means that the downsides of asset bundling will almost always outweigh the benefits of delivering more granular resources.

Leverage server push

The majority of resources that were previously inlined with HTTP 1.x can and should be delivered via server push. By doing so, each resource can be cached individually by the client and reused across different pages, instead of being embedded in each and every page.

For best performance, consolidate as many resources as possible on the same origin. Domain sharding is a performance anti-pattern for HTTP 2.0 and will hurt performance of the protocol: this is a critical first step. From there, a more gradual migration can take place. Bundled assets do not affect performance of the HTTP 2.0 protocol itself, but they can have a negative impact on cache performance and execution speed.

 For a reminder of the negative costs of concatenation and spriting, see "Concatenation and Spriting" on page 201 and "Calculating Image Memory Requirements" on page 203.

Similarly, inlined resources can be replaced with server push to further improve cache performance on the client, without incurring any extra network latency; see "Implementing HTTP 2.0 server push" on page 221. In fact, the use of server push may offer the most benefits for mobile clients, due to the high cost of network roundtrips on 3G and 4G networks.

Bundling and Protocol Overhead of HTTP 2.0

Lack of multiplexing and high per-request protocol overhead of HTTP 1.x are the primary reasons for asset bundling techniques such as concatenation and asset bundling. With HTTP 2.0, multiplexing is no longer a concern, and header compression dramatically reduces the metadata overhead of each HTTP request. As such, this eliminates the need for asset bundling in most cases.

However, while the request overhead is reduced, it is still not zero, and in cases where certain resources are always used together and updates are infrequent, use of bundling can still deliver performance benefits. Just keep in mind that such cases are an exception, not the rule. Measure their impact and apply accordingly.

Dual-Protocol Application Strategies

Unfortunately, the upgrade to HTTP 2.0 won't happen overnight. As a result, many applications will have to carefully consider the trade-offs of dual-protocol deployment strategies: the same application code can be delivered over HTTP 1.x and HTTP 2.0, without any modifications. However, aggressive optimization for HTTP 1.x can hurt HTTP 2.0 performance and vice versa.

If the application controls both the server and the client, then it is in a position to dictate the protocol in use—that's the simplest case. Most applications do not and cannot control the client and will have to use a hybrid or an automated strategy to accommodate both versions of the protocol. Let's evaluate some options:

Same application code, dual-protocol deployment
> The same application code can be delivered over HTTP 1.x and HTTP 2.0. As a result, you may not get the best performance out of either, but it may be the most pragmatic way to get *good enough* performance on both, where *good enough* should be carefully measured with respect to each individual application. With this strategy, a good first step is to eliminate domain sharding to enable efficient HTTP 2.0 delivery. From there, as more users migrate toward HTTP 2.0, you can also undo the resource bundling techniques and start to leverage server push where possible.

Split application code, dual-protocol deployment
> Different versions of the application can be delivered based on the version of the protocol in use. This increases operational complexity but in practice may be a reasonable strategy for many applications—e.g., an edge server responsible for terminating the connection can direct the client request to an appropriate server based on the version of negotiated protocol.

Dynamic HTTP 1.x and HTTP 2.0 optimization
> Some automated web optimization frameworks, and open source and commercial products, can perform dynamic rewriting (concatenation, spriting, sharding, and so on) of the delivered application code when the request is served. In that case, the server could also take into account the negotiated version of the protocol and dynamically apply the appropriate optimization strategy.

HTTP 2.0, single-protocol deployment
> If the application controls both the server and the client, then there is no reason why HTTP 2.0 cannot be used exclusively. In fact, if such an option is available, then this should be the default strategy.

The route you choose will depend on the current infrastructure, the complexity of the application, and the demographics of your users. Ironically, it is the applications that have invested the most effort into HTTP 1.x optimization that will have the hardest time to manage this migration. Alternatively, if you control the client, have an automated application optimization solution in place, or are not using any 1.x-specific optimizations in your existing application, then you can safely bet on HTTP 2.0 and not look back.

Dynamic Optimization with PageSpeed

Google's PageSpeed Optimization Libraries (PSOL) provide an open source implementation of over 40 various "web optimization filters," which can be integrated into any server runtime and applied dynamically to any application.

Backed by PSOL libraries under the hood, the mod_pagespeed (Apache) and ngx_pagespeed (Nginx) modules can both dynamically rewrite and optimize each delivered asset based on specified optimization filters—e.g., resource inlining, minification, concatenation, asset sharding, and many others. Each optimization is applied dynamically (and cached) at request time, which means that the entire optimization process is fully automated.

Because the optimization is performed dynamically, the server can also adjust the optimization strategy based on the version of protocol in use and even the type and version of user agent. For example, the mod_pagespeed module can be configured to skip certain optimizations when an HTTP 2.0 client is connected:

```
# Disable concatenation for SPDY/HTTP 2.0 clients
<ModPagespeedIf spdy>
  ModPagespeedDisableFilters combine_css,combine_javascript
</ModPagespeedIf>

# Shard assets for HTTP 1.x clients only
<ModPagespeedIf !spdy>
  ModPagespeedShardDomain www.site.com s1.site.com,s2.site.com
</ModPagespeedIf>
```

An automated web optimization product, such as PageSpeed, can offer the benefits of optimized performance without the hassle of worrying about specific optimizations for each protocol—a solution worth investigating.

Translating 1.x to 2.0 and Back

In addition to thinking about a dual-protocol application optimization strategy, many existing deployments may need an intermediate path for their application servers: an end-to-end HTTP 2.0 stack is the end goal for best performance, but a translation layer (Figure 13-2) can enable existing 1.x servers to take advantage of HTTP 2.0 as well.

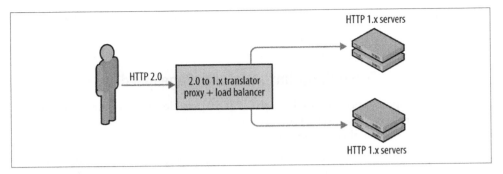

Figure 13-2. HTTP 2.0 to 1.x translation: streams converted to 1.x requests

An intermediate server can accept an HTTP 2.0 session, process it, and dispatch 1.x formatted requests to existing infrastructure. Then, once it receives the response, it can convert it back to HTTP 2.0 and respond back to the client. In many cases this is the simplest way to get started with HTTP 2.0, as it allows us to reuse our existing 1.x infrastructure with minimum or zero modification.

 Most web servers with HTTP 2.0 support provide a 2.0 to 1.x translation mechanism by default: the 2.0 session is terminated at the server (e.g., Apache, Nginx), and if the server is configured as a reverse proxy, then 1.x requests are dispatched to individual application servers.

However, the 2.0 to 1.x convenience path should not be mistaken for a good long-term strategy; in many ways, this workflow is exactly backward. Instead of converting an optimized, multiplexed session into a series of 1.x requests, and thereby deoptimizing the session within our own infrastructure, we should be doing the opposite: converting inbound 1.x client requests to 2.0 streams, and standardizing our application infrastructure to speak 2.0 in all cases.

To get the best performance, and to enable the low latency and real-time Web, we should demand our internal infrastructure to meet the following criteria:

- Load balancer and proxy connections to application servers should be persistent.
- Request and response streaming and multiplexing should be the default.
- Communication with application servers should be message-oriented.
- Communication between clients and application servers should be bidirectional.

An end-to-end HTTP 2.0 session meets all of these criteria and enables low latency delivery to the client, as well as within our own data centers: there is no longer a need for custom RPC layers and mechanisms to communicate between internal services to get the desired performance. In short, don't downgrade 2.0 to 1.x; that's not a good long-term strategy. Instead upgrade 1.x to 2.0 to get the best performance.

Evaluating Server Quality and Performance

The quality of implementation of the HTTP 2.0 server will have a significant impact on the performance of the client. A well-tuned HTTP server has always been important, but the performance benefits of prioritization, server push, and multiplexing are all closely tied to the quality of the implemented logic in the server:

- HTTP 2.0 server must understand stream priorities.
- HTTP 2.0 server must prioritize response processing and delivery.
- HTTP 2.0 server must support server push.
- HTTP 2.0 server should provide different push strategy implementations.

A naive implementation of an HTTP 2.0 server may "speak" the protocol, but without explicit awareness of request priorities, and server push, will deliver suboptimal performance—e.g., saturate the bandwidth by sending large, static image files, while the client is blocked on other critical resources, such as CSS and JavaScript.

> To get the best possible performance, an HTTP 2.0 client has to be "optimistic": it should send all requests as soon as possible and defer to the server to optimize delivery. Hence, the performance of an HTTP 2.0 client is even more dependent on the server than before.

Similarly, different servers may offer different mechanisms and strategies for leveraging server push; see "Implementing HTTP 2.0 server push" on page 221. It is not an understatement to say that the performance of your application will be closely tied to the quality of your HTTP 2.0 server.

> Given the fast-evolving nature of HTTP 2.0 and SPDY, different server implementations (Apache, Nginx, Jetty, etc.) are all at different stages in their HTTP 2.0 implementations. Check the appropriate documentation and release notes for supported features and latest news.

Speaking 2.0 with and without TLS

In practice, due to many incompatible intermediaries, early HTTP 2.0 deployments will have to be delivered over an encrypted channel, which leaves us with two options of where the ALPN negotiation and TLS termination can occur:

- The TLS connection can be terminated at the HTTP 2.0 server.
- The TLS connection can be terminated upstream (e.g., load balancer).

The first case requires that the HTTP 2.0 server is able to handle TLS, but otherwise is simple. The second case is far more interesting: the TLS+ALPN handshake can be terminated by an upstream proxy (Figure 13-3), at which point another encrypted tunnel can be established, or unencrypted HTTP 2.0 frames can be sent directly to the server.

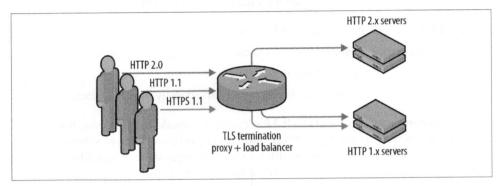

Figure 13-3. TLS+ALPN aware load-balancer

The choice of using a secure or an unencrypted tunnel for communication between the proxy and the application server is up to the application: as long as we control the internal infrastructure, we can guarantee that the unencrypted frames won't be modified or dropped. As a result, while most HTTP 2.0 servers should support TLS+ALPN negotiation, they should also be able to talk to HTTP 2.0 without encryption.

Further, a smart load balancer can also use the TLS+ALPN negotiation mechanism to selectively route the different clients to different servers, based on the version of the negotiated protocol!

 HAProxy, a popular open source load balancer, supports both NPN negotiation and routing based on the negotiated protocol. For a hands-on look, see "Simple SPDY and NPN Negotiation with HAProxy" (*http://hpbn.co/haproxy-npn*).

Load Balancers, Proxies, and Application Servers

Depending on the existing infrastructure in place, as well as the complexity and scale of the application, your infrastructure may need one or more load balancers (Figure 13-4) or HTTP 2.0-aware proxies.

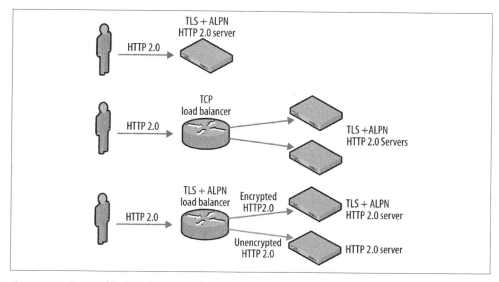

Figure 13-4. Load balancing and TLS termination strategies

In the simplest case, the HTTP 2.0 server is accessible directly by the client and is responsible for terminating the TLS connection, performing the ALPN negotiation, and servicing all inbound requests.

However, a single server is insufficient for larger applications, which require that we introduce a load balancer to split the inbound traffic. In this case, the load balancer could terminate the TLS connection (see preceding section), or it can be configured as a TCP proxy and pass the encrypted data directly to the application server.

> Many cloud providers offer HTTP and TCP load balancers as a service. However, while most support TLS termination, they may not provide ALPN negotiation, which is a requirement for HTTP 2.0 over TLS. In these cases, the load balancer should be configured as a TCP proxy: pass the encrypted data to the application server and let it perform the TLS+ALPN negotiation.

In practice, the most important questions to answer are which component of your infrastructure will terminate the TLS connection and whether it is capable of performing the necessary ALPN negotiation:

- To enable HTTP 2.0 over TLS, the termination server must support ALPN.
- Terminate TLS as close to the user as possible; see "Early Termination" on page 65.

- If ALPN support is unavailable, then use TCP load-balancing mode.
- If ALPN support is unavailable and TCP load balancing is not possible, then you have to fall back to HTTP Upgrade flow over an unencrypted channel; see "Efficient HTTP 2.0 Upgrade and Discovery" on page 224.

Browser APIs and Protocols

PART IV
Browser APIs and Protocols

CHAPTER 14

Primer on Browser Networking

A modern browser is a platform specifically designed for fast, efficient, and secure delivery of web applications. In fact, under the hood, a modern browser is an entire operating system with hundreds of components: process management, security sandboxes, layers of optimization caches, JavaScript VMs, graphics rendering and GPU pipelines, storage, sensors, audio and video, networking, and much more.

Not surprisingly, the overall performance of the browser, and any application that it runs, is determined by a number of components: parsing, layout, style calculation of HTML and CSS, JavaScript execution speed, rendering pipelines, and of course the networking stack. Each component plays a critical role, but networking often doubly so, since if the browser is blocked on the network, waiting for the resources to arrive, then all other steps are blocked!

As a result, it is not surprising to discover that the networking stack of a modern browser is much more than a simple socket manager. From the outside, it may present itself as a simple resource-fetching mechanism, but from the inside it is its own platform (Figure 14-1), with its own optimization criteria, APIs, and services.

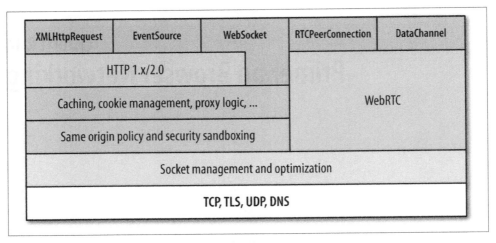

Figure 14-1. High-level browser networking APIs, protocols, and services

When designing a web application, we don't have to worry about the individual TCP or UDP sockets; the browser manages that for us. Further, the network stack takes care of imposing the right connection limits, formatting our requests, sandboxing individual applications from one another, dealing with proxies, caching, and much more. In turn, with all of this complexity removed, our applications can focus on the application logic.

However, out of sight does not mean out of mind! As we saw, understanding the performance characteristics of TCP, HTTP, and mobile networks can help us build faster applications. Similarly, understanding how to optimize for the various browser networking APIs, protocols, and services can make a dramatic difference in performance of any application.

Connection Management and Optimization

Web applications running in the browser do not manage the lifecycle of individual network sockets, and that's a good thing. By deferring this work to the browser, we allow it to automate a number of critical performance optimizations, such as socket reuse, request prioritization and late binding, protocol negotiation, enforcing connection limits, and much more. In fact, the browser intentionally separates the *request management* lifecycle from *socket management*. This is a subtle but critical distinction.

Sockets are organized in pools (Figure 14-2), which are grouped by origin, and each pool enforces its own connection limits and security constraints. Pending requests are queued, prioritized, and then bound to individual sockets in the pool. Consequently, unless the server intentionally closes the connection, the same socket can be automatically reused across multiple requests!

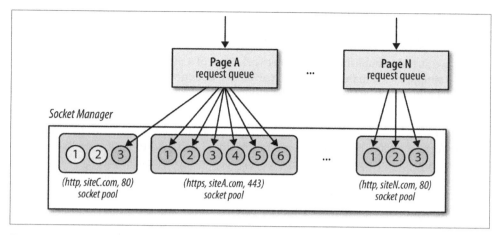

Figure 14-2. Auto-managed socket pools are shared among all browser processes

Origin
:   A triple of application protocol, domain name, and port number—e.g., (http, www.example.com, 80) and (https, www.example.com, 443) are considered as different origins.

Socket pool
:   A group of sockets belonging to the same origin. In practice, all major browsers limit the maximum pool size to six sockets.

Automatic socket pooling automates TCP connection reuse, which offers significant performance benefits; see "Benefits of Keepalive Connections" on page 189. However, that's not all. This architecture also enables a number of additional optimization opportunities:

- The browser can service queued requests in priority order.
- The browser can reuse sockets to minimize latency and improve throughput.
- The browser can be proactive in opening sockets in anticipation of request.
- The browser can optimize when idle sockets are closed.
- The browser can optimize bandwidth allocation across all sockets.

In short, the browser networking stack is our strategic ally on our quest to deliver high-performance applications. None of the functionality we have covered requires any work on our behalf! However, that's not to say that we can't help the browser. Design decisions in our applications that determine the network communication patterns, type and frequency of transfers, choice of protocols, and tuning and optimization of our server stacks play critical roles in the end performance of every application.

Speculative Networking Optimization in Google Chrome

We have already established that the network stack of a modern browser is much more than a simple socket manager. However, even that does not do full justice to some of the optimization techniques performed by modern browsers.

For example, Google Chrome browser gets faster as you use it. Chrome learns the topology of visited sites and typical browsing patterns and then leverages this information to perform a variety of "speculative optimizations" designed to anticipate likely user actions and eliminate unnecessary network latency: DNS pre-resolving, TCP pre-connect, page pre-rendering, and more. Simple actions, such as a mouse hover over a link can trigger a signal from the browser to the network stack "predictor," which may then select the best optimization based on past performance data!

For more details, see our earlier discussion on "Browser Optimization" on page 183. And if you're curious to learn more about Chrome's networking optimization, check out "High Performance Networking in Google Chrome" (*http://hpbn.co/chrome-networking*).

Network Security and Sandboxing

Deferring management of individual sockets serves another important purpose: it allows the browser to sandbox and enforce a consistent set of security and policy constraints on untrusted application code. For example, the browser does not permit direct API access to raw network sockets, as that would allow a malicious application to initiate arbitrary connections to any host—e.g., run a port scan, connect to a mail server and start sending unintended messages, and so on.

Connection limits
> Browser manages all open socket pools and enforces connection limits to protect both the client and server from resource exhaustion.

Request formatting and response processing
> Browser formats all outgoing requests to enforce consistent and well-formed protocol semantics to protect the server. Similarly, response decoding is done automatically to protect the user from malicious servers.

TLS negotiation
> Browser performs the TLS handshake and performs the necessary verification checks of the certificates. The user is warned when and if any of the verification fails—e.g., server is using a self-signed certificate.

Same-origin policy
> Browser enforces constraints on which requests can be initiated by the application and to which origin.

The previous list is not complete, but it highlights the principle of "least privilege" at work. The browser exposes only the APIs and resources that are necessary for the application code: the application supplies the data and URL, and the browser formats the request and handles the full lifecycle of each connection.

It is worth noting that there is no single "same-origin policy." Instead, there is a set of related mechanisms that enforce restrictions on DOM access, cookie and session state management, networking, and other components of the browser.

A full discussion on browser security requires its own separate book. If you are curious, Michal Zalewski's *The Tangled Web: A Guide to Securing Modern Web Applications* is a fantastic resource.

Resource and Client State Caching

The best and fastest request is a request not made. Prior to dispatching a request, the browser automatically checks its resource cache, performs the necessary validation checks, and returns a local copy of the resources if the specified constraints are satisfied. Similarly, if a local resource is not available in cache, then a network request is made and the response is automatically placed in cache for subsequent access if permitted.

- The browser automatically evaluates caching directives on each resource.
- The browser automatically revalidates expired resources when possible.
- The browser automatically manages the size of cache and resource eviction.

Managing an efficient and optimized resource cache is hard. Thankfully, the browser takes care of all of the complexity on our behalf, and all we need to do is ensure that our servers are returning the appropriate cache directives; see "Cache Resources on the Client" on page 236. You are providing Cache-Control, ETag, and Last-Modified response headers for all the resources on your pages, right?

Finally, an often-overlooked but critical function of the browser is to provide authentication, session, and cookie management. The browser maintains separate "cookie jars" for each origin, provides necessary application and server APIs to read and write new cookie, session, and authentication data and automatically appends and processes appropriate HTTP headers to automate the entire process on our behalf.

A simple but illustrative example of the convenience of deferring session state management to the browser: an authenticated session can be shared across multiple tabs or browser windows, and vice versa; a sign-out action in a single tab will invalidate open sessions in all other open windows.

Application APIs and Protocols

Walking up the ladder of provided network services we finally arrive at the application APIs and protocols. As we saw, the lower layers provide a wide array of critical services: socket and connection management, request and response processing, enforcement of various security policies, caching, and much more. Every time we initiate an HTTP or an XMLHttpRequest, a long-lived Server-Sent Events or WebSocket session, or open a WebRTC connection, we are interacting with some or all of these underlying services.

There is no one best protocol or API. Every nontrivial application will require a mix of different transports based on a variety of requirements: interaction with the browser cache, protocol overhead, message latency, reliability, type of data transfer, and more. Some protocols may offer low-latency delivery (e.g., Server-Sent Events, WebSocket), but may not meet other critical criteria, such as the ability to leverage the browser cache or support efficient binary transfers in all cases.

Table 14-1. High-level features of XHR, SSE, and WebSocket

	XMLHttpRequest	Server-Sent Events	WebSocket
Request streaming	no	no	yes
Response streaming	limited	yes	yes
Framing mechanism	HTTP	event stream	binary framing
Binary data transfers	yes	no (base64)	yes
Compression	yes	yes	limited
Application transport protocol	HTTP	HTTP	WebSocket
Network transport protocol	TCP	TCP	TCP

 We are intentionally omitting WebRTC from this comparison, as its peer-to-peer delivery model offers a significant departure from XHR, SSE, and WebSocket protocols.

This comparison of high-level features is incomplete—that's the subject of the following chapters—but serves as a good illustration of the many differences among each protocol. Understanding the pros, cons, and trade-offs of each, and matching them to the requirements of our applications, can make all the difference between a high-performance application and a consistently poor experience for the user.

CHAPTER 15

XMLHttpRequest

XMLHttpRequest (XHR) is a browser-level API that enables the client to script data transfers via JavaScript. XHR made its first debut in Internet Explorer 5, became one of the key technologies behind the Asynchronous JavaScript and XML (AJAX) revolution, and is now a fundamental building block of nearly every modern web application.

> XMLHTTP changed everything. It put the "D" in DHTML. It allowed us to asynchronously get data from the server and preserve document state on the client... The Outlook Web Access (OWA) team's desire to build a rich Win32 like application in a browser pushed the technology into IE that allowed AJAX to become a reality.
>
> — Jim Van Eaton
> *Outlook Web Access: A catalyst for web evolution*

Prior to XHR, the web page had to be refreshed to send or fetch any state updates between the client and server. With XHR, this workflow could be done asynchronously and under full control of the application JavaScript code. XHR is what enabled us to make the leap from building pages to building interactive web applications in the browser.

However, the power of XHR is not only that it enabled asynchronous communication within the browser, but also that it made it simple. XHR is an application API provided by the browser, which is to say that the browser automatically takes care of all the low-level connection management, protocol negotiation, formatting of HTTP requests, and much more:

- The browser manages connection establishment, pooling, and termination.
- The browser determines the best HTTP(S) transport (HTTP 1.0, 1.1, 2.0).
- The browser handles HTTP caching, redirects, and content-type negotiation.
- The browser enforces security, authentication, and privacy constraints.
- *And more...*

Free from worrying about all the low-level details, our applications can focus on the business logic of initiating requests, managing their progress, and processing returned data from the server. The combination of a simple API and its ubiquitous availability across all the browsers makes XHR the "Swiss Army knife" of networking in the browser.

As a result, nearly every networking use case (scripted downloads, uploads, streaming, and even real-time notifications) can and have been built on top of XHR. Of course, this doesn't mean that XHR is the most efficient transport in each case—in fact, as we will see, far from it—but it is nonetheless often used as a fallback transport for older clients, which may not have access to newer browser networking APIs. With that in mind, let's take a closer look at the latest capabilities of XHR, its use cases, and performance do's and don'ts.

An exhaustive analysis of the full XHR API and its capabilities is outside the scope of our discussion—our focus is on performance! Refer to the official W3C standard for an overview of the XMLHttpRequest API (*http://www.w3.org/TR/XMLHttpRequest/*).

Brief History of XHR

Despite its name, XHR was never intended to be tied to XML specifically. The XML prefix is a vestige of a decision to ship the first version of what became known as XHR as part of the MSXML library in Internet Explorer 5:

> This was the good-old-days when critical features were crammed in just days before a release...I realized that the MSXML library shipped with IE and I had some good contacts over in the XML team who would probably help out—I got in touch with Jean Paoli who was running that team at the time and we pretty quickly struck a deal to ship the thing as part of the MSXML library. Which is the real explanation of where the name XMLHTTP comes from—the thing is mostly about HTTP and doesn't have any specific tie to XML other than that was the easiest excuse for shipping it so I needed to cram XML into the name.
>
> — Alex Hopmann
> *The story of XMLHTTP*

Mozilla modeled its own implementation of XHR against Microsoft's and exposed it via the XMLHttpRequest interface. Safari, Opera, and other browsers followed, and XHR became a de facto standard in all major browsers—hence the name and why it stuck. In fact, the official W3C Working Draft specification for XHR was only published in 2006, well after XHR came into widespread use!

However, despite its popularity and key role in the AJAX revolution, the early versions of XHR provided limited capabilities: text-based-only data transfers, restricted support for handling uploads, and inability to handle cross-domain requests. To address these shortcomings, the "XMLHttpRequest Level 2" draft was published in 2008, which added a number of new features:

- Support for request timeouts
- Support for binary and text-based data transfers
- Support for application override of media type and encoding of responses
- Support for monitoring progress events of each request
- Support for efficient file uploads
- Support for safe cross-origin requests

In 2011, "XMLHttpRequest Level 2" specification was merged with the original XMLHttpRequest working draft. Hence, while you will often find references to XHR version or level 1 and 2, these distinctions are no longer relevant; today, there is only one, unified XHR specification. In fact, all the new XHR2 features and capabilities are offered via the same XMLHttpRequest API: same interface, more features.

New XHR2 features are now supported by all the modern browsers; see caniuse.com/xhr2. Hence, whenever we refer to XHR, we are implicitly referring to the XHR2 standard.

Cross-Origin Resource Sharing (CORS)

XHR is a browser-level API that automatically handles myriad low-level details such as caching, handling redirects, content negotiation, authentication, and much more. This serves a dual purpose. First, it makes the application APIs much easier to work with, allowing us to focus on the business logic. But, second, it allows the browser to sandbox and enforce a set of security and policy constraints on the application code.

The XHR interface enforces strict HTTP semantics on each request: the application supplies the data and URL, and the browser formats the request and handles the full lifecycle of each connection. Similarly, while the XHR API allows the application to add custom HTTP headers (via the setRequestHeader() method), there are a number of protected headers that are off-limits to application code:

- Accept-Charset, Accept-Encoding, Access-Control-*
- Host, Upgrade, Connection, Referer, Origin
- Cookie, Sec-*, Proxy-*, and a dozen others…

The browser will refuse to override any of the unsafe headers, which guarantees that the application cannot impersonate a fake user-agent, user, or the origin from where the request is being made. In fact, protecting the origin header is especially important, as it is the key piece of the "same-origin policy" applied to all XHR requests.

 An "origin" is defined as a triple of application protocol, domain name, and port number—e.g., (http, example.com, 80) and (https, example.com, 443) are considered as different origins. For more details see The Web Origin Concept (*http://tools.ietf.org/html/draft-abarth-origin*).

The motivation for the same-origin policy is simple: the browser stores user data, such as authentication tokens, cookies, and other private metadata, which cannot be leaked across different applications—e.g., without the same origin sandbox an arbitrary script on *example.com* could access and manipulate users' data on *thirdparty.com*!

To address this specific problem, early versions of XHR were restricted to same-origin requests only, where the requesting origin had to match the origin of the requested resource: an XHR initiated from *example.com* could request another resource only from the same *example.com* origin. Alternatively, if the same origin precondition failed, then the browser would simply refuse to initiate the XHR request and raise an error.

However, while necessary, the same-origin policy also places severe restrictions on the usefulness of XHR: what if the server wants to offer a resource to a script running in a different origin? That's where "Cross-Origin Resource Sharing" (CORS) comes in! CORS provides a secure opt-in mechanism for client-side cross-origin requests:

```
// script origin: (http, example.com, 80)
var xhr = new XMLHttpRequest();
xhr.open('GET', '/resource.js'); ❶
xhr.onload = function() { ... };
xhr.send();

var cors_xhr = new XMLHttpRequest();
cors_xhr.open('GET', 'http://thirdparty.com/resource.js'); ❷
cors_xhr.onload = function() { ... };
cors_xhr.send();
```

❶ Same-origin XHR request

❷ Cross-origin XHR request

CORS requests use the same XHR API, with the only difference that the URL to the requested resource is associated with a different origin from where the script is being executed: in the previous example, the script is executed from *(http, example.com, 80)*, and the second XHR request is accessing resource.js from *(http, thirdparty.com, 80)*.

The opt-in authentication mechanism for the CORS request is handled at a lower layer: when the request is made, the browser automatically appends the protected *Origin* HTTP header, which advertises the origin from where the request is being made. In turn, the remote server is then able to examine the *Origin* header and decide if it should allow the request by returning an *Access-Control-Allow-Origin* header in its response:

```
=> Request
GET /resource.js HTTP/1.1
Host: thirdparty.com
Origin: http://example.com ❶
...

<= Response
HTTP/1.1 200 OK
Access-Control-Allow-Origin: http://example.com ❷
...
```

❶ Origin header is automatically set by the browser.

❷ Opt-in header is set by the server.

In the preceding example, *thirdparty.com* decided to opt into cross-origin resource sharing with *example.com* by returning an appropriate access control header in its response. Alternatively, if it wanted to disallow access, it could simply omit the *Access-Control-Allow-Origin* header, and the client's browser would automatically fail the sent request.

 If the third-party server is not CORS aware, then the client request will fail, as the client always verifies the presence of the opt-in header. As a special case, CORS also allows the server to return a wildcard (`Access-Control-Allow-Origin: *`) to indicate that it allows access from any origin. However, think twice before enabling this policy!

With that, we are all done, right? Turns out, not quite, as CORS takes a number of additional security precautions to ensure that the server is CORS aware:

- CORS requests omit user credentials such as cookies and HTTP authentication.
- The client is limited to issuing "simple cross-origin requests," which restricts both the allowed methods (GET, POST, HEAD) and access to HTTP headers that can be sent and read by the XHR.

To enable cookies and HTTP authentication, the client must set an extra property (`withCredentials`) on the XHR object when making the request, and the server must also respond with an appropriate header (*Access-Control-Allow-Credentials*) to indicate that it is knowingly allowing the application to include private user data. Similarly, if the client needs to write or read custom HTTP headers or wants to use a "non-simple method" for the request, then it must first ask for permission from the third-party server by issuing a preflight request:

```
=> Preflight request
OPTIONS /resource.js HTTP/1.1 ❶
Host: thirdparty.com
Origin: http://example.com
Access-Control-Request-Method: POST
Access-Control-Request-Headers: My-Custom-Header
...

<= Preflight response
HTTP/1.1 200 OK ❷
Access-Control-Allow-Origin: http://example.com
Access-Control-Allow-Methods: GET, POST, PUT
Access-Control-Allow-Headers: My-Custom-Header
...

(actual HTTP request) ❸
```

❶ Preflight OPTIONS request to verify permissions
❷ Successful preflight response from third-party origin
❸ Actual CORS request

The official W3C CORS specification defines when and where a preflight request must be used: "simple" requests can skip it, but there are a variety of conditions that will trigger it and add a minimum of a full roundtrip of network latency to verify permissions. The good news is, once a preflight request is made, it can be cached by the client to avoid the same verification on each request.

CORS is supported by all modern browsers; see caniuse.com/cors. For a deep dive on various CORS policies and implementation refer to the official W3C standard (*http://www.w3.org/TR/cors/*).

Downloading Data with XHR

XHR can transfer both text-based and binary data. In fact, the browser offers automatic encoding and decoding for a variety of native data types, which allows the application to pass these types directly to XHR to be properly encoded, and vice versa, for the types to be automatically decoded by the browser:

`ArrayBuffer`
> Fixed-length binary data buffer

`Blob`
> Binary large object of immutable data

`Document`
> Parsed HTML or XML document

`JSON`
> JavaScript object representing a simple data structure

`Text`
> A simple text string

Either the browser can rely on the HTTP content-type negotiation to infer the appropriate data type (e.g., decode an *application/json* response into a JSON object), or the application can explicitly override the data type when initiating the XHR request:

```
var xhr = new XMLHttpRequest();
xhr.open('GET', '/images/photo.webp');
xhr.responseType = 'blob'; ❶

xhr.onload = function() {
  if (this.status == 200) {
    var img = document.createElement('img');
    img.src = window.URL.createObjectURL(this.response); ❷
    img.onload = function() {
        window.URL.revokeObjectURL(this.src); ❸
    }
    document.body.appendChild(img);
  }
};

xhr.send();
```

❶ Set return data type to blob

❷ Create unique object URI from blob and set as image source

❸ Release the object URI once image is loaded

Note that we are transferring an image asset in its native format, without relying on base64 encoding, and adding an image element to the page without relying on data URIs. There is no network transmission overhead or encoding overhead when handling the received binary data in JavaScript! XHR API allows us to script efficient, dynamic applications, regardless of the data type, right from JavaScript.

The blob interface is part of the HTML5 File API and acts as an opaque reference for an arbitrary chunk of data (binary or text). By itself, a blob reference has limited functionality: you can query its size, MIME type, and split it into smaller blobs. However, its real role is to serve as an efficient interchange mechanism between various JavaScript APIs.

Uploading Data with XHR

Uploading data via XHR is just as simple and efficient for all data types. In fact, the code is effectively the same, with the only difference that we also pass in a data object when calling *send()* on the XHR request. The rest is handled by the browser:

```
var xhr = new XMLHttpRequest();
xhr.open('POST','/upload');
xhr.onload = function() { ... };
xhr.send("text string"); ❶

var formData = new FormData(); ❷
formData.append('id', 123456);
formData.append('topic', 'performance');

var xhr = new XMLHttpRequest();
xhr.open('POST', '/upload');
xhr.onload = function() { ... };
xhr.send(formData); ❸

var xhr = new XMLHttpRequest();
xhr.open('POST', '/upload');
xhr.onload = function() { ... };
var uInt8Array = new Uint8Array([1, 2, 3]); ❹
xhr.send(uInt8Array.buffer); ❺
```

❶ Upload a simple text string to the server

❷ Create a dynamic form via FormData API

❸ Upload multipart/form-data object to the server

❹ Create a typed array (ArrayBuffer) of unsigned, 8-byte integers

❺ Upload chunk of bytes to the server

The XHR *send()* method accepts one of DOMString, Document, FormData, Blob, File, or ArrayBuffer objects, automatically performs the appropriate encoding, sets the appropriate HTTP content-type, and dispatches the request. Need to send a binary blob or upload a file provided by the user? Simple: grab a reference to the object and pass it to XHR. In fact, with a little extra work, we can also split a large file into smaller chunks:

```
var blob = ...;  ❶

const BYTES_PER_CHUNK = 1024 * 1024;  ❷
const SIZE = blob.size;

var start = 0;
var end = BYTES_PER_CHUNK;

while(start < SIZE) {  ❸
  var xhr = new XMLHttpRequest();
  xhr.open('POST', '/upload');
  xhr.onload = function() { ... };

  xhr.setRequestHeader('Content-Range', start+'-'+end+'/'+SIZE);  ❹
  xhr.send(blob.slice(start, end));  ❺

  start = end;
  end = start + BYTES_PER_CHUNK;
}
```

❶ An arbitrary blob of data (binary or text)

❷ Set chunk size to 1 MB

❸ Iterate over provided data in 1MB increments

❹ Advertise the uploaded range of data (start-end/total)

❺ Upload 1 MB slice of data via XHR

XHR does not support request streaming, which means that we must provide the full payload when calling *send()*. However, this example illustrates a simple application workaround: the file is split and uploaded in chunks via multiple XHR requests. This implementation pattern is by no means a replacement for a true request streaming API, but it is nonetheless a viable solution for some applications.

> Slicing large file uploads is a good technique to provide more robust API where connectivity is unstable or intermittent—e.g., if a chunk fails due to dropped connection, the application can retry, or resume the upload later instead of restarting the full transfer from the start.

Monitoring Download and Upload Progress

Network connectivity can be intermittent, and latency and bandwidth are highly variable. So how do we know if an XHR request has succeeded, timed out, or failed? The XHR object provides a convenient API for listening to progress events (Table 15-1), which indicate the current status of the request.

Table 15-1. XHR progress events

Event type	Description	Times fired
loadstart	Transfer has begun	once
progress	Transfer is in progress	zero or more
error	Transfer has failed	zero or once
abort	Transfer is terminated	zero or once
load	Transfer is successful	zero or once
loadend	Transfer has finished	once

Each XHR transfer begins with a *loadstart* and finishes with a *loadend* event, and in between, one or more additional events are fired to indicate the status of the transfer. Hence, to monitor progress the application can register a set of JavaScript event listeners on the XHR object:

```
var xhr = new XMLHttpRequest();
xhr.open('GET','/resource');
xhr.timeout = 5000; ❶

xhr.addEventListener('load', function() { ... }); ❷
xhr.addEventListener('error', function() { ... }); ❸

var onProgressHandler = function(event) {
  if(event.lengthComputable) {
    var progress = (event.loaded / event.total) * 100; ❹
    ...
  }
}

xhr.upload.addEventListener('progress', onProgressHandler); ❺
xhr.addEventListener('progress', onProgressHandler); ❻
xhr.send();
```

❶   Set request timeout to 5,000 ms (default: no timeout)

❷   Register callback for successful request

❸   Register callback for failed request

❹   Compute transfer progress

❺   Register callback for upload progress events

❻   Register callback for download progress events

Either the *load* or *error* event will fire once to indicate the final status of the XHR transfer, whereas the *progress* event can fire any number of times and provides a convenient API for tracking transfer status: we can compare the *loaded* attribute against *total* to estimate the amount of transferred data.

To estimate the amount of transferred data, the server must provide a content length in its response: we can't estimate progress of chunked transfers, since by definition, the total size of the response is unknown.

Also, XHR requests do not have a default timeout, which means that a request can be "in progress" indefinitely. As a best practice, always set a meaningful timeout for your application and handle the error!

Streaming Data with XHR

In some cases an application may need or want to process a stream of data incrementally: upload the data to the server as it becomes available on the client, or process the downloaded data as it arrives from the server. Unfortunately, while this is an important use case, today there is no simple, efficient, cross-browser API for XHR streaming:

- The *send* method expects the full payload in case of uploads.
- The *response*, *responseText*, and *responseXML* attributes are not designed for streaming.

Streaming has never been an official use case within the official XHR specification. As a result, short of manually splitting an upload into smaller, individual XHRs, there is no API for streaming data from client to server. Similarly, while the XHR2 specification does provide some ability to read a partial response from the server, the implementation is inefficient and very limited. That's the bad news.

The good news is that there is hope on the horizon! Lack of streaming support as a first-class use case for XHR is a well-recognized limitation, and there is work in progress to address the problem:

> Web applications should have the ability to acquire and manipulate data in a wide variety of forms, including as a sequence of data made available over time. This specification defines the basic representation for Streams, errors raised by Streams, and programmatic ways to read and create Streams.
>
> — W3C Streams API

The combination of XHR and Streams API will enable efficient XHR streaming in the browser. However, the Streams API is still under active discussion, and is not yet available in any browser. So, with that, we're stuck, right? Well, not quite. As we noted earlier, streaming uploads with XHR is not an option, but we do have limited support for streaming downloads with XHR:

```
var xhr = new XMLHttpRequest();
xhr.open('GET', '/stream');
xhr.seenBytes = 0;

xhr.onreadystatechange = function() { ❶
```

```
    if(xhr.readyState > 2) {
      var newData = xhr.responseText.substr(xhr.seenBytes); ❷
      // process newData

      xhr.seenBytes = xhr.responseText.length; ❸
    }
};

xhr.send();
```

❶   Subscribe to state and progress notifications

❷   Extract new data from partial response

❸   Update processed byte offset

This example will work in most modern browsers. However, performance is not great, and there are a large number of implementation caveats and gotchas:

- Note that we are manually tracking the offset for seen bytes and then manually slicing the data: *responseText* is buffering the full response! For small transfers, this may not be an issue, but for larger downloads, and especially on memory-constrained devices such as mobile handsets, this is a problem. The only way to release the buffered response is to finish the request and open a new one.

- Partial response can be read only from the *responseText* attribute, which limits us to text-only transfers. There is no way to read partial response of a binary transfer.

- Once partial data is read, we must identify message boundaries: application logic must define its own data format and then buffer and parse the stream to extract individual messages.

- Browsers differ in how they buffer received data: some browsers may release data immediately, while others may buffer small responses and release them in larger chunks.

- Browsers differ in which content-types they allow to be read incrementally—e.g., some allow "text/html," while others will only work with "application/x-javascript."

In short, currently, XHR streaming is neither efficient nor convenient, and to make matters worse, the lack of a common specification also means that the implementations differ from browser to browser. As a result, at least until the Streams API is available, XHR is not a good fit for streaming.

No need to despair! While XHR may not meet the criteria, we do have other transports that are optimized for the streaming use case: Server-Sent Events offers a convenient API for streaming text-based data from server to client, and WebSocket offers efficient, bidirectional streaming for both binary and text-based data.

Proprietary APIs and Extensions for XHR Streaming

Both Firefox and Internet Explorer provide custom "streaming XHR extensions":

- Firefox supports `moz-chunked-text` and `moz-chunked-arraybuffer`.
- Internet Explorer supports `ms-stream`.

By setting the `responseType` attribute on the XHR object to one of the preceding types, both browsers will avoid buffering the full response and will also allow a binary response to be read incrementally from the XHR object. Unfortunately, there are no equivalent APIs in Chrome, Opera, or other popular browsers. As a result, XHR streaming is still an impractical transport for cross-browser applications.

Real-Time Notifications and Delivery

XHR enables a simple and efficient way to synchronize client updates with the server: whenever necessary, an XHR request is dispatched by the client to update the appropriate data on the server. However, the same problem, but in reverse, is much harder. If data is updated on the server, how does the server notify the client?

HTTP does not provide any way for the server to initiate a new connection to the client. As a result, to receive real-time notifications, the client must either poll the server for updates or leverage a streaming transport to allow the server to push new notifications as they become available. Unfortunately, as we saw in the preceding section, support for XHR streaming is limited, which leaves us with XHR polling.

"Real-time" has different meanings for different applications: some applications demand submillisecond overhead, while others may be just fine with delays measured in minutes. To determine the optimal transport, first define clear latency and overhead targets for your application!

Polling with XHR

One of the simplest strategies to retrieve updates from the server is to have the client do a periodic check: the client can initiate a background XHR request on a periodic interval (poll the server) to check for updates. If new data is available on the server, then it is returned in the response, and otherwise the response is empty.

Polling is simple to implement but frequently is also very inefficient. The choice of the polling interval is critical: long polling intervals translate to delayed delivery of updates, whereas short intervals result in unnecessary traffic and high overhead both for the client and the server. Let's consider the simplest possible example:

```
function checkUpdates(url) {
  var xhr = new XMLHttpRequest();
  xhr.open('GET', url);
  xhr.onload = function() { ... }; ❶
  xhr.send();
}

setInterval(checkUpdates('/updates'), 60000); ❷
```

❶ Process received updates from server

❷ Issue an XHR request every 60 seconds

- Each XHR request is a standalone HTTP request, and on average, HTTP incurs ~800 bytes of overhead (without HTTP cookies) for request/response headers.
- Periodic checks work well when data arrives at predictable intervals. Unfortunately, predictable arrival rates are an exception, not the norm. Consequently, periodic polling will introduce additional latency delays between the message being available on the server and its delivery to the client.
- Unless thought through carefully, polling often becomes a costly performance anti-pattern on wireless networks; see "Eliminate Periodic and Inefficient Data Transfers" on page 142. Waking up the radio consumes a lot of battery power!

What is the optimal polling interval? There isn't one. The frequency depends on the requirements of the application, and there is an inherent trade-off between efficiency and message latency. As a result, polling is a good fit for applications where polling intervals are long, new events are arriving at a predictable rate, and the transferred payloads are large. This combination offsets the extra HTTP overhead and minimizes message delivery delays.

Modeling Performance of XHR Polling

To illustrate the trade-off between latency and overhead of XHR polling, let's consider a simple email application that is using XHR polling to check for message updates on the server. The implementation is as follows:

- Every 60 seconds the client sends an XHR to check for updates.
- Each XHR request includes the most recent message ID known by the client.
- The server compares the client ID against its list of messages.
- The server responds with a list of new messages or an empty list (no updates).

What is the average message latency delay?

> If a new message arrives on the server just before the client checks for updates, then the delay is minimal—just the latency between client and server. Conversely, the same new message can arrive moments after the client check, in which case the message will have to wait until the next client check (60 seconds). Hence, if the message arrival rate is random, then an average message would wait for 30 seconds on the server before the client gets it.

What is the overhead of polling?

> An average HTTP 1.x request adds 800 bytes of request and response overhead (see "Measuring and Controlling Protocol Overhead" on page 200). Because the client is logged in, we will also have an extra authentication cookie and the message ID; let's say this adds another 50 bytes. Hence, a request that returns no new messages will incur 850 bytes! Now imagine we have 10,000 clients, all polling on a 60-second interval:

$$\left(\frac{850 \text{ bytes} \times 8 \text{ bits} \times 10,000}{60 \text{ seconds}} \right) \approx 1.13 \text{ Mbps}$$

> Each client sends 850 bytes of data on each request, which translates to 167 requests per second and a sustained rate of 1.13 Mbps of ingress throughput on the server! And that's a constant rate without actually delivering any new messages to any of the clients.

Is the 30-second delay too high? We can decrease the polling interval, but in doing so, we would incur higher throughput and overhead: the same 10,000 clients, but on a 1-second interval, would generate over 60 Mbps of throughput! In short, unless the polling intervals are long, polling is expensive.

Long-Polling with XHR

The challenge with periodic polling is that there is potential for many unnecessary and empty checks. With that in mind, what if we made a slight modification (Figure 15-1) to the polling workflow: instead of returning an empty response when no updates are available, could we keep the connection idle until an update is available?

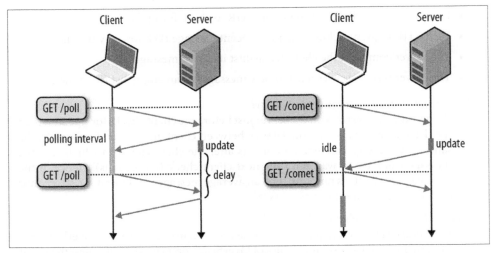

Figure 15-1. Polling (left) vs. long-polling (right) latency

 The technique of leveraging a long-held HTTP request ("a hanging GET") to allow the server to push data to the browser is commonly known as "Comet." However, you may also encounter it under other names, such as "reverse AJAX," "AJAX push," and "HTTP push."

By holding the connection open until an update is available (long-polling), data can be sent immediately to the client once it becomes available on the server. As a result, long-polling offers the best-case scenario for message latency, and it also eliminates empty checks, which reduces the number of XHR requests and the overall overhead of polling. Once an update is delivered, the long-poll request is finished and the client can issue another long-poll request and wait for the next available message:

```
function checkUpdates(url) {
  var xhr = new XMLHttpRequest();
  xhr.open('GET', url);
  xhr.onload = function() { ❶

    ...
    checkUpdates('/updates'); ❷
  };
```

```
    xhr.send();
}

checkUpdates('/updates'); ❸
```

❶ Process received updates and open new long-poll XHR

❷ Issue long-poll request for next update (and loop forever)

❸ Issue initial long-poll XHR request

With that, is long-polling always a better choice than periodic polling? Unless the message arrival rate is known and constant, long-polling will always deliver better message latency. If that's the primary criteria, then long-polling is the winner.

On the other hand, the overhead discussion requires a more nuanced view. First, note that each delivered message still incurs the same HTTP overhead; each new message is a standalone HTTP request. However, if the message arrival rate is high, then long-polling will issue more XHR requests than periodic polling!

Long-polling dynamically adapts to the message arrival rate by minimizing message latency, which is a behavior you may or may not want. If there is some tolerance for message latency, then polling may be a more efficient transport—e.g., if the update rate is high, then polling provides a simple "message aggregation" mechanism, which can reduce the number of requests and improve battery life on mobile handsets.

 In practice, not all messages have the same priority or latency requirements. As a result, you may want to consider a mix of strategies: aggregate low-priority updates on the server, and trigger immediate delivery for high priority updates; see "Nagle and Efficient Server Push" on page 143.

Facebook Chat via XHR Long-Polling

In practice, long-polling has become one of the most widely used methods for delivering real-time notifications via XHR. While it may not be the most efficient transport, it is simple, robust, and supported by any XHR-capable browser. Popular products such as Facebook's Chat were first deployed in 2008 via this very method:

> The method we chose to get text from one user to another involves loading an iframe on each Facebook page, and having that iframe's JavaScript make an HTTP GET request over a persistent connection that doesn't return until the server has data for the client. The request gets reestablished if it's interrupted or times out. This isn't by any means a new technique: it's a variation of Comet, specifically XHR long-polling, and/or BOSH.

— Facebook Chat
Facebook Engineering Blog

Today, we can deliver the same functionality much more efficiently via Server-Sent Events and WebSocket. Having said that, XHR is still a common fallback strategy for many real-time frameworks. If all else fails, long-polling to the rescue!

XHR Use Cases and Performance

XMLHttpRequest is what enabled us to make the leap from building pages to building interactive web applications in the browser. First, it enabled asynchronous communication within the browser, but just as importantly, it also made the process simple. Dispatching and controlling a scripted HTTP request takes just a few lines of JavaScript code, and the browser handles all the rest:

- Browser formats the HTTP request and parses the response.
- Browser enforces relevant security (same-origin) policies.
- Browser handles content negotiation (e.g., gzip).
- Browser handles request and response caching.
- Browser handles authentication, redirects, and more...

As such, XHR is a versatile and a high-performance transport for any transfers that follow the HTTP request-response cycle. Need to fetch a resource that requires authentication, should be compressed while in transfer, and should be cached for future lookups? The browser takes care of all of this and more, allowing us to focus on the application logic!

However, XHR also has its limitations. As we saw, streaming has never been an official use case in the XHR standard, and the support is limited: streaming with XHR is neither efficient nor convenient. Different browsers have different behaviors, and efficient binary streaming is impossible. In short, XHR is not a good fit for streaming.

Similarly, there is no one best strategy for delivering real-time updates with XHR. Periodic polling incurs high overhead and message latency delays. Long-polling delivers low latency but still has the same per-message overhead; each message is its own HTTP request. To have both low latency and low overhead, we need XHR streaming!

As a result, while XHR is a popular mechanism for "real-time" delivery, it may not be the best-performing transport for the job. Modern browsers support both simpler and more efficient options, such as Server-Sent Events and WebSocket. Hence, unless you have a specific reason why XHR polling is required, use them.

CHAPTER 16

Server-Sent Events (SSE)

Server-Sent Events enables efficient server-to-client streaming of text-based event data —e.g., real-time notifications or updates generated on the server. To meet this goal, SSE introduces two components: a new EventSource interface in the browser, which allows the client to receive push notifications from the server as DOM events, and the "event stream" data format, which is used to deliver the individual updates.

The combination of the EventSource API in the browser and the well-defined event stream data format is what makes SSE both an efficient and an indispensable tool for handling real-time data in the browser:

- Low latency delivery via a single, long-lived connection
- Efficient browser message parsing with no unbounded buffers
- Automatic tracking of last seen message and auto reconnect
- Client message notifications as DOM events

Under the hood, SSE provides an efficient, cross-browser implementation of XHR streaming; the actual delivery of the messages is done over a single, long-lived HTTP connection. However, unlike dealing XHR streaming on our own, the browser handles all the connection management and message parsing, allowing our applications to focus on the business logic! In short, SSE makes working with real-time data simple and efficient. Let's take a look under the hood.

EventSource API

The EventSource interface abstracts all the low-level connection establishment and message parsing behind a simple browser API. To get started, we simply need to specify the URL of the SSE event stream resource and register the appropriate JavaScript event listeners on the object:

```
var source = new EventSource("/path/to/stream-url"); ❶

source.onopen = function () { ... }; ❷
source.onerror = function () { ... }; ❸

source.addEventListener("foo", function (event) { ❹
  processFoo(event.data);
});

source.onmessage = function (event) {  ❺
  log_message(event.id, event.data);

  if (event.id == "CLOSE") {
    source.close(); ❻
  }
}
```

❶ Open new SSE connection to stream endpoint

❷ Optional callback, invoked when connection is established

❸ Optional callback, invoked if the connection fails

❹ Subscribe to event of type "foo"; invoke custom logic

❺ Subscribe to all events without an explicit type

❻ Close SSE connection if server sends a "CLOSE" message ID

 EventSource can stream event data from remote origins by leveraging the same CORS permission and opt-in workflow as a regular XHR.

That's all there is to it for the client API. The implementation logic is handled for us: the connection is negotiated on our behalf, received data is parsed incrementally, message boundaries are identified, and finally a DOM event is fired by the browser. EventSource interface allows the application to focus on the business logic: open new connection, process received event notifications, terminate stream when finished.

 SSE provides a memory-efficient implementation of XHR streaming. Unlike a raw XHR connection, which buffers the full received response until the connection is dropped, an SSE connection can discard processed messages without accumulating all of them in memory.

As icing on the cake, the EventSource interface also provides auto-reconnect and tracking of the last seen message: if the connection is dropped, EventSource will automatically

reconnect to the server and optionally advertise the ID of the last seen message, such that the stream can be resumed and lost messages can be retransmitted.

How does the browser know the ID, type, and boundary of each message? This is where the event stream protocol comes in. The combination of a simple client API and a well-defined data format is what allows us to offload the bulk of the work to the browser. The two go hand in hand, even though the low-level data protocol is completely transparent to the application in the browser.

Emulating EventSource with Custom JavaScript

SSE was an early addition to the HTML5 specification and is natively supported by most modern browsers. The two notable omissions, as of early 2013, are Internet Explorer and the stock Android browser. For the latest status, see caniuse.com/eventsource.

However, the good news is the EventSource interface is simple enough such that it can be emulated via an optional JavaScript library (i.e., a "polyfill") for browsers that do not support it natively. Similarly, the delivery of the event stream can be implemented on top of existing XHR mechanisms:

```
if (!window.EventSource) {
  // load JavaScript polyfill library
}

var source = new EventSource("/event-stream-endpoint");
...
```

The benefit of using a polyfill library is that it allows our applications to, once again, focus on the application logic, instead of worrying about the browser quirks and implementation status. Having said that, while a polyfill will provide a consistent API, be aware that the underlying XHR transport will not be as efficient:

- XHR polling will incur message delays and high request overhead.
- XHR long-polling minimizes latency delays but has high request overhead.
- XHR streaming support is limited and buffers all the data in memory.

Without native support for efficient XHR streaming of event stream data, the polyfill library can fallback to polling, long-polling, or XHR streaming, each of which has its own performance costs. For a full discussion, refer to "Real-Time Notifications and Delivery" on page 273.

In short, check the implementation of your polyfill library to ensure that it meets your performance goals! Many of the most popular libraries (e.g., jQuery.EventSource) use XHR polling to emulate the SSE transport—simple, but also an inefficient transport.

Event Stream Protocol

An SSE event stream is delivered as a streaming HTTP response: the client initiates a regular HTTP request, the server responds with a custom *"text/event-stream"* content-type, and then streams the UTF-8 encoded event data. However, even that sounds too complicated, so an example is in order:

```
=> Request
GET /stream HTTP/1.1 ❶
Host: example.com
Accept: text/event-stream

<= Response
HTTP/1.1 200 OK ❷
Connection: keep-alive
Content-Type: text/event-stream
Transfer-Encoding: chunked

retry: 15000 ❸

data: First message is a simple string. ❹

data: {"message": "JSON payload"} ❺

event: foo ❻
data: Message of type "foo"

id: 42 ❼
event: bar
data: Multi-line message of
data: type "bar" and id "42"

id: 43 ❽
data: Last message, id "43"
```

❶   Client connection initiated via EventSource interface

❷   Server response with "text/event-stream" content-type

❸   Server sets client reconnect interval (15s) if the connection drops

❹   Simple text event with no message type

❺   JSON payload with no message type

❻   Simple text event of type "foo"

❼   Multiline event with message ID and type

❽   Simple text event with optional ID

The event-stream protocol is trivial to understand and implement:

- Event payload is the value of one or more adjacent `data` fields.

- Event may carry an optional ID and an event type string.
- Event boundaries are marked by newlines.

On the receiving end, the EventSource interface parses the incoming stream by looking for newline separators, extracts the payload from data fields, checks for optional ID and type, and finally dispatches a DOM event to notify the application. If a type is present, then a custom DOM event is fired, and otherwise the generic "onmessage" callback is invoked; see "EventSource API" on page 279 for both cases.

UTF-8 Encoding and Binary Transfers with SSE

EventSource does not perform any additional processing on the actual payload: the message is extracted from one or more data fields, concatenated together and passed directly to the application. As such, the server can push any text-based format (e.g., a simple string, JSON payload, etc.), and the application must decode it on its own.

Having said that, note that all event source data is UTF-8 encoded: SSE is not meant as a mechanism for transferring binary payloads! If necessary, one could base64 encode an arbitrary binary object to make it SSE friendly, but doing so would incur high (33%) byte overhead; see "Resource Inlining" on page 204.

Concerned by high overhead of UTF-8 on the wire? An SSE connection is a streaming HTTP response, which means that it can be compressed (i.e., gziped), just as any other HTTP response while in flight! While SSE is not meant for delivery of binary data, it is nonetheless an efficient transport: ensure that your server is applying gzip compression on the SSE stream.

Lack of support for binary streaming is not an oversight. SSE was specifically designed as a simple, efficient, server-to-client transport for text-based data. If you need to transfer binary payloads, then a WebSocket is the right tool for the job.

Finally, in addition to automatic event parsing, SSE provides built-in support for reestablishing dropped connections, as well as recovery of messages the client may have missed while disconnected. By default, if the connection is dropped, then the browser will automatically reestablish the connection. The SSE specification recommends a 2–3 second delay, which is a common default for most browsers, but the server can also set a custom interval at any point by sending a retry command to the client.

Similarly, the server can also associate an arbitrary ID string with each message. The browser automatically remembers the last seen ID and will automatically append a "Last-Event-ID" HTTP header with the remembered value when issuing a reconnect request. Here's an example:

```
(existing SSE connection)
retry: 4500 ❶
```

```
id: 43 ❷
data: Lorem ipsum

(connection dropped)
(4500 ms later)

=> Request
GET /stream HTTP/1.1 ❸
Host: example.com
Accept: text/event-stream
Last-Event-ID: 43

<= Response
HTTP/1.1 200 OK ❹
Content-Type: text/event-stream
Connection: keep-alive
Transfer-Encoding: chunked

id: 44 ❺
data: dolor sit amet
```

❶ Server sets the client reconnect interval to 4.5 seconds

❷ Simple text event, ID: 43

❸ Automatic client reconnect request with last seen event ID

❹ Server response with "text/event-stream" content-type

❺ Simple text event, ID: 44

The client application does not need to provide any extra logic to reestablish the connection or remember the last seen event ID. The entire workflow is handled by the browser, and we rely on the server to handle the recovery. Specifically, depending on the requirements of the application and the data stream, the server can implement several different strategies:

- If lost messages are acceptable, then no event IDs or special logic is required: simply let the client reconnect and resume the stream.

- If message recovery is required, then the server needs to specify IDs for relevant events, such that the client can report the last seen ID when reconnecting. Also, the server needs to implement some form of a local cache to recover and retransmit missed messages to the client.

The exact implementation details of how far back the messages are persisted are, of course, specific to the requirements of the application. Further, note that the ID is an optional event stream field. Hence, the server can also choose to checkpoint specific messages or milestones in the delivered event stream. In short, evaluate your requirements, and implement the appropriate logic on the server.

SSE Use Cases and Performance

SSE is a high-performance transport for server-to-client streaming of text-based real-time data: messages can be pushed the moment they become available on the server (low latency), there is minimum message overhead (long-lived connection, event-stream protocol, and gzip compression), the browser handles all the message parsing, and there are no unbounded buffers. Add to that a convenient EventSource API with auto-reconnect and message notifications as DOM events, and SSE becomes an indispensable tool for working with real-time data!

There are two key limitations to SSE. First, it is server-to-client only and hence does not address the request streaming use case—e.g., streaming a large upload to the server. Second, the event-stream protocol is specifically designed to transfer UTF-8 data: binary streaming, while possible, is inefficient.

Having said that, the UTF-8 limitation can often be resolved at the application layer: SSE delivers a notification to the application about a new binary asset available on the server, and the application dispatches an XHR request to fetch it. While this incurs an extra roundtrip of latency, it also has the benefit of leveraging the numerous services provided by the XHR: response caching, transfer-encoding (compression), and so on. If an asset is streamed, it cannot be cached by the browser cache.

 Real-time push, just as polling, can have a large negative impact on battery life. First, consider batching messages to avoid waking up the radio. Second, eliminate unnecessary keepalives; an SSE connection is not "dropped" while the radio is idle. For more details, see "Eliminate Periodic and Inefficient Data Transfers" on page 142.

SSE Streaming over TLS

SSE provides a simple and convenient real-time transport on top of a regular HTTP connection, which makes it simple to deploy on the server and to polyfill on the client. However, existing network middleware, such as proxy servers and firewalls, which are not SSE aware, may still cause problems: intermediaries may choose to buffer the event-stream data, which will translate to increased latency or an outright broken SSE connection.

As a result, if you experience this or similar problems, you may want to consider delivering an SSE event-stream over a TLS connection; see "Proxies, Intermediaries, TLS, and New Protocols on the Web" on page 50.

CHAPTER 17

WebSocket

WebSocket enables bidirectional, message-oriented streaming of text and binary data between client and server. It is the closest API to a raw network socket in the browser. Except a WebSocket connection is also much more than a network socket, as the browser abstracts all the complexity behind a simple API and provides a number of additional services:

- Connection negotiation and same-origin policy enforcement
- Interoperability with existing HTTP infrastructure
- Message-oriented communication and efficient message framing
- Subprotocol negotiation and extensibility

WebSocket is one of the most versatile and flexible transports available in the browser. The simple and minimal API enables us to layer and deliver arbitrary application protocols between client and server—anything from simple JSON payloads to custom binary message formats—in a streaming fashion, where either side can send data at any time.

However, the trade-off with custom protocols is that they are, well, custom. The application must account for missing state management, compression, caching, and other services otherwise provided by the browser. There are always design constraints and performance trade-offs, and leveraging WebSocket is no exception. In short, WebSocket is not a replacement for HTTP, XHR, or SSE, and for best performance it is critical that we leverage the strengths of each transport.

 WebSocket is a set of multiple standards: the WebSocket API is defined by the W3C, and the WebSocket protocol (RFC 6455) and its extensions are defined by the HyBi Working Group (IETF).

WebSocket API

The WebSocket API provided by the browser is remarkably small and simple. Once again, all the low-level details of connection management and message processing are taken care of by the browser. To initiate a new connection, we need the URL of a WebSocket resource and a few application callbacks:

```
var ws = new WebSocket('wss://example.com/socket'); ❶

ws.onerror = function (error) { ... } ❷
ws.onclose = function () { ... } ❸

ws.onopen = function () { ❹
  ws.send("Connection established. Hello server!"); ❺
}

ws.onmessage = function(msg) { ❻
  if(msg.data instanceof Blob) { ❼
    processBlob(msg.data);
  } else {
    processText(msg.data);
  }
}
```

❶   Open a new secure WebSocket connection (wss)

❷   Optional callback, invoked if a connection error has occurred

❸   Optional callback, invoked when the connection is terminated

❹   Optional callback, invoked when a WebSocket connection is established

❺   Client-initiated message to the server

❻   A callback function invoked for each new message from the server

❼   Invoke binary or text processing logic for the received message

The API speaks for itself. In fact, it should look very similar to the EventSource API we saw in the preceding chapter. This is intentional, as WebSocket offers similar and extended functionality. Having said that, there are a number of important differences as well. Let's take a look at them one by one.

Emulating WebSocket

WebSocket protocol has undergone a number of revisions, implementation rollbacks, and security investigations. However, the good news is that the latest version (v13) defined by RFC6455 is now supported by all modern browsers. The only notable omission is the Android browser. For the latest status, see *http://caniuse.com/websockets*.

Similar to the SSE polyfill strategy ("Emulating EventSource with Custom JavaScript" on page 281), the WebSocket browser API can be emulated via an optional JavaScript library. However, the hard part with emulating WebSockets is not the API, but the transport! As a result, the choice of the polyfill library and its fallback transport (XHR polling, EventSource, iframe polling, etc.) will have significant impact on the performance of an emulated WebSocket session.

To simplify cross-browser deployment, popular libraries such as SockJS provide an implementation of WebSocket-like object in the browser but also go one step further by providing a custom server that implements support for WebSocket and a variety of alternative transports. The combination of a custom server and client is what enables "seamless fallback": the performance suffers, but the application API remains the same.

Other libraries, such as Socket.IO, go even further by implementing additional features, such as heartbeats, timeouts, support for automatic reconnects, and more, in addition to a multitransport fallback functionality.

When considering a polyfill library or a "real-time framework," such as Socket.IO, pay close attention to the underlying implementation and configuration of the client and server: always leverage the native WebSocket interface for best performance, and ensure that fallback transports meet your performance goals.

WS and WSS URL Schemes

The WebSocket resource URL uses its own custom scheme: *ws* for plain-text communication (e.g., *ws://example.com/socket*), and *wss* when an encrypted channel (TCP +TLS) is required. Why the custom scheme, instead of the familiar *http*?

The primary use case for the WebSocket protocol is to provide an optimized, bidirectional communication channel between applications running in the browser and the server. However, the WebSocket wire protocol can be used outside the browser and could be negotiated via a non-HTTP exchange. As a result, the HyBi Working Group chose to adopt a custom URL scheme.

Despite the non-HTTP negotiation option enabled by the custom scheme, in practice there are no existing standards for alternative handshake mechanisms for establishing a WebSocket session.

Receiving Text and Binary Data

WebSocket communication consists of messages and application code and does not need to worry about buffering, parsing, and reconstructing received data. For example, if the server sends a 1 MB payload, the application's onmessage callback will be called only when the entire message is available on the client.

Further, the WebSocket protocol makes no assumptions and places no constraints on the application payload: both text and binary data are fair game. Internally, the protocol tracks only two pieces of information about the message: the length of payload as a variable-length field and the type of payload to distinguish UTF-8 from binary transfers.

When a new message is received by the browser, it is automatically converted to a DOMString object for text-based data, or a Blob object for binary data, and then passed directly to the application. The only other option, which acts as performance hint and optimization for the client, is to tell the browser to convert the received binary data to an ArrayBuffer instead of Blob:

```
var ws = new WebSocket('wss://example.com/socket');
ws.binaryType = "arraybuffer"; ❶

ws.onmessage = function(msg) {
  if(msg.data instanceof ArrayBuffer) {
    processArrayBuffer(msg.data);
  } else {
    processText(msg.data);
  }
}
```

❶ Force an ArrayBuffer conversion when a binary message is received

> User agents can use this as a hint for how to handle incoming binary data: if the attribute is set to "blob", it is safe to spool it to disk, and if it is set to "arraybuffer", it is likely more efficient to keep the data in memory. Naturally, user agents are encouraged to use more subtle heuristics to decide whether to keep incoming data in memory or not...
>
> — The WebSocket API
> *W3C Candidate Recommendation*

A Blob object represents a file-like object of immutable, raw data. If you do not need to modify the data and do not need to slice it into smaller chunks, then it is the optimal format—e.g., you can pass the entire Blob object to an image tag (see the example in "Downloading Data with XHR" on page 266). On the other hand, if you need to perform additional processing on the binary data, then ArrayBuffer is likely the better fit.

An ArrayBuffer is a generic, fixed-length binary data buffer. However, an ArrayBuffer can be used to create one or more ArrayBufferView objects, each of which can present the contents of the buffer in a specific format. For example, let's assume we have the following C-like binary data structure:

```
struct someStruct {
  char username[16];
  unsigned short id;
  float scores[32];
};
```

Given an ArrayBuffer object of this type, we can create multiple views into the same buffer, each with its own offset and data type:

```
var buffer = msg.data;

var usernameView = new Uint8Array(buffer, 0, 16);
var idView = new Uint16Array(buffer, 16, 1);
var scoresView = new Float32Array(buffer, 18, 32);

console.log("ID: " + idView[0] + " username: " + usernameView[0]);
for (var j = 0; j < 32; j++) { console.log(scoresView[j]) }
```

Each view takes the parent buffer, starting byte offset, and number of elements to process —the offset is calculated based on the size of the preceding fields. As a result, ArrayBuffer and WebSocket give our applications all the necessary tools to stream and process binary data within the browser.

Sending Text and Binary Data

Once a WebSocket connection is established, the client can send and receive UTF-8 and binary messages at will. WebSocket offers a bidirectional communication channel, which allows message delivery in both directions over the same TCP connection:

```
var ws = new WebSocket('wss://example.com/socket');

ws.onopen = function () {
  socket.send("Hello server!"); ❶
  socket.send(JSON.stringify({'msg': 'payload'})); ❷

  var buffer = new ArrayBuffer(128);
  socket.send(buffer); ❸

  var intview = new Uint32Array(buffer);
  socket.send(intview); ❹

  var blob = new Blob([buffer]);
```

```
    socket.send(blob);  ❺
  }
```

❶   Send a UTF-8 encoded text message

❷   Send a UTF-8 encoded JSON payload

❸   Send the ArrayBuffer contents as binary payload

❹   Send the ArrayBufferView contents as binary payload

❺   Send the Blob contents as binary payload

The WebSocket API accepts a DOMString object, which is encoded as UTF-8 on the wire, or one of ArrayBuffer, ArrayBufferView, or Blob objects for binary transfers. However, note that the latter binary options are simply an API convenience: on the wire, a WebSocket frame is either marked as binary or text via a single bit. Hence, if the application, or the server, need other content-type information about the payload, then they must use an additional mechanism to communicate this data.

The *send()* method is asynchronous: the provided data is queued by the client, and the function returns immediately. As a result, especially when transferring large payloads, do not mistake the fast return for a signal that the data has been sent! To monitor the amount of data queued by the browser, the application can query the bufferedA mount attribute on the socket:

```
var ws = new WebSocket('wss://example.com/socket');

ws.onopen = function () {
  subscribeToApplicationUpdates(function(evt) { ❶
    if (ws.bufferedAmount == 0) ❷
      ws.send(evt.data); ❸
  });
};
```

❶   Subscribe to application updates (e.g., game state changes)

❷   Check the amount of buffered data on the client

❸   Send the next update if the buffer is empty

The preceding example attempts to send application updates to the server, but only if the previous messages have been drained from the client's buffer. Why bother with such checks? All WebSocket messages are delivered in the exact order in which they are queued by the client. As a result, a large backlog of queued messages, or even a single large message, will delay delivery of messages queued behind it—head-of-line blocking!

To work around this problem, the application can split large messages into smaller chunks, monitor the bufferedAmount value carefully to avoid head-of-line blocking, and even implement its own priority queue for pending messages instead of blindly queuing them all on the socket.

Many applications generate multiple classes of messages: high-priority updates, such as control traffic, and low-priority updates, such as background transfers. To optimize delivery, the application should pay close attention to how and when each type of message is queued on the socket!

Subprotocol Negotiation

WebSocket protocol makes no assumptions about the format of each message: a single bit tracks whether the message contains text or binary data, such that it can be efficiently decoded by the client and server, but otherwise the message contents are opaque.

Further, unlike HTTP or XHR requests, which communicate additional metadata via HTTP headers of each request and response, there is no such equivalent mechanism for a WebSocket message. As a result, if additional metadata about the message is required, then the client and server must agree to implement their own subprotocol to communicate this data:

- The client and server can agree on a fixed message format upfront—e.g., all communication will be done via JSON-encoded messages or a custom binary format, and necessary message metadata will be part of the encoded structure.

- If the client and server need to transfer different data types, then they can agree on a consistent message header, which can be used to communicate the instructions to decode the remainder of the payload.

- A mix of text and binary messages can be used to communicate the payload and metadata information—e.g., a text message can communicate an equivalent of HTTP headers, followed by a binary message with the application payload.

This list is just a small sample of possible strategies. The flexibility and low overhead of a WebSocket message come at the cost of extra application logic. However, message serialization and management of metadata are only part of the problem! Once we determine the serialization format for our messages, how do we ensure that both client and server understand each other, and how do we keep them in sync?

Thankfully, WebSocket provides a simple and convenient *subprotocol negotiation* API to address the second problem. The client can advertise which protocols it supports to the server as part of its initial connection handshake:

```
var ws = new WebSocket('wss://example.com/socket',
                       ['appProtocol', 'appProtocol-v2']); ❶

ws.onopen = function () {
  if (ws.protocol == 'appProtocol-v2') { ❷
    ...
  } else {
```

```
      . . .
   }
 }
```

❶   Array of subprotocols to advertise during WebSocket handshake

❷   Check the subprotocol chosen by the server

As the preceding example illustrates, the WebSocket constructor accepts an optional array of subprotocol names, which allows the client to advertise the list of protocols it understands or is willing to use for this connection. The specified list is sent to the server, and the server is allowed to pick one of the protocols advertised by the client.

If the subprotocol negotiation is successful, then the onopen callback is fired on the client, and the application can query the protocol attribute on the WebSocket object to determine the chosen protocol. On the other hand, if the server does not support any of the client protocols advertised by the client, then the WebSocket handshake is incomplete: the onerror callback is invoked, and the connection is terminated.

> The subprotocol names are defined by the application and are sent as specified to the server during the initial HTTP handshake. Other then that, the specified subprotocol has no effect on the core WebSocket API.

WebSocket Protocol

The WebSocket wire protocol (RFC 6455) developed by the HyBi Working Group consists of two high-level components: the opening HTTP handshake used to negotiate the parameters of the connection and a binary message framing mechanism to allow for low overhead, message-based delivery of both text and binary data.

> The WebSocket Protocol attempts to address the goals of existing bidirectional HTTP technologies in the context of the existing HTTP infrastructure; as such, it is designed to work over HTTP ports 80 and 443... However, the design does not limit WebSocket to HTTP, and future implementations could use a simpler handshake over a dedicated port without reinventing the entire protocol.
>
> — WebSocket Protocol
> *RFC 6455*

WebSocket protocol is a fully functional, standalone protocol that can be used outside the browser. Having said that, its primary application is as a bidirectional transport for browser-based applications.

Binary Framing Layer

Client and server WebSocket applications communicate via a message-oriented API: the sender provides an arbitrary UTF-8 or binary payload, and the receiver is notified of its delivery when the entire message is available. To enable this, WebSocket uses a custom binary framing format (Figure 17-1), which splits each application message into one or more *frames*, transports them to the destination, reassembles them, and finally notifies the receiver once the entire message has been received.

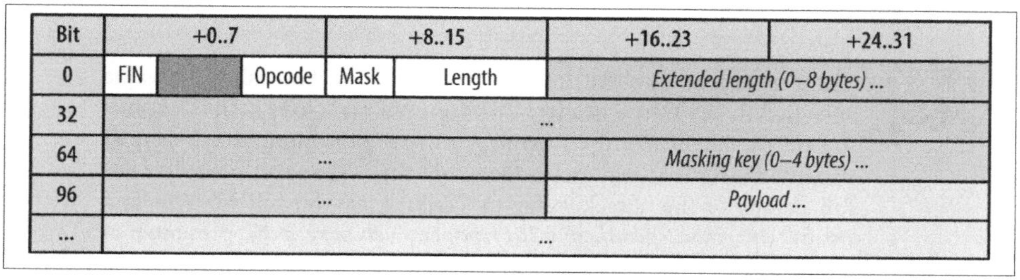

Bit	+0..7		Opcode	Mask	Length	+16..23	+24..31
0	FIN		Opcode	Mask	Length	Extended length (0–8 bytes) ...	
32						...	
64			...			Masking key (0–4 bytes) ...	
96			...			Payload ...	
...						...	

Figure 17-1. WebSocket frame: 2–14 bytes + payload

Frame
> The smallest unit of communication, each containing a variable-length frame header and a payload that may carry all or part of the application message.

Message
> A complete sequence of frames that map to a logical application message.

The decision to fragment an application message into multiple frames is made by the underlying implementation of the client and server framing code. Hence, the applications remain blissfully unaware of the individual WebSocket frames or how the framing is performed. Having said that, it is still useful to understand the highlights of how each WebSocket frame is represented on the wire:

- The first bit of each frame (FIN) indicates whether the frame is a final fragment of a message. A message may consist of just a single frame.

- The opcode (4 bits) indicates type of transferred frame: text (1) or binary (2) for transferring application data or a control frame such as connection close (8), ping (9), and pong (10) for connection liveness checks.

- The mask bit indicates whether the payload is masked (for messages sent from the client to the server only).

- Payload length is represented as a variable-length field:
  - If 0–125, then that is the payload length.

— If 126, then the following 2 bytes represent a 16-bit unsigned integer indicating the frame length.

— If 127, then the following 8 bytes represent a 64-bit unsigned integer indicating the frame length.

- Masking key contains a 32-bit value used to mask the payload.
- Payload contains the application data and custom extension data if the client and server negotiated an extension when the connection was established.

 The payload of all client-initiated frames is *masked* using the value specified in the frame header: this prevents malicious scripts executing on the client from performing a cache poisoning attack against intermediaries that may not understand the WebSocket protocol. For full details of this attack, refer to "Talking to Yourself for Fun and Profit" (*http://w2spconf.com/2011/papers/websocket.pdf*), presented at W2SP 2011.

As a result, each server-sent WebSocket frame incurs 2–10 bytes of framing overhead. The client must also send a masking key, which adds an extra 4 bytes to the header, resulting in 6–14 bytes over overhead. No other metadata, such as header fields or other information about the payload, is available: all WebSocket communication is performed by exchanging frames that treat the payload as an opaque blob of application data.

WebSocket Multiplexing and Head-of-Line Blocking

WebSocket is susceptible to head-of-line blocking: messages can be split into one or more frames, but frames from different messages can't be interleaved, as there is no equivalent to a "stream ID" found in the HTTP 2.0 framing mechanism; see "Streams, Messages, and Frames" on page 212).

As a result, a large message, even when split into multiple WebSocket frames, will block the delivery of frames associated with other messages. If your application is delivering latency-sensitive data, be careful about the payload size of each message and consider splitting large messages into multiple application messages!

The lack of multiplexing in core WebSocket specification also means that each Web-Socket connection requires a dedicated TCP connection, which may become a potential problem for HTTP 1.x deployments due to a restricted number of connections per origin maintained by the browser; see "Exhausting Client and Server Resources" on page 197.

On the bright side, the new "Multiplexing Extension for WebSockets" developed by the HyBi Working Group addresses the latter limitation:

> With this extension, one TCP connection can provide multiple virtual WebSocket connections by encapsulating frames tagged with a channel ID... The multiplexing extension maintains separate logical channels, each of which provides fully the logical equivalent of an independent WebSocket connection, including separate handshake headers.
>
> — WebSocket Multiplexing (Draft 10)

With this extension in place, multiple WebSocket connections (channels) can be multiplexed over the same TCP connection. However, each individual channel is still susceptible to head-of-line blocking! Hence, one potential workaround is to use different channels, or dedicated TCP connections, to multiplex multiple messages in parallel.

Finally, note that the preceding extension is necessary only for HTTP 1.x connections. While no official specification is yet available for transporting WebSocket frames with HTTP 2.0, doing so would be much easier: HTTP 2.0 has built-in stream multiplexing, and multiple WebSocket connections could be transported within a single session by encapsulating WebSocket frames within the HTTP 2.0 framing mechanism.

Protocol Extensions

WebSocket specification allows for protocol extensions: the wire format and the semantics of the WebSocket protocol can be extended with new opcodes and data fields. While somewhat unusual, this is a very powerful feature, as it allows the client and server to implement additional functionality on top of the base WebSocket framing layer without requiring any intervention or cooperation from the application code.

What are some examples of WebSocket protocol extensions? The HyBi Working Group, which is responsible for the development of the WebSocket specification, lists two official extensions in development:

"A Multiplexing Extension for WebSockets"
This extension provides a way for separate logical WebSocket connections to share an underlying transport connection.

"Compression Extensions for WebSocket"
A framework for creating WebSocket extensions that add compression functionality to the WebSocket Protocol.

As we noted earlier, each WebSocket connection requires a dedicated TCP connection, which is inefficient. Multiplexing extension addresses this problem by extending each WebSocket frame with an additional "channel ID" to allow multiple virtual WebSocket channels to share a single TCP connection.

Similarly, the base WebSocket specification provides no mechanism or provisions for compression of transferred data: each frame carries payload data as provided by the application. As a result, while this may not be a problem for optimized binary data structures, this can result in high byte transfer overhead unless the application implements its own data compression and decompression logic. In effect, compression extension enables an equivalent of transfer-encoding negotiation provided by HTTP.

To enable one or more extensions, the client must advertise them in the initial Upgrade handshake, and the server must select and acknowledge the extensions that will be used for the lifetime of the negotiated connection. For a hands-on example, let's now take a closer look at the Upgrade sequence.

WebSocket Multiplexing and Compression in the Wild

As of mid-2013, WebSocket multiplexing is not yet supported by any popular browser. Similarly, there is limited support for compression: Google Chrome and the latest Web-Kit browsers may advertise an "x-webkit-deflate-frame" extension to the server. However, deflate-frame is based on an outdated revision of the standard and will be deprecated in the future.

As the name implies, per-frame compresses the payload contents on a frame-by-frame basis, which is suboptimal for large messages that may be split between multiple frames. As a result, latest revisions of the compression extension have switched to per-message compression—that's the good news. The bad news is per-message compression is still experimental and is not yet available in any popular browser.

As a result, the application should pay close attention to the content-type of transferred data and apply its own compression where applicable. That is, at least until native Web-Socket compression support is available widely across all the popular browsers. This is especially important for mobile applications, where each unnecessary byte carries high costs to the user.

HTTP Upgrade Negotiation

The WebSocket protocol delivers a lot of powerful features: message-oriented communication, its own binary framing layer, subprotocol negotiation, optional protocol extensions, and more. As a result, before any messages can be exchanged, the client and server must negotiate the appropriate parameters to establish the connection.

Leveraging HTTP to perform the handshake offers several advantages. First, it makes WebSockets compatible with existing HTTP infrastructure: WebSocket servers can run on port 80 and 443, which are frequently the only open ports for the client. Second, it allows us to reuse and extend the HTTP Upgrade flow with custom WebSocket headers to perform the negotiation:

Sec-WebSocket-Version
> Sent by the client to indicate version ("13" for RFC6455) of the WebSocket protocol it wants to use. If the server does not support the client version, then it must reply with a list of supported versions.

Sec-WebSocket-Key

An auto-generated key sent by the client, which acts as a "challenge" to the server to prove that the server supports the requested version of the protocol.

Sec-WebSocket-Accept

Server response that contains signed value of Sec-WebSocket-Key, proving that it understands the requested protocol version.

Sec-WebSocket-Protocol

Used to negotiate the application subprotocol: client advertises the list of supported protocols; server must reply with a single protocol name.

Sec-WebSocket-Extensions

Used to negotiate WebSocket extensions to be used for this connection: client advertises supported extensions, and the server confirms one or more extensions by returning the same header.

With that, we now have all the necessary pieces to perform an HTTP Upgrade and negotiate a new WebSocket connection between the client and server:

```
GET /socket HTTP/1.1
Host: thirdparty.com
Origin: http://example.com
Connection: Upgrade
Upgrade: websocket ❶
Sec-WebSocket-Version: 13 ❷
Sec-WebSocket-Key: dGhlIHNhbXBsZSBub25jZQ== ❸
Sec-WebSocket-Protocol: appProtocol, appProtocol-v2 ❹
Sec-WebSocket-Extensions: x-webkit-deflate-message, x-custom-extension ❺
```

❶ Request to perform an upgrade to the WebSocket protocol

❷ WebSocket protocol version used by the client

❸ Auto-generated key to verify server protocol support

❹ Optional list of subprotocols specified by the application

❺ Optional list of protocol extensions supported by the client

Just like any other client-initiated connection in the browser, WebSocket requests are subject to the same-origin policy: the browser automatically appends the Origin header to the upgrade handshake, and the remote server can use CORS to accept or deny the cross origin request; see "Cross-Origin Resource Sharing (CORS)" on page 263. To complete the handshake, the server must return a successful "Switching Protocols" response and confirm the selected options advertised by the client:

```
HTTP/1.1 101 Switching Protocols ❶
Upgrade: websocket
Connection: Upgrade
Access-Control-Allow-Origin: http://example.com ❷
```

```
Sec-WebSocket-Accept: s3pPLMBiTxaQ9kYGzzhZRbK+xOo= ❸
Sec-WebSocket-Protocol: appProtocol-v2 ❹
Sec-WebSocket-Extensions: x-custom-extension ❺
```

❶   101 response code confirming WebSocket upgrade

❷   CORS header indicating opt-in for cross-origin connection

❸   Signed Key value proving protocol support

❹   Application subprotocol selected by the server

❺   List of WebSocket extensions selected by the server

 All RFC6455-compatible WebSocket servers use the same algorithm to compute the answer to the client challenge: the contents of the Sec-WebSocket-Key are concatenated with a unique GUID string defined in the standard, a SHA1 hash is computed, and the resulting string is base-64 encoded and sent back to the client.

At a minimum, a successful WebSocket handshake must contain the protocol version and an auto-generated challenge value sent by the client, followed by a 101 HTTP response code (Switching Protocols) from the server with a hashed challenge-response to confirm the selected protocol version:

- Client must send Sec-WebSocket-Version and Sec-WebSocket-Key.

- Server must confirm the protocol by returning Sec-WebSocket-Accept.

- Client may send a list of application subprotocols via Sec-WebSocket-Protocol.

- Server must select one of the advertised subprotocols and return it via Sec-WebSocket-Protocol. If the server does not support any, then the connection is aborted.

- Client may send a list of protocol extensions in Sec-WebSocket-Extensions.

- Server may confirm one or more selected extensions via Sec-WebSocket-Extensions. If no extensions are provided, then the connection proceeds without them.

Finally, once the preceding handshake is complete, and if the handshake is successful, the connection can now be used as a two-way communication channel for exchanging WebSocket messages. From here on, there is no other explicit HTTP communication between the client and server, and the WebSocket protocol takes over.

Proxies, Intermediaries, and WebSockets

In practice, for security and policy reasons, many users have a restricted set of open ports—specifically port 80 (HTTP), and port 443 (HTTPS). As a result, WebSocket negotiation is performed via the HTTP Upgrade flow to ensure the best compatibility with existing network policies and infrastructure.

However, as we noted earlier in "Proxies, Intermediaries, TLS, and New Protocols on the Web" on page 50, many existing HTTP intermediaries may not understand the new WebSocket protocol, which can lead to a variety of failure cases: blind connection upgrades, unintended buffering of WebSocket frames, content modification without understanding of the protocol, misclassification of WebSocket traffic as compromised HTTP connections, and so on.

The WebSocket Key and Accept handshake addresses some of these problems: it is a security policy against servers and intermediaries that may blindly "upgrade" the connection without actually understanding the WebSocket protocol. However, while this precaution addresses some deployment issues with explicit proxies, it is nonetheless insufficient for "transparent proxies," which may analyze and modify the data on the wire without notice.

The workaround? Establish a secure end-to-end tunnel—i.e., use WSS! By negotiating a TLS session prior to performing the HTTP Upgrade handshake, the client and server establish an encrypted tunnel, which resolves all of the previously listed concerns. This is especially true for mobile clients, whose traffic often passes through a variety of proxy services that may not play well with WebSocket.

WebSocket Use Cases and Performance

WebSocket API provides a simple interface for bidirectional, message-oriented streaming of text and binary data between client and server: pass in a WebSocket URL to the constructor, set up a few JavaScript callback functions, and we are up and running—the rest is handled by the browser. Add to that the WebSocket protocol, which offers binary framing, extensibility, and subprotocol negotiation, and WebSocket becomes a perfect fit for delivering custom application protocols in the browser.

However, just as with any discussion on performance, while the implementation complexity of the WebSocket protocol is hidden from the application, it nonetheless has important performance implications for how and when WebSocket should be used. WebSocket is not a replacement for XHR or SSE, and for best performance it is critical that we leverage the strengths of each transport!

Refer to "XHR Use Cases and Performance" on page 278 and "SSE Use Cases and Performance" on page 285 for a review of the performance characteristics of each transport.

Request and Response Streaming

WebSocket is the only transport that allows bidirectional communication over the same TCP connection (Figure 17-2): the client and server can exchange messages at will. As a result, WebSocket provides low latency delivery of text and binary application data in both directions.

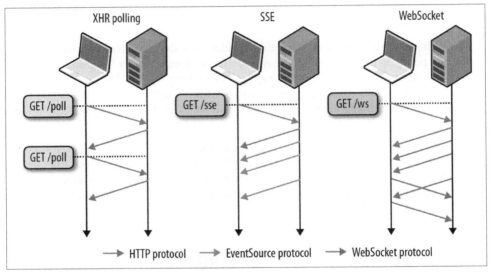

Figure 17-2. Communication flow of XHR, SSE, and WebSocket

- XHR is optimized for "transactional" request-response communication: the client sends the full, well-formed HTTP request to the server, and the server responds with a full response. There is no support for request streaming, and until the Streams API is available, no reliable cross-browser response streaming API.

- SSE enables efficient, low-latency server-to-client streaming of text-based data: the client initiates the SSE connection, and the server uses the event source protocol to stream updates to the client. The client can't send any data to the server after the initial handshake.

Propagation and Queuing Latency

Switching transports from XHR to SSE or WebSocket does not decrease the roundtrip between client and server! Regardless of the transport, the *propagation latency* of the data packets is the same. However, aside from propagation latency, there is also the *queuing latency*: the time the message has to wait on the client or server before it can be routed to the other party.

In the case of XHR polling, the queuing latency is a function of the client polling interval: the message may be available on the server, but it cannot be sent until the next client XHR request; see "Modeling Performance of XHR Polling" on page 275. By contrast, both SSE and WebSocket use a persistent connection, which allows the server to dispatch the message (and client, in the case of WebSocket), the moment it becomes available.

As a result, "low-latency delivery" for SSE and WebSocket is specifically referring to the elimination of message queuing latency. We have not yet figured out how to make Web-Socket data packets travel faster than the speed of light!

Message Overhead

Once a WebSocket connection is established, the client and server exchange data via the WebSocket protocol: application messages are split into one or more frames, each of which adds from 2 to 14 bytes of overhead. Further, because the framing is done via a custom binary format, both UTF-8 and binary application data can be efficiently encoded via the same mechanism. How does that compare with XHR and SSE?

- SSE adds as little as 5 bytes per message but is restricted to UTF-8 content only; see "Event Stream Protocol" on page 282.

- HTTP 1.x requests (XHR or otherwise) will carry an additional 500–800 bytes of HTTP metadata, plus cookies; see "Measuring and Controlling Protocol Overhead" on page 200.

- HTTP 2.0 compresses the HTTP metadata, which significantly reduces the overhead; see "Header Compression" on page 222. In fact, if the headers do not change between requests, the overhead can be as low as 8 bytes!

Keep in mind that these overhead numbers do not include the overhead of IP, TCP, and TLS framing, which add 60–100 bytes of combined overhead per message, regardless of the application protocol; see "TLS Record Size" on page 68.

Data Efficiency and Compression

Every XHR request can negotiate the optimal transfer encoding format (e.g., gzip for text-based data), via regular HTTP negotiation. Similarly, because SSE is restricted to UTF-8–only transfers, the event stream data can be efficiently compressed by applying gzip across the entire session.

With WebSocket, the situation is more complex: WebSocket can transfer both text and binary data, and as a result it doesn't make sense to compress the entire session. The binary payloads may be compressed already! As a result, WebSocket must implement its own compression mechanism and selectively apply it to each message.

The good news is the HyBi working group is developing the per-message compression extension for the WebSocket protocol. However, it is not yet available in any of the browsers. As a result, unless the application implements its own compression logic by carefully optimizing its binary payloads (see "Decoding Binary Data with JavaScript" on page 291) and implementing its own compression logic for text-based messages, it may incur high byte overhead on the transferred data!

> Chrome and some WebKit-based browsers support an older revision (per-frame compression) of the compression extension to the WebSocket protocol; see "WebSocket Multiplexing and Compression in the Wild" on page 298.

Custom Application Protocols

The browser is optimized for HTTP data transfers: it understands the protocol, and it provides a wide array of services, such as authentication, caching, compression, and much more. As a result, XHR requests inherit all of this functionality for free.

By contrast, streaming allows us to deliver custom protocols between client and server, but at the cost of bypassing many of the services provided by the browser: the initial HTTP handshake may be able to perform some negotiation of the parameters of the connection, but once the session is established, all further data streamed between the client and server is opaque to the browser. As a result, the flexibility of delivering a custom protocol also has its downsides, and the application may have to implement its own logic to fill in the missing gaps: caching, state management, delivery of message metadata, and so on!

> The initial HTTP Upgrade handshake does allow the server to leverage the existing HTTP cookie mechanism to validate the user. If the validation fails, the server can decline the WebSocket upgrade.

Leveraging Browser and Intermediary Caches

Using regular HTTP has significant advantages. Ask yourself a simple question: would the client benefit from caching the received data? Or could an intermediary optimize the delivery of the asset if it could cache it?

For example, WebSocket supports binary transfers, which allows the application to stream arbitrary image formats with no overhead—nice win! However, the fact that the image is delivered within a custom protocol means that it won't be cached by the browser cache, or any intermediary (e.g., a CDN). As a result, you may incur unnecessary transfers to the client and much higher traffic to the origin servers. The same logic applies to all other data formats: video, text, and so on.

As a result, make sure you choose the right transport for the job! A simple but effective strategy to address these concerns could be to use the WebSocket session to deliver non-cacheable data, such as real-time updates and application "control" messages, which can trigger XHR requests to fetch other assets via the HTTP protocol.

Deploying WebSocket Infrastructure

HTTP is optimized for short and bursty transfers. As a result, many of the servers, proxies, and other intermediaries are often configured to aggressively timeout idle HTTP connections, which, of course, is exactly what we don't want to see for long-lived WebSocket sessions. To address this, there are three pieces to consider:

- Routers, load-balancers, and proxies within own network
- Transparent and explicit proxies in external network (e.g., ISP and carrier proxies)
- Routers, firewalls, and proxies within the client's network

We have no control over the policy of the client's network. In fact, some networks may block WebSocket traffic entirely, which is why you may need a fallback strategy. Similarly, we don't have control over the proxies on the external network. However, this is where TLS may help! By tunneling over a secure end-to-end connection, WebSocket traffic can bypass all the intermediate proxies.

Using TLS does not prevent the intermediary from timing out an idle TCP connection. However, in practice, it significantly increases the success rate of negotiating the WebSocket session and often also helps to extend the connection timeout intervals.

Finally, there is the infrastructure that we deploy and manage ourselves, which also often requires attention and tuning. As easy as it is to blame the client or external networks, all too often the problem is close to home. Each load-balancer, router, proxy, and web server in the serving path must be tuned to allow long-lived connections.

For example, Nginx 1.3.13+ can proxy WebSocket traffic, but defaults to aggressive 60-second timeouts! To increase the limit, we must explicitly define the longer timeouts:

```
location /websocket {
    proxy_pass http://backend;
    proxy_http_version 1.1;
    proxy_set_header Upgrade $http_upgrade;
    proxy_set_header Connection "upgrade";
    proxy_read_timeout 3600; ❶
    proxy_send_timeout 3600; ❷
}
```

❶   Set 60-minute timeout between reads

❷   Set 60-minute timeout between writes

Similarly, it is not uncommon to have a load balancer, such as HAProxy, in front of one or more Nginx servers. Not surprisingly, we need to apply similar explicit configuration here as well—e.g., for HAProxy:

```
defaults http
    timeout connect 30s
    timeout client  30s
    timeout server  30s
    timeout tunnel  1h  ❶
```

❶   60-minute inactivity timeout for tunnels

The gotcha with the preceding example is the extra "tunnel" timeout. In HAProxy the connect, client, and server timeouts are applied only to the initial HTTP Upgrade handshake, but once the upgrade is complete, the timeout is controlled by the tunnel value.

Nginx and HAProxy are just two of hundreds of different servers, proxies, and load balancers running in our data centers. We can't enumerate all the configuration possibilities in these pages. The previous examples are just an illustration that most infrastructure requires custom configuration to handle long-lived sessions. Hence, before implementing application keepalives, double-check your infrastructure first.

 Long-lived and idle sessions occupy memory and socket resources on all the intermediate servers. Hence, short timeouts are often justified as a security, resource, and operational precaution. Deploying Web-Socket, SSE, and HTTP 2.0, each of which relies on long-lived sessions, brings its own class of new operational challenges.

Performance Checklist

Deploying a high-performance WebSocket service requires careful tuning and consideration, both on the client and on the server. A short list of criteria to put on the agenda:

- Use secure WebSocket (WSS over TLS) for reliable deployments.
- Pay close attention to polyfill performance (if necessary).
- Leverage subprotocol negotiation to determine the application protocol.
- Optimize binary payloads to minimize transfer size.
- Consider compressing UTF-8 content to minimize transfer size.
- Set the right binary type for received binary payloads.
- Monitor the amount of buffered data on the client.
- Split large application messages to avoid head-of-line blocking.
- Leverage other transports where applicable.

Last, but definitely not least, optimize for mobile! Real-time push can be a costly performance anti-pattern on mobile handsets, where battery life is always at a premium. That's not to say that WebSocket should not be used on mobile. To the contrary, it can be a highly efficient transport, but make sure to account for its requirements:

- "Preserve Battery Power" on page 140
- "Eliminate Periodic and Inefficient Data Transfers" on page 142
- "Nagle and Efficient Server Push" on page 143
- "Eliminate Unnecessary Application Keepalives" on page 144

CHAPTER 18

WebRTC

Web Real-Time Communication (WebRTC) is a collection of standards, protocols, and JavaScript APIs, the combination of which enables peer-to-peer audio, video, and data sharing between browsers (peers). Instead of relying on third-party plug-ins or proprietary software, WebRTC turns real-time communication into a standard feature that any web application can leverage via a simple JavaScript API.

Delivering rich, high-quality, RTC applications such as audio and video teleconferencing and peer-to-peer data exchange requires a lot of new functionality in the browser: audio and video processing capabilities, new application APIs, and support for half a dozen new network protocols. Thankfully, the browser abstracts most of this complexity behind three primary APIs:

- `MediaStream`: acquisition of audio and video streams
- `RTCPeerConnection`: communication of audio and video data
- `RTCDataChannel`: communication of arbitrary application data

All it takes is a dozen lines of JavaScript code, and any web application can enable a rich teleconferencing experience with peer-to-peer data transfers. That's the promise and the power of WebRTC! However, the listed APIs are also just the tip of the iceberg: signaling, peer discovery, connection negotiation, security, and entire layers of new protocols are just a few components required to bring it all together.

Not surprisingly, the architecture and the protocols powering WebRTC also determine its performance characteristics: connection setup latency, protocol overhead, and delivery semantics, to name a few. In fact, unlike all other browser communication, WebRTC transports its data over UDP. However, UDP is also just a starting point. It takes a lot more than raw UDP to make real-time communication in the browser a reality. Let's take a closer look.

Standard under construction

WebRTC is already enabled for 1B+ users: the latest Chrome and Firefox browsers provide WebRTC support to all of their users! Having said that, WebRTC is also under active construction, both at the browser API level and at the transport and protocol levels. As a result, the specific APIs and protocols discussed in the following chapters may still change in the future.

Standards and Development of WebRTC

Enabling real-time communication in the browser is an ambitious undertaking, and arguably, one of the most significant additions to the web platform since its very beginning. WebRTC breaks away from the familiar client-to-server communication model, which results in a full re-engineering of the networking layer in the browser, and also brings a whole new media stack, which is required to enable efficient, real-time processing of audio and video.

As a result, the WebRTC architecture consists of over a dozen different standards, covering both the application and browser APIs, as well as many different protocols and data formats required to make it work:

- Web Real-Time Communications (WEBRTC) W3C Working Group is responsible for defining the browser APIs.
- Real-Time Communication in Web-browsers (RTCWEB) is the IETF Working Group responsible for defining the protocols, data formats, security, and all other necessary aspects to enable peer-to-peer communication in the browser.

WebRTC is not a blank-slate standard. While its primary purpose is to enable real-time communication between browsers, it is also designed such that it can be integrated with existing communication systems: voice over IP (VOIP), various SIP clients, and even the public switched telephone network (PSTN), just to name a few. The WebRTC standards do not define any specific interoperability requirements, or APIs, but they do try to reuse the same concepts and protocols where possible.

In other words, WebRTC is not only about bringing real-time communication to the browser, but also about bringing all the capabilities of the Web to the telecommunications world—a $4.7 trillion industry in 2012! Not surprisingly, this is a significant development and one that many existing telecom vendors, businesses, and startups are following closely. WebRTC is much more than just another browser API.

Audio and Video Engines

Enabling a rich teleconferencing experience in the browser requires that the browser be able to access the system hardware to capture both audio and video—no third-party plug-ins or custom drivers, just a simple and a consistent API. However, raw audio and video streams are also not sufficient on their own: each stream must be processed to enhance quality, synchronized, and the output bitrate must adjust to the continuously fluctuating bandwidth and latency between the clients.

On the receiving end, the process is reversed, and the client must decode the streams in real-time and be able to adjust to network jitter and latency delays. In short, capturing and processing audio and video is a complex problem. However, the good news is that WebRTC brings fully featured audio and video engines to the browser (Figure 18-1), which take care of all the signal processing, and more, on our behalf.

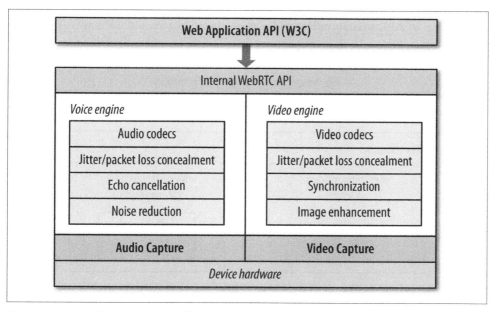

Figure 18-1. WebRTC audio and video engines

 The full implementation and technical details of the audio and video engines is easily a topic for a dedicated book, and is outside the scope of our discussion. To learn more, head to *http://www.webrtc.org*.

The acquired audio stream is processed for noise reduction and echo cancellation, then automatically encoded with one of the optimized narrowband or wideband audio codecs. Finally, a special error-concealment algorithm is used to hide the negative effects of network jitter and packet loss—that's just the highlights! The video engine performs similar processing by optimizing image quality, picking the optimal compression and codec settings, applying jitter and packet-loss concealment, and more.

All of the processing is done directly by the browser, and even more importantly, the browser dynamically adjusts its processing pipeline to account for the continuously changing parameters of the audio and video streams and networking conditions. Once all of this work is done, the web application receives the optimized media stream, which it can then output to the local screen and speakers, forward to its peers, or post-process using one of the HTML5 media APIs!

Acquiring Audio and Video with getUserMedia

The Media Capture and Streams W3C specification defines a set of new JavaScript APIs that enable the application to request audio and video streams from the platform, as well as a set of APIs to manipulate and process the acquired media streams. The Media Stream object (Figure 18-2) is the primary interface that enables all of this functionality.

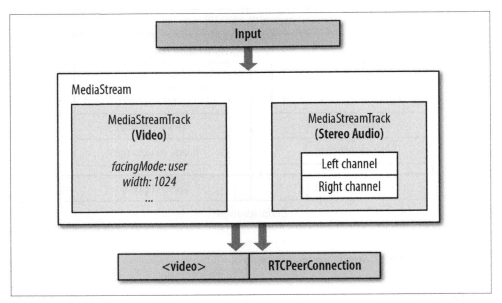

Figure 18-2. MediaStream carries one or more synchronized tracks

- The MediaStream object consists of one or more individual tracks (MediaStream-Track).
- Tracks within a MediaStream object are synchronized with one another.

- The input source can be a physical device, such as a microphone, webcam or a local or remote file from the user's hard drive or a remote network peer.
- The output of a MediaStream can be sent to one or more destinations: a local video or audio element, JavaScript code for post-processing, or a remote peer.

A MediaStream object represents a real-time media stream and allows the application code to acquire data, manipulate individual tracks, and specify outputs. All the audio and video processing, such as noise cancellation, equalization, image enhancement, and more are automatically handled by the audio and video engines.

However, the features of the acquired media stream are constrained by the capabilities of the input source: a microphone can emit only an audio stream, and some webcams can produce higher-resolution video streams than others. As a result, when requesting media streams in the browser, the getUserMedia() API allows us to specify a list of mandatory and optional constraints to match the needs of the application:

```
<video autoplay></video> ❶

<script>
  var constraints = {
    audio: true, ❷
    video: { ❸
      mandatory: {  ❹
        width: { min: 320 },
        height: { min: 180 }
      },
      optional: [  ❺
        { width: { max: 1280 }},
        { frameRate: 30 },
        { facingMode: "user" }
      ]
    }
  }

  navigator.getUserMedia(constraints, gotStream, logError);  ❻

  function gotStream(stream) { ❼
    var video = document.querySelector('video');
    video.src = window.URL.createObjectURL(stream);
  }

  function logError(error) { ... }
</script>
```

❶ HTML video output element

❷ Request a mandatory audio track

❸ Request a mandatory video track

❹ List of mandatory constraints for video track

❺ Array of optional constraints for video track

❻ Request audio and video streams from the browser

❼ Callback function to process acquired MediaStream

This example illustrates one of the more elaborate scenarios: we are requesting audio and video tracks, and we are specifying both the minimum resolution and type of camera that must be used, as well as a list of optional constraints for 720p HD video! The getUserMedia() API is responsible for requesting access to the microphone and camera from the user, and acquiring the streams that match the specified constraints—that's the whirlwind tour.

The provided APIs also enable the application to manipulate individual tracks, clone them, modify constraints, and more. Further, once the stream is acquired, we can feed it into a variety of other browser APIs:

- Web Audio API enables processing of audio in the browser.
- Canvas API enables capture and post-processing of individual video frames.
- CSS3 and WebGL APIs can apply a variety of 2D/3D effects on the output stream.

To make a long story short, getUserMedia() is a simple API to acquire audio and video streams from the underlying platform. The media is automatically optimized, encoded, and decoded by the WebRTC audio and video engines and is then routed to one or more outputs. With that, we are halfway to building a real-time teleconferencing application —we just need to route the data to a peer!

 For a full list of capabilities of the Media Capture and Streams APIs, head to the official W3C standard (*http://www.w3.org/TR/ mediacapture-streams*).

Audio (OPUS) and Video (VP8) Bitrates

When requesting audio and video from the browser, pay careful attention to the size and quality of the streams. While the hardware may be capable of capturing HD quality streams, the CPU and bandwidth must be able to keep up! Current WebRTC implementations use Opus and VP8 codecs:

- The Opus codec is used for audio and supports constant and variable bitrate encoding and requires 6–510 Kbit/s of bandwidth. The good news is that the codec can switch seamlessly and adapt to variable bandwidth.

- The VP8 codec used for video encoding also requires 100–2,000+ Kbit/s of bandwidth, and the bitrate depends on the quality of the streams:

  — 720p at 30 FPS: 1.0~2.0 Mbps

  — 360p at 30 FPS: 0.5~1.0 Mbps

  — 180p at 30 FPS: 0.1~0.5 Mbps

As a result, a single-party HD call can require up to 2.5+ Mbps of network bandwidth. Add a few more peers, and the quality must drop to account for the extra bandwidth and CPU, GPU, and memory processing requirements.

Real-Time Network Transports

Real-time communication is time-sensitive; that should come as no surprise. As a result, audio and video streaming applications are designed to tolerate intermittent packet loss: the audio and video codecs can fill in small data gaps, often with minimal impact on the output quality. Similarly, applications must implement their own logic to recover from lost or delayed packets carrying other types of application data. Timeliness and low latency can be more important than reliability.

 Audio and video streaming in particular have to adapt to the unique properties of our brains. Turns out we are very good at filling in the gaps but highly sensitive to latency delays. Add some variable delays into an audio stream, and "it just won't feel right," but drop a few samples in between, and most of us won't even notice!

The requirement for timeliness over reliability is the primary reason why the UDP protocol is a preferred transport for delivery of real-time data. TCP delivers a reliable, ordered stream of data: if an intermediate packet is lost, then TCP buffers all the packets after it, waits for a retransmission, and then delivers the stream in order to the application. By comparison, UDP offers the following "non-services":

No guarantee of message delivery
No acknowledgments, retransmissions, or timeouts.

No guarantee of order of delivery
No packet sequence numbers, no reordering, no head-of-line blocking.

No connection state tracking
No connection establishment or teardown state machines.

No congestion control
No built-in client or network feedback mechanisms.

Before we go any further, you may want to revisit Chapter 3 and in particular the section "Null Protocol Services" on page 36, for a refresher on the inner workings (or lack thereof) of UDP.

UDP offers no promises on reliability or order of the data, and delivers each packet to the application the moment it arrives. In effect, it is a thin wrapper around the best-effort delivery model offered by the IP layer of our network stacks.

WebRTC uses UDP at the transport layer: latency and timeliness are critical. With that, we can just fire off our audio, video, and application UDP packets, and we are good to go, right? Well, not quite. We also need mechanisms to traverse the many layers of NATs and firewalls, negotiate the parameters for each stream, provide encryption of user data, implement congestion and flow control, and more!

UDP is the foundation for real-time communication in the browser, but to meet all the requirements of WebRTC, the browser also needs a large supporting cast (Figure 18-3) of protocols and services above it.

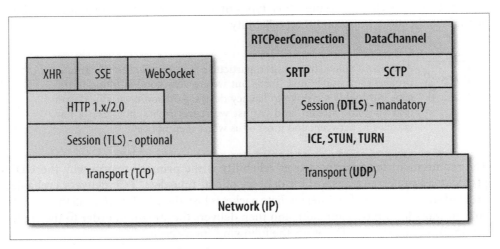

Figure 18-3. WebRTC protocol stack

- ICE: Interactive Connectivity Establishment (RFC 5245)
  - STUN: Session Traversal Utilities for NAT (RFC 5389)
  - TURN: Traversal Using Relays around NAT (RFC 5766)
- SDP: Session Description Protocol (RFC 4566)
- DTLS: Datagram Transport Layer Security (RFC 6347)
- SCTP: Stream Control Transport Protocol (RFC 4960)
- SRTP: Secure Real-Time Transport Protocol (RFC 3711)

ICE, STUN, and TURN are necessary to establish and maintain a peer-to-peer connection over UDP. DTLS is used to secure all data transfers between peers; encryption is a mandatory feature of WebRTC. Finally, SCTP and SRTP are the application protocols used to multiplex the different streams, provide congestion and flow control, and provide partially reliable delivery and other additional services on top of UDP.

Yes, that is a complicated stack, and not surprisingly, before we can talk about the end-to-end performance, we need to understand how each works under the hood. It will be a whirlwind tour, but that's our focus for the remainder of the chapter. Let's dive in.

We didn't forget about SDP! As we will see, SDP is a data format used to negotiate the parameters of the peer-to-peer connection. However, the SDP "offer" and "answer" are communicated out of band, which is why SDP is missing from the protocol diagram.

Brief Introduction to RTCPeerConnection API

Despite the many protocols involved in setting up and maintaining a peer-to-peer connection, the application API exposed by the browser is relatively simple. The RTCPeer Connection interface (Figure 18-4) is responsible for managing the full life cycle of each peer-to-peer connection.

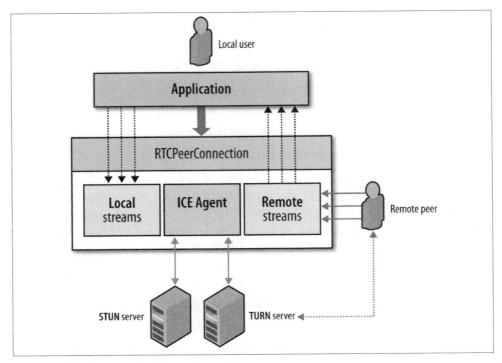

Figure 18-4. RTCPeerConnection API

- RTCPeerConnection manages the full ICE workflow for NAT traversal.
- RTCPeerConnection sends automatic (STUN) keepalives between peers.
- RTCPeerConnection keeps track of local streams.
- RTCPeerConnection keeps track of remote streams.
- RTCPeerConnection triggers automatic stream renegotiation as required.
- RTCPeerConnection provides necessary APIs to generate the connection offer, accept the answer, allows us to query the connection for its current state, and more.

In short, RTCPeerConnection encapsulates all the connection setup, management, and state within a single interface. However, before we dive into the details of each configuration option of the RTCPeerConnection API, we need to understand signaling and negotiation, the offer-answer workflow, and ICE traversal. Let's take it step by step.

DataChannel

DataChannel API enables exchange of arbitrary application data between peers—think WebSocket, but peer-to-peer, and with customizable delivery properties of the underlying transport. Each DataChannel can be configured to provide the following:

- Reliable or partially reliable delivery of sent messages
- In-order or out-of-order delivery of sent messages

Unreliable, out-of-order delivery is equivalent to raw UDP semantics. The message may make it, or it may not, and order is not important. However, we can also configure the channel to be "partially reliable" by specifying the maximum number of retransmissions or setting a time limit for retransmissions: the WebRTC stack will handle the acknowledgments and timeouts!

Each configuration of the channel has its own performance characteristics and limitations, a topic we will cover in depth later. Let's keep going.

Establishing a Peer-to-Peer Connection

Initiating a peer-to-peer connection requires (much) more work than opening an XHR, EventSource, or a new WebSocket session: the latter three rely on a well-defined HTTP handshake mechanism to negotiate the parameters of the connection, and all three implicitly assume that the destination server is reachable by the client—i.e., the server has a publicly routable IP address or the client and server are located on the same internal network.

By contrast, it is likely that the two WebRTC peers are within their own, distinct private networks and behind one or more layers of NATs. As a result, neither peer is directly reachable by the other. To initiate a session, we must first gather the possible IP and port candidates for each peer, traverse the NATs, and then run the connectivity checks to find the ones that work, and even then, there are no guarantees that we will succeed.

Refer to "UDP and Network Address Translators" on page 38 and "NAT Traversal" on page 40 for an in-depth discussion of the challenges posed by NATs for UDP and peer-to-peer communication in particular.

However, while NAT traversal is an issue we must deal with, we may have gotten ahead of ourselves already. When we open an HTTP connection to a server, there is an implicit assumption that the server is listening for our handshake; it may wish to decline it, but it is nonetheless always listening for new connections. Unfortunately, the same can't be said about a remote peer: the peer may be offline or unreachable, busy, or simply not interested in initiating a connection with the other party.

As a result, in order to establish a successful peer-to-peer connection, we must first solve several additional problems:

1. We must notify the other peer of the intent to open a peer-to-peer connection, such that it knows to start listening for incoming packets.

2. We must identify potential routing paths for the peer-to-peer connection on both sides of the connection and relay this information between peers.

3. We must exchange the necessary information about the parameters of the different media and data streams—protocols, encodings used, and so on.

The good news is that WebRTC solves one of the problems on our behalf: the built-in ICE protocol performs the necessary routing and connectivity checks. However, the delivery of notifications (signaling) and initial session negotiation is left to the application.

Signaling and Session Negotiation

Before any connectivity checks or session negotiation can occur, we must find out if the other peer is reachable and if it is willing to establish the connection. We must extend an offer, and the peer must return an answer (Figure 18-5). However, now we have a dilemma: if the other peer is not listening for incoming packets, how do we notify it of our intent? At a minimum, we need a shared signaling channel.

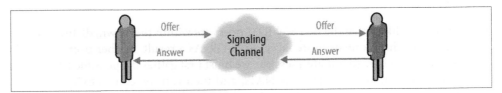

Figure 18-5. Shared signaling channel

WebRTC defers the choice of signaling transport and protocol to the application; the standard intentionally does not provide any recommendations or implementation for the signaling stack. Why? This allows interoperability with a variety of other signaling protocols powering existing communications infrastructure, such as the following:

Session Initiation Protocol (SIP)
    Application-level signaling protocol, widely used for voice over IP (VoIP) and videoconferencing over IP networks.

Jingle

> Signaling extension for the XMPP protocol, used for session control of voice over IP and videoconferencing over IP networks.

ISDN User Part (ISUP)

> Signaling protocol used for setup of telephone calls in many public switched telephone networks around the globe.

 A "signaling channel" can be as simple as a shout across the room—that is, if your intended peer is within shouting distance! The choice of the signaling medium and the protocol is left to the application.

A WebRTC application can choose to use any of the existing signaling protocols and gateways (Figure 18-6) to negotiate a call or a video conference with an existing communication system—e.g., initiate a "telephone" call with a PSTN client! Alternatively, it can choose to implement its own signaling service with a custom protocol.

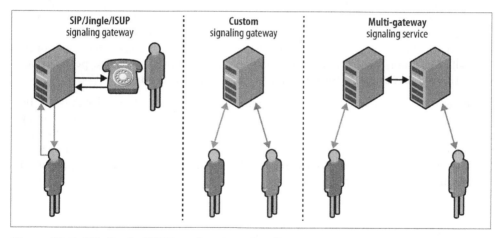

Figure 18-6. SIP, Jingle, ISUP, and custom signaling gateways

The signaling server can act as a gateway to an existing communications network, in which case it is the responsibility of the network to notify the target peer of a connection offer and then route the answer back to the WebRTC client initiating the exchange. Alternatively, the application can also use its own custom signaling channel, which may consist of one or more servers and a custom protocol to communicate the messages: if both peers are connected to the same signaling service, then the service can shuttle messages between them.

Skype is a great example of a peer-to-peer system with custom signaling: the audio and video communication are peer-to-peer, but Skype users have to connect to Skype's signaling servers, which use their own proprietary protocol, to help initiate the peer-to-peer connection.

Selecting a Signaling Service

WebRTC enables peer-to-peer communication, but every WebRTC application will also need a signaling server to negotiate and establish the connection. What are our options?

There is a growing list of existing communication gateways that can interoperate with WebRTC. For example, Asterisk is a popular, free, and open source framework that is used by both individual businesses and large carriers around the world for their telecommunication needs. As an option, Asterisk has a WebSocket module, which will allow SIP to be used as a signaling protocol: the browser establishes a WebSocket connection to the Asterisk gateway, and the two exchange SIP messages to negotiate the session!

Alternatively, the application can easily develop and deploy a custom signaling gateway if interoperability with other networks is not required. For example, a website may choose to offer peer-to-peer audio, video, and data exchange to its users: the site is already tracking which users are logged in, and it can keep signaling connections open to all of its online users. Then, when two peers want to initiate a peer-to-peer session, the site's servers can relay the signaling messages between clients.

There is no single correct choice for a signaling gateway: the choice depends on the requirements of the application. However, before you set out to invent your own, survey the available commercial and open source options first! And, of course, pay close attention to the underlying signaling transport, as it may have significant impact on both the latency of the signaling channel and the client and server overhead; see "Application APIs and Protocols" on page 258.

Session Description Protocol (SDP)

Assuming the application implements a shared signaling channel, we can now perform the first steps required to initiate a WebRTC connection:

```
var signalingChannel = new SignalingChannel(); ❶
var pc = new RTCPeerConnection({}); ❷

navigator.getUserMedia({ "audio": true }, gotStream, logError);  ❸

function gotStream(stream) {
  pc.addstream(stream); ❹

  pc.createOffer(function(offer) { ❺
```

```
      pc.setLocalDescription(offer); ❻
      signalingChannel.send(offer.sdp); ❼
    });
  }

  function logError() { ... }
```

❶   Initialize the shared signaling channel

❷   Initialize the RTCPeerConnection object

❸   Request audio stream from the browser

❹   Register local audio stream with RTCPeerConnection object

❺   Create SDP (offer) description of the peer connection

❻   Apply generated SDP as local description of peer connection

❼   Send generated SDP offer to remote peer via signaling channel

 We will be using unprefixed APIs in our examples, as they are defined by the W3C standard. Until the browser implementations are finalized, you may need to adjust the code for your favorite browser.

WebRTC uses *Session Description Protocol* (SDP) to describe the parameters of the peer-to-peer connection. SDP does not deliver any media itself; instead it is used to describe the "session profile," which represents a list of properties of the connection: types of media to be exchanged (audio, video, and application data), network transports, used codecs and their settings, bandwidth information, and other metadata.

In the preceding example, once a local audio stream is registered with the RTCPeerConnection object, we call `createOffer()` to generate the SDP description of the intended session. What does the generated SDP contain? Let's take a look:

```
(... snip ...)
m=audio 1 RTP/SAVPF 111 ... ❶
a=extmap:1 urn:ietf:params:rtp-hdrext:ssrc-audio-level
a=candidate:1862263974 1 udp 2113937151 192.168.1.73 60834 typ host ... ❷
a=mid:audio
a=rtpmap:111 opus/48000/2 ❸
a=fmtp:111 minptime=10
(... snip ...)
```

❶   Secure audio profile with feedback

❷   Candidate IP, port, and protocol for the media stream

❸   Opus codec and basic configuration

SDP is a simple text-based protocol (RFC 4568) for describing the properties of the intended session; in the previous case, it provides a description of the acquired audio stream. The good news is, WebRTC applications do not have to deal with SDP directly. The JavaScript Session Establishment Protocol (JSEP) abstracts all the inner workings of SDP behind a few simple method calls on the RTCPeerConnection object.

Once the offer is generated, it can be sent to the remote peer via the signaling channel. Once again, how the SDP is encoded is up to the application: the SDP string can be transferred directly as shown earlier (as a simple text blob), or it can be encoded in any other format—e.g., the Jingle protocol provides a mapping from SDP to XMPP (XML) stanzas.

To establish a peer-to-peer connection, both peers must follow a symmetric workflow (Figure 18-7) to exchange SDP descriptions of their respective audio, video, and other data streams.

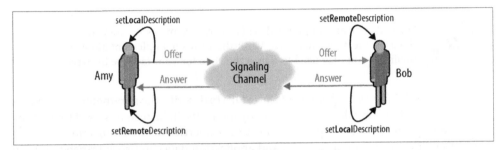

Figure 18-7. Offer/answer SDP exchange between peers

1. The initiator (Amy) registers one or more streams with her local RTCPeerConnection object, creates an offer, and sets it as her "local description" of the session.

2. Amy then sends the generated session offer to the other peer (Bob).

3. Once the offer is received by Bob, he sets Amy's description as the "remote description" of the session, registers his own streams with his own RTCPeerConnection object, generates the "answer" SDP description, and sets it as the "local description" of the session—phew!

4. Bob then sends the generated session answer back to Amy.

5. Once Bob's SDP answer is received by Amy, she sets his answer as the "remote description" of her original session.

With that, once the SDP session descriptions have been exchanged via the signaling channel, both parties have now negotiated the type of streams to be exchanged, and their settings. We are almost ready to begin our peer-to-peer communication! Now, there is just one more detail to take care of: connectivity checks and NAT traversal.

Interactive Connectivity Establishment (ICE)

In order to establish a peer-to-peer connection, by definition, the peers must be able to route packets to each other. A trivial statement on the surface, but hard to achieve in practice due to the numerous layers of firewalls and NAT devices between most peers; see "UDP and Network Address Translators" on page 38.

First, let's consider the trivial case, where both peers are located on the same internal network, and there are no firewalls or NATs between them. To establish the connection, each peer can simply query its operating system for its IP address (or multiple, if there are multiple network interfaces), append the provided IP and port tuples to the generated SDP strings, and forward it to the other peer. Once the SDP exchange is complete, both peers can initiate a direct peer-to-peer connection.

 The earlier "SDP example" illustrates the preceding scenario: the a=candidate line lists a private (192.168.x.x) IP address for the peer initiating the session; see "Reserved Private Network Ranges" on page 39.

So far, so good. However, what would happen if one or both of the peers were on distinct private networks? We could repeat the preceding workflow, discover and embed the private IP addresses of each peer, but the peer-to-peer connections would obviously fail! What we need is a public routing path between the peers. Thankfully, the WebRTC framework manages most of this complexity on our behalf:

- Each RTCPeerConnection connection object contains an "ICE agent."
- ICE agent is responsible for gathering local IP, port tuples (candidates).
- ICE agent is responsible for performing connectivity checks between peers.
- ICE agent is responsible for sending connection keepalives.

Once a session description (local or remote) is set, local ICE agent automatically begins the process of discovering all the possible candidate IP, port tuples for the local peer:

1. ICE agent queries the operating system for local IP addresses.
2. If configured, ICE agent queries an external STUN server to retrieve the public IP and port tuple of the peer.
3. If configured, ICE agent appends the TURN server as a last resort candidate. If the peer-to-peer connection fails, the data will be relayed through the specified intermediary.

If you have ever had to answer the "What is my public IP address?" question, then you've effectively performed a manual "STUN lookup." The STUN protocol allows the browser to learn if it's behind a NAT and to discover its public IP and port; see "STUN, TURN, and ICE" on page 41.

Whenever a new candidate (an IP, port tuple) is discovered, the agent automatically registers it with the RTCPeerConnection object and notifies the application via a callback function (onicecandidate). Once the ICE gathering is complete, the same callback is fired to notify the application. Let's extend our earlier example to work with ICE:

```
var ice = {"iceServers": [
              {"url": "stun:stun.l.google.com:19302"}, ❶
              {"url": "turn:user@turnserver.com", "credential": "pass"} ❷
         ]};

var signalingChannel = new SignalingChannel();
var pc = new RTCPeerConnection(ice);

navigator.getUserMedia({ "audio": true }, gotStream, logError);

function gotStream(stream) {
  pc.addstream(stream);

  pc.createOffer(function(offer) {
    pc.setLocalDescription(offer); ❸
  });
}

pc.onicecandidate = function(evt) {
  if (evt.target.iceGatheringState == "complete") { ❹
      local.createOffer(function(offer) {
        console.log("Offer with ICE candidates: " + offer.sdp);
        signalingChannel.send(offer.sdp); ❺
      });
  }
}

...

// Offer with ICE candidates:
// a=candidate:1862263974 1 udp 2113937151 192.168.1.73 60834 typ host ... ❻
// a=candidate:2565840242 1 udp 1845501695 50.76.44.100 60834 typ srflx ... ❼
```

❶   STUN server, configured to use Google's public test server

❷   TURN server for relaying data if peer-to-peer connection fails

❸   Apply local session description: initiates ICE gathering process

❹ Subscribe to ICE events and listen for ICE gathering completion

❺ Regenerate the SDP offer (now with discovered ICE candidates)

❻ Private ICE candidate (192.168.1.73:60834) for the peer

❼ Public ICE candidate (50.76.44.100:69834) returned by the STUN server

> The previous example uses Google's public demo STUN server. Unfortunately, STUN alone may not be sufficient (see "STUN and TURN in Practice" on page 43), and you may also need to provide a TURN server to guarantee connectivity for peers that cannot establish a direct peer-to-peer connection (~8% of users).

As the example illustrates, the ICE agent handles most of the complexity on our behalf: the ICE gathering process is triggered automatically, STUN lookups are performed in the background, and the discovered candidates are registered with the RTCPeerConnection object. Once the process is complete, we can generate the SDP offer and use the signaling channel to deliver it to the other peer.

Then, once the ICE candidates are received by the other peer, we are ready to begin the second phase of establishing a peer-to-peer connection: once the remote session description is set on the RTCPeerConnection object, which now contains a list of candidate IP and port tuples for the other peer, the ICE agent begins connectivity checks (Figure 18-8) to see if it can reach the other party.

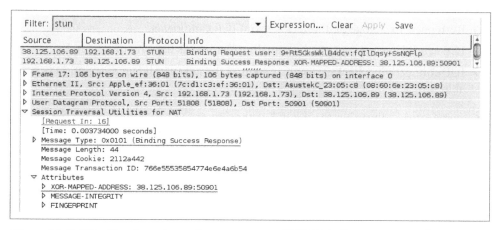

Figure 18-8. WireShark capture of a peer-to-peer STUN binding request and response

The ICE agent sends a message (a STUN binding request), which the other peer must acknowledge with a successful STUN response. If this completes, then we finally have a routing path for a peer-to-peer connection! Conversely, if all candidates fail, then either the RTCPeerConnection is marked as failed, or the connection falls back to a TURN relay server to establish the connection.

 The ICE agent automatically ranks and prioritizes the order in which the candidate connection checks are performed: local IP addresses are checked first, then public, and TURN is used as a last resort. Once a connection is established, the ICE agent continues to issue periodic STUN requests to the other peer. This serves as a connection keepalive.

Phew! As we said at the beginning of this section, initiating a peer-to-peer connection requires (much) more work than opening an XHR, EventSource, or a new WebSocket session. The good news is, most of this work is done on our behalf by the browser. However, for performance reasons, it is important to keep in mind that the process may incur multiple roundtrips between the STUN servers and between the individual peers before we can begin transmitting data—that is, assuming ICE negotiation is successful.

Incremental Provisioning (Trickle ICE)

The ICE gathering process is anything but instantaneous: retrieving local IP addresses is fast, but querying the STUN server requires a roundtrip to the external server, followed by another round of STUN connectivity checks between the individual peers. Trickle ICE is an extension to the ICE protocol that allows incremental gathering and connectivity checks between the peers. The core idea is very simple:

- Both peers exchange SDP offers without ICE candidates.
- ICE candidates are sent via the signaling channel as they are discovered.
- ICE connectivity checks are run as soon as the new candidate description is available.

In short, instead of waiting for the ICE gathering process to complete, we rely on the signaling channel to deliver incremental updates to the other peer, which helps accelerate the process. The WebRTC implementation is also fairly simple:

```
var ice = {"iceServers": [
            {"url": "stun:stun.l.google.com:19302"},
            {"url": "turn:user@turnserver.com", "credential": "pass"}
        ]};

var pc = new RTCPeerConnection(ice);
navigator.getUserMedia({ "audio": true }, gotStream, logError);

function gotStream(stream) {
  pc.addstream(stream);
```

```
  pc.createOffer(function(offer) {
    pc.setLocalDescription(offer);
    signalingChannel.send(offer.sdp); ❶
  });
}

pc.onicecandidate = function(evt) {
  if (evt.candidate) {
    signalingChannel.send(evt.candidate); ❷
  }
}

signalingChannel.onmessage = function(msg) {
  if (msg.candidate) {
    pc.addIceCandidate(msg.candidate); ❸
  }
}
```

❶   Send SDP offer without ICE candidates

❷   Send individual ICE candidate as it is discovered by local ICE agent

❸   Register remote ICE candidate and begin connectivity checks

Trickle ICE generates more traffic over the signaling channel, but it can yield a significant improvement in the time required to initiate the peer-to-peer connection. For this reason, it is also the recommended strategy for all WebRTC applications: send the offer as soon as possible, and then *trickle* ICE candidates as they are discovered.

Tracking ICE Gathering and Connectivity Status

The built-in ICE framework manages candidate discovery, connectivity checks, keep-alives, and more. If all works well, then all of this work is completely transparent to the application: the only thing we have to do is specify the STUN and TURN servers when initializing the RTCPeerConnection object. However, not all connections will succeed, and it is important to be able to isolate and resolve the problem. To do so, we can query the status of the ICE agent and subscribe to its notifications:

```
var ice = {"iceServers": [
            {"url": "stun:stun.l.google.com:19302"},
            {"url": "turn:user@turnserver.com", "credential": "pass"}
          ]};

var pc = new RTCPeerConnection(ice);

logStatus("ICE gathering state: "  + pc.iceGatheringState); ❶
pc.onicecandidate = function(evt) { ❷
   logStatus("ICE gathering state change: " + evt.target.iceGatheringState);
}
```

```
    logStatus("ICE connection state: " + pc.iceConnectionState); ❸
    pc.oniceconnectionstatechange = function(evt) { ❹
      logStatus("ICE connection state change: " + evt.target.iceConnectionState);
    }
```

❶   Log current ICE gathering state

❷   Subscribe to ICE gathering events

❸   Log current ICE connection state

❹   Subscribe to ICE connection state events

The `iceGatheringState` attribute, as its name implies, reports the status of the candidate gathering process for the local peer. As a result, it can be in three different states:

new   The object was just created and no networking has occurred yet.

gathering The ICE agent is in the process of gathering local candidates.

complete   The ICE agent has completed the gathering process.

On the other hand, the `iceConnectionState` attribute reports the status of the peer-to-peer connection (Figure 18-9), which can be in one of seven possible states:

new

> The ICE agent is gathering candidates and/or waiting for remote candidates to be supplied.

checking

> The ICE agent has received remote candidates on at least one component and is checking candidate pairs but has not yet found a connection. In addition to checking, it may also still be gathering.

connected

> The ICE agent has found a usable connection for all components but is still checking other candidate pairs to see if there is a better connection. It may also still be gathering.

completed

> The ICE agent has finished gathering and checking and found a connection for all components.

failed

> The ICE agent is finished checking all candidate pairs and failed to find a connection for at least one component. Connections may have been found for some components.

`disconnected`

Liveness checks have failed for one or more components. This is more aggressive than failed and may trigger intermittently (and resolve itself without action) on a flaky network.

`closed`

The ICE agent has shut down and is no longer responding to STUN requests.

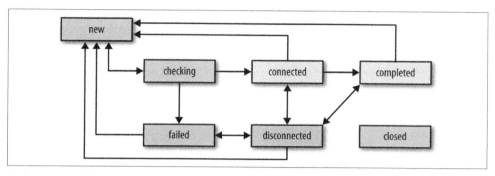

Figure 18-9. ICE agent connectivity states and transitions

A WebRTC session may require multiple streams for delivering audio, video, and application data. As a result, a successful connection is one that is able to establish connectivity for all the requested streams. Further, due to the unreliable nature of peer-to-peer connectivity, there are no guarantees that once the connection is established that it will stay that way: the connection may periodically flip between connected and disconnected states while the ICE agent attempts to find the best possible path to re-establish connectivity.

 The first and primary goal for the ICE agent is to identify a viable routing path between the peers. However, it doesn't stop there. Even once connected, the ICE agent may periodically try other candidates to see if it can deliver better performance via an alternate route.

Inspecting WebRTC Connection Status with Google Chrome

Google Chrome provides a simple and very useful tool to investigate the entire workflow and state of any WebRTC connection: open a new tab and load `chrome://webrtc-internals`. There, you can inspect (Figure 18-10) all of the open peer-to-peer connections, inspect the exchanged SDP descriptions, and more.

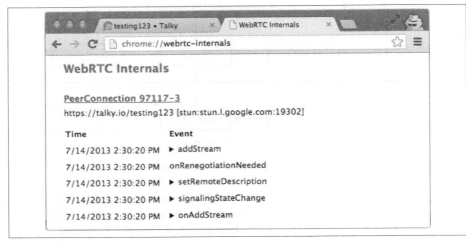

Figure 18-10. chrome://webrtc-internals

Chrome will also report a number of statistics for each stream, such as available bandwidth, latency, bitrate of the encoded video and audio streams, and more. Even if you are not developing a WebRTC application, start a WebRTC session with a friend or between multiple browser windows, and head to `chrome://webrtc-internals`; it is an indispensable tool for familiarizing yourself with the internals of WebRTC.

Putting It All Together

We have covered a lot of ground: we've discussed signaling, the offer-answer workflow, session parameter negotiation with SDP, and took a deep dive into the inner workings of the ICE protocol required to establish a peer-to-peer connection. Finally, we now have all the necessary pieces to initiate a peer-to-peer connection over WebRTC.

Initiating a WebRTC connection

We have been filling in all the necessary pieces bit by bit throughout the preceding pages, but now let's take a look at a complete example for the peer responsible for initiating the WebRTC connection:

```
<video id="local_video" autoplay></video> ❶
<video id="remote_video" autoplay></video> ❷

<script>
  var ice = {"iceServers": [
                {"url": "stun:stunserver.com:12345"},
                {"url": "turn:user@turnserver.com", "credential": "pass"}
            ]};

  var signalingChannel = new SignalingChannel(); ❸
  var pc = new RTCPeerConnection(ice); ❹

  navigator.getUserMedia({ "audio": true, "video": true }, gotStream, logError); ❺

  function gotStream(evt) {
    pc.addstream(evt.stream); ❻

    var local_video = document.getElementById('local_video');
    local_video.src = window.URL.createObjectURL(evt.stream); ❼

    pc.createOffer(function(offer) { ❽
      pc.setLocalDescription(offer);
      signalingChannel.send(offer.sdp);
    });
  }

  pc.onicecandidate = function(evt) { ❾
    if (evt.candidate) {
      signalingChannel.send(evt.candidate);
    }
  }

  signalingChannel.onmessage = function(msg) { ❿
    if (msg.candidate) {
      pc.addIceCandidate(msg.candidate);
    }
  }

  pc.onaddstream = function (evt) { ⓫
    var remote_video = document.getElementById('remote_video');
    remote_video.src = window.URL.createObjectURL(evt.stream);
  }

  function logError() { ... }
</script>
```

❶ Video element for output of local stream

❷ Video element for output of remote stream

❸ Initialize shared signaling channel

❹ Initialize peer connection object

⑤ Acquire local audio and video streams

⑥ Register local MediaStream with peer connection

⑦ Output local video stream to video element (self view)

⑧ Generate SDP offer describing peer connection and send to peer

⑨ Trickle ICE candidates to the peer via the signaling channel

⑩ Register remote ICE candidate to begin connectivity checks

⑪ Output remote video stream to video element (remote view)

The entire process can be a bit daunting on the first pass, but now that we understand how all the pieces work, it is fairly straightforward: initialize the peer connection and the signaling channel, acquire and register media streams, send the offer, trickle ICE candidates, and finally output the acquired media streams. A more complete implementation can also register additional callbacks to track ICE gathering and connection states and provide more feedback to the user.

> Once the connection is established, the application can still add and remove streams from the RTCPeerConnection object. Each time this happens, an automatic SDP renegotiation is invoked, and the same initialization procedure is repeated.

Responding to a WebRTC connection

The process to answer the request for a new WebRTC connection is very similar, with the only major difference being that most of the logic is executed when the signaling channel delivers the SDP offer. Let's take a hands-on look:

```
<video id="local_video" autoplay></video>
<video id="remote_video" autoplay></video>

<script>
  var signalingChannel = new SignalingChannel();

  var pc = null;
  var ice = {"iceServers": [
              {"url": "stun:stunserver.com:12345"},
              {"url": "turn:user@turnserver.com", "credential": "pass"}
            ]};

  signalingChannel.onmessage = function(msg) {
    if (msg.offer) { ❶
      pc = new RTCPeerConnection(ice);
      pc.setRemoteDescription(msg.offer);

      navigator.getUserMedia({ "audio": true, "video": true },
```

```
      gotStream, logError);

    } else if (msg.candidate) { ❷
      pc.addIceCandidate(msg.candidate);
    }
  }

  function gotStream(evt) {
    pc.addstream(evt.stream);

    var local_video = document.getElementById('local_video');
    local_video.src = window.URL.createObjectURL(evt.stream);

    pc.createAnswer(function(answer) { ❸
      pc.setLocalDescription(answer);
      signalingChannel.send(answer.sdp);
    });
  }

  pc.onicecandidate = function(evt) {
    if (evt.candidate) {
      signalingChannel.send(evt.candidate);
    }
  }

  pc.onaddstream = function (evt) {
    var remote_video = document.getElementById('remote_video');
    remote_video.src = window.URL.createObjectURL(evt.stream);
  }

  function logError() { ... }
</script>
```

❶ Listen and process remote offers delivered via signaling channel

❷ Register remote ICE candidate to begin connectivity checks

❸ Generate SDP answer describing peer connection and send to peer

Not surprisingly, the code looks very similar. The only major difference, aside from initiating the peer connection workflow based on an offer message delivered via the shared signaling channel, is that the preceding code is generating an SDP answer (via createAnswer) instead of an offer object. Otherwise, the process is symmetric: initialize the peer connection, acquire and register media streams, send the answer, trickle ICE candidates, and finally output the acquired media streams.

With that, we can copy the code, add an implementation for the signaling channel, and we have a real-time, peer-to-peer video and audio session videoconferencing application running in the browser—not bad for fewer than 100 lines of JavaScript code!

Initiating a WebRTC Session with SimpleWebRTC

In practice, the previous code can be made much simpler. Our example manually wires up all the necessary pieces, but there is no reason why most of this work cannot be wrapped by another library. As a practical example, the *simpleWebRTC* library does just that:

```
<script src="http://simplewebrtc.com/latest.js"></script>

<div id="local_video"></div>
<div id="remote_video"></div>

<script>
  var webrtc = new WebRTC({
    localVideoEl: "local_video",
    remoteVideosEl: "remote_video",
    autoRequestMedia: true
  });

  webrtc.on("readyToCall", function () {
      webrtc.joinRoom("your awesome room name");
  });
</script>
```

The JavaScript delivers the same videoconferencing experience as our earlier example. However, there is no magic; SimpleWebRTC simply makes a number of decisions on our behalf. Under the hood it initializes the RTCPeerConnection with a public STUN server for NAT traversal, requests audio and video streams with getUserMedia, and initiates a WebSocket connection to its own signaling servers. The only decision left to the application is to define the "room name," which the peers must agree on to initiate the peer-to-peer connection.

Check out the documentation for simpleWebRTC (*http://www.simplewebrtc.com*). As a bonus, the project also provides an open source signaling server, which you can run yourself or use as a reference for implementing your own version.

Delivering Media and Application Data

Establishing a peer-to-peer connection takes quite a bit of work. However, even once the clients complete the answer-offer workflow and each client performs its NAT traversals and STUN connectivity checks, we are still only halfway up our WebRTC protocol stack (Figure 18-3). At this point, both peers have raw UDP connections open to each other, which provides a no-frills datagram transport, but as we know that is not sufficient on its own; see "Optimizing for UDP" on page 44.

Without flow control, congestion control, error checking, and some mechanism for bandwidth and latency estimation, we can easily overwhelm the network, which would lead to degraded performance for both peers and those around them. Further, UDP transfers data in the clear, whereas WebRTC requires that we encrypt all communication! To address this, WebRTC layers several additional protocols on top of UDP to fill in the gaps:

- Datagram Transport Layer Security (DTLS) is used to negotiate the secret keys for encrypting media data and for secure transport of application data.
- Secure Real-Time Transport (SRTP) is used to transport audio and video streams.
- Stream Control Transport Protocol (SCTP) is used to transport application data.

Secure Communication with DTLS

WebRTC specification requires that all transferred data—audio, video, and custom application payloads—must be encrypted while in transit. The Transport Layer Security protocol would, of course, be a perfect fit, except that it cannot be used over UDP, as it relies on reliable and in-order delivery offered by TCP. Instead, WebRTC uses DTLS, which provides equivalent security guarantees.

DTLS is deliberately designed to be as similar to TLS as possible. In fact, DTLS *is* TLS, but with a minimal number of modifications to make it compatible with datagram transport offered by UDP. Specifically, DTLS addresses the following problems:

1. TLS requires reliable, in-order, and fragmentation friendly delivery of handshake records to negotiate the tunnel.
2. TLS integrity checks may fail if records are fragmented across multiple packets.
3. TLS integrity checks may fail if records are processed out of order.

Refer to "TLS Handshake" on page 50 and "TLS Record Protocol" on page 62 for a full discussion on the handshake sequence and layout of the record protocol.

There are no simple workarounds for fixing the TLS handshake sequence: each record serves a purpose, each must be sent in the exact order required by the handshake algorithm, and some records may easily span multiple packets. As a result, DTLS implements a "mini-TCP" (Figure 18-11) just for the handshake sequence.

```
 ▷ User Datagram Protocol, Src Port: 54153 (54153), Dst Port: 64964 (64964)
 ▽ Datagram Transport Layer Security
    ▽ DTLSv1.0 Record Layer: Handshake Protocol: Client Hello
         Content Type: Handshake (22)
         Version: DTLS 1.0 (0xfeff)
         Epoch: 0
       ┤ Sequence Number: 1
         Length: 146
       ▽ Handshake Protocol: Client Hello
            Handshake Type: Client Hello (1)
            Length: 134
            Message Sequence: 0
          │ Fragment Offset: 0
          │ Fragment Length: 134
            Version: DTLS 1.0 (0xfeff)
```

Figure 18-11. DTLS handshake records carry sequence and fragment offsets

DTLS extends the base TLS record protocol by adding an explicit fragment offset and sequence number for each handshake record. This addresses the in-order delivery requirement and allows large records to be fragmented across packets and reassembled by the other peer. DTLS handshake records are transmitted in the exact order specified by the TLS protocol; any other order is an error. Finally, DTLS must also deal with packet loss: both sides use simple timers to retransmit handshake records if the reply is not received within an expected interval.

The combination of the record sequence number, offset, and retransmission timer allows DTLS to perform the handshake (Figure 18-12) over UDP. To complete this sequence, both network peers generate self-signed certificates and then follow the regular TLS handshake protocol.

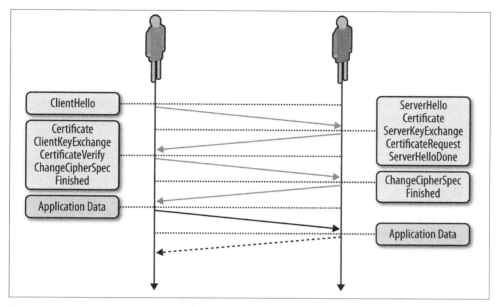

Figure 18-12. Peer-to-peer handshake over DTLS

The DTLS handshake requires two roundtrips to complete—an important aspect to keep in mind, as it adds extra latency to setup of the peer-to-peer connection.

The WebRTC client automatically generates self-signed certificates for each peer. As a result, there is no certificate chain to verify. DTLS provides encryption and integrity, but defers authentication to the application; see "Encryption, Authentication, and Integrity" on page 48. Finally, with the handshake requirements satisfied, DTLS adds two important rules to account for possible fragmentation and out-of-order processing of regular records:

- DTLS records must fit into a single network packet.
- A block cipher must be used for encrypting record data.

A regular TLS record can be up to 16 KB in size. TCP handles the fragmentation and reassembly, but UDP provides no such services. As a result, to preserve the out-of-order and best-effort semantics of the UDP protocol, each DTLS record carrying application data must fit into a single UDP packet. Similarly, stream ciphers are disallowed because they implicitly rely on in-order delivery of record data.

Identity and Authentication

The DTLS handshake performed between two WebRTC clients relies on self-signed certificates. As a result, the certificates themselves cannot be used to authenticate the peer, as there is no explicit chain of trust (see "Chain of Trust and Certificate Authorities" on page 57) to verify. If required, the WebRTC application must perform its own authentication and identity verification of the participating peers:

- A web application can use its existing identity verification system (e.g., require login to authenticate the user) prior to setting up the WebRTC session.
- Alternatively, each participating peer can specify its "identity provider" when generating the SDP offer/answer. Then, when the SDP message is received, the opposing peer can contact the specified identity provider to verify the received certificate.

The latter "identity provider" mechanism is still under active discussion and development in the W3C WebRTC working group. Consult the specification and the mailing list for the latest implementation status.

Delivering Media with SRTP and SRTCP

WebRTC provides media acquisition and delivery as a fully managed service: from camera to the network, and from network to the screen. The WebRTC application specifies the media constraints to acquire the streams and then registers them with the RTCPeerConnection object (Figure 18-13). From there, the rest is handled by the WebRTC media and network engines provided by the browser: encoding optimization, dealing with packet loss, network jitter, error recovery, flow, control, and more.

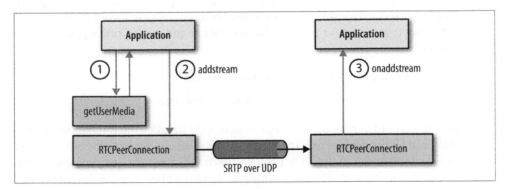

Figure 18-13. Audio and video delivery via SRTP over UDP

The implication of this architecture is that beyond specifying the initial constraints of the acquired media streams (e.g., 720p vs. 360p video), the application does not have any direct control over how the video is optimized or delivered to the other peer. This design choice is intentional: delivering a high-quality, real-time audio and video stream over an unreliable transport with fluctuating bandwidth and packet latency is a non-trivial problem. The browser solves it for us:

- Regardless of the quality and size of provided media streams, the network stack implements its own flow and congestion control algorithms: every connection starts by streaming audio and video at a low bitrate (<500 Kbps) and then begins to adjust the quality of the streams to match the available bandwidth.

- The media and network engines dynamically adjust the quality of the streams throughout the lifespan of the connection to adapt to the continuously changing network weather: bandwidth fluctuations, packet loss, and network jitter. In other words, WebRTC implements its own variant of adaptive streaming (see "Adaptive Bitrate Streaming" on page 97).

The WebRTC network engine cannot guarantee that an HD video stream provided by the application will be delivered at its highest quality: there may be insufficient bandwidth between the peers or high packet loss. Instead, the engine will attempt to adapt the provided stream to match the current conditions of the network.

 An audio or video stream may be delivered at a lower quality than that of the original stream acquired by the application. However, the inverse is not true: WebRTC will not upgrade the quality of the stream. If the application provides a 360p video constraint, then that serves as a cap on the amount of bandwidth that will be used.

How does WebRTC optimize and adapt the quality of each media stream? Turns out WebRTC is not the first application to run up against the challenge of implementing real-time audio and video delivery over IP networks. As a result, WebRTC is reusing existing transport protocols used by VoIP phones, communication gateways, and numerous commercial and open source communication services:

Secure Real-time Transport Protocol (SRTP)
Secure profile of the standardized format for delivery of real-time data, such as audio and video over IP networks.

Secure Real-time Control Transport Protocol (SRTCP)
Secure profile of the control protocol for delivery of sender and receiver statistics and control information for an SRTP flow.

Real-Time Transport Protocol (RTP) is defined by RFC 3550. However, WebRTC requires that all communication must be encrypted while in transit. As a result, WebRTC uses the "secure profile" (RFC 3711) of RTP—hence the S in SRTP and SRTCP.

SRTP defines a standard packet format (Figure 18-14) for delivering audio and video over IP networks. By itself, SRTP does not provide any mechanism or guarantees on timeliness, reliability, or error recovery of the transferred data. Instead, it simply wraps the digitized audio samples and video frames with additional metadata to assist the receiver in processing each stream.

Bit	+0..7				+8..15		+16..23	+24..31
0	V	P	X	CC	M	Payload Type	Sequence number	
32	Timestamp							
64	Synchronization source (SSRC) identifier							
+32	Contributing source (CSRC) identifier (optional)							
+32	RTP extension (optional)							
+N	*Encrypted RTP payload ...*							
...	SRTP MKI (optional) + Authentication Tag (optional)							

Figure 18-14. SRTP header (12 bytes + payload and optional fields)

- Each SRTP packet carries an auto-incrementing sequence number, which enables the receiver to detect and account for out-of-order delivery of media data.

- Each SRTP packet carries a timestamp, which represents the sampling time of the first byte of the media payload. This timestamp is used for synchronization of different media streams—e.g., audio and video tracks.

- Each SRTP packet carries an SSRC identifier, which is a unique stream ID used to associate each packet with an individual media stream.

- Each SRTP packet may contain other optional metadata.

- Each SRTP packet carries an encrypted media payload and an authentication tag, which verifies the integrity of the delivered packet.

The SRTP packet provides all the essential information required by the media engine for real-time playback of the stream. However, the responsibility to control how the individual SRTP packets are delivered falls to the SRTCP protocol, which implements a separate, out-of-band feedback channel for each media stream.

SRTCP tracks the number of sent and lost bytes and packets, last received sequence number, inter-arrival jitter for each SRTP packet, and other SRTP statistics. Then, periodically, both peers exchange this data and use it to adjust the sending rate, encoding quality, and other parameters of each stream.

In short, SRTP and SRTCP run directly over UDP and work together to adapt and optimize the real-time delivery of the audio and video streams provided by the application. The WebRTC application is never exposed to the internals of SRTP or SRTCP protocols: if you are building a custom WebRTC client, then you will have to deal with these protocols directly, but otherwise, the browser implements all the necessary infrastructure on your behalf.

 Curious to see SRTCP statistics for your WebRTC session? Check the latency, bitrate, and bandwidth reports in Chrome; see "Inspecting WebRTC Connection Status with Google Chrome" on page 332.

Adapting SRTP and SRTCP for WebRTC

Our whirlwind tour of SRTP and SRTCP covers the highlights of each protocol, but for implementers, there are many additional details that must be taken into account to make these protocols compatible with WebRTC requirements:

- Both SRTP and SRTCP encrypt application payload data (a WebRTC requirement), but neither protocol provides a mechanism to negotiate the secret keys! This is why the DTLS handshake must run first: the DTLS handshake establishes a shared secret between the peers, which is then reused as keying material within SRTP and SRTCP.

- Both SRTP and SRTCP require separate ports for each individual stream, which of course is a problem for clients behind NATs and firewalls. To address this, WebRTC uses an additional multiplexing extension to enable the delivery of multiple streams (and their control channels) on the same destination port.

- The IETF working group is also developing new congestion-control algorithms, which leverage the SRTCP feedback to optimize the delivery of audio and video streams generated by WebRTC applications.

In short, there is a lot more to it than simply firing off UDP packets with digitized audio and video data! Thankfully, the WebRTC media and network engines handle all of this complexity on our behalf. Adapting and improving SRTP and SRTCP performance is an area of ongoing research both at the standards level and for the implementers.

Delivering application data with SCTP

In addition to transferring audio and video data, WebRTC allows peer-to-peer transfers of arbitrary application data via the DataChannel API. The SRTP protocol we covered in the previous section is specifically designed for media transfers and unfortunately is not a suitable transport for application data. As a result, DataChannel relies on the Stream Control Transmission Protocol (SCTP), which runs on top (Figure 18-3) of the established DTLS tunnel between the peers.

However, before we dive into the SCTP protocol itself, let's first examine the WebRTC requirements for the RTCDataChannel interface and its transport protocol:

- Transport must support multiplexing of multiple independent channels.
  - Each channel must support in-order or out-of-order delivery.
  - Each channel must support reliable or unreliable delivery.
  - Each channel may have a priority level defined by the application.
- Transport must provide a message-oriented API.
  - Each application message may be fragmented and reassembled by the transport.
- Transport must implement flow and congestion control mechanisms.
- Transport must provide confidentiality and integrity of transferred data.

The good news is that the use of DTLS already satisfies the last criteria: all application data is encrypted within the payload of the record, and confidentiality and integrity are guaranteed. However, the remaining requirements are a nontrivial set to satisfy! UDP provides unreliable, out-of-order datagram delivery, but we also need TCP-like reliable delivery, channel multiplexing, priority support, message fragmentation, and more. That's where SCTP comes in.

Table 18-1. Comparing TCP vs. UDP vs. SCTP

	TCP	UDP	SCTP
Reliability	reliable	unreliable	configurable
Delivery	ordered	unordered	configurable
Transmission	byte-oriented	message-oriented	message-oriented
Flow control	yes	no	yes
Congestion control	yes	no	yes

> SCTP is a transport protocol, similar to TCP and UDP, which can run directly on top of the IP protocol. However, in the case of WebRTC, SCTP is tunneled over a secure DTLS tunnel, which itself runs on top of UDP.

SCTP provides the best features of TCP and UDP: message-oriented API, configurable reliability and delivery semantics, and built-in flow and congestion-control mechanisms. A full analysis of the protocol is outside the scope of our discussion, but, briefly, let's introduce some SCTP concepts and terminology:

Association
> A synonym for a connection.

Stream
> A unidirectional channel within which application messages are delivered in sequence, unless the channel is configured to use the unordered delivery service.

Message
> Application data submitted to the protocol.

Chunk
> The smallest unit of communication within an SCTP packet.

A single SCTP association between two endpoints may carry multiple independent streams, each of which communicates by transferring application messages. In turn, each message may be split into one or more chunks, which are delivered within SCTP packets (Figure 18-15) and then get reassembled at the other end.

Does this description sound familiar? It definitely should! The terms are different, but the core concepts are identical to those of the HTTP 2.0 framing layer; see "Streams, Messages, and Frames" on page 212. The difference here is that SCTP implements this functionality at a "lower layer," which enables efficient transfer and multiplexing of arbitrary application data.

Bit	+0..7	+8..15				+16..23	+24..31
0	Source Port					Destination Port	
32	Verification Tag						
64	Checksum						
96	Type (o)	Reserved	U	B	E	Length	
128	Transmission sequence number (TSN)						
160	Stream identifier					Stream sequence number	
192	Payload protocol identifier (PPID)						
224	Payload						

Figure 18-15. SCTP header and data chunk

An SCTP packet consists of a common header and one or more control or data chunks. The header carries 12 bytes of data, which identify the source and destination ports, a randomly generated verification tag for the current SCTP association, and the checksum for the entire packet. Following the header, the packet carries one or more control or data chunks; the previous diagram is showing an SCTP packet with a single data chunk:

- All data chunks have a 0×0 data type.
- The unordered (U) bit indicates whether this is an unordered DATA chunk.
- B and E bits are used to indicate the beginning and end of a message split across multiple chunks: B=1, E=0 indicates the first fragment of a message; B=0, E=0 indicates a middle piece; B=0, E=1 indicates the last fragment; B=1, E=1 indicates an unfragmented message.
- Length indicates the size of the DATA chunk, which includes the header—i.e., 16 bytes for chunk header, plus size of payload data.
- *Transmission sequence number (TSN)* is a 32-bit number used internally by SCTP to acknowledge receipt of the packet and detect duplicate deliveries.
- *Stream identifier* indicates the stream to which the chunk belongs.
- *Stream sequence number* is an auto-incremented message number for the associated stream; fragmented messages carry the same sequence number.
- *Payload protocol identifier (PPID)* is a custom field filled in by the application to communicate additional metadata about the transferred chunk.

 DataChannel uses the PPID field in the SCTP header to communicate the type of transferred data: 0×51 for UTF-8 and 0×52 for binary application payloads.

That's a lot of detail to absorb in one go. Let's review it once again, this time in the context of the earlier WebRTC and DataChannel API requirements:

- The SCTP header contains a few redundant fields: we are tunneling SCTP over UDP, which already specifies the source and destination ports (Figure 3-2).
- SCTP handles message fragmentation with the help of the B, E and TSN fields in the header: each chunk indicates its position (first, middle, or last), and the TSN value is used to order the middle chunks.
- SCTP supports stream multiplexing: each stream has a unique stream identifier, which is used to associate each data chunk with one of the active streams.

- SCTP assigns an individual sequence number to each application message, which allows it to provide in-order delivery semantics. Optionally, if the unordered bit is set, then SCTP continues to use the sequence number to handle message fragmentation, but can deliver individual messages out of order.

 In total, SCTP adds 28 bytes of overhead to each data chunk: 12 bytes for the common header and 16 bytes for the data chunk header followed by the application payload.

How does an SCTP negotiate the starting parameters for the association? Each SCTP connection requires a handshake sequence similar to TCP! Similarly, SCTP also implements TCP-friendly flow and congestion control mechanisms: both protocols use the same initial congestion window size and implement similar logic to grow and reduce the congestion window once the connection enters the congestion-avoidance phase.

 For a review on TCP handshake latencies, slow-start, and flow control, refer to Chapter 2. The SCTP handshake and congestion and flow-control algorithms used for WebRTC are different but serve the same purpose and have similar costs and performance implications.

We are getting close to satisfying all the WebRTC requirements, but unfortunately, even with all of that functionality, we are still short of a few required features:

1. The base SCTP standard (RFC 4960) provides a mechanism for unordered delivery of messages but no facilities for configuring the reliability of each message. To address this, WebRTC clients must also use the "Partial Reliability Extension" (RFC 3758), which extends the SCTP protocol and allows the sender to implement custom delivery guarantees, a critical feature for DataChannel.

2. SCTP does not provide any facilities for prioritizing individual streams; there are no fields within the protocol to carry the priority. As a result, this functionality has to be implemented higher in the stack.

In short, SCTP provides similar services as TCP, but because it is tunneled over UDP and is implemented by the WebRTC client, it offers a much more powerful API: in-order and out-of-order delivery, partial reliability, message-oriented API, and more. At the same time, SCTP is also subject to handshake latencies, slow-start, and flow and congestion control—all critical components to consider when thinking about performance of the DataChannel API.

Challenges with "Naked SCTP"

The use of a message-oriented API is what allows SCTP to avoid the head-of-line blocking problem of stream-oriented protocols like TCP; see "Head-of-Line Blocking" on page 30. Similarly, this same mechanism is what enables SCTP to allow configurable delivery models: in-order vs. out-of-order and reliable vs. partially reliable delivery.

With that in mind, why not just switch all communication to SCTP and run it directly on top of the IP protocol? Doing so would eliminate the need for UDP and also resolve the outstanding issues for delivery of HTTP 2.0 over TCP; see "Packet Loss, high-RTT Links, and HTTP 2.0 Performance" on page 218. In fact, SCTP would automatically resolve most of the issues addressed by HTTP 2.0; we could dramatically simplify the HTTP protocol as well!

Alas, existing routers and NAT devices simply don't handle SCTP correctly, which makes it near impossible to use SCTP as a "naked transport protocol" on the public Internet. As a result, WebRTC tunnels SCTP over UDP and DTLS. The protocol is implemented in "user space" by the WebRTC client.

In a controlled environment, such as an internal network, SCTP can deliver great results; e.g., many mobile carriers use SCTP to transport data from the radio tower and through their core networks until the packets have to exit to the public Internet. For more discussions on the topic, refer to *http://tools.ietf.org/html/draft-ietf-behave-sctpnat*.

DataChannel

DataChannel enables bidirectional exchange of arbitrary application data between peers —think WebSocket, but peer-to-peer, and with customizable delivery properties of the underlying transport. Once the RTCPeerConnection is established, connected peers can open one or more channels to exchange text or binary data:

```
function handleChannel(chan) { ❶
  chan.onerror = function(error) { ... }
  chan.onclose = function() { ... }

  chan.onopen = function(evt) {
    chan.send("DataChannel connection established. Hello peer!")
  }

  chan.onmessage = function(msg) {
    if(msg.data instanceof Blob) {
      processBlob(msg.data);
    } else {
      processText(msg.data);
    }
  }
}
```

```
}

var signalingChannel = new SignalingChannel();
var pc = new RTCPeerConnection(iceConfig);

var dc = pc.createDataChannel("namedChannel", {reliable: false}); ❷

... ❸

handleChannel(dc); ❹
pc.onDataChannel = handleChannel; ❺
```

❶   Register WebSocket-like callbacks on DataChannel object

❷   Initialize new DataChannel with best-effort delivery semantics

❸   Regular RTCPeerConnection offer/answer code

❹   Register callbacks on locally initialized DataChannel

❺   Register callbacks on DataChannel initiated by remote peer

The DataChannel API intentionally mirrors that of WebSocket: each established channel fires the same onerror, onclose, onopen, and onmessage callbacks, as well as exposes the same binaryType, bufferedAmount, and protocol fields on the channel.

However, because DataChannel is peer-to-peer and runs over a more flexible transport protocol, it also offers a number of additional features not available to WebSocket. The preceding code example highlights some of the most important differences:

- Unlike the WebSocket constructor, which expects the URL of the WebSocket server, DataChannel is a factory method on the RTCPeerConnection object.

- Unlike WebSocket, either peer can initiate a new DataChannel session: the onData Channel callback is fired when a new DataChannel session is established.

- Unlike WebSocket, which runs on top of reliable and in-order TCP transport, each DataChannel can be configured with custom delivery and reliability semantics.

DataChannel vs. WebSocket APIs

DataChannel API is a superset of the WebSocket API. As a result, all of our previous discussions about the WebSocket callbacks, flags, optimizations for processing of text and binary data, and subprotocol negotiation are directly applicable to the DataChannel API; refer to "WebSocket API" on page 288.

Table 18-2. WebSocket vs. DataChannel

	WebSocket	DataChannel
Encryption	configurable	always
Reliability	reliable	configurable
Delivery	ordered	configurable
Multiplexed	no (extension)	yes
Transmission	message-oriented	message-oriented
Binary transfers	yes	yes
UTF-8 transfers	yes	yes
Compression	no (extension)	no

The biggest difference between WebSocket and DataChannel is, of course, the underlying transport. WebSocket runs on top of TCP, which provides reliable and in-order delivery of each message, whereas DataChannel is layered on top of three protocols:

- UDP provides peer-to-peer connectivity.
- DTLS provides encryption of transferred data.
- SCTP provides multiplexing, flow and congestion control, and other features.

DataChannel can be configured to deliver the same reliability and in-order message guarantees as WebSocket. Although, more importantly, the real power of DataChannel is precisely due to the fact that it doesn't have to follow the in-order and reliable delivery semantics! Each channel can specify its own delivery and reliability requirements, and the data can be transferred directly peer to peer.

Setup and Negotiation

Regardless of the type of transferred data—audio, video, or application data—the two participating peers must first complete the full offer/answer workflow, negotiate the used protocols and ports, and successfully complete their connectivity checks; see "Establishing a Peer-to-Peer Connection" on page 319.

In fact, as we now know, media transfers run over SRTP, whereas DataChannel uses the SCTP protocol. As a result, when the initiating peer first makes the connection offer, or when the answer is generated by the other peer, the two must specifically advertise the parameters for the SCTP association within the generated SDP strings:

```
(... snip ...)
m=application 1 DTLS/SCTP 5000 ❶
c=IN IP4 0.0.0.0 ❷
a=mid:data
a=fmtp:5000 protocol=webrtc-datachannel; streams=10 ❸
(... snip ...)
```

❶　Advertise intent to use SCTP over DTLS

❷　0.0.0.0 candidate indicates use of trickle ICE

❸　DataChannel protocol over SCTP with up to 10 parallel streams

As previously, the RTCPeerConnection object handles all the necessary generation of the SDP parameters as long as one of the peers registers a DataChannel prior to generating the SDP description of the session. In fact, the application can establish a data-only peer-to-peer connection by setting explicit constraints to disable audio and video transfers:

```
var signalingChannel = new SignalingChannel();
var pc = new RTCPeerConnection(iceConfig);

var dc = pc.createDataChannel("namedChannel", {reliable: false}); ❶

var mediaConstraints = { ❷
  mandatory: {
      OfferToReceiveAudio: false,
      OfferToReceiveVideo: false
  }
};

pc.createOffer(function(offer) { ... }, null, mediaConstraints); ❸

...
```

❶　Register new unreliable DataChannel with RTCPeerConnection

❷　Set media constraints to disable audio and video transfers

❸　Generate data-only offer

With the SCTP parameters negotiated between the peers, we are almost ready to begin exchanging application data. Notice that the SDP snippet we saw earlier doesn't mention anything about the parameters of each DataChannel—e.g., protocol, reliability, or in-order or out-of-order flags. As a result, before any application data can be sent, the WebRTC client initiating the connection also sends a DATA_CHANNEL_OPEN message

(Figure 18-16) which describes the type, reliability, used application protocol, and other parameters of the channel.

Bit	+0..7	+8..15	+16..23	+24..31
0	Message Type (0x3)	Channel Type	Priority	
32	Reliability			
64	Label length		Protocol length	
...	*Label ...*			
...	*Protocol ...*			

Figure 18-16. DATA_CHANNEL_OPEN message initiates new channel

> The DATA_CHANNEL_OPEN message is similar to the HEADERS frame in HTTP 2.0: it implicitly opens a new stream, and data frames can be sent immediately after it; see "Initiating a New Stream" on page 229. For more information on the DataChannel protocol, refer to *http://tools.ietf.org/html/draft-jesup-rtcweb-data-protocol*.

Once the channel parameters are communicated, both peers can begin exchanging application data. Under the hood, each established channel is delivered as an independent SCTP stream: the channels are multiplexed over the same SCTP association, which avoids head-of-line blocking between the different streams and allows for simultaneous delivery of multiple channels over the same SCTP association.

Out-of-Band Channel Negotiation

DataChannel also allows out-of-band negotiation of channel parameters. When calling the createDataChannel method, the application can set the negotiated parameter to true, which skips the automatic dispatch of the DATA_CHANNEL_OPEN message. However, when doing so, both peers also have to specify the same id parameter, which is otherwise automatically generated by the browser:

```
signalingChannel.send({ ❶
  newchannel: true,
  label: "negotiated channel",
  options: {
    negotiated: true,
    id: 10, ❷
    reliable: true,
    ordered: true,
    protocol: "appProtocol-v3"
  }
```

```
  });

  signalingChannel.onmessage = function(msg) {
    if (msg.newchannel) { ❸
      dc = pc.createDataChannel(msg.label, msg.options);
    }
  }
```

❶   Send channel configuration via signaling channel to the other peer

❷   Unique, application-specified channel ID (integer)

❸   Initialize new DataChannel using received parameters

In practice, there are no additional performance benefits to using out-of-band negotiation with few participating peers. Let the RTCPeerConnection object handle the negotiation for you. However, where this workflow can be useful is in cases with many
participating peers, where the signaling server can generate the same description and
simultaneously distribute it to all the participating parties.

Configuring Message Order and Reliability

DataChannel enables peer-to-peer transfers of arbitrary application data via a
WebSocket-compatible API: this by itself is a unique and a powerful feature. However,
DataChannel also offers a much more flexible transport, which allows us to customize
the delivery semantics of each channel to match the requirements of the application and
the type of data being transferred.

- DataChannel can provide in-order or out-of-order delivery of messages.
- DataChannel can provide reliable or partially reliable delivery of messages.

Configuring the channel to use in-order and reliable delivery is, of course, equivalent
to TCP: the same delivery guarantees as a regular WebSocket connection. However, and
this is where it starts to get really interesting, DataChannel also offers two different
policies for configuring partial reliability of each channel:

Partially reliable delivery with retransmit
   Messages will not be retransmitted more times than specified by the application.

Partially reliable delivery with timeout
   Messages will not be retransmitted after a specified lifetime (in milliseconds) by the
   application.

Both strategies are implemented by the WebRTC client, which means that all the application has to do is decide on the appropriate delivery model and set the right parameters on the channel. There is no need to manage application timers or retransmission counters. Let's take a closer look at our configuration options:

Table 18-3. DataChannel reliability and delivery configurations

	Ordered	Reliable	Partial reliability policy
Ordered + reliable	yes	yes	n/a
Unordered + reliable	no	yes	n/a
Ordered + partially reliable (retransmit)	yes	partial	retransmission count
Unordered + partially reliable (retransmit)	no	partial	retransmission count
Ordered + partially reliable (timed)	yes	partial	timeout (ms)
Unordered + partially reliable (timed)	no	partial	timeout (ms)

Ordered and reliable delivery is self-explanatory: it's TCP. On the other hand, unordered and reliable delivery is already much more interesting—it's TCP, but without the head-of-line blocking problem; see "Head-of-Line Blocking" on page 30.

When configuring a partially reliable channel, it is important to keep in mind that the two retransmission strategies are mutually exclusive. The application can specify either a timeout or a retransmission count, but not both; doing so will raise an error. With that, let's take a look at the JavaScript API for configuring the channel:

```
conf = {}; ❶
conf = { ordered: false }; ❷
conf = { ordered: true,  maxRetransmits: customNum }; ❸
conf = { ordered: false, maxRetransmits: customNum }; ❹
conf = { ordered: true,  maxRetransmitTime: customMs }; ❺
conf = { ordered: false, maxRetransmitTime: customMs }; ❻

conf = { ordered: false, maxRetransmits: 0 }; ❼

var signalingChannel = new SignalingChannel();
var pc = new RTCPeerConnection(iceConfig);

...

var dc = pc.createDataChannel("namedChannel", conf); ❽

if (dc.reliable) {
  ...
} else {
  ...
}
```

❶ Default to ordered and reliable delivery (TCP)

❷ Reliable, unordered delivery

❸ Ordered, partially reliable with custom retransmit count

❹ Unordered, partially reliable with custom retransmit count

⑤ Ordered, partially reliable with custom retransmit timeout

⑥ Unordered, partially reliable with custom retransmit timeout

⑦ Unordered, unreliable delivery (UDP)

⑧ Initialize DataChannel with specified order and reliability configuration

 Once a DataChannel is initialized, the application can access the max Retransmits and maxRetransmitTime as read-only attributes. Also, as a convenience, the DataChannel provides a reliable attribute, which returns false if either of the partial-reliability strategies are used.

Each DataChannel can be configured with custom order and reliability parameters, and the peers can open multiple channels, all of which will be multiplexed over the same SCTP association. As a result, each channel is independent of the others, and the peers can use different channels for different types of data—e.g., reliable and in-order delivery for peer-to-peer chat and partially reliable and out-of-order delivery for transient or low-priority application updates.

Partially Reliable Delivery and Message Size

The use of a partially reliable channel requires additional design consideration from the application. Specifically, the application must pay close attention to the message size: nothing is stopping the application from passing in a large message, which will be fragmented across multiple packets, but doing so will likely yield very poor results. To illustrate this in action, let's assume the following scenario:

- Two peers have negotiated an out-of-order, unreliable DataChannel.
  — The channel is configured with maxRetransmits set to 0, aka plain UDP.
- The packet loss between the peers is ~1%.
- One of the peers is trying to send a large, 120 KB message.

WebRTC clients set the maximum transmission unit for an SCTP packet to 1,280 bytes, which is the minimum and recommended MTU for an IPv6 packet. But we must also account for the overhead of IP, UDP, DTLS, and SCTP protocols: 20–40 bytes, 8 bytes, 20–40 bytes, and 28 bytes, respectively. Let's round this up to ~130 bytes of overhead, which leaves us with ~1,150 bytes of payload data per packet and a total of 107 packets to deliver the 120 KB application message.

So far so good, but the packet loss probability for each individual packet is 1%. As a result, if we fire off all 107 packets over the unreliable channel, we are now looking at a very high probability of losing at least one of them en route! What will happen in this case? Even if all but one of the packets make it, the entire message will be dropped.

To address this, an application has two strategies: it can add a retransmit strategy (based on count or timeout), and it can decrease the size of the transferred message. In fact, for best results, it should do both.

- When using an unreliable channel, ideally, each message should fit into a single packet; the message should be less than 1,150 bytes in size.
- If a message cannot fit into a single packet, then a retransmit strategy should be used to improve the odds of delivering the message.

Packet-loss rates and latency between the peers are unpredictable and vary based on current network weather. As a result, there is no one single and optimal setting for the retransmit count or timeout values. To deliver the best results over an unreliable channel, keep the messages as small as possible.

WebRTC Use Cases and Performance

Implementing a low-latency, peer-to-peer transport is a nontrivial engineering challenge: there are NAT traversals and connectivity checks, signaling, security, congestion control, and myriad other details to take care of. WebRTC handles all of the above and more, on our behalf, which is why it is arguably one of the most significant additions to the web platform since its inception. In fact, it's not just the individual pieces offered by WebRTC, but the fact that all the components work together to deliver a simple and unified API for building peer-to-peer applications in the browser.

However, even with all the built-in services, designing efficient and high-performance peer-to-peer applications still requires a great amount of careful thought and planning: peer-to-peer does not mean high performance on its own. If anything, the increased variability in bandwidth and latency between the peers, and the high demands of media transfers, as well as the peculiarities of unreliable delivery, make it an even harder engineering challenge.

Audio, Video, and Data Streaming

Peer-to-peer audio and video streaming are one of the central use cases for WebRTC: getUserMedia API enables the application to acquire the media streams, and the built-in audio and video engines handle the optimization, error recovery, and synchronization between streams. However, it is important to keep in mind that even with aggressive optimization and compression, audio and video delivery are still likely to be constrained by latency and bandwidth:

- An HD quality streams requires 1–2 Mbps of bandwidth; see "Audio (OPUS) and Video (VP8) Bitrates" on page 314.
- The global average bandwidth as of Q1 2013 is just 3.1 Mbps; see Table 1-2.
- An HD stream requires, at a minimum, a 3.5G+ connection; see Table 7-2.

The good news is that the average bandwidth capacity is continuing to grow around the world: users are switching to broadband, and 3.5G+ and 4G adoption is ramping up. However, even with optimistic growth projections, while HD streaming is now becoming viable, it is not a guarantee! Similarly, latency is a perennial problem, especially for real-time delivery, and doubly so for mobile clients. 4G will definitely help, but 3G networks are not going away anytime soon either.

> To complicate matters further, the connections offered by most ISPs and mobile carriers are not symmetric: most users have significantly higher downlink throughput than uplink throughput. In fact, 10-to-1 relationships are not uncommon—e.g., 10 Mbps down, 1 Mbps up.

The net result is that you should not be surprised to see a single, peer-to-peer audio and video stream saturate a significant amount of users' bandwidth, especially for mobile clients. Thinking of providing a multiparty stream? You will likely need to do some careful planning for the amount of available bandwidth:

- A mobile client may be able to download an HD-quality stream (1 Mbps+) but may need to send a lower-quality stream due to lower uplink throughput; different parties can stream at different bitrates.
- The audio and video streams may need to share bandwidth with other applications and data transfers—e.g., one or more DataChannel sessions.
- Bandwidth and latency are always changing regardless of the type of connectivity —wired or wireless—or the generation of the network, and the application must be able to adapt to these conditions.

The good news is that the WebRTC audio and video engines work together with the underlying network transport to probe the available bandwidth and optimize delivery of the media streams. However, DataChannel transfers require additional application logic: the application must monitor the amount of buffered data and be ready to adjust as needed.

When acquiring the audio and video streams, make sure to set the video constraints to match the use case; see "Acquiring Audio and Video with getUserMedia" on page 312.

Multiparty Architectures

A single peer-to-peer connection with bidirectional HD media streams can easily use up a significant fraction of users' bandwidth. As a result, multiparty applications should carefully consider the architecture (Figure 18-17) of how the individual streams are aggregated and distributed between the peers.

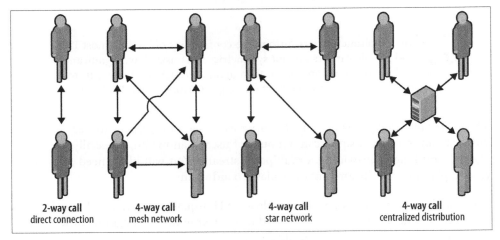

Figure 18-17. Distribution architecture for an N-way call

One-to-one connections are easy to manage and deploy: the peers talk directly to each other and no further optimization is required. However, extending the same strategy to an N-way call, where each peer is responsible for connecting to every other party (a mesh network) would result in $N - 1$ connections for each peer, and a total of $N \times (N - 1)$ connections! If bandwidth is at a premium, as it often is due to the much lower uplink speeds, then this type of architecture will quickly saturate most users' links with just a few participants.

While mesh networks are easy to set up, they are often inefficient for multiparty systems. To address this, an alternative strategy is to use a "star" topology instead, where the individual peers connect to a "supernode," which is then responsible for distributing the streams to all connected parties. This way only one peer has to pay the cost of handling and distributing $N - 1$ streams, and everyone else talks directly to the supernode.

A supernode can be another peer, or it can be a dedicated service specifically optimized for processing and distributing real-time data; which strategy is more appropriate depends on the context and the application. In the simplest case, the initiator can act as a supernode—simple, and it might just work. A better strategy might be to pick the peer with the best available throughput, but that also requires additional "election" and signaling mechanisms.

 The criteria and the process for picking the supernode is left up to the application, which by itself can be a big engineering challenge. WebRTC does not provide any infrastructure to assist in this process.

Finally, the supernode could be a dedicated and even a third-party service. WebRTC enables peer-to-peer communication, but this does not mean that there is no room for centralized infrastructure! Individual peers can establish peer connections with a proxy server and still get the benefit of both the WebRTC transport infrastructure and the additional services offered by the server.

Peer-to-Peer Optimization as a Service

Many existing videoconferencing solutions (e.g., Google's Hangouts) rely on "proxy servers" to aggregate the individual media streams, composite them, and then distribute the optimized versions to all the connected parties. Delivering a single stream reduces the amount of bandwidth and the amount of CPU and GPU resources required by each peer; each client sees only one stream instead of $N - 1$!

Similarly, a game server can aggregate updates from all the players and filter and distribute only the necessary updates; e.g., it won't send updates for players that are out of view or otherwise don't affect the other player.

Two-party streaming is simple and efficient to deploy, whereas multiparty architectures require a lot more thought and planning. As much as WebRTC is about enabling direct peer-to-peer communication, it is also a catalyst for a wide variety of services, both commercial and open source, that will help make it more efficient and feature-rich.

Infrastructure and Capacity Planning

In addition to planning and anticipating the bandwidth requirements of individual peer connections, every WebRTC application will require some centralized infrastructure for signaling, NAT and firewall traversal, identity verification, and other additional services offered by the application.

WebRTC defers all signaling to the application, which means that the application must at a minimum provide the ability to send and receive messages to the other peer. The number of users and the volume of signaling data sent will vary by the protocol, encoding of the data, and frequency of updates. Similarly the latency of the signaling service will have a great impact on the "call setup" time, especially when Trickle ICE is used, and other signaling exchanges.

- Use a low-latency transport, such as WebSocket or SSE with XHR.
- Estimate and provision sufficient capacity to handle the necessary signaling rate for all users of your application.
- Optionally, once the peer connection is established, the peers can switch to Data-Channel for signaling. This can help offload the amount of signaling traffic that must be handled by the central server and also reduce latency for signaling communication.

Due to the prevalence of NATs and firewalls, most WebRTC applications will require a STUN server to perform the necessary IP lookups to establish the peer-to-peer connection. The good news is that the STUN server is used only for connection setup, but nonetheless, it must speak the STUN protocol and be provisioned to handle the necessary query load.

- Unless the WebRTC application is specifically designed to be used within the same internal network, always provide a STUN server when initiating the RTCPeerConnection object; otherwise, most connections will simply fail.
- Unlike the signaling server, which can use any protocol, the STUN server must respond to, well, STUN requests. You will need a public server or will have to provision your own; *stund* is a popular open source implementation.

Even with STUN in place, 8%–10% of peer-to-peer connections will likely fail due to the peculiarities of their network policies. For example, a network administrator could block UDP outright for all the users on the network; see "STUN and TURN in Practice" on page 43. As a result, to deliver a reliable experience, the application may also need a TURN server to relay the data between the peers.

- Relaying peer connections is suboptimal: there is an extra network hop, and with each stream streaming at 1+ Mbps, it is easy to saturate the capacity of any service. As a result, TURN is always used as a last resort and requires careful capacity planning by the application.

Multiparty services may require centralized infrastructure to help optimize the delivery of many streams and provide additional services as part of the RTC experience. In some ways, multiparty gateways serve the same role as TURN but in this case for different reasons. Having said that, unlike TURN servers, which act as simple packet proxies, a "smart proxy" may require significantly more CPU and GPU resources to process each individual stream prior to forwarding the final output to each connected party.

Data Efficiency and Compression

WebRTC audio and video engines will dynamically adjust the bitrate of the media streams to match the conditions of the network link between the peers. The application can set and update the media constraints (e.g., video resolution, framerate, and so on), and the engines do the rest—this part is easy.

Unfortunately, the same can't be said for DataChannel, which is designed to transport arbitrary application data. Similar to WebSocket, the DataChannel API will accept binary and UTF-8–encoded application data, but it does not apply any further processing to reduce the size of transferred data: it is the responsibility of the WebRTC application to optimize the binary payloads and compress the UTF-8 content.

Further, unlike WebSocket, which runs on top of a reliable and in-order transport, WebRTC applications must account for both the extra overhead incurred by the UDP, DTLS, and SCTP protocols and the peculiarities of data delivery over a partially reliable transport; see "Partially Reliable Delivery and Message Size" on page 355.

 WebSocket offers a protocol extension that provides automatic compression of transferred data. Alas, there is no equivalent for WebRTC; all messages are transferred as they are provided by the application.

Performance Checklist

Peer-to-peer architectures pose their own unique set of performance challenges for the application. Direct, one-to-one communication is relatively straightforward, but things get much more complex when more than two parties are involved, at least as far as performance is concerned. A short list of criteria to put on the agenda:

Signaling service

- Use a low-latency transport.
- Provision sufficient capacity.
- Consider using signaling over DataChannel once connection is established.

Firewall and NAT traversal

- Provide a STUN server when initiating RTCPeerConnection.
- Use trickle ICE whenever possible—more signaling, but faster setup.
- Provide a TURN server for relaying failed peer-to-peer connections.

- Anticipate and provision sufficient capacity for TURN relays.

Data distribution
- Consider using a supernode or a dedicated intermediary for large multiparty communication.
- Consider optimizing the received data on the intermediary prior to forwarding it to the other peers.

Data efficiency
- Specify appropriate media constraints for voice and video streams.
- Optimize binary payloads sent over DataChannel.
- Consider compressing UTF-8 content sent over DataChannel.
- Monitor the amount of buffered data on the DataChannel and adapt to changes in the conditions of the network link.

Delivery and reliability
- Use out-of-order delivery to avoid head-of-line blocking.
- If in-order delivery is used, minimize the message size to reduce the impact of head-of-line blocking.
- Send small messages (< 1,150 bytes) to minimize the impact of packet loss on fragmented application messages.
- Set appropriate retransmission count and timeouts for partially reliable delivery. The "right" settings depend on message size, type of application data, and latency between the peers.

Index

We'd like to hear your suggestions for improving our indexes. Send email to index@oreilly.com.

security, 256–257
stack, 255
browser request prioritization, in HTTP 2.0, 216
browser(s)
 authentication management, 257
 caches, 305
 certificates, 59
 cookie management, 257
 graphics rendering pipelines, 253
 JavaScript VMs, 253
 media engines in, 340–343
 multiplexing support in, 298
 networking engines in, 340–343
 optimization caches, 253
 optimizing for, 183–185
 performance, 253
 process management, 253
 security sandboxes, 253
 session management, 257
 storage, 253
bufferbloat, 6
bundling notifications, 142
byte-stream oriented protocol, 37

C

cache lifetime, 236
Cache-Control header, 236
caching
 client state, 257–258
 resources, 257–258
 resources on client, 236–237
 on smart phones, 237
caching data, 66
calculating image memory requirements, 203
Canvas API, 314
capacity planning, WebRTC and, 359–361
Carrier Sense Multiple Access (CSMA), 90
CDMA-based networks, 103
 limitations, 121
cell DCH
 transition from cell FACH to, 120
 UMTS RRC State Machine, 119
cell FACH
 transition from cell DCH to, 120
 UMTS RRC State Machine, 119
cell-breathing, 86
cellular connections, worldwide, 99
Cerf, Vint, 13

certificate authorities, 57–60
 Certificate Revocation List (CRL), 61
certificate authorities (CA), 59
Certificate Revocation List (CRL), 61
certificates
 browser, 59
 Certificate Revocation List (CRL), 61
 check status, 61
 errors, 72
 invalidating, 61
 manually specified, 59
 operating system, 59
 reduce size of, 71
 revocation, 61–62
 root authority, 60
 self-signed, 340
chain of trust, 57–60
 DTLS and, 340
 establishing, 58
 length of, and performance, 70–71
 WebRTC and, 340
channels, 9
checksum, 36
chosen network latencies, 193
Chrome (Google)
 inspecting WebRTC connections with, 332
 optimizations in, 184
 RTC support in, 310
 speculative networking optimization in, 256
 WebP and, 238
 WebRTC support, 310
client connection limit, 198
client requests, 72
client state caching, 257–258
cloud providers, 249
CoDel actvie queue management algorithm, 6
coding HTTP 2.0 headers, 222
Collision Detection (CSMA/CD), 90
combining CSS files, 201
combining JavaScript files, 201
communication
 HTTP 2.0, 213
 limits set by, 233
 physical properties of, 233
 scheduling, 90
 transactional request-response, 302
compressing assets, 236
compressing text-based assets, 188
concatenation, 201, 243

Evolved Packet Core (EPC), 125, 127
execution performance
    CSS bundle size vs., 203
    JavaScript bundle size vs., 203
Extended Validation (EV), 71
extensions
    HTTP, 50
    Wi-Fi Multimedia (WMM), 92

F

Facebook, 64
Facebook Chat and XHR long-polling, 277
fail fast mechanism, 226
fast recovery algorithm, 19
fast retransmit algorithm, 19
Federal Communication Commission (FCC), 82
fetching resources, 176
    using a proxy server to, 66
    using CDN to, 66
file formats, 237
    WebP, 238
Firefox, RTC support in, 310
first in, first out (FIFO), 192
first-hop latency, measuring, 94
fixed length fields, 229
fixing perfromance regressions, 179
flow control, 19
    HTTP 2.0 and, 207
    in HTTP 2.0, 218–219
    regulation by, 219
flow control window (rwnd), 28
forced pushes, 221
formatting requests, 254
formula for domain sharding, 199
fragmenting application messages, 295
frame aggregation, 95
frames, 213
    GOAWAY, 228
    HTTP 2.0 types, 227
    implementing, 228
    PUSH PROMISE, 221
    settings, 220
    WebSocket, 295
frequency ranges, 82
front-end performance, 174

G

General Packet Radio Service (GPRS), 101

generations of mobile networks, 99
GET method, 156
Gettys, Jim, 6
getUserMedia API, 312–314
    constraints on, specifying, 313
globally unique IPs, 38
Gmail, 204
goals of HTTP 2.0, 207
goals of SPDY, 208
GOAWAY frame, 228
Google, 43, 64, 69
    STUN test servers, 327
Google Search, optimizing TTFB for, 185
Gs of mobile networks, 99–111
    2 (second generation), 100–101
    3 (third generation), 101–105
GSM (Global System for Mobile communications), 100
Gzip, 70
    assets, 188

H

handshake
    DTLS, 338, 340
    HTTP Upgrade, 304
    Key and Accept, 301
    TCP, 16
    TCP, three-way, 14–16
    TLS, 50–55
    WebSocket, 301
hanging XHR, 198
Hangouts (Google), 359
HAProxy, 248
head-of-line blocking, 30–32, 195, 296–297
    DataChannel and, 354
    HTTP 2.0 and, 215, 218
    SCTP and, 348
    TCP, 30–32
    WebSocket protocol, 296–297
headers
    Cache-Control, 236
    compression, in HTTP 2.0, 222–224
    Cookie, 239
    ETag, 236
    HTTP 2.0 and, 222
    WebSocket, 298
    XHR, 263
heterogeneous networks (HetNets), 133–135
    deploying, 133

TCP timeouts and, 40
native applications, push delivery and, 142
Navigation Timing API, 179
  benefits of, 180
  Resource Timing vs., 182
navigator.onLine notifications, 147
near-far problem, 86
negotiating TLS tunnels, 52
negotiating tunnels, 50
Netscape, 47
Network Address Translators (see NAT)
Network Control Program (NCP), 17
network latency, 174
  chosen, 193
network requests
  concatenation, 201
  decoupling from user interactions, 146
  spriting, 201
network roundtrips, 145
network sockets, lifecycle of, 254
network weather, 11
networking
  bandwidth, 9–12
  browsers, 253
  connection management, 254–256
  latency and, 4–9
  performance, 140
  real-time transports for, 315–319
  sandboxing, 256–257
  secure communications, 337–340
  security, 256–257
  speed, 3–12
new protocols, 50
new request latencies, 131
Next Protocol Negotiation (NPN), 54
  ALPN and, 54
NFC, 79
NoAck, 114
non-text assets, resource inlining, 205
notifications, bundling, 142
notifications, real time, 273–278
  long-polling, 276–278
  polling and, 274–275
null protocol service, 35
  UDP as, 36–38

O

OCSP (Online Certificate Status Protocol), 62
  CRL vs., 62

size, 72
  stapling, 71–72
offloading to Wi-Fi, 96
one-way latency, user-plane, 111
Online Certificate Status Protocol (OCSP), 62
Ookla, 10
OpenSSL buffers, 69
operating system certificates, 59
opt-in authentication mechanism, 265
optical fibers, 9
  advantages of, 9
optimizations
  application layer, 202
  document aware, 183
  evergreen, 188, 241
  for mobile networks, 139–151
  for TCP, 32–34
  for TLS, 63–72
  for UDP, 44–45
  for Wi-Fi, 95–97
  in Google Chrome, 184
  interaction, 165
  JavaScript execution, 176
  mobile networks, 234
  PageSpeed, 245
  protocol, 139
  resource inlining, 204
  speculative, 183
  TTFB for Google Search, 185
  web filters, 245
optimized resource caching, 257
OPUS bitrate codec, 314
organizing socket pools, 254
origins, 264
out-of-band negotiation, 352

P

packet flow
  between private networks, 325–332
  initiating requests on mobile networks, 129–131
  on mobile networks, 129–133
packet gateway (PGW), 125
packet loss, 31
  DTLS and, 338
  on Wi-Fi networks, 94–95
  partially reliable channels and, 355–356
  with TCP on wireless networks, 95
packet trace files, 142

public key cryptography
    performance of, 52
    symmetric vs., 52
push deliver, native applications and, 142
push delivery, 142
PUSH PROMISE frames, 221

Q

Quality of Service (QoS), 92
queuing delay, 5
queuing latency, 303

R

radio capabilities, 111
radio interface, using, 140
Radio Resource Controller (RRC), 113–123
    scheduling and, 115
radio specification of mobile devices, 113
RAN (Radio Access Network), 101, 123–125
Real-Time Communication in Web-browsers
    (RTCWEB), 310
real-time frameworks, 289
real-user measurement (RUM), 179
    analyzing, 181
receive windows (rwnd), 17
reduced protocol overhead, 202
reducing DNS lookups, 187, 235
reducing latency, 207
reduction of signal power, 85
regulation by flow control, 219
reliable attribute (DataChannel), 355
render trees, 168
replicating data, 66
request bytes, streamlining, 238–239
request formatting, 256
request prioritization, 215–217
request streaming, XHR and, 269
request/response multiplexing, 214–215
requirements, User Equipment category, 111
researching HTTP 2.0, 218
resource caching, 257–258
    efficient, 257
    optimized, 257
resource inlining, 221
    in HTTP 1.x, 204–205
    non-text assets and, 205
    text-based assets and, 205
Resource Timing, 182

resource waterfall, 171
resource(s)
    loading, 240
    prefetching, 183
    prioritization, 183
    waterfalls, 168–175
response processing, 256
response times, 239
responseType attribute, 273
responsive design, 139
root certificate authority, 60
routers, SCTP and, 348
RRC (Radio Resource Controller), 113–123
    EV-DO state machines for, 120–121
    LTE, state machine for, 116–118
    periodic transfers and, 121–123
    radio power requirements and, 115–116
    state transitions, accounting for, 146
RRC Connected, 117
RRC Idle, 117
RTCDataChannel API, 309
    WebRTC requirements for, 344
RTCPeerConnection API, 309, 317–318
    adding/removing streams from, 334
    createOffer(), 323
    ICE protocol and, 325–332
    JSEP and, 324
RTCWEB (Real-Time Communication in Web-
    browsers), 310

S

same-origin policy, 257, 264
    restrictions of, 264
    WebSocket, 299
sandboxing, 254, 256–257
scheduling communication, 90
    RRC and, 115
scheduling Wi-Fi transmissions, 94
SCTP, 344–348
    and head-of-line blocking, 348
    framing layer vs., 345
    naked, 348
    packet format, 345
SDP, 322–324
    createOffer() and, 323
    Jingle protocol and, 324
    mapping to XMPP, 324
Secure Real-time Control Transport Protocol
    (see SRTCP)

X

About the Author

Ilya Grigorik is a web performance engineer and developer advocate at Google where he works to make the Web faster by building and driving adoption of performance best practices at Google and beyond.

Colophon

The animal on the cover of *High Performance Browser Networking* is a Madagascar harrier (*Circus macrosceles*). The harrier is primarily found on the Comoro Islands and Madagascar, though due to various threats, including habitat loss and degradation, populations are declining. Recently found to be rarer than previously thought, this bird's broad distribution occurs at low densities with a total population estimated in the range of 250–500 mature individuals.

Associated with the wetlands of Madagascar, the harrier's favored hunting grounds are primarily vegetation-lined lakes, marshes, coastal wetlands, and rice paddies. The harrier hunts small invertebrates and insects, including small birds, snakes, lizards, rodents, and domestic chickens. Its appetite for domestic chickens (accounting for only 1% of the species' prey) is cause for persecution of the species by the local people.

During the dry season—late August and September—the harrier begins its mating season. By the start of the rainy season, incubation (~32–34 days) has passed and nestlings fledge at around 42–45 days. However, the harrier reproduction rates remain low, averaging at 0.9 young fledged per breeding attempt and a success rate of three-quarter of nests. This poor nesting success—owing partly to egg-hunting and nest destruction by local people—can also be attributed to regular and comprehensive burning of grasslands and marshes for the purposes of fresh grazing and land clearing, which often coincides with the species' breeding season. Populations continue to dwindle as interests conflict: the harrier requiring undisturbed and unaltered savannah, and increasing human land-use activities in many areas of Madagascar.

Several conservation actions proposed include performing further surveys to confirm the size of the total population; studying the population's dynamics; obtaining more accurate information regarding nesting success; reducing burning at key sites, especially during breeding season; and identifying and establishing protected areas of key nesting sites.

The cover image is from *Histoire Naturelle, Ornithologie, Bernard Direxit*. The cover font is Adobe ITC Garamond. The text font is Adobe Minion Pro; the heading font is Adobe Myriad Condensed; and the code font is Dalton Maag's Ubuntu Mono.

Have it your way.

Get even more for your money.

Join the O'Reilly Community, and register the O'Reilly books you own. It's free, and you'll get:

- $4.99 ebook upgrade offer
- 40% upgrade offer on O'Reilly print books
- Membership discounts on books and events
- Free lifetime updates to ebooks and videos
- Multiple ebook formats, DRM FREE
- Participation in the O'Reilly community
- Newsletters
- Account management
- 100% Satisfaction Guarantee

Signing up is easy:

1. Go to: oreilly.com/go/register
2. Create an O'Reilly login.
3. Provide your address.
4. Register your books.

Note: English-language books only

To order books online:
oreilly.com/store

For questions about products or an order:
orders@oreilly.com

To sign up to get topic-specific email announcements and/or news about upcoming books, conferences, special offers, and new technologies:
elists@oreilly.com

For technical questions about book content:
booktech@oreilly.com

To submit new book proposals to our editors:
proposals@oreilly.com

O'Reilly books are available in multiple DRM-free ebook formats. For more information:
oreilly.com/ebooks

O'REILLY®

Spreading the knowledge of innovators

oreilly.com

CPSIA information can be obtained at www.ICGtesting.com
Printed in the USA
LVOW03s1519240414

383102LV00008B/14/P